Oxford Studies in Lexicography and Lexicology

Series Editors
Richard W. Bailey, Noel Osselton, and Gabriele Stein

Fixed Expressions and
Idioms in English

Fixed Expressions and Idioms in English

A Corpus-Based Approach

ROSAMUND MOON

CLARENDON PRESS · OXFORD
1998

Oxford University Press, Great Clarendon Street, Oxford OX2 6DP

Oxford New York

Athens Auckland Bangkok Bogota Bombay Buenos Aires
Calcutta Cape Town Dar es Salaam Delhi Florence Hong Kong Istanbul
Karachi Kuala Lumpur Madras Madrid Melbourne Mexico City
Nairobi Paris Singapore Taipei Tokyo Toronto Warsaw

and associated companies in
Berlin Ibadan

Oxford is a registered trade mark of Oxford University Press

Published in the United States
by Oxford University Press Inc., New York

British Library Cataloguing in Publication Data
Data available

Library of Congress Cataloging in Publication Data
Fixed expressions and idioms in English:
a corpus-based approach / Rosamund Moon.
(Oxford studies in lexicography and lexicology)
1. English language–Discourse analysis.   2. English language-
-Terms and phrases.   3. English language–Lexicology.   4. English
language–Idioms.   5. Figures of speech.   I. Title.   II. Series.
PE1422.M66   1988   420.1'41–dc21   97-46861
ISBN 0–19–823614–X

1 3 5 7 9 10 8 6 4 2

Typeset by J&L Composition Ltd, Filey, North Yorkshire
Printed in Great Britain on acid-free paper by
Biddles Ltd, Guildford and King's Lynn

Acknowledgements

This book is based on my doctoral thesis, submitted at the University of Birmingham in 1994, and I must acknowledge the many people who helped me with the thesis and with this book. First and foremost is my Ph.D. supervisor, Malcolm Coulthard; also Michael McCarthy and John Sinclair, who jointly supervised the thesis in its early stages. I must also thank former colleagues in the Dictionaries Department of Oxford University Press, especially Patrick Hanks and Sue Atkins; former colleagues on the Hector Project at Digital Equipment Corporation's Systems Research Center in Palo Alto, California, Mary-Claire van Leunen, Lucille Glassman, Cynthia Hibbard, James R. Meehan, and Loretta Guarino Reid, and also Bob Taylor, director of SRC, and Mike Burrows; and colleagues at Cobuild, University of Birmingham, especially Gwyneth Fox, Jeremy Clear, Ramesh Krishnamurthy, and Tim Lane. Many other people gave me help and advice on specific points or pointed out additional examples or approaches, and I should especially like to thank Nick Alt, Pierre Arnaud, Ian G. Batten, Henri Béjoint, Ken Church, Murray Knowles, Bill Louw, and Eugene Winter. Finally, I should like to thank the Series Editors for their invaluable comments and suggestions; and Frances Morphy, Leonie Hayler, and Virginia Williams for seeing this book through to publication.

Contents

Copyrights

Conventions

Unattested and hypothetical words, expressions, and constructions are preceded by an asterisk: hence *shooted the breeze, *out of public. An asterisk is also used, following the base form of a word, to denote any and all of its inflectional forms: hence *call** implies *call, calls, called, calling.*

Ellipses in illustrative examples are normally indicated by . . .; however, in the transcriptions of spoken interaction, . . . is used to indicate hesitation or a pause. Indication is not given in the transcriptions in OHPC of the source of non-verbal noises such as *um*.

The fixed expressions, idioms, or other words being illustrated in examples are highlighted for ease of reference: the original typography is not reproduced.

SOMEONE, SOMETHING, ADJECTIVE, VERB, and so on are used in lists of expressions to represent variables. X, Y, and Z are sometimes used, for clarity, instead of SOMEONE to represent human subjects or objects of verbs and so on.

I

Introduction and Background

This is a text-based account of English fixed expressions and idioms. It sets out to describe the characteristics, behaviour, and usage of fixed expressions and idioms as observed in text, in particular in corpus text. My central contention is that such items can only be properly described and understood if they are considered together with the contexts in which they occur: I take it for granted that this should involve corpus evidence. I will report on the frequencies, forms, and functions of fixed expressions and idioms, drawing data from a database of several thousand such items, which I investigated by means of an 18 million-word corpus of contemporary English, the Oxford Hector Pilot Corpus. Discussions will be augmented as appropriate from other text sources, in particular The Bank of English. I will then explore use and function further, in order to ascertain the discoursal behaviour and roles of fixed expressions and idioms: this discussion will also centre on data from corpora and other texts.

This study of fixed expressions and idioms is essentially descriptive, not theoretical, but I will make reference to relevant discussions in the literature, and I will begin by examining in the first two chapters some of the theoretical issues involved. The field of phraseology has of course been extensively researched, and Cowie and Howarth (1996) provide a recent select bibliography. Traditional approaches in phraseology have been theory driven, often concerned with typology, semantics, and syntactic behaviour: the chief exceptions have been sociolinguistic studies. Corpus data provides the opportunity to corroborate or modify theoretical models, but detailed corpus-driven studies are still few and far between. Many earlier ones have focused on combinatorial aspects of lexis, as evidenced in lexicogrammatical patterning, and the statistics of collocation, or on the problems of automatically processing multi-word lexical items; more recent studies have tended to focus on particular kinds of item or on particular problems. I aim to be broader in scope, providing an overview and benchmarking data.

This book is therefore intended as a contribution to the systematic description of one part of the English lexicon.

Terminology in this field has always been problematic, and extended discussions of the problem include those by Gläser (1984), Čermák (1988), Nunberg *et al.* (1994), Barkema (1996*b*), and Cowie (forthcoming). There is no generally agreed common vocabulary. Different terms are sometimes used to describe identical or very similar kinds of unit; at the same time, a single term may be used to denote very different phenomena. It is therefore essential to clarify the kinds of unit and phenomenon which I will be discussing.

1.1.1 *Fixed Expressions and the Scope of this Book*

Fixed expression is a very general but convenient term, adopted from Alexander (1978, 1979), Carter (1987), and others, and used to cover several kinds of phrasal lexeme, phraseological unit, or multi-word lexical item: that is, holistic units of two or more words. These include:

> frozen collocations
> grammatically ill-formed collocations
> proverbs
> routine formulae
> sayings
> similes

Fixed expression also subsumes **idioms**, which I will discuss separately in Section 1.1.2. In Section 1.4, I will set out a more detailed typology, and discuss subordinate terms in use. **Fixed expression**, like idiom, is unsatisfactory as a term, since it will be seen that many fixed expressions of these types are not actually fixed; however, I will retain it for simplicity's sake. I will hereafter refer to fixed expressions (including idioms) as **FEIs**.

The set of FEIs to be examined covers only some of the range of phraseological units in English. I am deliberately avoiding four particular kinds of item. These are **compound nouns, adjectives,** and **verbs** such as *civil servant, self-raising,* and *rubber-stamp*; **phrasal verbs** such as *make up* and *stick out*; **foreign phrases** such as *fait accompli, che sarà sarà,* and *caveat emptor*; and **multi-word inflectional forms** of verbs, adjectives, and adverbs such as *had* *been lying* and *more careful(ly)*. (The interest in compound words seems to me to rest largely in morphology, and multi-word inflectional forms are simply part of the grammar of English. I am excluding phrasal verbs and foreign phrases because I need to set limits. Phrasal verbs are easily separable on lexicogrammatical grounds, but otherwise show a similar range of idiomaticity types to FEIs.)

1.1.2 *Idiom*

Idiom is an ambiguous term, used in conflicting ways. In lay or general use, **idiom** has two main meanings. First, **idiom** is a particular manner of expressing something in language, music, art, and so on, which characterizes a person or group:[1]

. . . the most fantastic [performance] I have seen in the strict **idiom** of the music hall comedian. (OHPC: journalism)

The portraits of women in the garden of M. Forest that Lautrec sent to Les Vingt, and a number of similar portrayals which should be placed with them, demonstrate his continuing interest in an Impressionist **idiom** of plein-air painting. (OHPC non-fiction)

But, as the show's own cliche-riddled **idiom** would have it, it's all a lost cause and a crying shame. (OHPC: journalism)

Such uses can be related to the concept of **idiomaticity** in general and to Sinclair's **idiom principle** (1987), which will be discussed in Section 2.1.1.

Secondly (and much less commonly in English), an **idiom** is a particular lexical collocation or phrasal lexeme, peculiar to a language:

The French translations, however, of my English speeches were superb (except for rare instances where the translator was unfamiliar with some out-of-the-way English **idiom** I had used). (OHPC: non-fiction)

Opposition leaders would then organise mass demonstrations and the king would choose a new ministry, charging it with the preliminary task of holding (or 'making', in the expressive Romanian **idiom**) fresh elections. (OHPC: journalism)

---

[1] Examples are all taken from authentic data. OHPC is the Oxford Hector Pilot Corpus, the main corpus used: see Section 3.2. BofE is The Bank of English, a 323 million-word corpus of British, American, and (some) Australian English, including both written text and transcribed speech. Examples from these corpora will normally be classified according to the following broad genres: print journalism (newspapers and periodicals); non-fiction; fiction; and (types of) spoken interaction.

These uses are related to **idiom** as both a superordinate and a hyponymic term for a lexical combination, thus further confusing the matter.

Narrower uses restrict **idiom** to a particular kind of unit: one that is fixed and semantically opaque or metaphorical, or, traditionally, 'not the sum of its parts', for example, *kick the bucket* or *spill the beans*. Such units are sometimes called **pure idioms** (Fernando and Flavell 1981: *passim*; Cowie 1988: 133). Grammatically ill-formed items such as *by and large* are sometimes excluded from the category of idiom, as are transparent metaphors such as *skate on thin ice* and strings such as *move heaven and earth* which have no possible literal meaning.

In broader uses, **idiom** is a general term for many kinds of multi-word item, whether semantically opaque or not. Dictionaries in the Anglo-American tradition often call FEIs 'idioms', making no further typological classification. Makkai uses **idiom** to cover non-compositional polymorphemic words such as *blackbird* as well as collocations and constructions that are not freely formed (1972). Hockett's view is still broader, embracing even single morphemes, since their meanings cannot be deducible (1958: 171ff.). Their models of idiom are discussed in Section 1.3.1.

In some discussions of speech act theory, **idiom** is occasionally used to refer to a conventionalized formula with an illocutionary function: for example, *can you pass the salt?* (Sadock 1974; Morgan 1978). Sadock (1972) draws attention to the ambiguity of utterances which have more than one pragmatic function: ambiguity leads to status as idioms. Gibbs (1986*b*) draws attention to ways in which some indirect speech acts are conventionalized, hence identification of the conventionalized forms as idioms. Levinson (1983) and Coulthard (1985) point out practical problems with this classification: for example, the set of potential formulae is almost open-ended, and hearers/readers react to both surface form and underlying meaning. Formulae such as *can you pass the salt?* are rarely recognized as idioms in lexicology.

Fillmore *et al.* (1988) use **formal idiom** to refer to semi-grammatical structures such as 'NOUN1 *to* NOUN2'. These are syntagmatic equivalents to the sorts of lexico-semantic unit normally denoted by the term **idiom**. I will refer to such units typologically as **phraseological collocations** and structurally as **frames**, rather than idioms: see Sections 1.4.1 and 6.3.

The terminological situation cannot be easily resolved except by avoiding the term **idiom** altogether. While I will not use **idiom** as a formal category, I will make occasional use of **idiom** to refer loosely to semi-transparent and opaque metaphorical expressions such as *spill the beans* and *burn one's candle at both ends,* as opposed to other kinds of expression. In more general contexts, I will subsume **idiom** within the broader category of **FEI**.

Where I refer to discussions of FEIs in the literature, and where **idiom** is an individual's term of choice, I will retain **idiom** as a term in that context. In these circumstances, **idiom** should be interpreted in accordance with the writer's own definition of **idiom**.

1.1.3 *Other Terms*

While I am using **FEI**s as a general term, there are others in use, in addition to broader uses of **idiom**. **Phraseological unit** is used in some Slavonic and German linguistic traditions as a superordinate term for multi-word lexical items: see, for example, Gläser (1984: 348). Similarly, **phraseme** is sometimes used as a superordinate term outside Anglo-American traditions, for example Mel'čuk (1995). There are, however, other uses for both terms. For example, Vinogradov and Tschernischova restrict **phraseological unit** to more metaphorical items, and Amosova (1963) uses **phraseme** for multi-word items which are not pure idioms: see Klappenbach (1968: *passim*). **Phraseological unit** and **phraseme** can be identified with Lyons's **phrasal lexeme** (1977: 23).

In discussing individual cases of FEIs, I will use **tokens** to refer to instances realizing a particular item or **type**. I will use **lemma** to refer to the set of forms that realize an individual lexical item: that is, a base form and its inflections or orthographic variants. **Lemma** is broadly synonymous with **lexeme**, as used by Matthews (1974), Lyons (1977), and Cruse (1986), although their precise definitions vary. However, I will be using **lemma** simply to refer to a formal grouping, with no implication as to meaning, and **lexeme** to refer to a nexus of related senses realized by a single set of forms. Thus in my terms *bear* belongs to a single lemma, but two lexemes—a polysemous verb with meanings such as 'carry' and 'tolerate', and a polysemous noun of which the core meaning denotes an animal.

In discussing the contextual uses of FEIs, I will use **text** to refer to a particular stretch of language (whether written or spoken) that is complete in its own right, although it may form part of a larger text (for example, an article within a newspaper), and **discourse** to refer to a text in its situational, sociocultural, and ideological context. This distinction between **text** and **discourse** follows that drawn by Van Dijk (1977: 3) and Stubbs (1983: 9f.).

1.2 IDIOMATICITY

Idiomaticity is a universal linguistic phenomenon in natural languages, although the distinction between morphemes, words, and groups may be qualitatively different in non-Indo-European languages. (Dasgupta (1993) fails to find evidence of non-compositional phrases in Esperanto, specifically in scientific texts, although he notes that a few individual words are morphologically non-compositional.) Compare the creation of semi-idiomatic or idiom-like units by primates in animal language acquisition experiments. For example, Aitchison (1992: 40 ff.) reports formulations such as *banana which is green* 'cucumber', *eye hat* 'mask', and *white tiger* 'zebra'. Compare also the case in pidgins. For example, Romaine (1988: 35 ff.) reports combinations such as *gras bilong pisin* 'feather' in Tok Pisin, *kuku ania gauna* (literally 'smoke eat thing') 'pipe' in Hiri Motu, and *fellow belong open bottle* 'corkscrew' in Pacific Jargon English. These are all semi-compositional formulations, but they clearly show principles of analogy and motivation underlying attempts to overcome a restricted vocabulary.

Theoretical aspects of combination and collocation are explored in Chapter 2. As far as FEIs are concerned, it has to be emphasized that there is no unified phenomenon to describe but rather a complex of features that interact in various, often untidy, ways and represent a broad continuum between non-compositional (or idiomatic) and compositional groups of words. Compare the observations by Bolinger: 'There is no clear boundary between an idiom and a collocation or between a collocation and a freely generated phrase—only a continuum with greater density at one end and greater diffusion at the other, as would be expected of a system where at least some of the parts are acquired by the later analysis of earlier wholes' (1977: 168), and Fernando and Flavell: '. . . idiomaticity is a phenomenon too complex to be defined in terms of a single property. Idiomaticity is best defined by multiple criteria, each criterion representing a single property' (1981: 19). Compare too the multi-dimensional model set out by Barkema (1996*b*): he points out that traditional models promote one dimension of idiomaticity at the expense of others, and thereby neglect to account for the heterogeneity of units.

The fundamental question to be addressed is whether a string can be considered a unit or FEI. I will be taking three principal factors into account: **institutionalization**, **lexicogrammatical fixedness**, and **non-compositionality**. They form the criteria by which the holism of a string may be assessed.

1.2.1 *Institutionalization*

Institutionalization is the process by which a string or formulation becomes recognized and accepted as a lexical item of the language (Bauer 1983: 48 and *passim*): it is a necessary but not sufficient condition for a string to be classifiable as an FEI. In corpus terms, institutionalization is quantitative, and assessed by the frequency with which the string recurs: Chapter 4 reports the evidence from an 18 million-word corpus. However, corpus-derived statistics are no more representative than the corpus they relate to; furthermore, as will be seen, most FEIs occur infrequently. FEIs may be localized within certain sections of a language community, and peculiar to certain varieties or domains, but private FEIs such as familial euphemisms cannot be regarded as properly institutionalized. Diachrony is relevant: FEIs such as *put one's eyes together* 'fall asleep', *swim between two waters* 'be impartial', and *fall in hand* 'come to blows, quarrel' are no longer current in the lexicon, but were institutionalized in former times. See Barkema (1996*b*: 132 f.) for further discussion of this point.

1.2.2 *Lexicogrammatical Fixedness*

Lexicogrammatical fixedness—or formal rigidity—implies some degree of lexicogrammatical defectiveness in units, for example with preferred lexical realizations and often restrictions on aspect, mood, or voice. Classic examples are *call the shots, kith and kin*, and *shoot the breeze*. Corpus evidence provides evidence of such patterns, preferences, and restrictions, although at the same time it shows that variation is much commoner than some models suggest: see Chapters 5 and 6 for discussion of transformations and variations.

Fixedness is complex. Institutionalization or recurrence of a fully frozen string does not necessarily indicate status as an FEI. For example, Renouf and Sinclair discuss fixed collocational frameworks in the Birmingham Collection of English Text (1991: 128 ff.), where many of the realizations of the frameworks are highly frequent but few can be considered holistic units: see further in Section 2.1. Compare also Choueka *et al.* (1983), who report that of the 50 commonest two-word combinations in a large corpus of Hebrew Rabbinical writing, none was an FEI: they refer to similar results from a French text. Conversely, by no means all FEIs are fully frozen strings. Institutionalization and fixedness are not sufficient criteria by themselves.

1.2.3 *Non-compositionality*

The **non-compositionality** of a string must be considered when
assessing its holism. It is typically regarded as a semantic criterion,
in the broadest sense, and semantic non-compositionality is the
archetypal form. The meaning arising from word-by-word interpretation of the string does not yield the institutionalized, accepted,
unitary meaning of the string: typical cases are metaphorical FEIs.
Institutionalized strings which are grammatically ill formed or
which contain lexis unique to the combination may also be considered non-compositional. Other cases involve what may be
termed pragmatic non-compositionality. The string is decodable
compositionally, but the unit has a special discoursal function.
Examples of this include proverbs, similes, and sayings.

The concept of **non-compositionality**, however, is problematic.
It is essentially idiolectal and synchronic. Moreover, apparently
holistic FEIs such as *spill the beans* and *rock the boat* are partly
compositional in relation to both syntactic structure and metaphoricality: we can understand and appreciate the pertinence of
the image. I will be discussing this further below but it must be said
here that there are strong arguments in the literature against the
analysis of idioms and other FEIs as monolithic non-compositional
gestalts. While I will retain **non-compositionality** as a basic criterion for identifying FEIs, it should be interpreted as indicating
that the component lexical items may have special meanings within
the context of the FEIs: not that the meanings can never be rationalized and analogized, nor that they are never found in other
collocations.

1.2.4 *Other Points*

There are three other criteria. First, I have made orthography a
criterion, in that FEIs should consist of—or be written as—two or
more words. This can be seen in computational terms as an indexing problem, perhaps arbitrary, arising from the need to ascertain
the extent of a lexical item. Not all studies use this as a criterion,
and in fact the blurring of the boundaries between single-word and
multi-word items can be seen when some FEIs have single-word
(often hyphenated) cognates: *break the ice, ice-breaker, ice-breaking*.

Secondly, there is a criterion of syntactic integrity. FEIs typically
form syntactic or grammatical units in their own right: adjuncts
(*through thick and thin*), complements (*long in the tooth*), nominal
groups (*a flash in the pan*), sentence adverbials (*by and large*), and so

on. They may also be realized as whole clauses or utterances (*sparks fly, don't count your chickens before they're hatched*), or verbs and their complementation (*bury the hatchet, stick to one's guns*). FEIs functioning as groups or clauses can be regarded within systemic grammar as exponents of rank-shift.

Thirdly, there is a phonological criterion. Where strings are ambiguous between compositional and non-compositional interpretations, intonation may distinguish: see Makkai (1972: 29), and also Bloomfield, who uses phonology to distinguish compounds from phrases (1935: 227f.). Van Lancker and Canter (1981) and Van Lancker *et al.* (1981) describe experiments and sets of results which suggest that when speakers produce disambiguated versions of potentially ambiguous sentence pairs, they give clues as to whether the intended meaning is idiomatic or literal: interword pauses and word durations are longer in literal readings, shorter in the idiomatic readings, thus reinforcing the holism of FEIs. The phonology and intonation of FEIs is itself a complex topic, requiring extensive oral data. I will not be attempting to describe it, and I will restrict my discussion of FEIs to their written forms and representations.

All the above-mentioned criteria are variables. In particular, institutionalization, fixedness, and non-compositionality distinguish FEIs from other strings, but they are not present to an equal extent in all items. There are degrees of institutionalization, from the extremely frequent *of course* to the fairly rare *cannot cut the mustard*; of fixedness, from the completely frozen *kith and kin* to the relatively flexible and variable *take stick from someone, get a lot of stick from someone, give someone stick*, and so on; and of non-compositionality, from the opaque *bite the bullet* to the transparent *enough is enough*. This means that it is difficult to identify cleanly discrete categories of FEI.

1.3 PHRASEOLOGICAL MODELS

Phraseological typologies have developed because of a need to account systematically for qualitatively different kinds of multi-word item (and sometimes polymorphemic word) within rule-based, or production-based, or meaning-based, models of language. Many classificatory attempts have focused on the identification and separation of pure idioms from other kinds of multi-word items, sometimes leading to neglect of other recurrent collocations and structures that are also problematic. Inevitably, different models foreground or prioritize different properties and best-case realizations of those properties. For example, semanticists are primarily interested in the meanings of FEIs, syntacticians in structures, sociolinguists in real-world usage, semioticians in symbolism, psycholinguists in processing, and so on. The following sections review briefly principal approaches to FEIs: more detailed critical accounts of models can be found in Makkai (1972), Fernando and Flavell (1981), Wood (1981), Čermák (1988), Barkema (1996*b*), and Howarth (1996).

1.3.1 *Broader and Semantic Approaches*

Many earlier, more traditional, models focus on semantic non-compositionality, or the unanalysability of units. Such models may be classified as structuralist in orientation, after Fernando and Flavell (1981: 10). In exploring the concept of **word**, Hockett sets up a reductionist model of the lexicon, with all irreducible elements—the exceptions to the rules of free composition—being **idioms** in his terms, whether they are morphemes, words, groups, clauses, or even exchanges (1958: 166–73). Significantly, in discussing the formation of idioms, he sees them as contextual and existential (as in the introduction and definition of a technical term, or in the reference of a pronoun or substitute), and finds idioms in semiotic systems other than language (1958: 303–9). His argument is important for a rigid view of the compositionality or otherwise of units, for the extension of 'idiom' to larger units such as clauses, and for establishing that idioms are not limited to the set lexical phrases listed in dictionaries, but may also arise from the discoursal situation. However, he does not account for the grading or variety of kinds of FEI, and his extension of idiom to morphemes and ad hoc formulations means that idiom becomes too broad to be a practical category.

Makkai's extensive study of the structure of FEIs in English is built round his own separation of **idioms** from **non–idioms**. This is essentially dichotomous, not permitting gradations, but it does involve the identification of two qualitatively different kinds of FEI, or idiom in his terms (a unit of at least two morphemes (1972: 38)). These are **idioms of encoding** and **idioms of decoding**: problems respectively of lexicogrammar and semantics (1972: 24f.). **Idioms of encoding** are 'phraseological peculiarities' or 'phraseological idioms' (1972: 56f.), involving collocational preferences and restrictions, such as the use of *at* in *he drove at 70 m.p.h.* **Idioms of decoding** are 'misleading' 'lexical clusters' such as *hot potato* and *fly off the handle*: these are naturally also idioms of encoding.

Concentrating on the latter group, he analyses them in the light of a stratificational model of language after Lamb (1962 and elsewhere) as belonging to one of two 'idiomaticity areas' in English: the lexemic and the sememic (overlapping with the hypersememic) (Makkai 1972: 117ff.). Broadly, lexemic idioms are problems of lexicogrammar and semantics, whereas sememic ones are problems of pragmatics and socioculture. Phrasal verbs, pure idioms such as *spill the beans*, and opaque compounds such as *forefinger* and *blackbird* are examples of lexemic idioms: proverbs and formulaic greetings are examples of sememic ones. Makkai then classifies lexemic idioms according to surface structure, copiously exemplifying his categories (1972: 191ff.). He discounts combinations such as *hue and cry* or *to and fro* which contain unique items, referring to them as 'pseudo-idioms' (1972: 123, 340, and *passim*) since they lack the essential ambiguity or misinformation factor which characterizes true idioms. Makkai's study has shortcomings: in particular, his attempts to classify FEIs rigorously prevent him from paying sufficient attention to other kinds of problematic collocation, and some of his distinctions are difficult to follow through, as Fernando and Flavell point out (1981: 8). However, it remains one of the most useful and detailed studies of the structures of English FEIs, and it continues to have a strong influence on other Anglo-American studies.

Mitchell offers a more lexicalist approach in his discussion of meaning and combination (1971). In particular, he distinguishes between collocations, colligations, idioms, and compounds, and he admits the existence of functional or pragmatic idioms—formulae and proverbs such as *who goes there?* or *waste not want not*—as well as semantically opaque idioms such as *kick the bucket* and *eat one's heart out* (1971: 58ff.). His paper is important because it attempts to separate out different sorts of lexical clustering within a Firthian framework, focusing on the chunking of language and recognizing the essentially woolly nature of the phenomenon. Mitchell's work is therefore valuable for corpus-based studies of FEIs, although, like Makkai, he does not provide a model that can be applied rigorously to the full range of FEIs and that accounts for all their features.

There are many studies which set out to define and distinguish **idiom** and to classify realizations of the category, and which can be grouped with broader and semantic approaches. Healey (1968) orients his model towards cross-cultural, lexicographical, and pedagogical applications. Working within the same stratificational framework as Makkai, he sets up a structural classification of FEIs, and takes into account transformational deficiencies. Fernando

(1978) carefully teases out the niceties of various categories of idiom, taking into account parallels in other languages, notably Sinhala, in order to identify pure idioms. Wood (1981) explores the syntactic, lexical, and semantic properties of FEIs in order to establish a narrow category of pure idioms but in doing so she effectively establishes a model of the gradations of semantic compositionality that characterize the full range of FEIs. Gläser (1988) discusses in depth the reference of idiom and characteristic transformational deficiencies of idioms, in order to explore the continuum of idiomaticity and establish a taxonomy of idioms and other FEIs. A number of studies use multiple criteria. For example, Allerton (1984) looks at the phenomenon in terms of levels (semantic, syntactic, locutional, and pragmatic) and of lexical co-occurrence restrictions, seeing a clear division between idiom and metaphor. Becker (1975) has six categories which are lexically or grammatically determined, but his explanations are in terms of their semantics, and he fits as naturally with semantic approaches as with other work in the syntactic/artificial intelligence traditions to which he also belongs: he sees his model as an attempt to organize facts rather than as a way of explaining them. These are all useful studies, rich with examples, but they mainly consider FEIs from the perspective of the lexicon, not text.

1.3.2 *Lexicalist Approaches*

A different tradition and approach is offered by Russian (or Soviet) linguists. Their aim is the description of phraseological units and structures: pure idioms are only one part of this, and they are equally interested in other sorts of collocation. It could be argued that they are seeking to identify the *lexical* primes of a language, rather than the *semantic* primes, and in this respect their work can be compared with collocational approaches: see Chapter 2.

Much of their work is available only in Russian and therefore relatively unknown: the output of the phraseologists Vinogradov and Babkin are cases in point. However, Weinreich gives an overview of Soviet phraseology and general lexicology (1963), and Klappenbach (1968) reviews the work and classifications of Vinogradov, Amosova, and Tschernischova, looking respectively at Russian, English, and German. Amosova (1963) attempts to distinguish carefully and rigorously between different kinds of phraseological unit by means of a 'context-logical analysis'. This gives primacy to considerations of context: whether potential units are ambiguous within their contexts and whether they can have their idiomatic or unitary meanings in other contexts. From this she separates out classes of pure idioms; of phrasemes (frozen collocations or compounds where one element has a meaning unique to the combination); of phraseoloids (restricted collocations where there is limited paradigmatic variability); and of fixed combinations (formulae or fixed collocations that are transparent).

Mel'čuk's extensive work in combinatorics, both within and outside the former Soviet Union, has led to applications in lexicography in the form of 'Explanatory Combinatorial Dictionaries' (ECDs) (Mel'čuk 1988) of Russian (Mel'čuk and Žolkovskii 1984) and of French (Mel'čuk *et al.* 1984 and continuing). In addition to teasing out and codifying the denotational and connotational semantics of lexemes, establishing their polysemous structure, and so on, he pays particular attention to the lexical and syntactic associations of words. In Mel'čuk 1995 he establishes distinctions between kinds of FEI ('phrasemes'), looking at them from an encoding point of view, rather than comprehension, and then builds his classifications into the framework of an ECD: he stresses that phrasemes constitute a huge proportion of text and of the lexicon. Mel'čuk's original distinction between collocation and idiomaticity is discussed by Weinreich (1969: 44f.): '(stability of) collocation' is 'a high degree of contextual restriction' whereas 'idiomaticity' is 'a strong restriction on the selection of a subsense': bondings that are qualitatively different although they may both be present. Čermák (1988) carefully explores issues relating to idioms and the ways in which they are to be distinguished from other collocations: he is considering this from the perspectives of Czech and English. He sets out criteria, pointing out that it is their interaction which is crucial, and links and critiques a number of theoretical models in setting out his own careful conclusions. See also Čermák (1994*b*), where he examines units from a cross-linguistic perspective.

This kind of approach has had influence elsewhere. It can be seen in Weinreich's attempt to reconcile FEIs (or idioms) within a TG (transformational–generative) model of grammar (1969): notably, he explores the interdependence of idiomaticity and polysemy, since it is only possible to have a robust understanding of whether a string has an idiomatic meaning if there is also a robust understanding of what is a non-idiomatic, generalizable meaning. In European phraseological studies, it has led to special attention being paid to collocational aspects of lexemes—for example, in Hausmann's discussions of collocations (1985 and elsewhere), particularly in relation to German, and in Benson *et al.*'s *The BBI Combinatory Dictionary of English* (1986).

The significance of this work is the status given to phraseological units other than pure idioms, and the range of types of fixed or semi-fixed collocations. It provides an intuitively more satisfying analysis of FEIs for those concerned with corpora and lexico-grammatical patterning or lexicographical analyses of a lexicon. The emphasis on collocations as opposed to pure idioms is supported by the relative frequencies of such kinds of unit, as will be seen in Chapter 4. It is difficult not to be impressed by work of this detail and delicacy, and there is certainly much to be considered by lexicographers and lexicologists—but yet again it may prove ultimately to be no more than an abstraction unless it can be shown to describe effectively the phenomena observed in real data.

1.3.3 *Syntactic Approaches*

Structuralist approaches such as those of Makkai and Healey categorize according to syntactic structure or function, but this is a secondary categorization of units already identified as non-compositional. In contrast, studies of FEIs from the perspective of transformational or transformational-generative (TG) grammar begin with syntax. The syntactic or grammatical aberrance or anomalousness of strings leads to their classification as non-compositional units: FEIs are regarded as exceptions to syntactic rules, or as unique realizations of rules. Because they are non-productive or only semi-productive, they cannot be generated freely, and productivity is part and parcel of TG models (Weinreich 1969: 24f.). Radford talks of sets or classes of anomalous expressions (1988: *passim*), and Harris talks of 'a finite learnable stock of "idiomatic" material' outside the rules of the language system (1991: 43). Attention often focuses on pure idioms, especially those which are semantically opaque or semi-transparent and which are homographic with compositional strings; also (but by no means always), on FEIs containing verbs with complementation, including phrasal verbs, since it is these clause-like structures which are more complex and interesting syntactically than lower-level phrases such as nominal groups and prepositional phrases.

Katz and Postal (1963) set out to integrate idioms into a TG model: their position is restated and updated by Katz (1973). Their starting-point is essentially the assertion that:

idioms are the 'exceptions that prove the rule': they do not get their meaning from the meanings of their syntactic parts. (Katz 1973: 358)

and their aim is to delimit:

some property of all and only idioms that can be stated in terms of the formal structure of grammars. (Katz 1973: 359)

In their 1963 paper, Katz and Postal distinguish between 'lexical idioms'—polymorphemic words or multi-word nouns, verbs, and so on—and 'phrasal idioms'—groups. The first group is recorded in the lexicon in the same way as ordinary words, but the second is recorded separately, in an 'idiom list'. This includes indications where the phrasal idioms are non-productive and transformations blocked.

Prior to Katz's restatement, two significant contributions appeared, both involving the notions of the idiom list and the necessity of indicating transformational deficiencies. Weinreich (1969) attempts to synthesize observations concerning the complexity of the range of types of FEI/idiom with the Katz–Postal and Chomskyan models, distinguishing between complex lexemes and idioms, and excluding from consideration well-formed compositional formulae. He posits an optional 'Idiom Comparison Rule' which matches terminal strings against an idiom list (optional to allow for literal counterparts to idioms). Idiom elements are marked as to which transformations are precluded. Fraser's paper (1970) sets out a hierarchy of seven degrees of idiom frozenness from L6 (completely free) to L0 (completely frozen): he argues that no true idioms can belong to level 6. Each entry in his idiom list is to be marked with its appropriate level of frozenness. Additional transformations are blocked as the degree of frozenness increases, following a regular sequence. Fraser accepts that assessments of frozenness are idiolectal, but maintains that the hierarchy holds good and leads to a better classification of the idiomaticity of units and their annotation within the idiom list. Katz (1973) raises objections to both these papers, and his careful description of the (±Idiom) feature is partly a response to them. See also Newmeyer (1972) for a discussion of FEIs and the ways in which they fit into TG models; Nunberg *et al.* (1994) for a detailed exploration of idioms in the light of syntactic models, showing up common patterns which explain some syntactic anomalies; Jackendoff (1995) for a review of received ideas about FEIs, with suggested revisions to received syntactic models; and Abeillé (1995) and Schenk (1995) for examinations of constraints on the syntactic behaviour of FEIs—Abeillé with reference to French and real data, Schenk mainly with reference to Dutch and some parallel cases in English.

There are three important results of such work. First, the observation and investigation of transformational deficiencies has influenced other phraseological work, not necessarily operating within a TG model of language, such as the models of Makkai (1972) and Wood (1981), and dictionaries such as *ODCIE*[2] which attempt to record the transformational potential and valency of phrasal lexemes.

Secondly, paying attention to the syntactic structure of FEIs and the marking of idiom-features ironically encourages awareness of compositionality as well as non-compositionality. For example, it can explain inflections as well as transformational deficiencies. To use Weinreich's example (1969: 55f.), the past tense inflection of *shoot the breeze* is *shot the breeze* rather than **shooted the breeze* or **shoot the breezed*.

Thirdly, the concept of the idiom list has been questioned, and psycholinguistic research suggests that FEIs may not be stored separately in the mental lexicon: see Section 2.2. However, it resurfaces in the look-up lists of exceptions—or FEIs—that are currently used as strategies for tagging and parsing of corpora and the identification of FEIs in corpora: see Section 3.3.

Syntactic approaches and models are effective in describing or characterizing the morphology of FEIs, but generally fail to account for the range of lexical patterning. Weinreich (1969) is an exception, as is Harris, who, describing his model of language as an orderly system, operating by rules, sees idioms and frozen expressions as cases of constraints or narrow selection in lexico-syntactic structures (1991: 67). One point to be made is that many studies are dealing with phrasal verbs as well as idioms; these undergo relatively different syntactic operations and processes, and so the generalizations and discussions may be irrelevant to FEIs of other kinds. Syntactic approaches often underplay the role of lexical patterning or the motivation underlying the development and usage of FEIs: Chafe (1968) and Fillmore *et al.* (1988) are partly reactions to this. One of the most serious flaws in syntax-based models of FEIs is that many are based on intuition and non-authentic data. This means that some of the assertions concerning transformational potential and syntactic defectiveness may

---

[2] Abbreviated titles of dictionaries are explained under References.

not be reliable: that is, they may not be borne out by real evidence.

1.3.4 *Functional Approaches*

Whereas the above approaches essentially concentrate on the internal features of FEIs and their roles within the lexicon, other more behaviourist approaches look at FEIs as encoding or enabling devices. In particular, there are psycholinguistic and collocational investigations of the way in which language is encoded in chunks rather than word by word: for example, Peters (1983) and Sinclair (1987) (see Chapter 2). Others have discussed the use of FEIs and routine formulae from discourse perspectives, as strategies for fostering interactions, as boundary markers or gambits and so on: for example, Coulmas (1979b, 1981), Drazdauskiene (1981), Strässler (1982), Pawley and Syder (1983), Carter (1987), Schiffrin (1987), Tannen (1989), Nattinger and DeCarrico (1992), McCarthy and Carter (1994), Drew and Holt (1995), and Aijmer (1996) (see Chapters 8, 9, and 10). An analogous approach is taken by Lattey (1986), who considers pure idioms and their like in terms of a pragmatic classification with the aim of showing how they fit into real-time discourse, although she is focusing on pragmatic concepts such as 'relationship with the world' rather than on interactional devices: her model is applied in a dictionary of FEIs (Lattey and Heike 1990).

These studies are important because they establish a broader and more holistic approach to strings, particularly as a phenomenon of discourse. At the same time, the lexicological category of FEIs cannot be said to be properly integrated within pragmatic descriptions of language. For example, Verschueren (1987: 90ff.) sets out taxonomies of lexical units which ignores multi-word units outside grammar and morphology.

1.3.5 *Lexicographical Approaches*

Inevitably, as a corpus lexicographer, I have been heavily influenced by dictionary constructs and frameworks: assembling a database of FEIs is essentially a lexicographical task. General dictionaries in the Anglo-American tradition have tended to be atheoretical (in contrast to dictionaries in the European tradition, influenced by Russian/Soviet phraseological models). While they list FEIs, they rarely categorize them, sometimes making no distinction between compounds, phrasal verbs, and other FEIs. Occasionally proverbs and sayings are labelled as such, but more often FEIs are treated together under a notional or actual label such as 'idioms' or 'phrases'.

The identification of FEIs in dictionaries is typically bound up with compositionality: it is the semantic anomalousness of FEIs which is their dominant criterial feature and which leads to their being recognized as lexical items. The continuum of idiomaticity or compositionality is accordingly misrepresented, since FEIs are entered in dictionaries as the result of binary decisions—either something is an FEI or it is not. Variations on canonical forms are typically under-reported, as are functions and syntactic behaviour. Such matters are not ignored by metalexicographers: for example, Zgusta (1971) and Svensén (1993) discuss the range of collocations and FEIs in their manuals of lexicography, and Béjoint (1994: 211 ff.) discusses the variability of idioms and the wider phenomenon of idiomaticity. Zgusta (1967) sets out nine criteria for distinguishing multi-word lexical items from free combinations—these mostly concern fixedness and non-compositionality, with single-word equivalents in English and other languages also being considered relevant. Such criteria, however, are more useful for distinguishing fixed compounds from recurrent collocations than for FEIs in general. In my own papers on FEIs and lexicography, I have discussed corpus evidence for FEIs, for example with reference to prioritization (1988) and variation (1996), and argued the case for the inclusion of pragmatic information (1992a, 1992b).

Perhaps the chief importance of dictionaries in relation to lexicology is that dictionaries set out to identify the lexical items of a language and the appropriate level—clause, group, structure, word, sense, morpheme—at which meanings are lexicalized or coded: see Section 2.3. FEIs are theoretically, therefore, those units which cannot be explained in terms of their components. This reflects Chomsky's characterization of the TG lexicon as 'the full set of irregularities of the language' (1965: 142), or Halliday's characterization of lexis as the most delicate form of grammar (1966 and elsewhere). Compare also Pawley (1986), who, discussing lexicalization, sees lexicographical views as corresponding more closely to lay views than grammatical or TG models do. Čermák (1994b: 185) points out that systematic lexicographical description shows up inadequacies in other models which were built around a few selected FEIs, rather than the whole lexicon. An important point is that while dictionaries themselves may be based on faulty assumptions or imperfect evidence, and the information that they provide is often partial, their inventories of FEIs are basic resources for lexicologists in the field.

1.4 A TYPOLOGY OF FEIS

Models and views such as those discussed above show that FEIs are not a unified phenomenon: there is no generally agreed set of categories, as well as no generally agreed set of terms. Moreover, no clear classifications are possible, although sets of tests may be applied to distinguish major groupings. Instead, it should be stressed that FEIs are non-compositional (to some extent); 'collocations' and 'idioms' represent two large and amorphous subgroups of FEIs on a continuum; transformational deficiencies are a feature of FEIs but not criterial; and discoursally or situationally constrained units should be considered FEIs.

When I set out to quantify and describe FEIs in English and needed a framework or typological model to apply, none of the typologies that I found in the literature worked adequately for the range I was investigating, and none accounted adequately for the degree of formal variation which I observed in the data. I therefore developed my own typology, which grew out of the established models in the literature and the data I encountered. This typology essentially involved identifying the reason or reasons why each potential FEI might be regarded *lexicographically* as a holistic unit: that is, whether the string is problematic and anomalous on grounds of lexicogrammar, pragmatics, or semantics. This led to three macrocategories: **anomalous collocations**, **formulae**, and **metaphors**. Each is a grouping of finer categories. They are shown in Table 1.1, and discussed further below.

TABLE 1.1. *Categories of FEIs*

problems of lexicogrammar	anomalous collocations	ill-formed collocations cranberry collocations defective collocations phraseological collocations
problems of pragmatics	formulae	simple formulae sayings proverbs (literal/metaphorical) similes
problems of semantics	metaphors	transparent metaphors semi-transparent metaphors opaque metaphors

TABLE 1.2. *Alternative grouping of FEIs*

phraseological collocations defective collocations	paradigmatically restricted
ill-formed collocations cranberry collocations	syntagmatically restricted
simple formulae sayings non-metaphorical proverbs	fixed, literal, discoursally meaningful
metaphorical proverbs similes transparent metaphors	non-literal, transparent
semi-transparent metaphors opaque metaphors	non-literal, non-transparent

This typology is simply a means to an end: a way of classifying a wide range of FEIs so that particular types of item (such as proverbs, or metaphors, or ill-formed FEIs) could be selected or excluded and so that global statements could be made about broad groupings of FEIs. The three macrocategories—anomalous collocations, formulae, and metaphors—represent the primary reason for identifying strings as FEIs, but clearly other groupings are possible. For example, the subtypes can be combined into five classifications, reflecting more delicately the cline between free combinations and semantically non-compositional units: see Table 1.2. However, I will be using the tripartite groupings anomalous collocations, formulae, and metaphors where no more delicate information is needed. In defence, it may be pointed out that distinctions between defective/phraseological collocations and ill-formed/cranberry collocations largely depend on polysemy and diachrony; that proverbs, whether literal or metaphorical, have much in common with each other pragmatically; and that the transparency or otherwise of metaphors is diachronically and idiolectally variable.

1.4.1 *Anomalous Collocations*

Strings classified as **anomalous collocations** are problematic in lexicogrammatical terms. They are syntagmatically or paradigmatically aberrant: they cannot therefore be decoded purely compositionally nor encoded freely. Further subclassification of anomalous collocations categorizes according to the nature of the anomaly.

The more straightforward subtypes are **ill-formed collocations** and **cranberry collocations**. **Ill-formed collocations** break the conventional grammatical rules of English. Common examples include *at all, by and large, of course, stay put,* and *thank you.* (Fillmore *et al.* (1988: 505) describe them as 'extragrammatical idioms'.) **Cranberry collocations** include items that are unique to the string and not found in other collocations: compare Makkai's term 'cranberry morph' for such items (1972: 43 and elsewhere), following discussion by Hockett (1958: 126–7) of 'unique morphemes', with the morpheme *cran-* in *cranberry* as exemplar.[3] Common examples include *in retrospect, kith and kin, on behalf of someone/ something, short shrift,* and *to and fro.*

Slightly more complicated is the subtype **defective collocations**. These are collocations that cannot be decoded purely compositionally either because a component item has a meaning not found in other collocations or contexts, although it has other compositional meanings, or because one or more of the component items is semantically depleted. Common examples include *at least, a foregone conclusion, in effect, beg the question,* and *in time.* Compare Cruse's term 'bound collocations' (1986: 41) for combinations such as *curry favour, foot the bill,* and *toe the line.*

The fourth subtype is **phraseological collocations**.[4] This is the weakest group and consists of cases where there is a limited paradigm in operation and other analogous strings may be found, but where the structure is not fully productive. Clear examples are sets such as *in action, into action,* and *out of action; on show* and *on display;* and *to a — degree* and *to a — extent.* Compare Fillmore *et al.*'s term 'formal idiom' (1988): an earlier term of Fillmore's is 'structural formula'.

1.4.2 *Formulae*

Strings classified as **formulae** are problematic because of their discoursal functions: they are specialized pragmatically. They generally conform to lexicogrammatical conventions of English, although a few are effectively truncated utterances. They are generally compositional semantically, although some similes and proverbs are obscure or metaphorical. Many of the units which

---

[3] Jackendoff (1995: 150) points out the recent extension of the *cran-* morpheme in *cran-apple juice*.

[4] This grouping is not to be confused with Weinreich's use of **phraseological collocation** to translate Vinogradov's term **sočetanija** (1963: 73)—'a closed set of word collocations of which only one [word] is basic and restricted, while the others are used freely'.

I have included here would fall into Mel'čuk's category of 'pragma-temes' (1995: 176ff.).

The most basic subtype is **simple formulae**, routine compositional strings that nevertheless have some special discoursal function or are iterative or emphatic, as well as syntagmatically fixed. Common examples are *alive and well, I'm sorry to say, not exactly, pick and choose,* and *you know.* Like phraseological collocations, these are very much in a grey area between free combinations and FEIs. The subtype **sayings** includes formulae such as quotations (typically unattributed and sometimes unattributable), catchphrases, and truisms: examples include *an eye for an eye —, curiouser and curiouser, don't let the bastards grind you down, that's the way the cookie crumbles,* and *home, James, and don't spare the horses.*

The subtype **proverbs** comprises traditional maxims with deontic functions. Metaphorical proverbs are distinguished from non-metaphorical ones, but, like Norrick (1985: 49), I consider the latter proverbs rather than sayings. Commoner examples of metaphorical proverbs are *every cloud has a silver lining* and *you can't have your cake and eat it*: of non-metaphorical ones, *enough is enough* and *first come first served.*

The fourth subtype is **similes**: institutionalized comparisons that are typically but not always transparent, and are signalled by *as* or *like.* Examples include *as good as gold, as old as the hills, like lambs to the slaughter,* and *live like a king.*

1.4.3 *Metaphors*

Strings classified as **metaphors** are non-compositional because of their semantics: they include pure idioms. Subclassification of metaphors reflects degrees of transparency, and it will be clear that such classification is subjective and represents a continuum rather than discrete categories. In the following subcategories, identification of metaphors as transparent, semi-transparent, or opaque proceeds from an assumed position of ignorance of meaning.

Transparent metaphors are those which are institutionalized but the image or vehicle (Leech 1969: 151) of the metaphor is such that the hearer/reader can be expected to be able to decode it successfully by means of his/her real-world knowledge. Commoner examples include *alarm bells ring, behind someone's back, breathe life into something, on (some)one's doorstep,* and *pack one's bags.*

Semi-transparent metaphors require some specialist knowledge in order to be decoded successfully. Not all speakers of a language may understand the reference or be able to make the required analogy; if the institutionalized idiomatic meaning is unknown, there may be two or more possible interpretations. Commoner examples include *grasp the nettle, on an even keel, the pecking order, throw in the towel,* and *under one's belt.* To expand on semi-transparency: *grasp the nettle* means something like 'tackle something difficult with determination and without delay' and with hindsight the metaphor in the string is relatively straightforward, but someone not knowing the expression might as easily interpret the metaphor as 'do something foolish which will have unpleasant consequences'. Similarly, *not be playing with a full deck* implies stupidity but could as easily imply dishonesty. Pulman (1993: 250–1) points out that someone unfamiliar with *put the cat among the pigeons* could interpret it as a metaphor reasonably accurately, but might erroneously infer connotations of cruelty, which are not present in the conventionalized idiomatic meaning.

Finally, **opaque metaphors**, pure idioms, are those where compositional decoding and interpretation of the image are practically or completely impossible without knowledge of the historical origins of the expression. Examples include *bite the bullet, kick the bucket, over the moon, red herring,* and *shoot the breeze.*

Division into types of metaphor according to transparency is inevitably idiolectal or idiosyncratic, and Titone and Connine (1994: 262) report only 40% reliable agreement in an investigation testing views of the compositionality of items. Moreover, opaque metaphors can be reinterpreted synchronically and analysed compositionally. For example, Jackendoff (1995: 151–2) discusses *eat humble pie,* seeing *humble* as a clear part of its meaning, interpreting *eat* as 'take something back' or 'accept', and finding only *pie* to be unmotivated or unexplained. Diachronically, the metaphor must be interpreted differently, with *humble pie* being a corruption of *umbles pie,* a pie made out of the entrails of deer or other animals, and served to people lowest hierarchically in a social situation. The source domain of the metaphor leads to connotations in the target domain of abasement and self-abasement: the humbleness which Jackendoff notes.

1.4.4 *Dual Classifications*

The above typology is not entirely satisfactory: groupings overlap, and it is often impossible to assign an FEI to a single category. I gave dual classifications in the database to FEIs which fell into more than one category. Around 25% of FEIs in the database have dual classifications of type, and 1% have three classifications.

TABLE 1.3. *Defective collocations: secondary subtypes*

formula	26%
phraseological collocation/frame	25%
transparent metaphor	20%
semi-transparent metaphor	14%
ill-formed collocation	13%

The need for dual classification arises when an FEI exhibits features of two different types. My main purpose in classifying FEIs was to see how far certain clusters of properties or of idiomaticity types correlate with distribution, syntax, and discourse function. To this end, the gross types—anomalous collocation, formula, and metaphor—provide a reasonable means of distinguishing and sorting the heterogeneous set of FEIs. When two or more classifications are given, the first is the one which seems more important. But a secondary purpose of classifying FEIs was to record membership of certain traditional classes of FEI—pure idioms, proverbs, 'cranberries', and so on. In cases where an FEI is metaphorical or proverbial, but also contains a unique lexical item or is grammatically ill formed, dual classification is desirable.

The commonest types of dual classification may be used to explore the boundaries between types and to locate the areas of greatest indeterminacy. In over 60% of dual classifications, one subtype is 'defective collocation', and nearly half of all classifications of 'defective collocation' are dual ones. The commonest of their secondary subtypes are as shown in Table 1.3. This shows that 'defective collocation' as a type is very much a ragbag, and reflects the uneasy status of some meanings of polysemous words: are they context-bound or do they have fully independent meanings? There appears to be some form of idiomatic or non-compositional bonding, but this cannot be identified precisely. For example, *admit defeat* was classified as a defective collocation since there is no real paradigm operating: it is decodable compositionally and so was classifiable as a formula too. FEIs such as *in a fix* and *on one's books* belong to phraseological paradigms, where other nouns can be substituted to give parallel expressions; at the same time, the senses of *fix* and *books* are not independent. Similar points can be made about cases of triple classification.

If 25% of classifications of typology are complex, 75% are straightforward and unique assignments are possible. In the majority of cases of multi-assignment, there is one clearly preferable assignment. On balance, a flexible system is preferable to a rigid one where only single classes are acceptable: it allows a greater range of information to be recorded and reflects the indisputable fuzziness of boundaries.

2

Collocation and Chunking

Corpus evidence demonstrates clearly that language is strongly patterned: many words occur repeatedly in certain lexicogrammatical patterns. This ties in with psycholinguistic research, which suggests that language is processed in chunks, at least part of the time, and with psycholinguistic–phonological arguments 'that the tone-group is the usual unit of neurolinguistic pre-preparation' (Laver 1970: 69), rather than individual sounds or words. The basic unit for encoding and decoding may therefore be the group, set phrase, or collocation, rather than the orthographic word. This is relevant to FEIs, as it may shed light on how they are processed and how they fossilize, as well as on their functions within discourse.

2.1 COLLOCATION

The term **collocation** is defined by Sinclair (1991: 170): 'Collocation is the occurrence of two or more words within a short space of each other in a text.' Collocation typically denotes frequently repeated or statistically significant co-occurrences, whether or not there are any special semantic bonds between collocating items. Corpora of ever-increasing sizes permit collocations to be studied more exhaustively, and statistics concerning collocation or derived from collocations accordingly become more robust (see Renouf (1987), who compares degrees of evidence in different-sized corpora). Terminological confusion may arise since **collocation** is sometimes used to designate weak kinds of FEI, in contradistinction to pure idioms. However, I will use **collocation** to designate simple co-occurrence of items, and **anomalous collocation** to designate a class of FEIs, with subtypes **ill-formed collocation, cranberry collocation, defective collocation,** and **phraseological collocation**: see Section 1.4.1.

Collocations are the surface, lexical evidence that words do not combine randomly but follow rules, principles, and real-world motivations. Different kinds of collocation reflect qualitatively different kinds of phenomenon: see, for example, Jones and Sinclair (1974). The simplest kind arises through semantics: co-occurrence of co-members of semantic fields, representing co-occurrence of the referents in the real world. For example, the lemma *jam* co-occurs significantly in OHPC with other words from the lexical set 'food', such as *tarts, butty, doughnuts, marmalade, apricot,* and *strawberry.* Such collocations may help identify topic or disambiguate polysemous words automatically in cases where the discoursal context has to be inferred: compare Lesk (1986), who uses collocation to disambiguate two homographic uses of *cone.*

A second kind of collocation arises where a word requires association with a member of a certain class or category of item. Such collocations are constrained lexicogrammatically as well as semantically. For example, *rancid* is typically associated with *butter, fat,* and foods containing butter or fat. In other cases, a word has a particular meaning only when it is in collocation with certain other words. Aisenstadt gives the example *face the truth/facts/problem* and so on, referring to such co-occurrences as **restricted collocations** (1979, 1981). Similarly, selection restrictions on verbs may specify certain kinds of subject or object: 'animate', 'liquid', 'vehicle', and so on: for example, the verb *drink* normally requires a human subject and a liquid as object. In all cases, the specified collocation slot can be realized by a proform, but where it is realized by a content word, the collocation can be observed and measured. In this way, collocates can be used to distinguish between quasi-synonyms: for example, Church and Hanks (1990) distinguish *strong* from *powerful* through automatic collocational analysis.

A third kind of collocation is syntactic, and arises where a verb, adjective, or nominalization requires complementation with, say, a specified particle. Such collocations—or colligations—are closer to other recurrent strings in text, grammatically well formed and highly frequent, but not necessarily holistic and independent. For example, Kjellmer (1987) describes recurrent strings such as *to be, one of,* and *had been* in the Brown corpus, and Altenberg (1991) describes recurrent strings such as *you know, yes yes, thank you very much,* and *are going to be* in the London–Lund corpus of spoken English. Similarly, Renouf and Sinclair (1991) describe collocational frameworks in the Birmingham Collection of English Text, such as *a/an—of, too—to,* and *many—of.* They observe what appear to be constraints in operation, and suggest that the examination of such frameworks may be a viable alternative approach to the study and explanation of patterning in language (1991: 143): collocation may be driving grammar rather than the other way round (1991: 133). This is explored further by Francis (1993), who describes a radical, corpus-driven grammar which takes lexis into account. It is a sort of generative lexicology, establishing the existence and significance of lexical and syntactic co-dependencies, restrictions, and repetitions. Many ordinary words or meanings of ordinary words occur primarily or exclusively in certain structures. This is important, as it demonstrates the absence of a clear-cut distinction between free combinations and phraseological units, as Francis points out. Even if a lexical selection is motivated by semantics, it carries with it various collocational and syntactic constraints: the selection of the co-text is not free. There are pre-ferred or typical locutions or structures, preferred ways of saying things.

Compositionality is an issue here, and must be considered in order to distinguish recurrent meaningful strings such as *for a long time* (with a frequency of around 16 per million in OHPC) from gestalts such as *enough is enough* (with a frequency of around 1 per million). *For a long time* is a grammatically regular structure, with paradigms operating at each slot in the nominal group (for example, *after a long time, for a short time, for ages, for a long while*). Similarly, the frame (*two/a hundred/many/*etc.) *years ago* has a frequency of around 160 per million, but it is compositional and not an FEI.

2.1.1 *Sinclair's 'Idiom Principle'*

Sinclair (1987) draws on observations of lexical patterning and co-occurrences, and postulates two principles underlying language: **the open choice principle** and **the idiom principle**. These are diametrically opposed, and both are required in order to account for language. The open choice principle 'is a way of seeing language text as the result of a very large number of complex choices. At each point where a unit is completed—a word or a phrase or a clause—a large range of choice opens up, and the only restraint is gramma-ticalness.' The idiom principle 'is that a language user has available to him or her a large number of semi-preconstructed phrases that constitute single choices, even though they might appear to be analysable into segments.' Thus at a point in text where the open choice model would suggest a large range of possible choices, the idiom principle restricts it dramatically over and above predictable semantic restraints that result from topic or situational context. A single choice in one slot may be made which dictates which ele-ments will fill the next slot or slots, and prevents the exercise of free choice. Sinclair illustrates this at its simplest level by the combination *of course*. Orthography and the open choice model would suggest that this sequence comprises two free choices, one at the *of* slot and one at the *course* slot.[1] The idiom principle on the other hand suggests that it is a single choice which coincidentally occupies two word spaces. This represents a lexicalist, holistic approach to language production and processing. Compare Čermák (1994*b*: 187), who discusses anomaly as analogy and forces underlying idioms, commenting: 'Idiomatics is a residual anomalous counterpart of the regular, that is, rule-governed combinations of the language.' It is important to note that Sinclair is interested in the statistics of the bonding between adjacent orthographic words here: that is, the statistical probability of the items co-occurring. An alternative view might consider *of course* as a single-word lexical item which happens to include a space as one of its component characters.

2.1.2 *The Idiom Principle, FEIs, and Discourse*

The idiom principle can be seen not only in fixed strings such as *of course*, but also in other kinds of phraseological unit. Greetings and social routines demonstrate the idiom principle: sociocultural rules of interaction restrict choices within an exchange which may be realized in fairly fixed formulations or lexicalizations (see Coulmas (1981: 1 ff.) and Hoey (1993) who draw attention to larger units or sequences of formulae, crossing turn boundaries). Sayings, similes, and proverbs also represent single choices, even when truncated or manipulated, and they may be prompted discoursally as stereotyped responses: for example, (*every cloud has*) *a silver lining* or *no news is good news* are predictable comments on common experiences. Routines, gambits, and other kinds of formula should also be mentioned. Some are fossilized, perhaps ill formed, and can be classified as FEIs, but others are only semi-fixed. Pawley and Syder (1983) describe and discuss what they term 'lexicalized sentence stems': recurrent clauses and other units that are enabling devices. These may vary from the purely compositional *can I come in?* or *are you ready?* to proverbs and similes such as *you can lead a horse to water but you can't make it/him drink* and *it's as easy as falling off a log*. They comment (1983: 208): 'Memorized clauses and clause-sequences form a high proportion of the fluent stretches of speech

---

[1] *Of* may be dropped in informal speech, as in *'I'm hoping everybody will enjoy it.'—'Course we will.'* or *'. . . I mean he wasn't brusque or rude or anything.'—'No.'—'Course I mean he'd been trained to er deal with people hadn't he.'*, both examples being taken from unscripted conversation in BofE.

heard in everyday conversation. In particular, we find that multi-clause fluent units—apparently exceptions to the one clause at a time constraint—generally consist partly or wholly of a familiar collocation. Speakers show a high degree of fluency when describing familiar experiences or activities in familiar phrases.' The same phenomenon is also described and discussed by, for example, Bolinger (1977), Sorhus (1977), Coulmas (1981), Cowie (1992), Nattinger and DeCarrico (1992), Willis (1993), and Howarth (1996), as well as by Renouf and Sinclair (1991). It is a clear manifestation of the operation of the idiom principle.

Lexis therefore patterns in chunks—formulae and collocations, and the like. Not all chunks are FEIs, which are particular sorts of collocation, single choices syntagmatically, restricted lexical choices paradigmatically, and motivated by discoursal considerations. FEIs demonstrate the idiom principle.

2.2 PSYCHOLINGUISTIC ASPECTS OF CHUNKING

Research into language acquisition suggests that language is learned, stored, retrieved, and produced in holophrases and other multi-word items, not just as individual words or terms. Peters (1983) observes widespread use of language routines in young children. She sets her work in the specific context of language development, but also sees the utility of such strings and routines as communicative strategies or 'shortcutting devices' for mature speakers (1983: 3). She argues that even when speakers analogize and become aware of the compositionality of units, the units may continue to be stored as complete or partial units, in addition to their component parts (1983: 90): they can therefore be retrieved and produced as units. She adds: 'The relation between syntax and lexicon may therefore be more fluid than is usually supposed . . . Syntax and lexicon are thus seen to be complementary in a dynamic and redundant way.' Peters also reports parallel findings by Wong Fillmore with respect to L2 speakers. Compare Bolander (1989) who looks at formulaic speech in adult language learners and argues that 'chunk processing' facilitates language processing in general and is a way of acquiring lexicogrammatical structures. Similarly, Bahns *et al.* (1986) look at formulae in child language learning, and argue that formulae are playing a crucial part. Yorio (1989) considers the role of 'conventionalized language' in second language acquisition, and sees a correlation between successful acquisition and the use of formulae. Krashen and Scarcella

(1978: 298) point out that the use of routines and formulae is only one form of L2 language acquisition, insufficient in itself for full competence, but comment on its usefulness 'for establishing social relations and encouraging intake'. Tannen (1989) also discusses prepatterning and repetition in language, and sees it as evidence of structure, rather than redundancy and repetition. In a study of translations by a group of students, Toury (1986: 89) observes that the most successful student segmented the source text into the largest chunks or strings. These studies and others reinforce the observations of collocationists, and support Sinclair's idiom principle.

Support does not only come from language acquisition work. In a series of papers, Kuiper and colleagues look at routine language in special speech situations. For example, Kuiper and Haggo (1984) comment on the use of formulae in cattle auctions, and Kuiper and Tillis (1985) comment on the use of formulae in tobacco auctions, although they comment that the faster the bidding, the fewer the formulae. See Kuiper (1996) for further discussion. Kiparsky (1976) points out correspondences between FEIs and the formulae of oral poetry, of significance and value in constructing classificatory models of poetic formulae.

In discussing the processing of semantically complex items, Jackendoff draws an analogy with chunking in music (1988: 125): 'Any musician can attest that one of the tricks to playing fast is to make larger and larger passages form simplex units from the point of view of awareness—to "chunk" the input and output. This suggests that processing speed is linked not so much to the gross measure of information processed as to the number of highest-level units that must be treated serially. Otherwise chunking wouldn't help.' This can be related to observations that telephone numbers, postcodes, and security codes are easier to remember as chunked groups than as series of individual letters or digits. This provides a motivation and function for the parallel agglomeration of (linguistic) units, as well as providing further evidence of the general applicability of an idiom principle.

2.2.1 *Processing of FEIs*

Research into the psycholinguistic processing of FEIs addresses questions such as how FEIs are recognized; how they are stored in the mental lexicon; whether idiomatic meanings are retrieved before, after, or simultaneously with literal meanings; and how variations and inflections are handled. These matters have not

been resolved, but a number of experiments support certain findings. General overviews of research are given in, for example,
Titone and Connine (1994), and earlier in Swinney and Cutler
(1979), Estill and Kemper (1982), and Schweigert and Moates
(1988): further work is discussed and reported in Cacciari and
Tabossi (1993). There is a huge body of literature demonstrating
repeated attempts to adjust or corroborate previous models and
findings. For the most part, research has concentrated on pure
idioms or metaphorical FEIs, although Botelho da Silva and Cutler
(1993) look at ill-formed FEIs, which they observe are commoner
in Portuguese, French, and German than in English.

It has to be said that from a corpus linguistics perspective, some
of the experiments are suspect. Much of the work elicits responses
on the basis of either decontextualized strings or fabricated texts
and contexts. Bobrow and Bell (1973), Ortony *et al.* (1978), and
Gibbs (1980) show that appropriateness of context, 'biassing' contexts, or contextual clues help to resolve ambiguity thus speeding
up the processing of ambiguous FEIs. However, 'biassing' contexts
given in other experiments—for example, to test perceptions concerning the compositionality of idioms—are so laden with contextual clues that they breach rules of naturalness (Sinclair 1984) and
cannot reflect ordinary language use. Cacciari and Tabossi (1988)
comment that some texts used in experiments contain too many
contextual clues, and Schweigert (1986: 44) that the full picture
may not emerge until better texts are used. Moreover, explorations
and discussions of variation and transformation are typically intuition-based rather than data-driven: they depend on invented examples and so may not reflect real usage. Fellbaum (1993: 278) is
rare in expressing concern at this. Yet many of the results are
interesting and relevant, and in principle, the use of some kind of
disambiguating context is entirely appropriate since in cases where
an FEI *is* genuinely ambiguous, with both literal and idiomatic
interpretations genuinely occurring, it is context which shows up
the intended meaning: see discussion of this point in Section 7.1.

Some physiological or neurological work relates to FEI processing. Van Lancker and Canter (1981) say that there is evidence
from aphasics that propositional (or freely formed) speech and
automatic (or routine) speech are controlled by different parts
of the brain. Burgess and Chiarello (1996) suggest that indirect
forms of language such as metaphorical language, inferences,
indirect speech acts, humour, and idioms are associated with
right-brain processing, whereas syntactic analysis is associated
with left-brain processing.

In attempting to deduce how FEIs are processed, models have been borrowed from TG. The notion of the 'idiom list' has been incorporated into the hypothesis that idioms are stored separately in the mental lexicon—effectively in a look-up list of fixed units, accessed when such a unit is encountered. Some models suggest that FEIs are stored as 'big words', perhaps marked with trans-formational deficiencies as in Fraser's model (1970). (Note that Aitchison (1987a: 13f.) argues from evidence for slips of the tongue 'polymorphemic words are retrieved from the mental lexicon as structural wholes'. Although she is primarily interested in language production here, not decoding, this may be seen as further evidence of the storage of at least some kinds of FEI as big words.) The earliest models and hypotheses, for example Bobrow and Bell (1973), broadly suggest that idioms are stored in a separate list, with analysis of the literal meaning occurring separately from the idiomatic meaning. The literal meaning is normally processed first, and when the processing fails to yield an interpretation for the context, the 'idiom list' is accessed: occasionally the idiom list may be accessed first. Swinney and Cutler (1979) refer to this view as the Idiom List Hypothesis or ILH. Swinney and Cutler reject ILH in favour of the Lexical Representation Hypothesis (LRH). According to LRH, idioms are stored and retrieved like single words and idiomatic and literal meanings are processed simultaneously. Their experiments support LRH, since they observe that subjects decode idiomatic meanings faster than literal ones. One reason for this is that accessing a list is likely to be faster than generating a word-by-word interpretation. Many others observe that idiomatic meanings are processed faster than literal ones, either agreeing that meanings begin to be processed simulta-neously or suggesting that idiomatic meanings are processed first with recourse to the literal only when an idiomatic interpretation fails: see Gibbs (1980, 1986a), Estill and Kemper (1982), Glass (1983), Gibbs and Gonzales (1985), Schweigert and Moates (1988), and Flores d'Arcais (1993). In an early paper in this field, Ortony *et al.* (1978) investigate the processing of metaphorical language and find that it takes no longer than literal, providing the context is appropriate: they do not find that any special proces-sing is needed. Cacciari and Tabossi (1988) reject both ILH and LRH, instead positing a notion of the 'key' word, a component word in an FEI that triggers recognition of the whole (1988: 678): 'Idioms are not encoded as separate entries in the mental lex-icon. Rather, their meaning is associated with particular config-urations of words and becomes available—in lexical processing terms, is accessed—whenever sufficient input has rendered the configuration recognizable.' This may account for recognition points in FEI processing and storage. As a model, it is attractively flexible and makes sense if analogies are drawn with looser collocations and wider phenomena of chunking in language or interpretations of utterances, seen from other perspectives. Needham's findings (1992) support those of Cacciari and Tabossi and other researchers by showing that literal processing of idioms is not necessarily completed: there is a point, he argues, at which literal processing is abandoned because an idiomatic meaning fits and is accepted.

An important factor is familiarity. Schweigert (1991) points out that informants' familiarity with the metaphorical meanings of idioms is a variable, as is the likelihood of the occurrence of their literal meanings. These variables influence whether or not the idiomatic meaning is processed first: for example, there is a contrast between an item like *go haywire* with no literal equivalent, and *in hot water*, which may genuinely be ambiguous between literal and idiomatic meanings. If informants know an FEI and its idiomatic meaning, self-evidently they are likely to process it more swiftly than if they do not. Experiments by Schweigert (1991), Cronk and Schweigert (1992), and Titone and Connine (1994) bear this out.[2] Familiarity with idiomatic and literal meanings is discussed further in Section 7.1.1, and the interpretation of unfamiliar items in Section 7.2.

Conclusions drawn from other experiments subvert traditional views of idioms as not the sums of their parts, and suggest partial compositionality (Gibbs *et al.* 1989*b*; Glucksberg 1993; Colombo 1993). Instead of, or as well as, their unitary value (*spill the beans* = 'disclose a secret'), the component words have idiomatic meanings (*spill* = 'disclose'; *beans* = 'secrets') which are activated when the expression is varied or exploited. Experiments show that variations and exploitations are successfully interpreted as idiomatic as swiftly as any literal interpretations, whereas deviations from canonical forms might have been expected to privilege literal readings: see, for example, Gibbs (1985), Gibbs *et al.* (1989*a*). This supports the 'key' word view of Cacciari and Tabossi. This is not to say that FEIs are entirely compositional: as Peters comments on routine formulae,

---

[2] A mildly complicating factor for speakers of British English who examine the data or who want to test or replicate results is that several American studies draw on lists of FEIs found in British dictionaries and include British-only FEIs or variations, which automatically get a lower familiarity rating from American informants than they would from a matched set of British informants.

units may be holistic as well as analysable. However, transformations of FEIs and other variations are partial evidence of compositionality. Conversely, compositionality explains the range of possible transformations: see, for example, Wasow *et al.* (1983) and Pulman (1993). Finally, further evidence in favour of compositionality is present in findings that, when confronted with unfamiliar FEIs, informants use analogy as a decoding strategy (see Bauer 1983: *passim*; Aitchison 1987*b*: 153 ff. for discussions of analogy), attempting to decompose the metaphor on the basis of better-known FEIs or metaphorical senses (Cacciari 1993; Flores d'Arcais 1993).

Relevant here are experiments concerning informants' intuitions about the metaphors involved in FEIs. Results show increasing awareness of metaphoricality of idioms and 'figurative competence' in children (Cacciari and Levorato 1989; Levorato 1993). Lakoff (1987: 447 ff.) reports surprising unanimity in informants concerning the prototypical mental image invoked by *keeping someone at arm's length* or *spilling the beans*. For example, most say of *spill the beans* that the beans are uncooked and in a container about the size of the human head; that they are supposed to be in the container; that the spilling is accidental; that the beans go all over the place and are never easy to retrieve; and that the spill is messy. Gibbs and O'Brien (1990) report further experiments concerning mental images that show uniform responses, with greater uniformity for idiomatic meanings than for literal ones. Such work relates to the research into cognitive prototypes and categories carried out by Rosch (for example, 1975), to the conceptual metaphors described in Lakoff and Johnson (1980) and Lakoff (1987) (see Section 7.5), and to idiom schemas (see Section 6.6). Stock *et al.* express scepticism about this (1993: 231 ff.), suggesting that the lost historical origins of metaphorical FEIs may explain as much as imposed conceptual-cognitive interpretations.

From all this, it appears that the 'big word' approach to FEIs— seeing FEIs as fundamentally the same as single-word items—is most appropriate for the most frozen of items such as *at least*, *of course*, and *good morning*, and the most opaque idioms, such as *shoot the breeze*, which permit only limited inflection and transformations. The compositionality attributed to other kinds of FEI explains not only variation and transformation but also the revitalization of the images that appear in exploitations. Thus analysing metaphorical FEIs as kinds of 'dead metaphor' (Cruse 1986: 41 ff.; Davidson 1979: 35 f.) is sometimes inappropriate. The images fossilized in FEIs are culturally significant, as Makkai argues (1993), particularly with respect to connotation and the evaluation implied. At the same time, images may not be invoked at all in ordinary non-introspective language use.

I do not want to do more here than report some of the findings of psycholinguistic research into FEIs. Until researchers work with authentically occurring texts, it is very difficult to see whether the various hypotheses accurately reflect what actually goes on during interpretation and processing in real language situations. Many experiments produce evidence concerning particular points, but taken as a set, nothing seems conclusive overall, other than that it is probable that different kinds of FEI require different kinds of processing strategy: a very bland statement. There are strong psycholinguistic arguments in favour of some measure of compositionality in FEIs; however, they do not necessarily contradict collocationist arguments concerning chunking.

2.3 LEXICALIZATION

Lexicalization (Bauer 1983: 48 ff.; Pawley 1986) is, with respect to FEIs, the process by which a string of words and morphemes becomes institutionalized as part of the language and develops its own specialist meaning or function. (See Bauer for fuller discussion of lexicalization, including different uses of terms, and compare also discussion of 'routinization' by Hopper and Closs Traugott (1993: 65).) Béjoint (1989: 1), preferring the term **codedness**, sees it as a crucial concept in determining the lexicon to be covered by a dictionary: 'Roughly, a sequence of graphemes or phonemes is coded if it is recognised as an "established" unit of the language by the members of the community. "Codedness" is an important notion in lexicography, because the word list of a dictionary can only be made up of coded units; if a dictionary recorded uncoded units, it would not be a dictionary at all.' In lexicographical terms, therefore, the coded units of a dictionary—the formal record of a lexicon—are those units, whether morphemes, words, or strings, which may be considered the factors of a language, to use a mathematical analogy. The word *beans* is capable of interpretation through lower-level units, the factors *bean* and the plural morpheme-*s*, whereas *spill the beans* may be compared to a prime number, and irreducible to factors. Clearly, the longer the string, the less likely it is to be non-compositional, in the same way that the density of prime numbers grows less as numbers grow larger.

In theory, a lexicographical analysis of the evidence for a

polysemous lemma should lead to an identification of the different senses and subsenses of the lemma, and the lexicogrammatical patterns associated with those senses. Any uses not explained by an understanding of those senses and the normal rule-governed combinatorial potential of the language may therefore come to be classified as lexicalized or coded units, 'fixed expressions', the exceptions to the rules. In practice, this is not so simple. It presupposes thorough awareness of the combinatorial principles of a language, and these are complicated by being not only syntactic but also lexical or collocational, with restrictions on the syntagmatic axis typically accompanied by restrictions on the paradigmatic axis and vice versa. In English, at any rate, such principles have not yet been codified and exhaustively described, in spite of the best lexicographical endeavours to make corpus-based starts in this direction. It is unlikely that the set of FEIs in English will be delimited until the syntagmatic and paradigmatic properties of individual words and individual meanings have been properly explored: see Čermák who makes similar comments (1994*b*: 188).

The problem can be exemplified by *fall*. One of its uses is as a pseudo-copula with an inchoative meaning: it is followed by an adjective or prepositional phrase with *in* or *into*. The following realizations of the structure occur 5 or more times in OHPC:

fall asleep
fall ill
fall in love
fall into disuse
fall into error
fall short of SOMETHING
fall silent
fall vacant

Fall into disrepair/disrepute/disfavour/neglect/arrears are also found. These adjectives and prepositional phrases largely refer to states that imply such things as helplessness, inertia, inactivity, or disuse, and this is a semantic semi-constraint on this use of *fall*. Although theoretically almost any such 'negative' word could be used, in practice only some are. These are not lexicalized units, but lexical preferences. *Short of* and *in love* are FEIs in their own right, but they occur in other structures and after other verbs, not just after *fall*.

More problematic cases are presented by peripheral uses of prepositions: that is, uses other than their primary functions of indicating space, time, instrumentality, purpose, or other kinds of circumstance. Most prepositions in most FEIs have meanings or functions which are decodable and analogous to other, entirely compositional formulations: principal counter-examples are such FEIs as *at all* and *of course*, which are unanalysable, at least in synchronic terms.[3] For example,

dip into ONE's pocket
for the time being
go by the book
in the line of fire
kill two birds with one stone
make a beeline for SOMETHING/SOMEWHERE
up the creek

The idiomaticity of these FEIs is generated by other elements in the expression, and an analysis of prepositional meaning makes this clear. However, there are cases of prepositional phrases where nouns are used in one of their regular meanings but pattern very strongly with a particular preposition used in one of its peripheral meanings: the strings seem fixed, and the high incidence of the pattern overshadows their compositionality. In this way, a regular collocational pattern comes to be classified as fully lexicalized. An example is the preposition *under*. A peripheral meaning of *under* may be paraphrased as 'subjected to' or 'constrained by': it can be illustrated by such collocations as *under enemy occupation* and *under Chinese rule*, and also occurs in these FEIs:

under SOMEONE's thumb
under lock and key
under orders
under the aegis of SOMEONE/SOMETHING
under the influence of SOMEONE/SOMETHING
under the sway of SOMEONE/SOMETHING

A further group of collocations including *under* consists of

under close watch
under consideration
under discussion
under examination
under observation
under scrutiny

Under here has a similar meaning: 'subjected to'. Although its complement is a process or activity rather than a controlling force, it too is an identifiable meaning or use of *under*. To take the case of *under scrutiny*, the collocation comprises over 20% of the evidence for *scrutiny* in OHPC. While it is grammatically well

---

[3] The uses of adverbial particles are more complex, and particle meaning in phrasal verbs is another matter altogether: see *CCDPV*; Sinclair (1991: 68 ff.); Ruhl (1977).

formed, a lexicographer analysing *scrutiny* might feel that the pattern is sufficiently strong to warrant consideration as a potential unit. Thus the observation of a prominent, asymmetrical collocation, in conjunction with an imperfect model of the phraseological frames of English, leads to its classification as an FEI. (See Nagy (1978) for further discussion of the *under* + NOUN frame: he argues that strings such as *under stress* cannot be considered idioms because 'the second word has its normal meaning, and the meaning of the first is predictable in terms transparent and often very general rules'.)

Similarly with *beyond*, which occurs, usually after a copula, in the frame 'beyond NOUN = verbal process':

    beyond belief
    beyond description
    beyond doubt
    beyond question
    beyond recognition
    beyond repair

Its meaning can be paraphrased crudely as 'impossible to believe/describe/doubt' and so on, or 'too great/much/bad to believe/describe/doubt'. These are units in so far as they are institutionalized, and they are formally rigid (although the nouns can be modified with *any* or *all* for intensification). *Beyond doubt*, *beyond question*, and perhaps *beyond belief* have developed pragmatic functions as epistemic modalizers: the others are compositional by virtue of established, discrete meanings of both preposition and noun. If they are recorded in a dictionary, it should be as patterns and not gestalts.

The lexicalization of FEIs therefore results from a three-way tension between the quantitative criterion of institutionalization, the lexicogrammatical criterion of fixedness, and the qualitative criterion of non-compositionality, but there are problems, as has been seen, with all these criteria. Institutionalization and frequency are not enough on their own. Fixedness can be misleading, and corpora provide evidence of the dynamism or instability of forms. Non-compositionality can be queried in a number of respects, and it is also dependent on the ways in which the meanings of individual words are analysed both in dictionaries and in notional lexicons.

While corpus and text evidence provide quantificational data concerning types, structures, and priorities, they call into question some inherited notions about FEIs. The very identification and classification of FEIs and the assessment of the extent of their lexicalization or codedness becomes indeterminate and arbitrary.

This serves as a caveat for the rest of this book, although the notion of FEI is retained. FEIs are institutionalized and coded culturally as well as lexically: FEIs are a phenomenon of discourse, not simply of the lexicon.

2.4 DIACHRONIC CONSIDERATIONS

This study is synchronic, but institutionalization is a diachronic process and historical aspects cannot be ignored. It is important to remember that much of the lexical, syntactic, and semantic anomalousness of FEIs results from historical processes. Cranberry collocations such as *to and fro* or *kith and kin* contain lexical items that formerly had wider currency. The ill-formed collocation *through thick and thin* is an ellipsis of *through thicket and thin wood*, and *of course* is an ellipsis of *a matter of course* or of the postnominal groups *of course and custom* and *of common course* (see *OED*). Other ill-formed collocations may be considered dialectally well formed: *for free* may be unacceptable in written standard English but conforms to a standard frame *for five pounds, for nothing*. Cutler (1982) correlates the age of FEIs and their transformational deficiencies, pointing out that some items originally had unstable or flexible forms, but they have frozen over time: Chapter 6 will look at variation and the unfreezing and destabilization of FEIs.

FEIs disappear, and others emerge. The stock of cranberry collocations increases when the real-world referents of component lexical items cease to exist or are superseded: for example, *not matter a brass farthing, bent as a nine-bob note*, or *don't spoil the ship for a ha'porth of tar*, to give three numismatics examples. Phraseological collocations are productive and formed by analogy, like most other kinds of neologism. Metaphors, initially transparent, come in from sporting, technical, and other specialist domains: for example, baseball metaphors such as *(way) out in left field*, *(not) get to first base*, or *touch base*, computing metaphors such as *garbage in garbage out*, and business metaphors such as *there's no such thing as a free lunch*. As neologisms become institutionalized and divorced from their original contexts of use, the explanation or motivation for the metaphor may become lost or obscure. They accordingly undergo processes of semantic depletion or semantic shift.

Some metaphorical FEIs and proverbs may be traced back to classical or Biblical sayings or historical events—*better late than never, all roads lead to Rome, an eye for an eye* (etc.), *a (lone) voice crying in the wilderness*, and *burn one's bridges/boats*—and Crystal lists FEIs first recorded in the Bible or in Shakespeare (1988: 198f.). The common European linguistic and cultural heritage has had a strong influence on English FEIs in the past; less so today, since the strongest influence appears now to be intervarietal, with American FEIs penetrating British English. Historically, however, many FEIs were formed through calquing. The peculiar valency of *beg the question* is the result of its being a calque, an imperfect and infelicitous translation of the Latin logic term *petitio principii* (itself recorded in *OED* from 1531 and glossed as 'begging or taking for granted of the beginning or of a principle' and a calque of a Greek term *to en arkhei aiteisthai*, 'the asking in the beginning'). This can be compared with the situation in bilingual Anglophone communities, where the other language influences the development of calques in a non-standard variety of English. For example, Odlin (1991) reports cases of Irish idioms being transferred into an indigenized form of English, as in *you couldn't make stiff on him* ('you couldn't make free with him'), which corresponds to *Ní fhéadfá bheith teann air*, literally 'Not could-you be stiff on-him'. Section 6.1.12 looks briefly at calques which exist in (more or less) standard English alongside their originals. All this ignores non-naturalized FEIs such as *al dente*, *mano a mano*, and *Vorsprung durch Technik* which are found in at least some registers or varieties of English. They constitute a restricted part of the lexicon, and I will not be discussing them.

More significant cross-linguistically or sociolinguistically is the way in which English FEIs are influencing other languages, entering those languages as calques. Significantly, Pedersen (1986: 129f.), Newmark (1991: 80), and Danchev (1993: 58ff.) see calquing as part of the dynamic development of languages, whereby foreign idioms and the like are incorporated into the lexicon, although the violations of perceived norms may cause problems. Pedersen cites as an example Danish *de er velkommen* 'you're welcome' to acknowledge thanks (compare Canadian French *bienvenue*). In another paper (1992), he lists recent borrowings from English into Danish, which he sees in the context of 'language approximation' within the European Union, whereby widely spoken languages such as English influence less widely spoken languages such as Danish. Amongst the calques are:

feje problemet under (gulv)tæppet 'sweep the problem under the carpet'
få fingeren ud 'get one's finger out'
for mange høvdinger og for få indianere 'too many chiefs and too few Indians'

Moberg (1996) reports on the same phenomenon in Swedish, where calques include *the ball is in someone's court, back to square one,* and *get cold feet.* Both Pedersen and Moberg list respectively Danish and Swedish calques of *be caught with one's pants/trousers down, keep a low profile,* and *not be one's cup of tea.* Moberg points out the oddness of the last within the context of a Swedish culture: similarly Pedersen points out the oddness of references to chiefs and Indians in a Danish culture. Danchev (1993) cites recent Bulgarian adoptions of translations of *let the cat out of the bag, (with) a long face,* and *rock the boat.* Danchev comments on the sociocultural significance of this: since 1989, the status of English has risen in Bulgaria and attitudes towards language change have relaxed, and the calques function as indicators of 'sociolinguistic prestige and group cohesion for people with a knowledge of English'.

In his preface to Danchev's paper, Lefevere sets borrowing of phrasemes or FEIs in a wider perspective, arguing that kinship between the FEIs of different languages is not a matter of etymology but of 'interactions on the personal, group, and national level' (1993: 57). This can be related to arguments that FEIs are realizations of intertextuality: see, for example, Hatim and Mason (1990: 132 and *passim*).

An obvious way in which English FEIs realize intertextuality is where catchphrases drawn from cinema, television, politics, journalism, and so on become institutionalized as sayings and other kinds of formula. This process can be observed in the following, of various vintages:

And now for something completely different
Didn't she do well
Go ahead, make my day
I think we should be told
I'll be back
I'll have what she's having
Pass the sick bag, Alice
That will do nicely
There is no alternative [abbreviated as TINA]
This could be the beginning of a beautiful friendship
the white heat of this revolution [usually, 'the white heat of the technological revolution']
We wuz robbed

A few recent institutionalized proverbs are attributable:

It takes two to tango (song by Hoffman and Manning)
When the going gets tough, the tough get going (popularized by Joseph Kennedy)
The opera isn't over until the fat lady sings (Dan Cook)

It is not certain exactly how catchphrases establish themselves as ritualistic FEIs, but in the clearest cases above, they are associated with a memorable event or film sequence, or consistent media use. They are repeated as boundary markers, commentary devices, greetings, and so on, and become situationally or culturally bound.

In other cases, FEIs become established as pithy ways of expressing and referring to concepts. Hyphenation is an indicator of the processes of institutionalization and lexicalization (Pawley 1986: 108). The catenation of strings into quasi-single words signals the writer's intention to consider a string as a unit, or his/her insecurity about the holism, in the same way that scare quotes signal a writer's insecurity about register or terminology. Some such strings found in OHPC are transformations of FEIs, typically as modifiers:

on a **first-come-first-served** basis
an emotive, **pulling-no-punches** oration
his **charity-begins-at-home** appeal
a **don't-take-no-for-an-answer** message

But others are neologistic:

It was a perfect '**I-never-thought-I'd-live-to-see-the-day** situation'.

Six months ago it [sc. a hotel] changed owners, but remained in the **hello-how-may-I-help-you** realm.

The chaos might amuse the man who belonged to the **live-fast-die-young-have-a-good-looking-corpse** school.

Not Ava, though, with her **nothing-is-but-theories-make-it-so** line.

Although these expressions are not fossilized, they represent the formulation and bonding of concepts. Some formulations are ephemeral and ad hoc; others allude to or reflect established cultural stereotypes. Underlying all this are processes of creativity and stability (Cowie 1988): Cowie observes patterns of semantic depletion in interaction-oriented FEIs and of semantic shift in more transactional ones (1988: 132f.). Taking this further, stability can be seen in repetitions, patterns, and collocations in general; creativity in variation and exploitation. The processes are interwoven in complex ways, and must be explored in the context of language as discourse.

3
Corpus and Computer

I take it as axiomatic that effective and robust descriptions of any kind of lexical item must be based on evidence, not intuition, and that corpora provide evidence of a suitable type and quality. At the heart of the study described in this book lies a database of several thousand FEIs, recording their features and characteristics as demonstrated in corpus data. This chapter briefly discusses the database, corpus, and some related computational issues. The following chapters set out the results of the research, and correlations to be drawn.

3.1 DATABASES OF FEIS

The concept of a database of FEIs is far from original. All dictionaries are essentially databases: there are also more focused databases, such as machine-readable dictionaries of FEIs or those set up to study Russian FEIs, reported in Telija and Doroshenko (1992), or Czech idioms for lexicographical purposes, reported in Čermák (1994*a*). Everaert and Kuiper (1996) report the construction of a database of 14,000 English phrasal lexical items, and another of 10,000 Dutch items: the exact typologies of these items is unstated, but the numbers involved suggest that they include phrasal verbs as well as proverbs and conventions. None of these resources exactly parallels each other: each records and prioritizes only certain kinds of information.

3.1.1 *The Set of FEIs*

A total of 6776 FEIs were recorded in the database. I intended to include, as far as possible, a large proportion of the commonest FEIs in current British English, together with some commoner FEIs from American English. The database does not of course record the complete set of the FEIs of English, which is uncharted, unquantified, and indeterminate.

It was not feasible to assemble a set of FEIs for this study purely by empirical means, for example, by examining corpus data either manually or automatically and retrieving all gestalts and only lexicalized or coded units. I therefore decided to use an existing published source as starting-point. However, most such sources—general dictionaries, or specialist dictionaries of idioms—record and perpetuate items not necessarily found in current English. Of the dictionaries available at the time, only *CCELD* (1987) set out to analyse from first principles all (or virtually all) tokens in a corpus of current and general English; the FEIs it included may be taken as a reasonable indication of which FEIs were actually in use in the 1980s. Furthermore, as one of the editors of *CCELD*, I was in a privileged position and knew how and why FEIs in *CCELD* were recorded in the way they were. I therefore built the database around those items which *CCELD* included and identified as 'phrases' in the grammatical coding. In the event, about 10% of the phrases in *CCELD* were rejected as not conforming to the types of FEI under consideration, or as being insufficiently fixed or non-compositional; about 14% of database FEIs do not occur in *CCELD*.

Some of these additions were proverbs from a comparative study of proverbs in French and English that I undertook with Pierre Arnaud in 1991–2, and reported in Arnaud and Moon (1993). The English component of the study examined 240 proverbs in the light of evidence in OHPC, recording in a subdatabase the frequency, and the forms, clause and text positions, and genres in which each example of each proverb occurred. These 240 proverbs consisted of those proverbs best attested in an informant study previously undertaken by Arnaud. Other additions came from elsewhere: FEIs observed in OHPC but not treated in *CCELD*, and FEIs encountered in everyday interaction and reading. In this way, FEIs, or strings manifesting characteristics of FEIs, were included on the basis of at least two out of three possible pieces of evidence: their occurrence in OHPC; their inclusion in a corpus-based dictionary; and their familiarity to informants.

3.1.2 *The Structure of the Database*

'Database' is technically a misnomer as far as my research was concerned, since my database consists computationally of a series of structured text files which could be manipulated by means of standard UNIX tools.[1] A detailed account of the database and report on the findings is given in Moon (1994*b*).

Different kinds of data relating to individual FEIs were recorded in up to 17 separate fields. Two fields were organizational, for example to handle miscellaneous comments concerning exploitation or peculiar distributions. Three fields related to form: the canonical or citation forms of FEIs, major lexicogrammatical variations, and information concerning the realizations of any open slots. One field recorded typology, following the model set out in Section 1.4, and another recorded frequency as observed in OHPC: see Chapter 4. Three fields related to syntax: the clausal functions of FEIs (according to a systemic model); passivization and other transformations and inflections; and significant collocations or colligations of FEIs. Syntactic characteristics of FEIs are discussed in Chapter 5.

Four fields looked more closely at the semantics of four syntactic classes of FEIs. Where the FEI consisted of a predicator and complementation, the verbal process was recorded, following Halliday's model (1985: 101ff.; 1994: 106ff.). Since in many cases, especially with metaphors, the surface process described in the lexis does not accord with the deep process inherent in the actual meaning, I recorded both surface and deep processes. Similarly, where FEIs functioned adjectivally, adverbially, or as nominal groups, I recorded the kind of attribute, circumstantial, or entity they denoted, together with any mismatches between surface lexis and deep meaning. Mismatches are discussed in Section 7.6. Two fields contained information about discoursal functions and pragmatics: that is, the typical function of the FEI in discourse, and the contribution made to text ideationally, interpersonally, or organizationally. The final field recorded attitude and evaluation, for example, positive or negative evaluation, ironic usage, or euphemistic or dysphemistic content. The data from these last three fields is discussed in Chapters 8, 9, and 10.

3.2 CORPUS AND TOOLS

Altenberg and Eeg-Olofsson discuss the need for corpus-based studies of FEIs (1990), commenting that there have been few to

---

[1] I am indebted to Ian G. Batten, who advised me on computational aspects of database design. I am also indebted to former colleagues at DEC/SRC on the Hector project, and in particular Mike Burrows, for their assistance with software.

date. Early work on FEIs was effectively based on the analysis of lists of known items, either observed in texts or in dictionaries (Meier 1975; Norrick 1985). Collection of data was an erratic process and depended on the quantity and type of the texts encountered or the accuracy of the dictionaries consulted. As a result, some studies of FEIs in English are flawed or unbalanced because rare, obsolete, or even spurious FEIs are given equal status with common, current ones. For example, hand-collected sets of citations cannot give robust information concerning relative frequencies.

Inevitably, the development of corpus linguistics and increasing use of large corpora in lexicology and lexicography is changing all this. One of the most important and basic pieces of information to be derived from a corpus concerns lexis: the frequencies and distributions of lemmas, and the forms and collocational patterns in which they occur. Profiles of the lexicon based on corpora can be used to prioritize: to distinguish the incontrovertibly significant from the marginal (and gradations between). This has clear applications in pedagogy, artificial intelligence, contrastive linguistics, and other fields. Collocational studies of corpora shed light on lexical behaviour and pave the way for smarter models of the interaction between syntagm and paradigm.

The linguistic phenomena attested in corpora can be used both to test existing abstract models and hypotheses concerning language, and to establish empirically new models and hypotheses through description. The second approach is characteristic of collocational studies, but most studies of FEIs follow the first since they are founded on and characterized by a priori assumptions. This is not necessarily bad: assumptions and hypotheses may require adjustment or modification, but they are not necessarily wrong. The literature of corpus linguistics shows decisively that there is a tension or conflict between received, introspection-derived beliefs about language and observed behaviour in corpora. One of the most significant results of corpus linguistics is the blurring of divisions and categories that were formerly thought discrete. This is reported, for example, by Sinclair (1986; 1991: 103), Halliday (1993), and, with particular reference to grammatical categories, by Aarts (cited in Aarts 1991: 45f.) and Sampson (1987: 219ff.): see Briscoe (1990) for comments on this last. In relation to FEIs, corpora show up clearly the fallacy of the notion of fixedness of form, and, I suggest, the notion that FEIs can be clearly distinguished from other kinds of linguistic item.

TABLE 3.1.   *Genres represented in OHPC*

newspaper journalism	59.5%
non-fiction	17.9%
fiction	10.9%
magazines and periodicals	6.6%
miscellaneous leaflets and printed matter	1.9%
transcribed speech and broadcasts	3.1%

3.2.1 *The Corpus*

The corpus of texts I used to investigate FEIs was OHPC, the Oxford Hector Pilot Corpus, which I had access to during the period when I was compiling the database. This corpus was assembled by Oxford University Press as the basis for a research collaboration between Oxford University Press and Digital Equipment Corporation's Systems Research Center in Palo Alto, California: I was one of the lexicographers involved in the project. OHPC was a subset of the Oxford Pilot Corpus, itself assembled by OUP as part of the British National Corpus initiative.[2]

The corpus consisted of just over 18 million words of predominantly British English, drawn from 159 texts. Its genre make-up was as shown in Table 3.1. Of the texts, 124, including all the newspapers, are from the period 1989–91. Only 5 of the remaining texts predated 1981: these comprised 2 novels, a biography, and 2 works of non-fiction, together accounting for about 2% of the corpus.

Halliday suggested in 1966 that a 20 million-word corpus would prove a suitable size for linguistic studies (1966: 159). It became clear in the course of the present study that OHPC was too small to give conclusive information concerning transformations, inflection potential, and variations; it merely suggested tendencies. A more suitably sized corpus would be at least an order of magnitude larger. Yet such very large corpora are problematic without efficient and flexible tools to interrogate them: see further below.

OHPC was clearly not a balanced corpus of English. There was far too little spoken data and far too great a proportion of journalism. The newspapers represented—The *Independent*, The *Guardian*, The *Financial Times*—were not demotic, although the 2.4 million words taken from local Oxford newspapers compensated a little for this. Results drawn from the data may therefore be skewed since it is undoubtedly the case that many FEIs have different distributions

---

[2] The compilation of the database of FEIs was not part of the Hector project, but simply took advantage of the availability of the corpus and software.

in different genres: see Section 4.9. In particular, the lack of spoken data meant that FEIs functioning as greetings, valedictions, and other speech acts had distorted frequencies, and were mainly represented in fictional dialogue.

I am *not* claiming in what follows that figures and statistics concerning events observed in OHPC are universal truths. However, I *am* claiming that figures and statistics can be regarded as reasonable benchmarks, which may then be tested against or compared with other corpora: compare Stubbs and Gerbig, who raise the issue of replicability of corpus studies (1993: 65). Some comparative frequencies are discussed in Section 4.8.

I am also claiming that, in spite of the shortcomings of OHPC, gross tendencies observed in it are likely to be observed too in other corpora. Thus FEIs occurring in OHPC with frequencies of 1 per million or more are likely to occur in other corpora of British English of the same period, albeit with different distributions. It is reasonably unlikely that FEIs with frequencies of 2 per million and above would fail to occur at all in comparable corpora. Similarly, it would be surprising if FEIs that do not occur in OHPC, or that occur with frequencies no better than chance, were then found to be highly frequent in comparable corpora. The vintage of corpora is important here: language changes rapidly with respect to FEIs.

3.2.2 *Searching the Corpus*

It is important to emphasize that the success of corpus investigations is entirely bound up with the effectiveness of the corpus tools. Unless these are flexible and powerful enough, searches will fail and results be distorted. Moreover, however much corpora provide data and strong evidence which can prove or disprove intuition, intuition is also necessary or variations will not all be found. Searches are deterministic, and only report what has been sought, not what should or could have been looked for.

The tools I used to interrogate OHPC had been developed by Digital's Systems Research Center, as part of the Hector project. The project and tools are described in detail in Glassman *et al.* (1992), Atkins (1992), and Guarino Reid and Meehan (1994). The tools were extremely flexible and delicate, and I have to date not found tools of their calibre elsewhere.

In most cases, when searching for FEI matches, fairly general queries proved as successful as more precisely framed ones. A specific query such as 'show all matches of the lemma **spill**, used as a verb, with the word **beans** occurring within a window of between 2 and 5 words of **spill**, and preceded immediately by **the**' yielded 7 matches, all containing the FEI *spill the beans*. So too did a search for matches between the lemma **spill**, with no wordclass specified, and the lemma **bean** occurring within the default window of 5 words—or even a window of 15 words. In another case, 23 matches resulted from a search for co-occurrences of *storm*, with noun inflections, and *weather*, with both noun and verb inflections, within a window of 5 words. Of these, 22 matches represented the FEI *weather the storm*, and only one contained the individual words, as nouns, coincidentally co-occurring but not in the syntagmatic structure *weather the storm*, even though both *storm* and *weather* are members of a single lexical set and so literal tokens might have been predicted to co-occur. Thus certain lemmas co-occur in OHPC only within FEIs, as if literal or non-idiomatic co-occurrences are blocked: see further in Section 7.1.1.

More loosely defined queries generally proved better for finding syntagmatic variations. In the case of cranberry collocations such as *grist for one's mill*, searching simply for the cranberry element was sufficient. Occasionally such searches yielded strong evidence of other structures or uses, resulting in redefinition of the string and loss of lexicalized or coded status. The collocation *do someone a disservice* is occasionally classified as an FEI on the grounds that *disservice* is unique to the combination; however, OHPC showed that it occurs in other structures and is therefore a restricted collocation, not an FEI.

One further feature in the Hector corpus tools proved valuable. It was possible to search for collocating words or lemmas, or for collocating wordclasses (for example, 'immediately preceded by a noun'): it was also possible to search for collocating words within lexical sets such as 'clothing' or 'food/drink' (for example, 'with a word denoting an article of clothing within a window of 5 words'). Some FEIs are regularly exploited or have thematically bound variations: they could be found by means of this tool more easily than by random searching for possible variations. For example, 49 matches resulted from a search for the lemma *spill* in collocation with a word denoting a kind of food/drink within a window of 5 words. Of these matches, 9 contained *spill** followed by *the*, 7 realizing *spill the beans*, as reported above. The eighth was *He spilled the large container of orange juice*, and the ninth was *before he can spill the pasta* which turned out to be an exploitation of the idiom in a review of a television comedy:

His old friend and partner in crime Georgio Bertoli (Steve O'Donnell) talks to the police in return for personal immunity and a Continental breakfast. Alarmed by this turn of events the Grand Master of the Freemasons (Nosher Powell) employs two inept hit men, Mig (Tim McInnerny) and Mog (Alexei Sayle), to kill Bertoli before he can **spill the pasta**. (OHPC: journalism)

Finding exploitations and variations of FEIs is the hardest part of corpus-based investigations, and ultimately a matter of serendipity. Searches are most successful when the query consists of two lexical words, fairly close together. Proverbs in particular are frequently truncated or exploited, as Arnaud and Moon report (1993), and several queries are needed to make sure that all variations have been located. Even then, some exploitations escape. For example, when I searched OHPC for different combinations and permutations of the lexical words in *a bird in the hand is worth two in the bush*, the only match of interest was a pub name *The Bird in Hand*, which might as easily allude to a falcon as to the proverb. However, I later found an exploitation of the proverb in

But it's easier, without a dog, to keep the lot you've penned in rather than run the risk of losing them. **A sheep in the pen is worth two in the field** could be our adaptation of the popular saw. (OHPC: journalism)

This sort of ad hoc exploitation is easy to miss.

3.3 COMPUTATIONAL ISSUES

Ideally, the FEIs in a corpus would be identified automatically by machine, thus removing human error or partiality from the equation. There is, however, no evidence that this is possible given the current state of the art. It is also difficult to see exactly how progress can be made. The problems arise because in so many cases FEIs are not predictable, not common, not fixed formally, and not fixed temporally (that is, they are often vogue items like slang). They are dynamic vocabulary items, whereas—at least at present—corpus processing requires givens and stability.

The size of the computer-held corpora used in linguistic research has increased over the last 30 years by orders of magnitude. Leech comments on how 'first-generation' corpora of up to 1 million words (such as the Brown and LOB corpora) have been succeeded by 'second-generation' corpora of 20 million or so words such as OHPC and the Birmingham Collection of English Text, and then by 'third-generation' corpora of hundreds of millions of words

(1991: 10). There is too much data for manual analysis, and pre-processing is required in order to make use of the information that such corpora contain. That is, routines are run over the data in order to identify certain features of the component text. At the most basic level, the text is indexed so that tokens of the same word type may be retrieved as a set. Beyond this, the most extensively developed and successful of the preprocessing or automatic routines involve the tagging of words with part-of-speech labels, the parsing of the sequences so tagged, and the identification of recurrent collocations. Research includes the tagging of the Brown corpus, reported in Greene and Rubin (1971) and of the LOB corpus, reported in Garside *et al.* (1987) and Garside (1987); taggers developed at AT&T Bell Labs, reported, for example, in Church (1988); taggers and parsers developed in Helsinki, reported, for example, in Voutilainen *et al.* (1992); research into collocations led by Sinclair and reported, for example, in Sinclair *et al.* (1970), Sinclair (1991), and Renouf and Sinclair (1991); and research into lexical statistics and the significances of collocations by Church and colleagues and reported in Church and Hanks (1990), Church *et al.* (1991), and Church *et al.* (1994). Such work has concentrated on formal aspects of corpora. Research into semantics—for example, the automatic disambiguation of homographic or polysemous words—has largely proceeded by distinguishing word uses on the basis of grammar or lexical collocation. However, routines are not yet robust or delicate enough to detect the more subtle polysemies recorded in dictionaries. Lexicographers using monolingual corpora to analyse lexis in order to write conventional (non-AI) dictionaries still largely rely on data that has been processed only in terms of form, syntactic function, and lexical collocation.

FEIs present a particular problem for preprocessing routines. Semantically and often syntactically they function as units rather than as arbitrary sequences, but they need not be contiguous or uninterrupted. They may be syntactically or lexically ill formed, breaking conventional grammatical rules or valency patterns. Higher-level automatic routines, attempting to establish meaning or topic, may be thrown by the lexico-semantic incongruence of FEIs in their contexts.

One solution adopted is the use of a preprocessing routine to identify and tag FEIs. These routines largely rely on the establishment of a look-up list of FEIs and then pattern matching: the text processed is searched for matches of the predefined listed strings, and occurrences are flagged as units. Preprocessing routines thus reflect the tradition of the notional or actual storage of FEIs as a separate part of the lexicon, as well as reflecting work on patterning and chunking in language in general. A number of routines of different kinds have been developed. The tagging of the LOB corpus was assisted by a program IDIOMTAG, described and discussed by Blackwell (1987) and McEnery (1992: 67) whereby holistic units such as *at first sight* and *to and fro* were tagged as such. This often involved the use of 'ditto tags', whereby subsequent elements in non-compositional units such as *at last* and *time and again* were linked to the first element and given a tag appropriate to the whole unit. Johansson and Hofland describe these units further (1989), and list 160 of them. The list of combinations includes foreign phrases such as *ultra vires* and compounds such as *button stitch* as well as FEIs, and it is clear that the list was only a tiny beginning to the efficient tagging of multi-word items in a corpus. Some further programs are described and discussed by Wilensky and Arens (1980), Kunst and Blank (1982), Chin (1992), Stock *et al.* (1993: 237f.), and Cignoni and Coffey (1995). Martin (1996: 88f.) gives an overview of the problems presented in computational processing of FEIs, and recent European work includes the DECIDE project.

Preprocessing routines work best in cases where the FEIs contain unique constituents or unique sequences, as with *to and fro* or *take umbrage,* or are completely frozen 'big words'. They work less well where FEIs have unpredictable transformational behaviour or where they are interrupted by non-canonical words. They work least well when the FEI has variant forms or is exploited. Stock *et al.* (1993) describe their program WEDNESDAY 2 which deals reasonably successfully with variant word order in FEIs as well as some other kinds of variation—although not exploitations. Gross (1993) describes a parsing model which improves the handling of variation in FEIs, particularly in the cases of sets such as *blow one's top/cork/stack* and of FEIs with interpolated items. Pulman (1993) rejects the notions of the look-up list and the canonical form, preferring instead a notion of lexical indexing, where each component is marked with its special features. Breidt *et al.* (1996) describe IDAREX, which involves the use of local grammars in which the morphological, syntactic, and sequencing properties for items are stated on an individual basis, in addition to some information concerning lexical variation (they do not specify how robust information concerning all this is to be acquired): the information is then accessed during the processing of text in order to identify FEIs.

A look-up list is based in the first place on secondary sources, albeit modified by an examination of a corpus, and this approach to corpus analysis is diametrically opposite to the kinds of empirical study being carried out on collocation. Ideally, any base look-up list of FEIs would be generated automatically or empirically, but this is hard to do. The use of secondary sources in establishing a base look-up list is unsatisfactory and a compromise; however, it allows a reasonably powerful processing tool to be developed and can of course be adjusted as information becomes available. Comparisons may be made with other work in natural-language processing, for example, work carried out on the automatic detection of metaphor and metonymy in text (Fass 1991; Martin 1990). Such work typically involves some pretraining such as access to a list of valencies of the literal meanings and interpretation of nouns and so on in terms of superordinates or *isa*-structures. Work by Church *et al.* on lexical substitutability (1994) can lead to the automatic detection of sets of collocates, for example the range of verbs used with a noun or vice versa, but again it starts from a manually observed 'good-case' pairing. Taggers themselves start from look-up tables of the word classes of particular words or sets of rules, and probabilities of polyfunctional words.

If look-up lists are incorporated into routines, the size of the list becomes important. The list of ditto tags used for the LOB corpus contained relatively few items, all 'big words'. Smith, in discussing the preprocessing of idioms, suggests that there are 4–5,000 common idioms in everyday use (1991: 64), although his definition of 'idiom' is fairly loose. In discussions with the Hector team at DEC/SRC concerning the value of fully tagging multi-word items, we decided that we should expect to find around 15,000 FEIs and phrasal verbs in a second-generation corpus of current British and American English: routines based on the results of the tagging would need to know at least that number of items in order to be effective. This figure would need to be increased for substantially bigger corpora such as BofE, probably to around 25,000, since many more randomly occurring low-frequency items would be observed.

A comparatively late development in the course of the Hector research collaboration between Oxford University Press and Digital Equipment Corporation was the introduction of 'z-tagging'. Tokens of individual types in OHPC were already being tagged in order to link tokens with the relevant sense in an electronic dictionary entry that synthesized the evidence found for the type in OHPC. In particular, each token of each FEI, phrasal verb, and

compound was given an individual sense tag (for each of its meanings if it was polysemous). With the introduction of z-tagging, the
main tag for each multi-word item was set at one of the elements:
the first word in a compound, the verb in a phrasal verb, and a fixed
lexical element in an idiom. All subsidiary items were then given
the same tag, suffixed with -z, thus binding all parts of all individual
tokens of individual lexical items, regardless of orthography. Had
OHPC been fully sense-tagged, it would have given a complete
record of the lexical items in the corpus, as opposed to the orthographic words. This would have interesting potential. It would be
possible to compute the proportion of words in text that form part
of complex lexical items, both in the corpus as a whole and in
individual texts or genres, thus measuring the density of such items
in text. The tagging of subsidiary elements in compounds and
phrasal verbs would enable lexicographers to analyse and describe
more efficiently the morphology and semantics of such items. One
of the aims of hand-tagging OHPC for sense and syntax was to use
the tagged corpus as a training corpus, to facilitate the automatic
analysis of an untagged corpus by recognition of recurrent patterns
associated with individual meanings (see Glassman *et al.* 1992;
compare Leech 1991: 18 and *passim*). The detailed tagging of
multi-word items would extend the kind of automatic analysis
possible. Finally, a fully sense-tagged corpus would make it possible
to compute the relative proportions of the FEI tokens, including
variations, and their homographic non-idiomatic strings. The
resulting data could be used to establish probabilistically the
likelihood of further tokens of individual strings in other corpora
being idiomatic or literal.

If preprocessing routines are to incorporate a look-up list, then
much of their success clearly depends on the robustness and completeness of the list. The better the list, the more likely FEI tokens
are to be detected. In particular, information concerning syntax,
transformations, variations, and non-canonical insertions would, as
Breidt *et al.* suggest, lead to more sophisticated matching procedures to be developed. However, this information needs to be
derived from robust sources such as large corpora, and not from
intuition nor from commercial dictionaries. Including data concerning the distribution of FEIs in a corpus would help in the
identification of FEIs in other corpora, through probability. Even
though many FEIs are rare and likely to occur only on a random
basis, information to the effect that an FEI *is* rare has itself some
predictive power.

There are several benefits of improved automatic routines for recognizing FEIs in text. First, it would improve the accuracy of tagging and parsing routines in general. Secondly, it would become possible to investigate more robustly the distribution of FEIs, and of different kinds of FEI, in specific genres, varieties, or idiolects (see Biber and Finegan (1991) for a discussion of the methodology of using corpora in large-scale studies of variation, and Crystal (1991) on stylistic profiling). This would lead to a better understanding of the lexicon and could be unified with work on the recurrent collocations of text and of specific text-genres. As work developed, information gathered could be fed back into the look-up list in order to modify, augment, and improve it. Thirdly, there are possible applications in machine translation (see Bar-Hillel (1955) and many writers since on the automatic translation of idioms). Finally, Meehan *et al.* (1993) describe other applications in natural-language processing such as a software product, functioning like a spell-checker or grammar-checker, to monitor the use of FEIs in text being composed. It would report aberrant or marked uses, abnormally high (or even low) densities of idioms, Americanisms and Briticisms, and so on. An extension of the FEI list would incorporate stock formulae—Pawley and Syder's 'lexicalized sentence stems' (1983), Coulmas's 'routine formulae' (1979*b*), Nattinger and DeCarrico's 'lexical phrases' (1992)—in order to exploit the recurrence of such formulae in speech recognition work. For example, many telephone calls involve the eliciting and giving of information and operate round simple exchange structures, realized by prefabricated routines and semi-institutionalized strings, or programmable data. The starting-point for all such work must be a detailed corpus-based, text-based description of FEIs, of the kind begun in my own study, and incorporating distributional, formal, semantic, and discoursal information.

4
Frequencies and FEIs

In setting out what I learned about the distribution of FEIs from investigating a corpus, I want to emphasize again the limitations of the study in order to contextualize my findings. OHPC was an idiosyncratic corpus, but useful as a means to an end. My findings were intended to be benchmarking statistics; to provide some framework which could be used in further studies—for example, of different corpora, whether matched typologically or constructed from different kinds of text. Some cross-corpus comparisons are given in the last sections of this chapter. It is my contention that the general tenor of the distributions I observed are borne out by other corpora, and anomalies can be explained.

4.1 FREQUENCY AND SIGNIFICANCE

One of my core aims in examining the evidence in OHPC was to gather data concerning the frequency of FEIs. However, frequency can be complex to assess. There are problems with deciding exactly which elements in an FEI should be regarded as part of the FEI. Auxiliaries, subjects, infinitive markers, and so on are part of the FEI clausally but not lexically; the status of the realizations of open slots is uncertain. Corpora are quantified in terms of individual words or tokens, and FEIs consist of at least two words, but FEI frequencies need to be calculated per lexical item rather than component word. I did not attempt to calculate what proportion of OHPC is made up of FEIs. A best guess would be between 4% and 5%: that is, 4–5% of corpus words are actually parts of FEIs of the kinds held in the database.

I set the significance threshold at 5. FEIs occurring 4 or fewer times in OHPC can be considered random events which might not be observed in another corpus, even one matched exactly as to size, genre distribution, and vintage. See discussion by Dunning (1992) on how statistics concerning very low-frequency items in corpora are likely to be inaccurate or may not be replicable.

The string *of course* occurs around 240 times per million words of OHPC. Basic probability theory can be used to assess the significance of this by calculating the difference between its observed frequency and its expected frequency. Expected frequency is calculated according to the formula given in Figure 4.1. The result gives the likelihood of events occurring at any given point in the corpus: events here are two-word sequences. This is realized in the case of *of course* as shown in Figure 4.2. The consecutive sequence *of course* might be predicted to occur around 228 times in the corpus, or just over 12 tokens per million words: a twentieth of its actual frequency.

$$\frac{\text{frequency word1}}{\text{tokens in corpus}} \times \frac{\text{frequency word2}}{\text{tokens in corpus}}$$

FIG. 4.1 Formula for predicting collocational frequency

$$\frac{539657}{18020163} \times \frac{7599}{18020163}$$

FIG. 4.2 Predicted frequency of *of course* in OHPC

Expected frequency for collocations that are not immediately adjacent are calculated as in Figure 4.3. The lemma *spill** may be predicted to occur within a window of two words of *beans* less than 0.01 times (see Figure 4.4). Its actual frequency in OHPC, excluding exploitations, is 7.

$$\frac{\text{frequency word1}}{\text{tokens in corpus}} \times \frac{\text{frequency word2}}{\text{tokens in corpus}} \times \text{window}$$

FIG. 4.3 Formula for predicting frequency of non-adjacent collocations

$$\frac{259}{18020163} \times \frac{332}{18020163} \times 2$$

FIG. 4.4 Predicted frequency of *spill the beans* in OHPC

These are crude measures of significance. More rigorous methods of calculating frequency use t-scores or mutual information: see Church *et al.* (1991) for detailed discussions of this, and

Choueka *et al.* (1983) for statistical calculations for Hebrew. It was, however, beyond the scope of the present study to calculate such significances routinely for all the FEIs investigated.

4.2 THE RECORDING OF FREQUENCY

The frequency of an FEI as recorded in the database is simply the number of times the string occurred in OHPC, including exploitations and variations. The frequencies of certain transformations were recorded separately (for example, the nominalization of *get one's wires crossed* as *crossed wires*), where that transformation seemed to be a separate lexical item. Frequencies of 17 and below—that is, less than 1 per million—were recorded as absolute figures; however, frequencies of 18 and above were given in bands, and these are set out in Table 4.1.

The banding of FEI frequencies in this way gives a more succinct picture of distribution than raw, ungrouped frequencies and it certainly simplified counting large numbers. However, with hindsight, it would have been preferable to give absolute figures for all FEIs, not just infrequent ones. The dividing-lines are arbitrary, and in terms of distribution, FEIs with frequencies at the top of a band have more in common with those at the lower end of the next highest band than with those at the lower end of their own band.

TABLE 4.1. *Frequency bands for FEIs*

Band	Rate of occurrence	Comment
I	zero tokens	insignificant frequencies,
II	1–4 tokens in OHPC	(below the significance threshold)
III	5–17 tokens in OHPC (less than 1 token per million)	low frequencies
IV	18–35, 1–2 tokens per million	
V	36–89, 2–5 tokens per million	medium frequencies
VI	90–179, 5–10 tokens per million	
VII	180–899, 10–50 tokens per million	
VIII	900–1799, 50–100 tokens per million	high frequencies
IX	1800+, 100 or more tokens per million	

4.3 OVERALL FREQUENCIES

Note that in the tables below, figures for FEIs falling within particular groupings or bands are represented as percentages, normally rounded to the nearest whole number. The spread of corpus frequencies among database FEIs was as shown in Table 4.2.Thus just under 40% of FEIs in the database occur with frequencies that must be considered no more significant than random chance, and over 70% of FEIs have frequencies of less than 1 per million tokens.

Zero frequency is ambiguous: it may signify either non-currency or simply a random failure to appear. Examples of FEIs with zero frequencies include:

bag and baggage
by hook or by crook
cupboard love
hang fire
kick the bucket
lose ONE's rag
one man's meat is another man's poison
out of practice
speak for yourself!
when the cat's away, the mice will play

In contrast, there are cases of FEIs which occur in OHPC with surprisingly high frequencies: for example, *a leopard does not change its spots* and *the die is cast* both have frequencies of around 0.55 per million. These reflect the kind of mannered, literary journalism in OHPC. They have lower frequencies in BofE, respectively 0.19 per million and 0.28 per million; however, most of the BofE tokens

TABLE 4.2. *FEIs and frequency ranges*

Frequency range	Proportion of FEIs
0	8%
1–4	32%
5–17	32%
1–2/million	12%
2–5/million	9%
5–10/million	4%
10–50/million	3%
50–100/million	<1%
over 100/million	<1%

occur in written British journalism, which corroborates the distribution observed in OHPC.

4.4 FREQUENCY AND GENERAL TYPOLOGY

Frequency can be correlated with typology (see Section 1.4). Percentages of database FEIs according to their general idiomaticity
type are as shown in Table 4.3. This only considers primary classifications and ignores secondary ones; however, if account is taken
of dual classifications, the proportions are very similar (see Table
4.4). Secondary classifications are ignored in the following sections.

Table 4.5 shows the percentages of FEIs in the database in each
frequency band, according to general typology. This shows that the
majority of metaphors have frequencies of less than 1 per million,
and that very common FEIs are likely to be anomalous collocations
of some kind. Figures correlating frequencies, typology, and syntax
are set out in Sections 5.2 and 5.3.

TABLE 4.3. *FEI proportions, according to idiomaticity type*

anomalous collocations	45.3%
formulae	21.3%
metaphors	33.4%

TABLE 4.4. *FEI proportions: idiomaticity type, including secondary classifications*

anomalous collocations	43%
formulae	21%
metaphors	36%

TABLE 4.5. *FEI proportions: frequency and idiomaticity type*

	Anomalous collocations	*Formulae*	*Metaphors*
0	2%	2%	3%
1–4	11%	8%	13%
5–17	15%	5%	13%
1–2/million	7%	2%	3%
2–5/million	6%	2%	1%
5–10/million	3%	<1%	<1%
10–50/million	2%	<1%	<1%
50–100/million	<1%	<0.1%	0
over 100/million	<1%	<0.1%	0

4.5 DISTRIBUTION OF ANOMALOUS COLLOCATIONS

The macrocategory of anomalous collocations includes the subcategories **ill formed** (*by and large, of course*); **cranberries** (*short shrift, to and fro*); **defective** (*at least, in effect*); and **phraseological** (*in action, on time*). The 3,068 database FEIs labelled as anomalous collocations occur in the proportions shown in Table 4.6.

Mapping types onto frequency bands gives the results shown in Table 4.7. The commonest type is overwhelmingly the defective collocation. Those FEIs which are grammatically ill formed or contain unique items largely have low frequencies.

4.6 DISTRIBUTION OF FORMULAE

The macrocategory of formulae includes **simple formulae** (*you know, not exactly*); **sayings** (*that's the way the cookie crumbles, an eye for an eye*); **proverbs** (*enough is enough, you can't have your cake and eat it*); and **similes** (*as good as gold, live like a king*). The 1,443 database FEIs labelled as formulae occur in the proportions shown in Table 4.8.

TABLE 4.6. *Subtypes of anomalous collocations*

ill-formed	10%
cranberries	4%
defective	62%
phraseological	24%

TABLE 4.7. *Anomalous collocations: frequency and subtype*

	Ill-formed	Cranberries	Defective	Phraseological
0	<1%	<1%	3%	1%
1–4	2%	1%	14%	5%
5–17	3%	1%	21%	7%
1–2/million	<1%	<1%	9%	3%
2–5/million	1%	<1%	8%	4%
5–10/million	<1%	<0.1%	3%	2%
10–50/million	<1%	<1%	3%	1%
50–100/million	<1%	0	<1%	<1%
over 100/million	<1%	0	<1%	<0.1%

TABLE 4.8. *Subtypes of formulae*

simple formulae	70%
sayings	2%
proverbs	19%
similes	9%

TABLE 4.9. *Formulae: frequency and subtype*

	Simple formulae	Sayings	Proverbs	Similes
0	5%	<0.1%	5%	2%
1–4	20%	1%	11%	6%
5–17	21%	<1%	3%	<1%
1–2/million	9%	<0.1%	<0.1%	<0.1%
2–5/million	8%	0	<0.1%	0
5–10/million	4%	0	0	0
10–50/million	3%	0	0	0
50–100/million	<0.1%	0	0	0
over 100/million	<0.1%	0	0	0

Of the proverbs, 59% are metaphorical, or involve some kind of metaphor, for example, *let sleeping dogs lie*, or *a leopard does not change its spots*: compare Norrick's study (1985) of proverbs which finds a comparable proportion of metaphorical proverbs in *ODEP* (1970). The comparisons in 33% of the similes are not transparent: for example, the motivations for *plain as a pikestaff* and *right as rain* are obscure or opaque.

Mapping types onto frequency bands give the results shown in Table 4.9. As far as proverbs, sayings, and similes are concerned, their occurrence or non-occurrence in corpora of this size is almost entirely a matter of chance.

4.7 DISTRIBUTION OF METAPHORS

The 2,265 metaphors were divided into three classes: transparent, semi-transparent, and opaque. The relative proportions are shown in Table 4.10. It is important to note that comparatively few metaphorical FEIs are opaque. The majority can be decoded through real-world knowledge: compare discussions concerning the compositionality of idioms. However, as I pointed out in Section 1.4.3,

TABLE 4.10. *Subtypes of metaphor*

transparent	37%
semi-transparent	51%
opaque	12%

TABLE 4.11. *Metaphors: frequency and subtype*

	Transparent	Semi-transparent	Opaque
0	2%	4%	2%
1–4	13%	21%	5%
5–17	14%	20%	4%
1–2/million	5%	5%	<1%
2–5/million	2%	2%	<0.1%
5–10/million	<1%	<1%	0
10–50/million	<1%	<0.1%	0
50–100/million	0	0	0
over 100/million	0	0	0

perceptions of the transparency or opacity of metaphors are subjective.

Distribution of metaphors is as shown in Table 4.11. Very few opaque metaphors occur in OHPC with frequencies greater than 1 per million; they include *bite the bullet, over the moon,* and *red herring*. In the far larger BofE, they are slightly less common, but still have frequencies of over 2 tokens per 3 million words. No metaphor occurs more frequently than 50 per million.

4.8 CORPUS COMPARISONS

Nobody would claim that OHPC is a balanced corpus, but then no corpus is perfect: even when they are perfectly balanced as to genre, text type, mode, speech situation, and topic or field, they still fail to do more than reflect a cross-section of the language that a cross-section of the community might have experienced at particular points in time. How robust are my findings? In order to monitor the reliability of OHPC with regard to the FEI frequencies, I selected a few FEIs and then checked them against other corpora, themselves not necessarily balanced. In this way, some idea of typicality or atypicality could be reached. Ken Church, AT&T

TABLE 4.12. *Corpora used by AT&T Bell Labs*

AP90	AP Newswire items, 1990	46,309,162 tokens
AP91	AP Newswire items, 1991	47,179,688 tokens
WSJ	*The Wall Street Journal*	61,821,228 tokens
CHE	Canadian Hansard, English version	18,043,261 tokens

TABLE 4.13. *Comparative corpus frequencies*

	OHPC	AP90	AP91	WSJ	CHE
spill* the beans	0.39	0.02	0.02	0.06	0.11
beg* the question	1	0.09	0	0.18	0.78
call* the shots	0.94	0.71	0.93	0.89	0.94
without exception	2	0.28	0.53	0.47	2.28
ups and downs	1.83	1.47	1.97	1.93	0.78
from afar	0.89	0.39	0.72	0.36	0.22
of course	242	28.98	34.32	67.88	282.17

Bell Labs, New Jersey, supplied data from the corpora shown in Table 4.12, of which the first three consist entirely of American journalism and the fourth of transcriptions of Canadian parliamentary proceedings. He ran strictly linear searches, as shown above with inflected items indicated by *. They are compared in Table 4.13 with figures for the identical searches in OHPC—itself heavily biased towards journalism, although British rather than American. Figures given are per million. Distribution is clearly variable: even the closely parallel AP Newswire corpora differ. It is noticeable that the differences are not consistent across all the tested FEIs. Some FEIs such as *call the shots* and *ups and downs* are fairly consistent, whereas *of course* is remarkably divergent. This will be discussed further in Section 4.9.

It can be seen further in a comparison between OHPC and the 323 million-word BofE, which is nearly 20 times larger. The same 7 FEIs were checked, although in this case it was possible to run non-linear searches, thus including transformed and interrupted tokens. Table 4.14 sets out comparisons: again, figures are per million. Frequencies in these two corpora still diverge, but to a lesser extent.

In Section 4.3, I listed 10 FEIs with zero frequencies in OHPC. They are all attested in BofE, but two (*bag and baggage* and *cupboard love*) occur with insignificant frequencies of respectively 7 and 6 tokens. The two commonest in BofE (*by hook or by crook* and *out of practice*) occur just over 50 times each in the corpus, that is 0.17 per million: this is still a very low frequency.

TABLE 4.14.   *Comparative corpus frequencies*

	OHPC	BofE
spill* the beans	0.39	0.63
beg* the question	2.5	1.4
call* the shots	0.94	1.22
without exception	2	1.17
ups and downs	1.83	2.59
from afar	0.89	0.98
of course	242	207

TABLE 4.15.   *Frequencies of FEIs in CCDI*

Frequency in 211m BofE	*Proportion of FEIs*
1–4 tokens	4%
5–20	27%
21–63	35%
64–125	17%
126+	17%

CCDI (1995) treats some 4,000 metaphorical FEIs, similes, and proverbs. The published text gives indications of frequencies as observed in BofE (211 million words at the time *CCDI* was written). There is slightly more information in the underlying electronic text, and this is set out in Table 4.15. It shows a distribution curve similar to that set out in Section 4.7.

It is worth mentioning a few quantitative surveys of FEIs which have appeared: mostly limited in scope, and mostly investigating spoken interaction. Norrick (1985: 6 f.) investigated English proverbs, and found only 2 tokens in *A Corpus of English Conversation* (Svartvik and Quirk 1980: 170,000 words). One of the proverb tokens was 'marginal', or manipulated. There was a much higher incidence of proverbs in the 557,514 words of transcribed speech in OHPC: 19 tokens of proverbs were found. Of these, 9 tokens were in their canonical forms, 3 had minor lexical or syntactic variations, and 4 were exploited or varied more radically. It is important to remember, however, that these are still very small numbers.

Akimoto (1983), stressing the importance of corpus-based studies, quantifies some 400 predicate FEIs in the Survey of English Usage (385,000 words) and an unspecified amount of 1970s journalism and other written material. His findings cannot be correlated precisely with those reported here. However, the commonest FEIs that he finds are *take place* (997 tokens); *take action* (595); *take part in*

(560); *play a part/role in* (546); and *take steps* (*to do something*) (272). These all occur with high frequencies in OHPC, although the relative proportions vary. In particular, *take place* has a frequency of over 100 per million, and *take part in* of between 50 per million and 100 per million. The same general tendencies are observed.

Strässler (1982: 77 ff.) reports on the distribution of idioms in a corpus of spoken English interaction of various types—some 106,000 words. He found 92 tokens of idioms in the corpus: an average of 1 idiom per 1,152 words that may be multiplied up to give 868 tokens per million words. Strässler's study centres on a very small sample of language—around 0.6% of the size of OHPC—that is itself neither balanced nor homogeneous and includes published transcriptions of trials and therapeutic sessions as well as transcriptions of privately recorded conversations. Strässler adopts a fairly narrow view of idiom, but amongst his set are a couple of misidentified instantial metaphors and even a literal string. It is therefore difficult to compare results. However, while my database does not record figures for genre, except in the case of proverbs, nor absolute figures for FEIs with frequencies of more than 1 per million, it is possible to make some extrapolations by looking simply at the distribution of metaphorical FEIs. Frequencies across the whole corpus can be calculated since absolute figures were recorded for lower frequencies (and the majority of metaphorical FEIs are infrequent), and distribution curves suggest mean frequencies for commoner ones. In all, 2,079 metaphorical FEIs were recorded as occurring at least once, and a cautious estimate of tokens in OHPC may be given as 22,000, or 1,222 tokens per million: around 40% higher than projections obtained from Strässler's analysis. The discrepancy would be greater if further categories of FEIs were taken into account, for example proverbs and similes. This suggests a distinction in the distributions of idioms in spoken and written texts.

Sorhus (1977) reports a remarkably high density of fixed expressions in her study of 131,536 words of spontaneous Canadian speech. She finds over 6,500 expressions, with the 19 commonest types having 2,643 tokens, and she calculates that 'the national Canadian average . . . [is] one fixed expression every five words' (1977: 217). She is primarily looking at fillers and formulae, however, and includes single word fillers and conventions such as *say*, *right*, *well*, and *please*. As before, it is difficult to compare results. *At times* and *of course* in her study appear to be significantly commoner than in OHPC. Most of her commonest FEIs (in my terms, not hers) also have high frequencies in OHPC: for example, *of course*, *at all*, and *at least*, and the fillers *I think* and *you know*. In contrast, *in fact* occurs very frequently in OHPC but does not feature in her list of commoner expressions. This may be a reflection of the precise genre and texts she is investigating; yet in BofE *in fact* is significantly commoner in unscripted conversation than in written texts.

Finally, Altenberg (1991) reports on a project to describe pre-patterning and recurrent combinations in the 500,000 word London–Lund corpus of spoken English. It investigated all types of combination, but a number of FEIs were observed. Only 5 of the most frequent combinations coincide with Sorhus's top 19: these are *at all*, *I think*, *thank you*, *you know*, and *you see*. *You know* is the commonest, with 152 tokens (1991: 77). Sorhus's figures suggest a frequency for *you know* nearly 9 times greater than this.

In most of these comparisons, it can be seen that the general tendencies I observed in OHPC are paralleled to some extent in other corpora. However, the difficulties of comparing results are obvious. Problems arise from different definitions of target units and different kinds of corpora, and even genre-specific corpora diverge. There may also be anomalous local densities, for example where an FEI is echoed within a text or discussed metalinguistically.

4.9 CORPORA AND GENRE

While some discrepancies between corpora can be attributed to time and language change, differences in genre composition of corpora cannot be ignored. Some genres are marked by relatively high densities of FEIs, others are not and may even seem to block the use of certain kinds of FEI such as highly marked metaphorical informational or evaluative FEIs. This is discussed by Gläser (1986), who sets out the need for a 'phraseo-stylistics', that is a consideration of phraseology from a stylistics perspective. For reasons of politeness, some FEIs are restricted to certain formality levels and situational contexts: this may also be seen in terms of tenor (for example, Halliday *et al.* 1964) and constraints enforced by the power relationships of the participants. For example, FEIs containing taboo or semi-taboo items, such as *for fuck's sake* or *talk through one's arse* are restricted to informal contexts, whereas some formulae such as *have the honour of—*, *it is one's honour to—*, and *your obedient servant* occur in the ritualistic procedures of formal situations. Similarly, catchphrases, other ephemeral formulae, and neologistic metaphors may distinguish subcultures. Changes in the type and density of FEIs may occur in different parts of a single discourse, in particular between different articles in a single edition of a newspaper. This can be seen as indicative of a kind of code-switching (Hudson 1980: 56–8; Wardhaugh 1986: 99 ff.), with corresponding notions of foregrounding or minimizing the dynamic communicative relationship of the discourse participants. A greater use of FEIs helps to bond speaker/writer and hearer/reader, and this is discussed further in Chapter 9.

Certain observations can be made concerning the genre distribution of FEIs, as this emerges from OHPC. The least genre-bound are those FEIs which organize discourse; the most are, unsurprisingly, those conventions and other formulae which are tied to spoken interaction. There is extensive use of FEIs in hortatory journalism, less so in simple expository texts such as news reports, where the density appears to vary according to topic and its seriousness. There is limited use of FEIs in non-fiction apart from organizational ones. While fictional dialogue provides many tokens of FEIs, these uses do not necessarily reflect uses in authentic dialogue and spoken interaction: fiction also seems to perpetuate expressions that may otherwise be found only rarely.

Some support for these assertions can be found in the distribution of proverb tokens in OHPC: broad genre classifications were recorded in the subdatabase of proverbs. In total, 702 tokens of 208 different proverbs were found, and their distribution was as shown in Table 4.16.

The point is further borne out by the case of *beg the question*, of which there are 45 tokens in OHPC: there are also 2 tokens of the transformation *question-begging*. Table 4.17 shows distribution in OHPC according to genre, and it sets observed frequency against the frequency which might be predicted from the relative proportions of text in OHPC. (*Question-begging* occurs once in a newspaper and once in non-fiction.) There are more tokens in non-fiction than might have been expected, although 11 of the 14 occur in only 3 sources, of which 1 is a philosophy text. The percentage of tokens occurring in the newspaper component of the corpus is exactly as

TABLE 4.16. *Distribution of proverb tokens in OHPC*

	Proportion of proverbs	*Proportion of OHPC*
spoken interaction	3%	3%
journalism	71%	66%
fiction	12%	11%
non-fiction	12%	18%
other written material	2%	2%

TABLE 4.17. *Distribution of* beg the question *in OHPC*

	Actual frequency	Predicted frequency
newspapers	27	27
periodicals	3	3
non-fiction	14	8
fiction	1	5
speech	0	1
other	0	1

TABLE 4.18. Beg the question *in OHPC newspapers*

	Actual frequency	Predicted frequency
Financial Times	1	<1
The *Guardian*	5	5
The *Independent*	21	17
Oxford Times/News	0	5

TABLE 4.19. *Distribution of* beg the question *in BofE*

	Actual frequency	Predicted frequency
newspapers	242	186
broadcast journalism	19	59
periodicals	93	68
conversation	13	27
fiction + non-fiction	83	104
other	3	9

predicted, but the distribution between different newspapers is uneven: see Table 4.18. These figures are too small to be conclusive, but suggest that *beg the question* is more likely to occur in 'serious' newspapers with a heavy component of discussion: compare the lower frequency in fiction and higher frequency in non-fiction. It suggests likely discourse types and contexts for the FEI. This is further supported by BofE, where the distribution of the 453 tokens of the FEI is as shown in Table 4.19. Representation in written journalism is higher than might be predicted, and higher than in OHPC. Representation in other written texts is lower than predicted, and lower than in OHPC; unfortunately, the distribution of tokens between fiction and non-fiction cannot be factored in. Representation in speech is also lower than predicted, as in OHPC, and this applies to the conversation subcorpus and to the sub-corpora of broadcast journalism. A closer look at sources in BofE shows up two further points. First, *beg the question* is significantly less common in American English. Its frequency in American sources is roughly 0.7 per million; in British ones, 1.62 per million; and in Australian sources (mainly journalism) 1.31 per million. Compare its frequency in the British OHPC of 2.5 per million, and its low frequencies in American corpora as reported in Section 4.8. Secondly, the distribution of *beg the question* in different journalism components of BofE is 2.8 per million in The *Independent*; 2.6 per million in The *Guardian*; 2.5 per million in The *New Scientist*; 2.3 per million in The *Economist*; and 2.0 per million in The *Times*. This suggests that *beg the question* is indeed commoner in 'serious' journalism.

Some journalistic subgenres are noted for especially high densities of FEIs. McCarthy (1992: 62f.) and McCarthy and Carter (1994: 113) draw attention to idioms and proverbs in horoscopes, and explain it in terms of the interpersonal relationship between astrologer–writer and reader, and of the necessary generality of the predictions. Horoscopes in OHPC certainly bear this out:

ARIES (Mar 21/Apr 20): **Honesty is the best possible policy** especially if you receive conflicting advice or instructions from colleagues or employers. Don't pretend to be something you're not or that you understand all you're told today or you could end up **with egg on your face**.

AQUARIUS (Jan 21/Feb 19): Don't believe anything you're told today until you see it written down **in black and white**, even then you should be cautious and **take a pinch of salt with** whatever you see or hear. A new era of expansion and enterprise is about to begin, but there's no need for you to **jump the gun** or make premature promises.

PISCES (Feb 20/Mar 20): You may be engrossed and enthralled about **the whys and wherefores** of a theoretical grand design or intellectual masterplan, but it's **the nuts and bolts of** daily tasks and chores that are most pressing Wednesday. Usually you've a bevy of buddies happy to help but you have to **show willing** and **pull your weight**.

Genre-based patterns can be seen in the comparative corpus frequencies set out in Section 4.8. *Call the shots* and *ups and downs* are relatively evenly distributed across corpora regardless of their composition. *Of course* has higher frequencies in corpora containing spoken interaction, and *from afar* in corpora containing fiction. *Beg the question* has already been discussed in detail. Some further genre-based comparisons can be made between OHPC and BofE with respect to just four of the FEIs, bearing in mind that the size and composition of the corpora are different and the numbers of FEI tokens involved are small: see Table 4.20. *Spill the beans, call the*

TABLE 4.20.　*Comparative corpus distributions*

	Proportion of genre in corpus	Proportion of FEI tokens in genre			
		spill the beans	*call the shots*	*ups and downs*	*from afar*
OHPC written journalism	66%	75%	83%	79%	62%
BofE written journalism	56%	77%	72%	66%	48%
OHPC spoken sources	3%	0%	0%	3%	0%
BofE spoken sources	19%	2%	13%	11%	8%
OHPC fiction + non-fiction	29%	25%	17%	18%	38%
BofE fiction + non-fiction	23%	21%	15%	23%	41%
OHPC other	2%	0%	0%	0%	0%
BofE other	2%	<1%	0%	1%	3%

shots, and *ups and downs* are consistently commoner in journalism. In contrast, *from afar* is commoner in fiction/non-fiction: slightly so in OHPC, more so in BofE (which contains substantially more fiction than OHPC). These findings suggest possible genre preferences for individual FEIs, relating to interpersonal conventions.

These FEIs are generally less common in spoken data than might be predicted. A number of people on different occasions have made the point that the low frequencies I found in OHPC for idioms, proverbs, and the like are misleading, that they simply result from the lack of conversational data in OHPC: conversation has, allegedly, a much greater density of those kinds of lexical item. All my investigations contradict this view. Obviously, some FEIs such as situational formulae and conventions feature more strongly in spoken discourse, but this appears not to be the case for idioms. Table 4.21 shows 24 FEIs, mainly idioms, giving their incidence per million in BofE as a whole, and also in its 20 million-word sub-corpus of unscripted conversation. Only five items are commoner in conversation: *behind the times* (marginally), *go (the) whole hog*, *out of the blue*, *over the moon*, and *red herring*. *Go (the) whole hog* has an inflated frequency because of repetitions by a single user in a single interaction. *Over the moon* is not found in American English: if only British and Australian sources in BofE are taken into account, its frequency in general text is 1.2 per million. It appears that people

TABLE 4.21. *Distributions (per million) of FEIs in BofE and conversation*

	BofE	Conversation
armed to the teeth	0.3/m	0
behind the times	0.3/m	0.4/m
bite the bullet	0.8/m	0.5/m
cut and dried	0.5/m	0.3/m
face the music	0.7/m	<0.1/m
foot the bill	1.8/m	0.6/m
get the picture	0.7/m	0.6/m
give/get the cold shoulder	0.5/m	0
go (the) whole hog	0.5/m	0.9/m
let the cat out of the bag	0.3/m	0.1/m
make no bones about	0.6/m	0.3/m
nip SOMETHING in the bud	0.6/m	0.4/m
on cloud nine	0.3/m	0.3/m
out of the blue	2.5/m	2.7/m
out of thin air	0.3/m	<0.1/m
over the hill	0.5/m	0.4/m
over the moon	1/m	1.3/m
pull ONE's punches	0.7/m	0.2/m
red herring	0.9/m	1.3/m
sour grapes	0.7/m	0.5/m
spin a yarn	0.3/m	0
swallow ONE's pride	0.4/m	0.1/m
(take SOMETHING with) a pinch/grain of salt	0.7/m	0.7/m
upset the applecart	0.3/m	0.3/m

may be impressionistically over-reporting high incidences of idioms in conversation. This may well be because of the saliency of idioms and the fact that they are marked lexical items. Further, some people may be overinfluenced by passive, ostensibly 'spoken-genre', speech situations such as dialogue in fiction, film, and television, where certain FEIs appear to be fossilized and used to develop or delineate character and to foster the development of the narrative. *Hold your horses* is a case in point, as its genre of choice is fabricated dialogue, not naturally occurring speech. This further confuses the picture with respect to the density of idioms in authentic conversation. At the same time, I must emphasize again that ordinary spoken interaction is very full of other kinds of fixed phrase and recurrent formulaic structuring devices: compare Aijmer

(1996) and Pawley and Syder (1983). It is clear that the exact densities and proportions of different kinds of item in different genres will only emerge after exhaustive corpus-based and text-based studies.

5
Lexical and Grammatical Form

This chapter looks at lexical and grammatical aspects of FEIs. One particular finding from OHPC—that the lexical forms of FEIs are much more unstable than is often thought—is so important and complex that I will deal with it separately in Chapter 6.

5.1 LEXIS AND ANOMALY

It is not at all surprising that the vocabulary of FEIs has a distribution that is different from that of the lexicon in general. A frequency list of the constituent words of database FEIs differs markedly from that for OHPC. This is, of course, not comparing like with like, but it gives some indication of words (and so concepts, images, and structures) which feature strongly in FEIs, or occur relatively more often in FEIs than in freely formed text. Just over 4,000 types or forms, unlemmatized, constitute the vocabulary of database FEIs, including variations. This is a remarkably small number, given that even a moderate-sized English dictionary includes 20–30,000 lemmas. Whole areas of the vocabulary—whole semantic fields—simply do not occur in FEIs. For example, *carbon, glass,* and *sulphur* are common substances, and common in the lexicon; *angry, sad,* and *beautiful* are common adjectives, describing common emotions or qualities; *chair, bowl, pencil,* and *newspaper* designate common everyday objects. However, they feature in few FEIs of any kind:

    people in glass houses shouldn't throw stones
    small is beautiful
    (not) a bowl of cherries
    have/put lead in ONE's pencil

5.1.1 *Word Rankings*

Table 5.1 shows the 20 commonest types occurring in database FEIs (in present tense, canonical forms), set against the 20

TABLE 5.1. *Frequency rankings of types in FEIs and OHPC*

Rank	FEIs	OHPC	Rank	FEIs	OHPC
1	the	the	11	at	on
2	a	of	12	out	The
3	in	to	13	with	with
4	of	and	14	it	it
5	to	a	15	has	be
6	on	in	16	takes	as
7	is	is	17	all	at
8	and	that	18	makes	by
9	as	for	19	not	I
10	for	was	20	no	he

TABLE 5.2. *Rankings of lexical types in FEIs and OHPC*

Rank	FEIs	OHPC	Rank	FEIs	OHPC
1	takes	time	11	mind	work
2	makes	first	12	comes	make
3	goes	people	13	life	good
4	way	new	14	hand	get
5	gets	last	15	head	British
6	time	years	16	day	go
7	good	year	17	go	take
8	puts	made	18	side	see
9	keeps	way	19	heart	know
10	gives	cent	20	eye	think

commonest orthographic types in OHPC.[1] There is considerable overlap. However, the 20 commonest lexical types occurring in the database FEIs and the 20 commonest lexical types in OHPC have less in common: see Table 5.2. (*Cent* in OHPC occurs almost entirely as part of the compound *per cent*.) Some contrasts result from inflection, but others suggest the comparative dominance in FEIs of delexical or support verbs and of nouns which have specific rather than general meanings. The former are characteristic of anomalous collocations, and the latter of metaphors. Table 5.3 sets out a comparison of the lexical types occurring at least 11 times in anomalous collocations and metaphors in the database. Verbs feature in both lists, but there are more nouns in the list for metaphors than in that for anomalous collocations: 50% more in fact. These

---

[1] These were indexed separately and not lemmatized, so that *the* and *The* are treated as individual items.

TABLE 5.3. *Frequencies of lexical types in anomalous collocations and metaphors*

Tokens	Anomalous collocations	Tokens	Metaphors	Tokens	Anomalous collocations	Tokens	Metaphors
101	makes	54	takes	15	name	17	hell
99	takes	52	goes	15	order	16	cold
59	way	50	gets	15	point	16	loses
52	goes	44	puts	14	go	16	mind
51	time	37	head	14	lets	15	ears
41	mind	31	makes	14	runs	15	runs
39	gives	31	way	14	turns	14	ear
38	keeps	30	hand	13	bad	14	mouth
37	gets	30	keeps	13	luck	14	teeth
36	good	26	comes	13	view	13	air
30	comes	26	gives	12	breath	13	blood
30	life	26	side	12	head	13	falls
28	puts	25	nose	12	lives	13	ground
23	hand	24	eye	12	question	13	pulls
22	word	23	turns	12	take	13	sets
21	day	22	heart	11	account	13	throws
20	last	22	plays	11	better	12	earth
19	first	21	face	11	breaks	12	home
19	matter	20	end	11	catches	12	light
18	place	19	line	11	hard	12	top
18	short	18	eyes	11	lays	12	water
18	full	18	hands	11	part	11	full
17	line	18	life	11	sets	11	holds
17	holds	17	feet	11	well	11	knocks
16	man	17	fire			11	neck

nouns often have precise referents such as *blood, nose,* and *water.* This can be related to the stereotypical concrete-to-abstract transfer which characterizes metaphors (Kronasser's law: see Kronasser 1952; Makkai 1972: 43). There are very few adjectives in the metaphors list: there are comparatively few adjectives in metaphorical FEIs in general. This may be because adjectives evaluate, describe, or identify in compositional language, but metaphorical FEIs are inherently evaluative or descriptive, and vague rather than identificatory, thus making, perhaps, constituent adjectives redundant.

5.1.2 *Median Lengths of FEIs*

The lengths of individual FEIs are important when calculating the densities of FEIs in text: for example, to assess densities of FEIs in different discourse types. The average length is 3.56 words, but my data suggests a strong correlation between length and frequency: commoner FEIs are shorter than infrequent ones (see Table 5.4)

5.1.3 *Cranberry Collocations*

While most lexemes in the general lexicon never occur in FEIs, a few never occur outside FEIs. Many of these are rare fossil words, or have been borrowed from other languages or varieties, and they include:

amok	run amok
cahoots	in cahoots with SOMEONE
dint	by dint of SOMETHING
dudgeon	in high dudgeon
fettle	in fine/good fettle
fro	to and fro

TABLE 5.4. *Correlation between FEI frequency and length*

Frequency range	Average number of words
0	4
1–4	3.96
5–17	3.54
1–2 million	3.16
2–5 million	2.93
5–10 million	2.83
10–50 million	2.68
50–100 million	2.36
100+ million	2

grist	grist to ONE's mill
haywire	go/be haywire
kibosh	put the kibosh on SOMETHING
kilter	out of kilter/off kilter
kith	kith and kin
loggerheads	at loggerheads
sleight	sleight of hand
snook	cock a snook
spic(k)	spic(k) and span
tenterhooks	on tenterhooks
trice	in a trice
umbrage	take umbrage
wend	wend ONE's way SOMEWHERE
yore	of yore

Fraser (1970: 31) comments that he has not found any cranberry FEIs which undergo transformations, although component verbs inflect. Certainly, neither OHPC or BofE shows, for example, any passive tokens of the superficially transitive *put the kibosh on*, *cock a snook*, or *take umbrage* (although BofE includes the journalistic formations *snook-cockers* and *snook-cocking*).

Another group of cranberry collocations contains lexemes which are unique to the FEI but homographic with other independent items:

beck	be at SOMEONE's beck and call
boot	to boot
cropper	come a cropper
curry	curry favour
hue	hue and cry
lurch	leave SOMEONE in the lurch
queer	queer SOMEONE's pitch
scruff	(by) the scruff of SOMEONE's neck
slouch	be no slouch (at SOMETHING)
truck	have no truck with SOMEONE/SOMETHING

Other cranberry collocations look less peculiar, because the cranberry items have compositional or familiar morphemic structures, but nevertheless now occur only in fixed strings:

accordance	in accordance with SOMETHING
amends	make amends (for SOMETHING)
gunpoint	at gunpoint
irrespective	irrespective of
outset	at/from the outset
retrospect	in retrospect
run-around	give SOMEONE the run-around

triplicate in triplicate
unbeknownst unbeknownst to SOMEONE

A few FEIs, grammatical in function and comparatively common, contain unanalysable or unique items:

behalf on SOMEONE's behalf, on behalf of SOMEONE
sake for SOMEONE'S/SOMETHING's sake,
for the sake of SOMEONE/SOMETHING
stead in SOMEONE's stead

This sort of description is essentially synchronic, reinforcing the idiosyncratic or 'peculiar' quality of many FEIs. It ignores the extent to which the collocations may be diachronically well formed and the cranberry elements unremarkable lexical items. For example, *OED* sets out evidence showing how *dint* had historically more general uses—meaning 'a blow' or 'the dealing of blows'—although these had more or less become obsolete by the publication of the relevant volume in 1897. Another sense—'dent' or 'impression'—is now, 100 years later, obsolete in many varieties of English, although it survives in Australian English and some other Englishes. This leaves only *by dint of* extant in standard British and American usage. In the case of *dudgeon*, *OED* suggests that from the time of its earliest citation in 1573 the word was typically found after the preposition *in* and often after an adjective such as *high, great,* or *deep.* Again, the uses have atrophied until only one form really remains. This shows the power of phraseological patterning. 'Cranberry' expressions result from phraseological attrition, from increasingly restricted lexical patterns. They should be considered as further manifestations of the patterning underlying lexical items of all kinds, and it is not helpful to view them as peculiar or distinct from other kinds of FEI or lexical item. They can be compared to foreign phrases, which are borrowed wholesale into English but retain their original wording and alien syntagmatic structure.

5.1.4 *Ill-Formed FEIs*

FEIs that cannot be parsed according to normal syntactic rules are non-compositional: the grammatical equivalents to cranberry FEIs ('extragrammatical idioms': Fillmore *et al.* 1988: 505). While their deviant structures may be fossils of earlier uses, they are aberrant in synchronic terms. Fraser (1970: 31) points out that, like cranberries, they never or only rarely undergo any transformations at all. Since many of them are unanalysable, it is not possible to analogize and perform transformations.

The ill-formedness of these FEIs often arises from odd phrase structures, ellipsis, or inflections, or from an archaic mood:

at all
be that as it may
be seeing you
by and by
by and large
come to think of it
come what may
curiouser and curiouser
dog eat dog
every which way
far be it from me
give SOMEONE what for
go for broke
hard done by
how come
how do you do?
I'll be blowed
let alone —
mind you
more fool you
needless to say
please God
point taken
quote unquote
shame on —
so long!
to do with
to each X's own
to the manner born
writ large

Other FEIs contain strange uses of wordclasses: in particular, a non-nominal word or sense may be used as a noun, or an adjective as an adverb:

all of a sudden
at the ready
beyond compare
do the dirty on SOMEONE
for free
have a down on SOMEONE
ifs and buts
in brief

in general
in the know
of late
of old
once in a while
on the alert
on the make
on the up and up
play fair
stand easy
state the obvious
swear blind
the back of beyond
the dos and don'ts
the ins and outs
the whys and wherefores
through thick and thin
trip the light fantastic

Sometimes, one or more component words deviate from their usual syntactic behaviour. In particular, countable nouns may be used without determiners in the singular, or verbs may be used in aberrant transitivity patterns:

bag and baggage
bring SOMEONE to book
(by) word of mouth
come a cropper
fight tooth and nail
(not) go a bundle on SOMETHING
go (the) whole hog
in all weathers
in case
keep body and soul together
put pen to paper
rain cats and dogs
sweat blood
stand SOMEONE in good stead
stay put
to hand
turn and turn about
under lock and key
to date

Other lexicogrammatical aberrations arise because the structures are correct syntagmatically but not paradigmatically, and so the valencies and collocational well-formedness are disturbed. Some

FEIs are literally impossible, and the grammar reinforces their violation of truth conditions:

clap eyes on SOMEONE
do a runner
live a lie
look daggers at SOMEONE
make heavy weather of SOMETHING
put ONE's best foot forward
turn turtle
when push comes to shove

In another kind of ill-formedness, determiners or proforms lack clear coreferentiality in their co-texts, thus enforcing retrieval of the reference directly from the institutionalized idiomatic meaning of the string: for example, *it* in *make it big* or *the* in *bite the bullet. The* is discussed further in Section 10.2.1.

Palmer draws attention to some aberrant uses of modal verbs in FEIs (1990: 71f. and 187): this can be considered another kind of ill-formedness. For example, *can* is used to convey commands of 'a brusque or somewhat impolite kind', as in *you can say that again* (discoursally an expressive rather than a directive). Similarly, *may/might* in *may/might (just) as well* are anomalous in that they do not convey their typical modal meanings but some sort of dynamic possibility: Palmer points out the uses may simply reflect the essential idiomaticity of the strings.

Frames and phraseological FEIs are discussed further in Section 6.3. Some can be considered grammatically ill formed if an isolationist compositional analysis is adopted. However, they actually demonstrate meaningful and analogizable patterns.

5.2 FREQUENCIES OF GRAMMATICAL TYPES

The database recorded grammatical type for each FEI, together with some information about inflections, transformations, colligations, and so on. Table 5.5 shows the percentages of database FEIs according to grammatical type: only canonical forms and principal syntactic functions are considered. Predicates are those FEIs which function as the predicate of a clause: that is, as a verb and its complementation. The commonest type is clearly the predicate FEI, followed by adjuncts and adverbials.

Table 5.6 shows the proportions for grammatical types, set against the 3 main idiomaticity types. Anomalous collocations cluster as predicates and adjuncts, formulae cluster as conventions, and

TABLE 5.5. *FEI proportions, according to grammatical type*

predicates	40%
nominal groups	9%
adjectival groups	2%
modifiers, quantifiers	1%
adjuncts, submodifiers	28%
sentence adverbials	5%
conventions, exclamations, and subordinate clauses	12%
fillers, others	1%

TABLE 5.6. *FEI proportions: idiomaticity and grammatical types*

	Anomalous collocations	Formulae	Metaphors
total in database	45.3%	21.3%	33.4%
predicates	17%	3%	20%
nominal groups	3%	2%	4%
adjectival groups	<1%	<1%	<1%
modifiers, quantifiers	<1%	<1%	<1%
adjuncts, submodifiers	18%	3%	7%
sentence adverbials	3%	2%	<1%
conventions, exclamations, and subordinate clauses	2%	9%	<1%
fillers, others	<1%	<1%	<0.1%

TABLE 5.7. *FEI proportions: frequency and grammatical type*

Frequency	<1/m	1–10/m	10+/m
total in database	72%	24%	4%
predicates	32%	8%	<1%
nominal groups	7%	2%	<0.1%
adjectival groups	2%	<1%	<0.1%
modifiers, quantifiers	<1%	<1%	<0.1%
adjuncts, submodifiers	17%	9%	2%
sentence adverbials	2%	2%	1%
conventions, exclamations, and subordinate clauses	11%	1%	<1%
fillers, others	<1%	<1%	<1%

metaphors cluster particularly as predicates. These tendencies are correlated with their discoursal uses in Chapter 8.

Table 5.7 sets grammatical types against broad frequency bands. These figures are unsurprising. FEIs with grammatical functions, such as sentence adverbials, are proportionally stronger in higher frequency ranges: something entirely in keeping with the relative frequencies of lexical and grammatical words in the general lexicon.

5.3 GRAMMATICAL TYPES AND STRUCTURES

The following sections look in more detail at the different grammatical types recorded in the database.

5.3.1 *Predicate FEIs*

Table 5.8 shows the 12 commonest patterns of predicate FEIs in the database, including variations: the majority are structurally simple. These patterns cover over 90% of all the FEIs, and just 3 patterns account for nearly 70%. No other pattern occurs in more than 1% of cases. The analysis is crude, however, and does not take into account more delicate case relationships: compare Jackendoff (1991: 234), who reports observations by Carrier and Randall concerning resultatives, as in *work one's fingers to the bone* and *eat someone out of house and home*, and compare discussions by Nunberg *et al.* (1994: 525 ff.) on agents, goals, and so on. The following gives examples of FEIs in these patterns:

TABLE 5.8. *Commonest structures of predicate FEIs*

Frequency	Structure
29%	subject + predicator + object
27%	subject + predicator + object + adjunct
13%	subject + predicator + adjunct
5%	subject + predicator + complement
3%	subject + predicator + adjunct + adjunct
3%	subject + predicator + complement + adjunct
2%	subject + predicator + indirect object + direct object
2%	subject + predicator + adjunct + object
2%	subject + predicator + object + catenated predicator
2%	subject + predicator + object + object complement
1%	(fully lexical) subject + predicator
1%	subject + predicator + object + adjunct + adjunct

subject+predicator+object

X admits defeat
X bends Y's ear
X bends the rules
X buries the hatchet
SOMETHING catches fire
X cools X's heels
X has second thoughts
X pulls X's weight
X steals Y's thunder
X takes aim

subject+predicator+object+adjunct

X brings Y to heel
X gets X's act together
X gets SOMETHING off the ground
SOMETHING has a bearing on SOMETHING
X keeps tabs on Y
X lays X's cards on the table
SOMETHING lends itself to SOMETHING
X puts X's finger on SOMETHING
X takes Y to task
SOMETHING takes X by surprise

subject+predicator+adjunct

X comes into X's own
X comes to grief
SOMETHING falls on deaf ears
X goes to ground
X rises to the occasion
X sticks to X's guns

subject+predicator+complement

SOMETHING comes true
X's days are numbered
X goes bust
SOMETHING is not X's cup of tea
SOMETHING is wearing thin
the coast is clear

subject+predicator+adjunct+adjunct

SOMETHING comes out in the wash
X comes up against a brick wall
X gets in on the act
X lives from hand to mouth

subject+predicator+complement+adjunct

X falls prey to SOMETHING/Y
X is a credit to Y
SOMETHING is music to X's ears

SOMETHING is uppermost in X's mind

subject+predicator+indirect object+direct object
X gives Y Y's head
X leads Y a (merry) dance
X shows Y the door
X teaches Y a lesson

subject+predicator+adjunct+object
X lets off steam
X pulls out all the stops
X puts in an appearance
X throws in the towel

subject+predicator+object+catenated predicator
X has an axe to grind
X has no business VERBing
X makes ends meet
X starts the ball rolling

subject+predicator+object+object complement
X calls a spade a spade
X has X's hands full
X keeps X's fingers crossed
X sets the record straight

subject+predicator
alarm bells ring
sparks fly
the penny drops
the plot thickens

subject+predicator+object+adjunct+adjunct
X gives SOMETHING/Y up as a bad job
X has SOMETHING down to a fine art
X pulls Xself up by X's bootstraps
SOMETHING/X rubs Y up the wrong way

5.3.2 *Nominal groups*

FEIs functioning as nominal groups are problematic since it is not always clear how to distinguish them from noun compounds: see Mitchell (1971: 60 ff.), Matthews (1974: 33 ff.), and Bloomfield (1935: 227f.), who uses phonology as a criterion. From a lexico-grammatical point of view, *civil servant*, *clothes horse*, *grizzly bear*, and *traffic jam* function in the same way as single-word nouns; possible hyphenation and pluralizability supports their classification as nouns. In contrast, *flash in the pan*, *thin end of the wedge*, *neck of the woods*, *trial and error*, and *blot on one's escutcheon* may be classified as FEIs. This is partly because they are more complex groups, partly because they are defective syntagmatically. They tend to be fossilized in particular clause positions or to have restrictions on colligating determiners or prepositions. Defectiveness, whether syntagmatic, inflectional, or collocational, is key in distinguishing between noun compounds and nominal FEIs. In general, fixed nominal groups classified here as FEIs are metaphorical, and they tend to be evaluative rather than simply descriptive or denotative.

Of FEIs functioning as nominal groups, 19% occurred in OHPC in all available clause positions—subject, complement, verbal object, and prepositional object:

> a bird's eye view, a —'s eye view
> bread and circuses
> chink in SOMEONE's armour
> the conventional wisdom
> the villain of the piece

Where nominal group FEIs were found in only one clause position in OHPC, this was usually that of copular complement: 21% occur only as complements:

> a blessing in disguise
> a dead loss
> a flash in the pan
> a foregone conclusion
> the thin end of the wedge

In all, 25% of nominal group FEIs were found in two clause positions in OHPC, usually two out of complement, object, and prepositional object. (A further 4% occurred in all three of these positions.) Where nominal group FEIs follow prepositions, the choice of preposition was sometimes highly restricted: for example *part and parcel of something* functioned either as a complement or as the object of *as*, after a verb such as *see*:

object or prepositional object
a clean sheet
a free hand
ivory tower
the straight and narrow
the whys and wherefores of SOMETHING

object or complement
a new lease of life
a world of difference
light at the end of the tunnel
the salt of the earth
the shape (and size) of things to come

complement or prepositional object
a wild goose chase
pie in the sky
sour grapes
Trojan horse
uncharted waters, uncharted territory

The preference therefore seems to be against subject position, and this in turn relates to the discoursal functions of these nominal groups in conveying new information and evaluations—which conventionally follow some sort of copula or are not sentence-initial.

5.3.3 *Predicative adjectival groups*

Database FEIs classified as adjectival groups occurred either postnominally or after a copula: prenominal adjectival groups were classified with other modifiers. This is an infrequent type. Most FEIs functioning as the complements of copulas are morphologically nominal groups or prepositional phrases, not adjectival groups:

alive and kicking
bone idle
cut and dried
dressed to kill
free and easy
long in the tooth
wet behind the ears
wide awake

5.3.4 *Modifiers*

A very small number of FEIs in the database functioned in prenominal position. They included expressions operating as quantifiers, deictics, and adjectival modifiers:

a thousand and one
all-singing all-dancing
any old
common or garden
dim and distant
hard and fast
precious little, precious few
the one and only

5.3.5 *Adjuncts*

FEIs functioning as adjuncts are generally prepositional phrases. The commonest prepositions heading them are shown in Table 5.9.

TABLE 5.9. *Commonest prepositions heading FEIs*

in	534
on	264
at	161
out of	90
to	73
for	65
by	55
with	44
under	43
of	37
from	35
up	26
off	25

Compound prepositions such as *in spite of* and *on behalf of* were analysed together with their objects, as adjuncts. Over 40% of adjunct FEIs occurred in OHPC after copulas as well as after other verbs. The majority of these FEIs describe manner, circumstances, or situations:[2]

above board
by heart
by the skin of ONE's teeth
from memory
high and dry
in cold blood
in from the cold
in secret
in the lead
in the pipeline
on horseback
out of the question
under the counter
under the weather
up for grabs
with ONE's bare hands

Only 1% express time or duration:

at once
at the outset
for good, for good and all
for the time being

---

[2] Metaphorical adjuncts are listed here according to their idiomatic meanings: mismatching between literal and metaphorical meanings is discussed in Section 7.6.4.

in the cold light of day
in the foreseeable future
in the fullness of time
on the spur of the moment

Nearly 4% express rate or frequency:

from time to time
little by little
like a bat out of hell
again and again, time and again
on occasions
once in a blue moon

Around 13% express position or direction:

at home
from afar
from side to side
in full view (of SOMETHING/SOMEONE)
in the open
side by side
the world over, the whole world over
within spitting distance

Around 5% express purpose, reason, cause, or result:

for the sake of SOMEONE/SOMETHING
in vain
on behalf of SOMEONE/SOMETHING
to be on the safe side
to smithereens
with a view to SOMETHING, with a view to VERBing

Around 7% express degree or extent: some of these also function as submodifiers of adjectives or adverbs. Compare Gross (1994: 233) who observes that a large proportion of his (French) multi-word frozen adverbials mean 'a lot' or 'strongly':

a touch
by far
far and away
from top to bottom
in a big way
through and through
to the hilt
well and truly

5.3.6 *Sentence Adverbials*

Of database FEIs functioning as sentence adverbials, disjuncts—metalinguistic comments or attitude markers—slightly outnumber conjuncts—connectors and boundary markers—in the ratio 6:4. However, in cases where sentence adverbials both comment and connect, the functions are often inseparable. Common disjuncts include:

> believe you me
> by definition
> for the most part
> in effect
> no doubt
> sooner or later
> to all intents and purposes
> to be sure

Common conjuncts include:

> by the way
> for example
> in other words
> on the one hand
> on the other hand, on the other
> so much for —
> talking of —
> to cut a long story short

Sentence adverbials with dual functions include:

> above all
> after all
> in any case
> in fact
> mind you
> on the contrary

These vary in degree and kind. *Above all* is a typical case, functioning both as a preface to a statement of the most important thing in a series and as a signal of its importance. Similarly, one use of *in fact* is to signal a correction or statement of a true state of affairs, as well as its truth value. FEIs functioning as sentence adverbials are discussed further in Chapters 8 and 10.

5.3.7 *Conventions, Exclamations, and Subordinate Clauses*

The commonest of these FEIs in everyday interaction are closed-set turns which encode greetings, apologies, refusals, expressions of sympathy, exhortations, and so on (see Section 8.5). They occurred relatively infrequently in OHPC, except in fictional dialogue, but their distribution was distorted because of the corpus composition:

by all means
don't mention it
excuse me
go for it!
good luck
good morning
never mind
no comment
no way
thank you

A number of FEIs express reactions and opinions. As with the preceding group, these were generally low frequency in OHPC:

about time, about time too
curiouser and curiouser
eat your heart out, —
it's nothing
pigs might fly
roll on —
those were the days
to hell with —
who cares?
you can say that again

Proverbs and many other sayings were classified as conventions (proverb tokens in OHPC frequently showed downgrading to predicates or nominal groups):

any port in a storm
don't let the bastards grind you down
enough is enough
every cloud has a silver lining
first come first served
it's the last straw that breaks the camel's back
it takes two to tango
the end justifies the means
you can't have your cake and eat it

FEIs functioning as main clauses were classified as predicate FEIs. However, a few FEIs functioned only as subordinate clauses, with the discoursal functions of adjuncts or disjuncts:

as if X owns the place
for all X knows, for all X cares
if the worst comes to the worst
until the cows come home
when push comes to shove
when the chips are down
while the going is good

5.3.8 *Other Classes*

Amongst FEIs falling into miscellaneous grammatical categories are a number of fillers and particles:

and so on, and so forth
and the like
at all
full stop
on earth
one — after another
or what?
quote unquote
sort of
you know

and a few compound conjunctions:

as if, as though
as long as, so long as
as soon as
if ever
in case
in order to, in order that
just because
much as
on condition that
so that, so as

5.4 INFLECTABILITY

It is normally the case with predicate FEIs that verbs inflect, although there may be restrictions on number, tense, aspect, voice, and mood. It is virtually always the case that items realizing open slots or supplying subjects, objects, and prepositional objects inflect fully. The exceptions largely involve requirements for inserted nouns to be plural:

in —s' midst, in the midst of —
to the exclusion of other/all —
X + Y talk turkey
X + Y lock horns (*compare* X locks horns with Y)
X + Y rub shoulders (*compare* X rubs shoulders with Y)

The problem of inflectability mainly involves the fixed nouns and adjectives in FEIs. There are few obvious patterns to detect, although nouns in non-metaphorical FEIs are more likely to inflect than ones in metaphors. *Bill*, *conclusion*, and *question* inflect normally in *foot the bill, a foregone conclusion,* and *beg the question.* Views advocating the (partial) compositionality of FEIs relate inflectability to the metaphoricality of the component items, but the relationship is complicated. The nouns in *kick the bucket, bite the bullet,* and *spill the beans* do not change, but both nouns pluralize in *have a chip on one's shoulder* and *(have) a frog in one's throat.*

In particular, nothing systematic accounts for the way in which words denoting parts of the body inflect in some FEIs, in accordance with the number of the grammatical subject or referend, but not in others. The problem is at its most acute where the FEI contains an item (often metonymic) such as *eye, ear,* or *hand,* which is singular in the FEI, but normally found in pairs in the real world. Taking the case of *ear,* the singular form occurs in 16 database FEIs:

a word in SOMEONE's ear
be beaming from ear to ear (and so on)
bend SOMEONE's ear
by ear
give SOMEONE a thick ear
go in one ear and out the other
(with) half an ear
in ONE's mind's ear (*compare* in ONE's mind's eye)
keep ONE's ear to the ground
lend SOMEONE an ear, lend an ear (and so on)
make a pig's ear of SOMETHING
out on ONE's ear
play SOMETHING by ear
turn a deaf ear (to SOMETHING)
with a flea in ONE's ear
you can't make a silk purse out of a sow's ear

Only 5 of these occurred 5 or more times in OHPC, and even the commonest, *bend someone's ear,* occurred only 11 times. Few tokens in OHPC happened to occur with plural subjects. *Lend an ear* and *play something by ear* each had 1 token with a plural subject, and *ear* remained singular in both cases (but compare *Friends, Romans, countrymen, lend me your ears*). *Keep one's ear to the ground* had 1 token with a mass subject (a newspaper, as metonym), and *ear* was singular. *Turn a deaf ear* had 2 tokens with plural subjects: *ear* was singular in one, plural in the other. *Bend someone's ear* occurred 5 times with plural subjects: *ear* was plural in 4 of them, and singular in the other. Only in the last case could there be seen anything like a conventionalized pluralization of the component noun.

McCawley (1971: 201f.) comments on the case of *pull someone's leg,* suggesting that *Thieu has pulled both Nixon's leg and Lodge's* is possible, but *Thieu has pulled both Nixon's leg and Lodge's leg* is not. He also points out a distinction between *He has pulled our legs* which (he claims) refers to separate occasions, and *He has pulled our leg* which refers to a single occasion affecting the plural referent of *our*. This is partially borne out by BofE. Where the affected is plural, *legs* is used more often than singular *leg*. Most uses refer to a collective experience, sometimes a recurrent experience. The distinction is perhaps that with the plural forms, the focus is on the individual experiencers, whereas with the singular, focus is on the mass:

A: I'm not sure really . . . whether . . . whether you're **pulling our legs** . . . or . . . or not.
B: Thi [*sic*] honestly this is absolutely serious.
A: No I mean
B: This is not a leg pull.
A: I mean are you **pulling our legs** when you say you don't really understand it and it puzzles you? (BofE: unscripted conversation)

Like a lot of Mt Isa old-timers, he'll yarn to visitors, happily **pulling their legs** a little, becoming just a little impatient [with] complaints about modern living in the outback. (BofE: journalism)

Ms Thomson is already making plans for next year's eisteddfod: 'It has proved so popular we must limit the number of acts but all children will take part.' It's a worthy cause but is Ms Thomson **pulling our leg** by saying the eisteddfod is part of the Excellence In Education In the Outback? (BofE: journalism)

While OHPC demonstrates some tendencies concerning inflectability, it is too small to be conclusive and a much larger corpus is needed. There seems to be genuine insecurity amongst speakers concerning pluralizations—the FEIs are comparatively infrequent, plural subjects are not that common, and the rules are not formalized.

A partial solution is suggested by the occasional use of an inserted plural marker. *Collective* is used as a grammatical device in metaphorical FEIs with plural subjects or referents and indeterminate rules for pluralization. *Corporate* is also used in this way, although in the examples cited below, this insertion is influenced by the management or business contexts. In all cases, the action denoted by the FEI is a mass experience or joint action, rather than affecting people individually:

But advertisers have since mostly seen that they have **shot themselves and viewers in their collective feet**. (OHPC: journalism)

The Curtain falls. The audience **rises to its collective feet** with cries of 'Bravo'. The critics predict a huge sell-out monster. (OHPC: journalism)

Banks, building societies and other high street lenders look set to **put a collective hand in their pockets** to help people in debt. (OHPC: journalism)

Every time we get to the end, no one can say anything for a few minutes. There's **a collective lump in the throat**—even when you're rushing through a rehearsal, working desperately hard. There's something that just hits you so hard. It just gets you right in the tripes. (OHPC: journalism)

The Soviet embassy already has to **grit its collective teeth** and accept the burden of its formal address: Andrei Sakharov Plaza, Washington DC. (OHPC: journalism)

Well, chap, **our buns could be in a collective sling**, if you know what I mean. (OHPC: fiction)

Tobacco was carrying health warnings in the West and it seemed prudent not to **put all your corporate eggs into one basket**. (OHPC: journalism)

The auction [of TV company franchises], when it comes next year, is sudden death for the losers; it is qualitatively different from the old review of the franchises where, provided **the corporate nose had been kept reasonably clean**, a renewal was virtually certain. (OHPC: journalism)

In fact, as *pocket* in the third example shows, the problem of pluralization is not entirely resolved.

5.4.1 *A Note on Tense and Mood*

I did not routinely record in the database the tenses in which FEIs occurred in OHPC: there was too little evidence, and genre influences choice. Similarly, I did not record mood choices of interrogative and imperative, except where they were fossilized and near-mandatory, nor the clause types in which FEIs occurred in OHPC (this could be significant since, although conventions such as speech formulae are typically fossilized in tense and person, they may inflect normally when reported). However, I monitored the distribution of proverbs in main and subordinate clauses in the separate study of proverbs which I undertook with Pierre Arnaud. I found that 20% of proverb tokens in OHPC occurred in subordinate clauses, typically report clauses. Most notably, 15 of the 18 tokens of *enough is enough* occurred in report clauses. In this way, the selection of the proverb represents a further level of distancing or interpretation on the part of the speaker/writer, reporting and sheltering behind received wisdom (see Chapter 9):

Mr Brittain added: 'How long heads are prepared to keep going is deba-table. There comes a point when we have to say **enough is enough**. (OHPC: journalism)

Dudgeon, who throughout his professional life stressed that **prevention is better than cure,** had the highly original idea that preliminary trials should be undertaken in closed religious communities. (OHPC: journalism)

You have to accept the notion that **two heads are better than one**. (OHPC: transcribed discussion)

Other choices such as passives and negatives are discussed in Section 5.6.

5.5 REGULAR SLOTS IN FEIS

In 48% of all database FEIs, there are slots to be filled according to context. Such slots include the subjects and direct or indirect objects of predicate FEIs; prepositional objects; possessives; reflex-ive pronouns; and locatives. More than half of FEIs with fillable slots have two or more slots:

X catches Y red-handed
X faces the music
X feels the pinch
X lines X's pockets
X takes Y for a ride
X takes a shine to Y
X ties Xself in knots
X/SOMETHING gets up Y's nose
at X's pleasure/at the pleasure of X
in X's heart of hearts
SOMETHING flies in the face of SOMETHING
SOMETHING sets X's teeth on edge

Nearly 10% of all database FEIs have 2 different human partici-pants. Only 4 have 3, and in the first 2, Y and Z can be realized as *them, their,* or a plural nominal group:

X drives a wedge between Y and Z
X knocks Y and Z's heads together
X leaves Y to Z's tender mercies
X robs Y to pay Z (variation of X robs Peter to pay Paul)

While SOMETHING is used as a convenient proform in the database to denote abstracts and inanimates, there are frequently semantic constraints on its realization:

SOMETHING goes to seed (literal use; SOMETHING = plant)
SOMETHING springs a leak (SOMETHING = boat or container)

TABLE 5.10. *Realizations of subject slots in FEIs*

human	76%
inanimate	11%
either human or inanimate	8%
animal	<1%
place	<1%

> SOMETHING is wearing thin (SOMETHING = feeling or joke or hackneyed story)
>
> X is prey to SOMETHING (SOMETHING = unpleasant event or situation)
>
> X pours cold water on SOMETHING (SOMETHING = idea or suggestion)
>
> X sets/puts SOMETHING in motion (SOMETHING = activity or situation)

Over 15% of database FEIs containing the marker SOMETHING are recorded as having mandatory constraints of this kind. The constraints may be broken instantially, as in:

> Is it too much to hope that MPs will **put the Bill out of its misery** tonight? (The *Guardian*, 25 May 1993)

where *the Bill* is personified.

The following sections look more closely at some of the available slots.

5.5.1 *Subject Slots*

Most predicate FEIs have fillable slots in subject position—the slots are not filled in nonfinite structures or agent-less passivizations—and there are normally selection restrictions on the realizations of these subjects. Supplied subjects are usually human. Figures for subject slots are shown in Table 5.10.

Looking simply at metaphors, the proportion of human subjects rises to 81%, with another 4% either human or inanimate.[3] An aspect to be explored with a larger corpus is whether there are restrictions on use with first/second/third person: see Section 9.2.1 for discussion of this in relation to face. Similarly, there may be gender constraints on subjects: for example, evidence in BofE suggests that *blow one's top* and *pull someone's leg* typically have men as actors/agents or grammatical subjects (compare *butter wouldn't melt in someone's mouth* which is used of women twice as commonly as men). It is not at all clear whether these are collocational constraints, in the same way that *dapper* and *portly* describe men rather

---

[3] Čermák (forthcoming) comments that the proportion of Czech idioms with human subjects is over 90%.

than women, or whether the corpus data is reflecting real-world sociocultural behaviours: this also needs further investigation.

Of the remaining predicate FEIs, around 4% have fixed lexical realizations of the subject, 1% have proforms such as *it, this,* and *that,* and 1% have existential *there.* (Proverbs in their canonical or original forms generally have fixed subjects, unless imperative, but I classified these as conventions rather than predicate FEIs.)

Where predicate FEIs have fixed subjects, around a quarter require the insertion of possessives. The metaphors in these FEIs often involve parts of the body:

X's bark is worse than X's bite
X's blood runs cold
X's ears are burning
X's face falls
X's hands are tied
X's heart is in X's mouth
X's lips are sealed
X's mind goes blank
X's number is up
X's word is X's bond

Possessives are discussed further in Section 5.5.3.

5.5.2 *Non-Subject Slots*

Approximately one-third of predicate FEIs in the database have open slots in direct, indirect, or prepositional object position. Realizations are distributed in the proportions shown in Table 5.11. This distribution differs sharply from that for subject position. It contrasts with the animacy status of fixed nouns in FEIs: these generally denote inanimates or animals. A similar observation is made by Gross (1994: 234) with respect to French FEIs.

Apart from the formula *who is X when X is at home?* (or *what's — when it is at home?*), no database FEI has a fixed subject and a fillable slot as the complement of a copula. This may reflect the fact that post-copular groups typically define or state fixed attributions and descriptions, rather than tying items anaphorically.

TABLE 5.11. *Realizations of non-subject slots in FEIs*

human	40%
inanimate	41%
either human or inanimate	14%
reflexive pronoun (human)	5%
reflexive pronoun (inanimate)	<1%

Similarly, Nunberg *et al.* (1994: 525) cite Marantz as saying that there are very few, if any, cases of FEIs with fixed subjects and fillable object slots: the only cases I found amongst database FEIs are *the world doesn't owe X a living, wild horses wouldn't make X* —, and *woe betide* —, which fit their characterization of exceptions as 'complete sentence frames'. Full-sentence proverbs would also fit here.

A very few FEIs contain obligatory adjuncts of position or direction, where the realization is not fixed: the rarity of these FEIs is pointed out by Kiparsky: see Nunberg *et al.* (1994: 527). The few examples I found tended to be anomalous collocations or to have preferred locative realizations:

ride roughshod over SOMEONE/SOMETHING
ride roughshod SOMEWHERE

set foot SOMEWHERE

set ONE's sights on SOMETHING
set ONE's sights SOMEWHERE

the buck stops here
the buck stops SOMEWHERE

There are, as Nunberg *et al.* (1994: 527) point out, many cases of FEIs which incorporate a prepositional phrase denoting location or direction and which require a noun to be supplied, for example *pour cold water on something, put the skids under someone,* and *put the wind up someone.*

5.5.3 *Possessives*

Around 14% of database FEIs contain slots fillable by possessives—possessive adjectives or possessive forms of nouns—which cue the FEI deictically into context. Two points are worth making. First, less than 15% of these FEIs were found in OHPC to have a recurrent variation with *of*:

at X's request, at the request of X
in honour of X/SOMETHING, in X's/SOMETHING's honour
in X's pocket, in the pocket of X
X clips Y's wings, X clips the wings of Y
X sees SOMETHING through Y's eyes, X sees SOMETHING through the eyes of Y

The variation is commoner in prepositional phrases than in predicative FEIs. Given that this is a very basic transformation in English, it is perhaps surprising that the figure is not higher. But the function of possessive structures with *of* is to introduce or clarify information concerning attribution, in contrast to prenominal possessives. Its infrequency in FEIs suggests that other kinds of information are being presented through the FEI: FEIs with possessives are not foregrounding attribution.

Secondly, it is understood that a slot indicated by X's or Y's is to be filled by a possessive adjective or noun. However, in some cases attribution can be realized by a classifying adjective, for example denoting membership of a group:

By **spiking Senna's guns**, Mansell will be helping his future team-mate bring the highly prized numbers one and two to Ferrari. (OHPC: journalism)

The rest of us could never make up our minds whether Sol had simply misunderstood Jackson (English was not his mother-tongue), or whether he had deliberately chosen this method of **spiking the Communist guns**. (OHPC: non-fiction)

Such modifiers are not usually noted as having the deictic functions conventionally associated with possessives.[4]

Jackendoff (1991: 298) refers to a personal communication from Farmer, where she points out that mandatory possessives may be lost when FEIs are passivized. Farmer's example is the restricted collocation *gnash one's teeth*, and her passivized example, *Many teeth were gnashed as the home town went down to defeat*, may or may not be authentic. I did not find any specific evidence to prove or disprove this in OHPC. However, BofE has 135 tokens for forms of this expression, of which 40% are active and retain the possessive. Some 50% of lines realize the transformed collocation (*weeping/wailing and*) *gnashing of teeth*, where the possessive never occurs. The remainder include 9 tokens of the transformation *teeth-gnashing*, 1 passive *teeth were gnashed*, and 1 intransitive *teeth . . . gnashing*: none includes a possessive, and this lends support to Farmer's observation. What seems to be going on here is that the transformations are effectively generalizations which broaden out the reference of the FEI, and so the loss of the specific possessive is a reflection of the loss of referential specificity.

---

[4] The last example continues with a further transformation/exploitation of the FEI, quoted in Section 5.6.5. However, this particular use seems plausible and is replicable, not anomalous.

5.5.4 *Open Slots*

Just over 10% of database FEIs have other kinds of slot to be filled. In about 2% of database FEIs, a verb is supplied, usually as an infinitive or *-ing* form:

in a position to VERB
in the process of VERBing
trust X to VERB!
X breaks X's back to VERB
X hasn't got the face to VERB

Many of these have variations where the verb alternates with a nominal group:

hell-bent on VERBing, hell-bent on SOMETHING
on the verge of SOMETHING, on the verge of VERBing
X goes all out for SOMETHING, X goes all out to VERB
X sets X's heart on SOMETHING, X sets X's heart on VERBing

Of the open slots in FEIs, 35% are prenominal and require filling with an adjective or quantifier:

in — parlance
SOMETHING/X strikes a — note
to a — degree
too — for words
X cuts a — figure
X makes — work of SOMETHING

In some cases, the open slot is optional. In other cases, there are preferred realizations, which may be considered canonical forms: see further in Section 6.1.6:

a bird's eye view, a worm's eye view, a —'s eye view
in fine fettle, in good fettle, in — fettle
SOMETHING/X opens old wounds, SOMETHING/X opens — wounds
too close for comfort, too — for comfort
X has a tough row to hoe, X has a — row to hoe
X leads Y a merry dance, X leads Y a — dance

Sometimes the word supplied provides the focus in a sentence adverbial, for example when stating the basis for an assertion:

at a — estimate
on a — estimate

from the point of view of —
from a — point of view
from the — point of view

in — terms
in terms of —

on a — basis

to a — degree

Such structures are discussed further in Section 8.6.1. A similar effect is created when FEIs are interrupted by non-canonical words: see Section 6.8.

Finally, some FEIs require the addition of a clause:

I'll be blowed if —

SOMETHING crosses X's mind, it crosses X's mind that —

there is no saying wh–

X can bet X's bottom dollar that —

X lays a pound to a penny that —

Such freely formed but mandatory clauses are not formally part of the FEI. The FEI will be lexically or grammatically ill formed (or have a different function or meaning) if the clause is missing, but there are few or no restrictions on its realization or content. Other kinds of optional structure are discussed in Section 5.7.

5.6 TRANSFORMATIONS

The transformation potential of FEIs—particularly idioms—has been extensively discussed in the literature: see Section 1.3.3 with respect to syntactic approaches. Cutler (1982) relates transformational deficiencies to diachronic developments. She finds some evidence in *OED* that the earliest examples of items investigated were less frozen in form, and that items became more fixed over time and as their literal equivalents disappeared: for example, *kick over the traces* and *let off steam*. Other studies relate transformational deficiencies to semantics, thus finding motivations for apparent anomalies (Newmeyer 1972, 1974; Lakoff 1987: 451; Mel'čuk 1995: 205 ff.) or arguing in favour of the notional compositionality of idioms (Wasow *et al.* 1983; Nunberg *et al.* 1994; Jackendoff 1991: 299). A number of studies consider the transformational deficiencies of idioms (in their terms) and use these deficiencies to distinguish idioms from non-idioms: however, target idioms are often items which could be classified as restricted collocations such as *crane one's neck* (Ross 1970), delexical structures such as *take a piss* (McCawley 1971), or phrasal verbs (Newmeyer 1972). These papers set out various observations of the systematicity which underlies some kinds of multi-word item but not necessarily all FEIs. The inclusion of phrasal verbs in the set of idioms has, moreover, resulted in a number of distractions in the literature, with the observation of regular syntactic procedures and unities of particle meaning diverting attention away from less regularizable items.

I have already pointed out that many studies of the transformation potential of FEIs are marred by a lack of authentic data or detailed examination of data: this is not to say that the authors are unaware of this (Fraser 1970; Newmeyer 1974; Fellbaum 1993), nor that transformational deficiencies are insignificant or non-existent. An alternative lexicalist or collocationist view would see transformational deficiencies in terms of preferred lexicogrammatical patterning, analogous to restrictions on ordinary senses of simple words: an approach more compatible with descriptivist corpus-based studies.

Transformations were recorded in the database as observed in OHPC: this was inevitably ad hoc. It would of course have been desirable to record transformations along the lines of Fraser's hierarchy of frozenness: see Fraser (1970: 39 and *passim*) and Section 1.3.3; however, OHPC was too small a corpus with too few tokens for many predicate FEIs to give conclusive information. For example, the absence of passive forms is negative evidence that proves nothing either way, and even where I found passivization, this may have been stylistic exploitation or nonce use. Transformations are clearly something to be investigated more fully with much larger corpora.

Two psycholinguistic studies investigated the acceptability of different transformations with respect to the maintenance of idiomatic meaning. Gibbs and Gonzales (1985) report that informants accepted nominalization most readily of all transformations: this corresponds to Fraser's weakest level, level 5, beyond which he claims items are not idioms. However, their ranking of other transformations did not correspond to Fraser. In contrast, Reagan (1987) finds an 86% agreement between informants and Fraser's hierarchy. In this vein, Pulman (1993: 252) suggests that some transformations of some FEIs could only permit literal interpretations (*The bucket was finally kicked by the old curmudgeon, It was among the pigeons that he put the cat, He was chasing a herring that was red*). These are unnatural and peculiar examples, and I personally find it hard to interpret either the first or third as literal, but Pulman's point may well be borne out by studies of very large tranches of data. Finally, another psycholinguistic point: Nunberg *et al.* (1994: 507) raise an important question when they ask how it is that speakers acquire knowledge of the transformational defectiveness of FEIs, when very clearly no rules for this are ever taught.

It may be that if language is acquired through lexicogrammatical patterns, in chunks, and not rules, 'knowledge' of transformational defectiveness may be acquired as part and parcel of the patterning.

5.6.1 *Polarity*

Negation is a very basic transformation. Around 5% of database FEIs are conventionally negative: that is, a negative is part of the canonical expression:

I kid you not
leave no stone unturned
make no odds
no laughing matter
not be SOMEONE's pigeon
not by any stretch of the imagination
not lift a finger
not much cop
not put a foot wrong
not worth a hill of beans
there is no time to lose
(there is) nothing new under the sun

A few other FEIs typically or mandatorily occur in (broad) negative environments. Sadock cites the case of *a red cent* (1974: 87), and some further examples include the emphasizers *at all* and *in the least* and also *pull one's weight, be the end of the world,* and *up to scratch,* which are all more commonly negative than positive.

Halliday and James report an investigation of polarity in the Birmingham Collection of English Text, finding that the proportion of positive to negative clauses is 87.6:12.4 (1993: 60 and *passim*), or roughly 7:1. I cannot say whether negated predicate FEIs occur in this proportion in OHPC, but it is unlikely to be substantially more, and it may well be substantially less. The polarity of proverb tokens in OHPC was recorded in the subdatabase of proverbs, and only 7% have reversed polarity. The typical case is where the canonical form is a negative imperative or modal (*Don't . . . , You can't . . .*): tokens are transformed to positive predicates, although a negative evaluation may still be implied:

He wanted to **have his cake and eat it**—somehow to marry Mrs. Simpson and yet to remain on the throne. (OHPC: non-fiction)

Well, Mr Patten will do his best to **make a silk purse out of a sow's ear,** and the audience will know it was not his idea. Nor, of course, was it Mr Lawson's. (OHPC: journalism)

I should have taken issue with and perhaps—for he is very intelligent—
I could have convinced him that he **had the cart before the horse**.
(OHPC: non-fiction)

In a few cases, proverb tokens have their conventional polarity, but
are then contradicted in their co-texts. Compare the subversions of
evaluations discussed in Section 9.1.3:

Variety, as the poet William Cowper first observed, **may be 'the very
spice of life'**. But in motor racing, the less the variety, the spicier the
contest. (OHPC: journalism)

Having always believed that **an apple a day kept the doctor away**, the
realisation that an apple a day might actually give my child cancer one day
was absolutely terrifying. (OHPC: journalism)

Some exploitations of proverbs effectively negate the proverb: in
particular *big is beautiful* as an exploitation of *small is beautiful*:

Big is beautiful in Admiral's Cup boats. In the Lymington IOR regatta,
the Danish 50-footer Andelsbanken IV and Alan Gray's similarly sized
Jamarella each placed first and second in the two races over the weekend,
a 22-mile Olympic course in Christchurch Bay and yesterday's 16-miler in
the Solent. (OHPC: journalism)

Compare the institutionalized reversals of FEIs which are discussed
in Section 6.7.

5.6.2 *Passivization*

I recorded around 15% of predicate FEIs in the database as passi-
vizing in OHPC, but lack of data means that this figure is not a
robust indication of passivization potential. While some FEIs are
never passivized, there are others where passive forms are at least as
common as active forms:

X bears SOMETHING in mind
SOMETHING is borne in mind

SOMETHING/X cuts Y short
Y is cut short

X hauls Y over the coals
Y is hauled over the coals

SOMETHING is nipped in the bud
X nips SOMETHING in the bud

X is rushed off X's feet
Y rushes X off X's feet

X makes X's mind up

X's mind is made up

X settles a score
a score is settled

SOMETHING/X stops Y in Y's tracks (and variations)
Y is stopped in Y's tracks

Reflexives occasionally alternate with passives:

X is armed to the teeth
X arms Xself to the teeth

X ties Xself in knots
X is tied up in knots

Nunberg *et al.* (1994: 520ff.) point out the infrequency of double passivization in idioms, where both direct object and prepositional/ indirect object can be thematized as the subject of a passive verb. They cite *take advantage of someone/something* as a rare counter-example, and I found few others in OHPC. These items are among the least idiom-like of FEIs:

X takes account of Y/SOMETHING
account is taken of Y/SOMETHING
Y/SOMETHING is taken account of

X pays lip service to SOMETHING
SOMETHING is paid lip service
lip service is paid to SOMETHING

X gives priority to SOMETHING
SOMETHING is given priority
priority is given to SOMETHING

See Nunberg *et al.* (1994: 532ff.) for lists of the passivizability of FEIs with *make* and *take*.

Some FEIs seem completely fossilized as passives. Others in the following list are technically passive constructions although they do not follow the auxiliary *be*: see Nunberg *et al.* (1994: 516ff.):

as/so far as X is concerned
a force to be reckoned with
chilled to the marrow/bone
cut and dried
X is damned if X is going to VERB
dressed to kill
X is frightened of X's own shadow
X gets shot of something, X is shot of something
X is hard done by
X is hard pressed/put/pushed to VERB
X is made of sterner stuff
SOMETHING/X is not all that SOMETHING/X is cracked up to be

SOMEWHERE is paved with gold
X is strapped for cash
X is tarred with the same brush as Y, X and Y are tarred with the same brush

In the following cases, OHPC offers no evidence of active forms: actives would probably require general or mass subjects such as *they*, rather than specific ones:

SOMETHING is cheered to the echo
X is laughed out of court
X is mentioned in despatches

A few FEIs are so strongly passive that active tokens appear as exploitations:

X is bitten by the — bug
the — bug bites X

X is hoist(ed) by X's own petard
SOMETHING/Y hoists X with X's own petard

the die is cast
X casts the die

It is not easy to define rules for the acceptability of passive forms, although semantics may well account for motivation. There are analogies with uses of the simple verb outside the FEI (particularly in the case of anomalous collocations), or with its deep meaning. Newmeyer (1974: 329f.) argues that *pull someone's leg*, *bury the hatchet*, and *spill the beans* are passivizable because their literal equivalents are passivizable and their idiomatic meanings contain passive-governing predicates; in contrast, the meanings of *kick the bucket* and *blow one's top* are one-place predicates. Evidence in BofE supports this to some extent. None of the 103 tokens of *blow one's top* is passive, and there are no passives amongst the 42 tokens of *kick the bucket* with idiomatic meaning: the sole passive token of this string has a literal meaning, whereas 7 of the 123 tokens of *bury the hatchet*, 15 of the 159 tokens of *pull someone's leg*, and 4 of the 198 tokens of *spill the beans* are passive. There may indeed be semantic motivations here, but phraseological patterning also plays a part. Cases like *spill the beans* show a strong fossilization in an active structure, irrespective of potential passives and deep semantics. This is another area which needs to be teased out more fully in the light of much larger corpora and robust models of case structures, verbal processes, and meanings.

5.6.3 *Nonfinite uses*

I did not specifically record information concerning occurrences of FEIs in nonfinite structures. In general, FEIs can be catenated as infinitives or *-ing* forms without destroying the gestalt:

Or some writers felt they had earned the right in the Seventies, and now had the duty, to participate in the reassessment of the Left, if necessary by **washing dirty linen in public**. Most writers have done a bit of both. I was more inclined to the latter than the former. (OHPC: journalism)

In some cases, nonfinite structures are commoner than finite ones. *Add insult to injury* occurs in OHPC in the forms shown in Table 5.12. Note that the infinitive form functions as a sentence adverbial:

Ron Atkinson's Sheffield Wednesday received a nasty shock away to Cambridge United in their fifth round tie, United going in front after eighteen minutes through Dublin, and Wednesday were to receive another rude shock seven minutes after the break when Philpot made it two nil. **To add insult to injury**, Taylor scored a third for Cambridge twelve minutes from time and then seconds from the final whistle Dublin scored a fourth for Cambridge United. (OHPC: transcribed broadcast journalism)

A much grander house, the property of a firm of solicitors, suffered similar treatment. Again, original, perfectly sound wooden parts were destroyed and, **to add insult to injury**, plastic, press-moulded doors inserted. (OHPC: journalism)

5.6.4 *Embedding*

Embedding involves the relegation of part of an FEI to a relative clause, perhaps elided, and dependent on a component noun in the FEI, or to a catenated infinitive or cleft or pseudocleft structure: see Newmeyer (1972: 300f.), Nunberg *et al.* (1994: 501). Some isolated examples from OHPC are:

Another straw at which we can clutch is that if real snow arrives in the near future it will be falling on cold slopes and so will last reasonably well. (OHPC: journalism)

TABLE 5.12. *Forms of* add insult to injury *in OHPC*

add* insult to injury	finite	12 tokens
add insult to injury	after modal verb	2 tokens
to add insult to injury	infinitive	11 tokens
adding insult to injury	nonfinite -ing form	5 tokens
adding of insult to injury	verbal noun	1 token

Yes, what's he doing about his words then? **Any actions that are speaking louder than his words?** (OHPC: transcribed radio broadcast)

It is not, however, easy to contemplate putting whole federations out of action. **That is a bullet on which the Arthur Golds of this world have steadfastly failed to bite.** (OHPC: journalism)

The question begged by all these glowing predictions is whether they will ever be fulfilled. (OHPC: journalism)

Establishing even a temporary England succession to No. 8 Dean Richards is as painful as the big man's dodgy shoulder and Dean Ryan's early return stirs up **waters they themselves have muddied** since David Egerton appeared against Fiji. (OHPC: journalism)

This may be **a hard bullet for the left to bite**, but there is no question of what families want. (OHPC: journalism)

These examples are discoursally well formed, and the embedding can be explained in terms of thematization and cohesion. However, such transformations are fairly rare amongst FEIs. The following examples are indeterminate. They may be transformations of *put up a fight*, *kick the habit*, and *be up to one's tricks*, and symptomatic of the weakening of the gestalts; alternatively they may simply evidence senses of *put up*, *kick*, and *(be) up to*:

The fight put up by the Health and Safety Commission to get more money saw niggardly extra funding at the end of the last year. (OHPC: journalism)

Apart from grey hair, a big distinction between the younger, more carefree student travellers and the escapees is that the latter have **a work habit which is hard to kick**. (OHPC: journalism)

Do you imagine I don't know **all the tricks you are up to**, Toby, all your little games? (OHPC: fiction)

5.6.5 *Pronominalization*

It is normally the case that fixed nominal groups in FEIs are not pronominalized. A few isolated cases such as *put one's foot in one's mouth/put one's foot in it* can be analysed as cases of variation rather than pronominalization: see Section 6.1.2. Fraser and Ross (1970: 264f.) observe that some FEIs, for example, *get wind of something* and *set fire to something*, can never be pronominalized, whereas others allow pronominalization where there is clear anaphoric reference. This relates to the question of idiomaticity type and the semantic depletion (in these cases) of the component verbs. Pulman comments that there is a correlation between pronominalization potential and potential for internal modification (1993:

253), so that, to use his examples, while *He turned the tables on me and then I turned them on him* is acceptable, *I'll keep an eye on him and one on her too* is not (although Malcolm Coulthard suggests (personal communication) that *I'll keep an eye on him while you keep one on her* is plausible). Alford points out (1971: 573) that a notice-advertisement *Nailbiters just can't kick it alone* is meaningless without knowledge of the expansion *kick the habit*, but that it is nevertheless an example of pronominalization with extratextual reference. See Nunberg *et al.* (1994: 501 ff.) for further discussion of pronominalization and ellipsis.

It may simply be that the tight relationship between lexicogrammatical form and meaning in FEIs precludes pronominalization which might obscure the gestalt. In the following isolated examples, the missing nominal group occurs in the immediately preceding text, and so the reference is clear:

Jonathan Gili's film for Forty Minutes 'All about Ambridge' (BBC 2), which fleshed out the bones of character outlines with a few actor's CVs and offered receding hairlines to set alongside the voices, should have clarified **the waters, but ended up muddying them** even further. (OHPC: journalism)

So Europe is being carried towards a durable system of fixed exchange rates on the tide of history. Mr Lawson **was swimming with that tide**. Mrs Thatcher **is swimming against it**. (OHPC: journalism)

The rest of us could never make up our minds whether Sol had simply misunderstood Jackson (English was not his mother-tongue), or whether he had deliberately chosen this method of **spiking the Communist guns**. In any event **it spiked them**. (OHPC: non-fiction)

Spin-doctors have been keen to point out that the two men have met six times at various summits, and that Canada's competent ambassador in Washington is the prime minister's nephew. Anyway, if there is **ice**, Mr Clinton **is breaking it** with a visit to the Canadian capital on February 23rd and 24th. (BofE: written journalism)

A: I've **got a bone to pick with you**.
B: What?
A: No, I'll **pick it with you** tomorrow. (telephone conversation: 1987)

Non-fixed nominal groups in FEIs can be pronominalized freely.

5.6.6 *Nominalization*

Chafe comments (1968: 111) that while (*Sam's*) *kicking the bucket* can be either literal or idiomatic, the nominalization (*Sam's*) *kicking of the bucket* enforces a literal interpretation. OHPC offers very few counter-examples for any FEI, and in the following case with a less opaque metaphor, there is no doubt that the idiomatic meaning is intended:

In 1980 there was widespread resentment—especially, but not only, in East Germany—of what was seen as an unnecessary **rocking of the boat**. (OHPC: journalism)

Nominalization of FEIs in OHPC is more commonly lexical or morphological than purely syntactic. There are three specific forms. In the first, the FEI is truncated and reduced to one of its clausal components, usually retaining allusion to the original whole:

a new broom sweeps clean	new broom
damn SOMEONE with faint praise	faint praise
every cloud has a silver lining	silver lining
have a bee in ONE's bonnet	a bee in one's bonnet
it's the last straw that breaks the camel's back	last/final straw
play second fiddle to SOMEONE	second fiddle

A new broom sweeps clean never occurs in its traditional full form in OHPC, only as *new broom*. However, it would be wrong to say that the proverb is now obsolete and *new broom* an entirely separate lexical item, as the following example shows:

Under **the sweep of William Glock's new broom** at the BBC, groups such as the Vesuvius and Melos ensembles had been catching up on modern developments throughout the decade; the London Symphony Orchestra was at its all-time peak and the metropolis seemed full of players who actually wanted to do new music. (OHPC: journalism)

In the second kind of nominalization, verbs occur as verbal nouns or participial adjectives, or they are replaced by cognate nouns:

come and go	coming and going
cry wolf	cries of wolf
ebb and flow	the ebb and flow of SOMETHING
grit ONE's teeth	(through) gritted teeth
kick SOMEONE in the teeth	a kick in the teeth
lose face	loss of face
rap SOMEONE on the knuckles	a rap on the knuckles
stab SOMEONE in the back	a stab in the back
turn up ONE's nose	upturned noses
waste ONE's breath	a waste of breath

In the third kind, a different lexical item altogether is formed, often involving the inversion of the original lexical elements:

blaze a trail	trail-blazer, trail-blazing
break the ice	ice-breaker
fly a kite	kite-flying
hold SOMEONE's hand (=support)	hand-holding
keep house	housekeeper
pick SOMEONE's pocket	pickpocket
stop the show	show-stopper
take the mickey	mickey-taker, mickey-taking
twist SOMEONE's arm	arm-twisting
wipe the slate clean	a clean slate

5.6.7 *Transformation to Adjectives*

Adverbial and nominal FEIs may be transformed into adjectives simply through clausal positioning: the transformations are often hyphenated (compare discussion in Section 2.4). For example, the adverbial (*a*)*round the clock* becomes *round-the-clock*, *face to face* becomes *face-to-face*, and *on the spot* becomes *on-the-spot*. Truncation is sometimes involved:

of all time	all-time
on the back of an envelope	back-of-envelope
on the spur of the moment	spur-of-the-moment
the cut and thrust of —	cut-and-thrust
with tongue in cheek	tongue-in-cheek

Some of the following examples are nonce-forms:

There are 30 places available on a **first come, first served** basis; the closing date is Friday 15 March. (OHPC: journalism)

Less well known, but in my opinion more interesting, is the fact that unofficial and unspoken nonaggression pacts, a **'live-and-let-live'** system, flourished all up and down the front lines for at least two years starting in 1914. (OHPC: non-fiction)

The world premiere of Holmboe's Twelfth, commissioned by the BBC Welsh Symphony Orchestra, was only the latest in a succession of Holmboe performances in Cardiff; and like much of his music it offered a hard-boned, **take-it-or-leave-it** image, with no nod in the direction of modernism or post-modernism or any other 'ism', but plenty of sheer good writing and strongly chiselled ideas. (OHPC: journalism)

This light **melt-in-the-mouth** meringue, filled with rich chocolate cream, is irresistible. (OHPC: journalism)

Less than famous London team burst into the light with a powerful, unusual dancefloor groover featuring an emotive, **pulling-no-punches** oration from a youth called Afolbi and clear, spirited singing from Allison Gordon. (OHPC: journalism)

As with nominalizations, other formations involve syntactic changes and inversion, and can be considered separate lexical items:

break the ice	ice-breaking
break the mould	mould-breaking
catch SOMEONE's eye	eye-catching
clear as crystal	crystal-clear
dry as a bone	bone-dry
lick SOMEONE's boots	boot-licking
live from hand to mouth	hand-to-mouth
mean well	well-meaning
ONE's mouth waters	mouth-watering
take ONE's breath away	breath-taking

Formations such as *crystal-clear, well-meaning, mouth-watering,* and *breath-taking* are overwhelmingly more common than the cognate FEIs.

5.6.8 *Transformation to Predicates*

Proverbs are frequently truncated or reduced to verbal groups and complementation, thus contextualizing something that is essentially or diachronically a statement of a universal truth or deontic. Such downgradings may become institutionalized as variations, or effectively supersede the proverbial form. In particular, all 11 tokens of *you can't have your cake and eat it* in OHPC and all 6 of *it's the exception that proves the rule* were downgraded. Some further proverbs that were commonly downgraded in OHPC include:

a drowning man will clutch at a straw	to clutch at straws
don't look a gift-horse in the mouth	to look a gift-horse in the mouth
don't put the cart before the horse	to put the cart before the horse
don't wash your dirty linen in public	to wash ONE's dirty linen in public
make hay while the sun shines	to make hay
the devil is not as black as he is painted	to (not) be as ADJECTIVE as ONE is painted

For example:

There is only one glimmer of hope, although pessimists say it could be **clutching at straws**. (OHPC: journalism)

Professor Matthew Meselson, a chemical weapons expert at Harvard, said the administration 'wants to **have its cake and eat it**, too'. (OHPC: journalism)

Yet Henderson is also fully capable of hitting home runs if he cannot get on base. Against a slow-moving catcher like the Giants' Terry Kennedy in the World Series, Henderson is expected to **make hay**. (OHPC: journalism)

Prohibitions in proverbs (*Don't* — or *You can't*) are carried over in downgradings in the form of evaluations, so that use of the predicates in positive clauses continues to convey speaker/writer's disapproval. See Sections 5.6.1 and 6.1.7 for further discussion and examples.

A rare but interesting type deserves brief mention. There are a few cases where predicate FEIs have cognate single-word verbs: *pick nits* and *nitpick*, *pinch pennies* and *penny-pinch*. In these particular cases, the single-word forms are more common, and are frequently found as participial adjectives or nouns (*nitpicking*, *penny-pinching*). The single-word forms are used to evaluate an activity negatively; however, the fuller forms are more neutral in orientation. Compare

The Mittelstand may have become too fixated on selling high-quality goods at premium prices. This works when the product is unique and the manufacturer invests enough to keep it that way. But when markets are shrinking and customers **are pinching pennies**, customers may suddenly migrate to cheaper rivals. (BofE: journalism)

and

Staff both at New York's Metropolitan Museum of Art and at London's British Museum are acutely nervous of **penny-pinching** governments with an increasingly utilitarian approach to the arts. (BofE: journalism)

It cannot therefore be assumed that evaluative orientation will be consistent across transformations.

5.7 COLLIGATIONS, COLLOCATIONS, AND OTHER STRUCTURES

The lexical boundaries of FEIs are often unclear. Many are associated with optional colligating structures:

blow the gaff
blow the gaff on SOMEONE

compound the felony
compound the felony by VERBing

look daggers
look daggers at SOMEONE

make amends
make amends for SOMETHING

on purpose
on purpose to VERB

pass the time of day
pass the time of day with SOMEONE

While the continuation is optional, the choice of preposition or structure is restricted. In other cases, FEIs collocate strongly with particular categories, structures, or lexical words, but the restrictions are not so tight, and to present them as part of the canonical form of the FEI would be to overstate the case: see Table 5.13. Syntactic, lexical, and semantic aspects of FEIs overlap here.

This can be seen further in cases where an FEI typically co-occurs with modals, and it becomes difficult to separate its meaning from the modality of the co-text. For example, 26 of the 29 tokens for *rock the boat* in OHPC are modalized, occurring in structures with modal verbs or other words expressing modal ideas of possibility, necessity, ability, and so on, or else occurring in imperative structures. Altogether, 14 tokens occur with negatives and several others with broad negatives or words with a negative semantic component such as *if, fewer, afraid*, and *lost*. The patterns can be represented as shown in Table 5.14. I am oversimplifying here, and some of the epistemic tokens imply intention and volition too. Nevertheless, there is a very strong pattern of *rock the boat* being used in negative contexts, typically with expressions of the improbability, inadvisability, or undesirability of rocking the boat, as the following examples show:

TABLE 5.13. *Collocations of FEIs*

FEI	Collocating word or structure
a nip in the air	*there is*
bolt upright	*sit*
for the worse	*change, take a turn*
hook, line, and sinker	*swallow, fall*
in the clear	*be, put*
make tracks	adjunct of direction
mile off	verb of perception
on loan	*to, from*
over the moon	adjunct, *when*+clause
pull ONE's weight	negative
to a fault	adjective
with a flea in ONE's ear	*send away*

TABLE 5.14.   Rock the boat: *collocating modals*

Modality type	Positive	(Broad) negative
epistemic	2	6
deontic	1	10
conative	1	1
volitive	0	5
none	3	0

Ms Morrell attempts damage limitation by telling her boss to keep his mouth shut and not **rock the boat**, but on he goes collecting more enemies and being let down by erstwhile friends. (OHPC: journalism)

We are represented by men hungry for high political office who will therefore not **rock the party boat**; men whose loyalty is to their political careers, not necessarily their constituents [etc.]. (OHPC: periodical cited in non-fiction)

Sadock (1974: 122) discusses the FEI *in the world* which functions as an emphasizer in *wh*-interrogatives structures, that is structures beginning with *who, what, where,* and so on. More particularly, *in the world* occurs in rhetorical questions where the speaker/writer wants to *hear* the answer rather than know it. They are indirect speech acts, expressives or directives, rather than simple requests for information:

This second tale brought me up short. I said: 'Where **in the world** did this proposal come from?' 'You'd be surprised.' (OHPC: biography)

As I thought about that perceptive question I realised its implications. Was the message or the product important enough to present properly? Did the result matter to those of us who were involved? And if it was important, to us and the country, why **in the world** weren't we snuffing out all those niggling grievances and getting on with the job of winning? (OHPC: non-fiction)

She was about to close her eyes again when she heard a far-off roaring. She sat up and frowned. What **in the world** could it be? She whimpered as the noise filled her ears. It was now unbelievably loud. (OHPC: fiction)

All this relates to colligating and collocating structures as observed. It does not begin to deal with FEIs where certain structures are precluded—in the same way that some transformations of FEIs are precluded. For example, Mel'čuk (1995: 206) points out that several FEIs meaning 'die', such as *kick the bucket, bite the dust,* and *snuff it,* cannot be associated with an indication of the cause of death, apparently for semantic reasons. I can find only one counter-example in BofE, and it comes from British journalism:

When AIDS started to be taken seriously (i.e. a cabinet minister **kicked the bucket with it**).

These kinds of restriction and preference operate on individual items, and so are described on an individual basis. Alt makes a more general point in discussing *to*-infinitive and *-ing* complementation of verbs, particularly *begin* (1991: 462 ff.). While in many cases, either structure is possible, often with little change in meaning other than change of aspect or focus, he observes that where FEIs, idiomatic phrasal verbs, and other kinds of institutionalized metaphors occur in the complements, the to-infinitive structure is preferred and the -ing structure may be blocked. For example, *this began to set my teeth on edge* (Birmingham Collection of English Text) is unlikely to have the variation **this began setting my teeth on edge*. Alt suggests that this can be explained in terms of stativity and idiomaticity, and it is clearly another aspect of FEIs needing detailed exploration.

Finally, a minor but none the less interesting phenomenon is when FEIs collocate with other FEIs. Francis points out that *be a case of* typically co-occurs in BofE with FEIs (1993: 145), functioning as a preface which compares a situation already established in the discourse with another one familiar to the reader/hearer. Her examples include *It's simply a case of keeping fingers crossed* and *For it may not just be a case of having egg on your face*. Another FEI where this happens is *not be one to —*, for example:

But Mr Baker **is not one to go out on a limb**—he is only too well aware that the Middle East is a graveyard of American peace proposals, many of them killed by Mr Shamir. (OHPC: journalism)

Charlton **is not one to lose sleep over** anything—apart, perhaps, from the one that got away—and the superior technique his players will encounter next summer leaves him utterly unconcerned. (OHPC: journalism)

With £10.8m turnover, Robinson **is not one to rest on laurels**: this afternoon will find him working in the Bath branch of Jigsaw, a few miles from his home in the village of Colherne. (OHPC: journalism)

See Section 10.5 for a discussion of colligating FEIs and other words which metalinguistically signal FEIs or other choices of lexis.

6

Variation

Corpus studies of FEIs show clearly that their forms are often unstable. Fixedness is a key property of FEIs, yet around 40% of database FEIs have lexical variations or strongly institutionalized transformations, and around 14% have two or more variations on their canonical forms. Of course, some FEIs are more fixed than others, and some, for example, *take place* and *at all*, do not vary at all; however, variation is very widespread. This is not a phenomenon confined to English, but has been reported by people involved in text-based or corpus-based studies of FEIs in other languages. For example, Clausén (1996) discusses it with respect to Swedish, and Cignoni and Coffey (1995) with respect to Italian: lexicographers working with Danish and Czech have also observed it (personal communications). Nor are all these variations ad hoc manipulations for stylistic effect. Such exploitations happen (see Section 6.7) and are very noticeable in text, but they are not the dominant type. Designating departures from canonical forms as 'artistic deformations' (Mel'čuk 1995: 213) or 'wordplay' (Schenk 1995: 257) underplays the prevalence and significance of the phenomenon of variation.

Variation is fairly consistent across FEI types: see Table 6.1. Variation is also relatively consistent across frequency bands. Table 6.2 shows what proportion of FEIs in each frequency band were found in OHPC with variations. In fact, the most deviant figure is for the least frequent FEIs, and this clearly reflects the fact that if

TABLE 6.1. *FEIs with variations, according to idiomaticity type*

	Proportion of FEIs in database	*Proportion of all FEIs with any variations*	*Proportion of all FEIs with 2 or more variations*
anomalous collocations	45.3%	47%	46%
formulae	21.3%	18%	19%
metaphors	33.4%	35%	35%

TABLE 6.2. *FEIs with variations, according to frequency*

	FEIs with variations	FEIs without variations
0	–	–
1–4	31%	69%
5–17	45%	55%
1–2/million	48%	52%
2–5/million	48%	52%
5–10/million	55%	45%
10–50/million	45%	55%
50–100/million	41%	59%
over 100/million	50%	50%

only one or two tokens of an expression were found, they were less likely to include variations: obviously, if I found no tokens at all, I found no variations. It is likely that larger corpora, with more tokens of FEIs, will throw up more examples of variation. These statistics are at variance with Čermák's assertion (1994c: 16) that 'the higher the idiom's frequency, the more the idiom is fixed (stable) and the less is the chance that there might be variations of it'; however, Barkema (1996a: 81) finds no relation between frequency and 'flexibility' in his examination of a large set of noun phrases, not all FEIs, in a 20 million-word corpus of English.

Correlating variation with grammatical type suggests that it is particularly strong with predicate FEIs, less strong with FEIs which are syntactically adjectival, nominal, or prepositional groups. Since frequency factors complicate further correlations, this should be seen as merely indicating a general tendency. Genre clearly plays a role too: while variations occur across the range of text types, it is often associated with journalism. Variations found in journalism cannot be dismissed out of hand as mannerism and journalese. In fact, journalism represents the cutting edge of language change, or the popularization of language change: variations fossilizing here may foreshadow what will later becomes institutionalized more widely.

All this calls into question the whole notion of fixedness, shedding doubt on the viability of the notion of the canonical form. In the course of this chapter, I shall set out evidence which suggests that the notion should be superseded, and newer models of FEIs developed in its stead. The line I shall take in exploring this issue may seem perverse or illogical, in view of my conclusions, since

I propose to start from the assumption that I myself started from and that studies of FEIs in general start from: the assumption that FEIs have fixed or canonical forms and that variations are to some extent derivative or deviant. It might also seem perverse or illogical that I persist with the term 'fixed expression', albeit disguised in FEI. However, this study is a descriptive account of one part of the English lexicon, and since there *are* received ideas and models, it seems more efficient to build on them in order to set out where, how, and why they need adjusting. With regard to the term 'FEI', I would defend it by saying that even in extreme cases there still remains some kind of fixedness, symmetry, or integrity: it is just that it is not always *lexical* fixedness.

One important issue must be raised at the outset. Statements about the incidence of variability presuppose that the variant forms of an individual expression are to be considered as variations rather than as separate expressions with coincidentally the same meaning and with some lexis in common. Thus pairs such as

    champ at the bit
    chafe at the bit

    hit the roof
    hit the ceiling

represent two expressions, each with an institutionalized variation, not four individual expressions. The problem is particularly acute with American/British pairings such as

    the shoe is on the other foot (AmE)
    the boot is on the other foot (BrE)

    blow off steam (AmE)
    let off steam (BrE)

where the parallels are obvious. It is valid to consider them as variations of each other, but it is equally valid to consider them as equivalent lexical items which are as discrete as *gasoline/petrol* or *apartment/flat*. I will take the line that broadly synonymous pairs or sets of FEIs with common or parallel lexis represent single FEIs or FEI clusters. This view allows newly encountered variant forms to be reconciled with those forms already found, providing further evidence of instability, rather than enforcing either their categorization as completely new items or else their dismissal as deviant.

Equally important is the matter of identifying the 'canonical' form of an FEI. There are two ways of considering a case such as

    have an axe to grind
    have no axe to grind
    with an axe to grind

without an axe to grind
with no axe to grind

Either this represents a variable FEI cluster, where there are several possible related forms, or a frozen, unvarying FEI nucleus *axe to grind* which collocates with preceding *have/with/without* and *a/no*. There are some advantages to seeing it as a frozen nucleus with a collocating structure, but I do not think that *axe to grind* is itself a very meaningful unit. In cases such as *champ/chafe at the bit* and *hit the roof/ceiling*, there is no meaningful lexical core.

The crucial point here is that very large numbers of FEIs do not have fixed forms, and it would be wrong to claim that they do. The evidence is simply against it. *Kick the bucket* is often cited as a prime example of an FEI where the lexis is completely frozen, and Newmeyer (1972: 297) argues that *kick the pail* would not have the same meaning as *kick the bucket*, but I have encountered both *kick the pail* and *kick the can* in real text, meaning 'die': both in American English. Sadock (1972: 332) and Ruhl (1977: 462) draw attention to dialectal uses of *kick*, *kick off*, and *kick in* meaning 'die'. *OED* includes eighteenth- and nineteenth-century examples of *kick* and *kick it* and twentieth-century examples of *kick off*, 'die'. These may be independent uses, or they may be contracted forms of either *kick the bucket* or *kick up one's heels*, with the same meaning 'die'. The main point here is that stability and frozenness can never be assumed, and change over time.

To be truly systematic, of course, categories of variation need to have some predictive power, and this is not always the case. What *can* be predicted is that FEIs, especially metaphorical ones, are likely to vary. Pulman's careful debunking of the notion of canonical form ends securely with: 'It thus seems legitimate to regard all idioms as being able in principle to occur in any syntactic configuration, and therefore we can put the responsibility for explaining why some variations sound better than others onto some future theory of information structuring in relation to syntax' (1993: 270). The same may apply to lexical configuration.

Some psycholinguistic studies have examined the effects that variations of all kinds have on processing and comprehension. Gibbs *et al.* (1989a) suggest that processing of variations is not hampered as long as the original metaphor is maintained, for example when words from the same semantic field are substituted. McGlone *et al.* (1994) suggest that informants use their knowledge of the canonical forms and literal meanings of the substituted words, in order to process variations and exploitations. Such variations take longer to deal with than canonical forms, and as long to process as literal meanings, but they are nevertheless not problematic.

This chapter will begin by looking at institutionalized variations. It will then consider more ad hoc variations, exploitations, and other manipulations. A perennial problem in the literature is that examples of variations, as with transformations, are often intuited rather than supported by real data. Here, all examples of variations are taken from OHPC, BofE, or other authentic text sources.

6.1 TYPES OF LEXICAL VARIATION

Variability can be explored formally, looking at the structural or syntactic ways in which FEIs vary. This is the approach followed by Thun (1975), who considers French FEIs, and also Negreneau (1975), who examines parallels and divergences between French and Romanian FEIs. It would be naive to suggest that all realizations of an FEI pair or cluster have precisely the same meaning or usage, as there may be shifts in focus, intensity, or distribution. However, it seems useful to group together FEIs which vary in a given syntactic or other way in order to systematize the phenomenon of variation as observed in corpora and other texts. It must be pointed out that this is ultimately surface description, and not all categories can be seen as evidencing any deeper sociocultural or other linguistic system at work.

In the following subsections, I will look at cases where variations relate to individual words within FEIs: more structural variations will be considered in Section 6.2.

6.1.1 *Verb Variation*

Verb variation is, in my data, the commonest type, and points clearly to instability in the forms of FEIs. It is not, however, a uniform phenomenon. While in many cases, the meaning of the whole is barely affected by variation, other variations reflect important syntacto-semantic distinctions.

In the following pairs or clusters, the verb varies, but there is no real change in meaning of the FEI, although there may be register distinctions. In only a few of these cases do alternating verbs reflect a superordinate/hyponym distinction:[1]

---

[1] In the following, I shall be giving examples of kinds of variation, not exhaustive lists.

fall/run foul of SOMEONE/SOMETHING
set/start the ball rolling
up/raise the ante
fit/fill the bill
rest/lean on ONE's oars
stick/stand out like a sore thumb
throw/toss in the towel
upset/overturn the applecart

Single verbs sometimes alternate with verb + particle combinations:

blow up in ONE's face, explode in ONE's face
down tools, lay down tools
lower/drop ONE's guard, let down ONE's guard
separate the sheep from the goats, sort out the sheep from the goats
step into SOMEONE's shoes, fill SOMEONE's shoes

The alternating verbs may not be synonymous in other contexts:

bend/stretch the rules
get/put SOMEONE's back up
look/shoot daggers at SOMEONE
say/kiss goodbye to SOMETHING
the dust settles/clears
twist/wrap SOMEONE around ONE's little finger

The alternating verbs sometimes show differences in focus or degree:

hang in the air, be left hanging in the air
keep/juggle the balls in the air
play/keep ONE's cards close to ONE's chest
throw/put SOMEONE off the scent

A more complicated case is the variant group *knock/lick/whip something into shape*. These are broadly interchangeable now, with the verbs notionally denoting 'beat, hit, force'; however, there is a discrete historical origin for *lick something into shape*, which allegedly refers to a traditional belief that cubs were born as shapeless masses and only took on recognizable forms when licked by the mother bears.

The copula *be* sometimes alternates with other verbs,

be/come within an ace of SOMETHING
be/come under fire
be/feel sorry for SOMEONE
be/get up to SOMETHING
be/look miles away

but in most of such cases, the FEIs are better analysed as adjectival groups or adjuncts.

While varying verbs are typically the main verbs in FEIs, they are occasionally catenated verbs:

come out swinging/fighting
make ONE's blood freeze/run cold

Other kinds of verb variation reflect grammatical variations, or variations in transitivity and other clausal processes. These are dealt with in Section 6.2.

6.1.2 *Noun Variation*

Variation of nouns in FEIs is only slightly less common than variation of verbs. In the simplest cases, the varying nouns are broadly synonymous:

a piece/slice of the action
a pot/crock of gold
a skeleton in the closet/cupboard
in full flow/spate/flood
run rings/circles round SOMEONE
tempt fate/providence
the calm/lull before the storm

The variation may take the form of singular or plural forms of the same noun:

at all events, at any event
break ranks/rank
not give a hoot, not give two hoots
skin and bone/bones
take the wind out of SOMEONE's sail/sails
test the water/test the waters
under plain cover, in plain covers

or of male/female noun equivalents:

jobs for the boys/girls
the man/woman in the street
you can't keep a good man/woman down

Variant nouns sometimes reflect general/specific distinctions. In the following cases, the second variation given is a hyponym or meronym of the first:

a ballpark figure/estimate
from head to foot/toe
hang on by ONE's fingertips/fingernails
hold a gun/pistol to SOMEONE's head
in the teeth of the wind/gale
lick SOMEONE's shoes/boots

put ONE's head/neck on the block
sing from the same song/hymn sheet
throw ONE's hat/cap into the ring

A specific noun may alternate with a proform or empty slot:

give SOMEONE an even break, give a sucker an even break
hitch ONE's wagon to SOMETHING, hitch ONE's wagon to a star
SOMETHING is not worth the candle, the game is not worth the candle
the wheel has come full circle, SOMETHING has come full circle

In the following, the proform is institutionalized:

pull SOMEONE's leg, pull the other one
put ONE's foot in it, put ONE's foot in ONE's mouth
rub SOMEONE's nose in it, rub SOMEONE's nose in the dirt

There are many cases where the nouns are not synonymous outside the FEIs, and may even belong to different semantic fields:

a cat on a hot tin roof, a cat on hot bricks
a tower/pillar of strength
burn ONE's boats/bridges
castles in the air/castles in Spain
lead SOMEONE a merry chase/dance
leave SOMEONE holding the baby/bag
miss the boat/bus
take the cake/biscuit
throw SOMEONE to the wolves/lions

In metaphorical FEIs, the nouns often appear to be the locus or focus of the metaphor. Variations do not have changed meanings, but mental images of the metaphor may differ considerably: for example, the images generated by *burn one's boats* and *burn one's bridges*. The distinctions are therefore greater than those between many verb variations, and there would be more reason to regard such pairs as discrete, but cognate, lexical items.

Further cases of noun variation are discussed in Section 6.3.

6.1.3 *Adjective and Modifier Variation*

Variation of adjectives in FEIs is considerably less common than that of verbs or nouns, but there are fewer component adjectives than nouns in FEIs. As before, the varying adjectives are sometimes broadly synonymous:

a bad/rotten apple
a level/even playing field
a hard/tough row to hoe
close/near to the bone
(as) easy/simple as falling off a log

the best/greatest thing since sliced bread

They may also have quite different meanings in other collocations:

bleed SOMEONE dry/white
hard/close/hot on the heels of SOMEONE/SOMETHING
on a short/tight leash
scream blue/bloody murder

The variation *handsome/pretty is as handsome/pretty does* occasionally reflects a gender distinction.

Semi-deictic *different* in FEIs sometimes alternates with *another* and *new*:

a different/another kettle of fish
a horse of a different/another colour
a new/different/whole other ball game

Variation of quantifiers and grammatical and other prenominal modifiers is systematic and predictable, in that conventional distinctions in meaning or emphasis are maintained:

all/more power to ONE's elbow
at all events, at any event
not a/one red cent
pull no punches, not pull ONE's/any punches
no/little love lost (between X and Y)
there are plenty more fish in the sea, there are other fish in the sea

However, there are a very few cases where there is no difference in meaning or reference, although the last of these connotes a distinction in attitude:

a fifth/third wheel
a nine-day/one-day wonder
ONE's better/other half

A number of open-slot FEIs require insertion of adjectives: see Section 5.5.4. In these cases the inserted adjectives make a substantial contribution to the specific meanings of the FEIs. Extraneous adjectives inserted in FEIs provide semantic focus or specialization: see Section 6.8. I will not discuss determiner variation in depth here, but it is worth pointing out that *the* is significant when it appears in FEIs which are not lexically cohesive (see Section 10.2.1), and that the majority of nominal FEIs are not associated with fixed determiners.

6.1.4 *Particle Variation*

In the following cases, variation of a prepositional or adverbial particle involves no apparent shift in meaning: the variations *from/ out of* or *round/around* are entirely conventional:

at/in a single sitting
a bolt from the blue, a bolt out of the blue
by/in leaps and bounds
in/at full throttle
on/along the right lines
out of thin air, from thin air
rap SOMEONE on/over the knuckles
go round/around in circles

Other variations, however, may reflect a shift in focus:

fray at/around the edges
with egg on ONE's face, with egg all over ONE's face
try SOMETHING on/out for size

Of the 533 database FEIs headed by *in*, 38 have dynamic transformations or variations in OHPC with *into*, and 37 have antonymous parallels with *out of*:

in arrears
into arrears

in leaf
into leaf

in debt
into debt
out of debt

in touch
into touch
out of touch

in keeping (with SOMETHING/SOMEONE)
out of keeping (with SOMETHING/SOMEONE)

There are sometimes marked distinctions in frequency within such sets. For example, *in keeping* is 8 times commoner than *out of keeping*: the antonym may also be constructed through negation as (*not*) *in keeping*. Such antonymous variations are discussed in Section 6.4.

6.1.5 *Conjunction Variation*

For the sake of completeness, here are a very few cases from my data where the conjunction in an FEI varies:

hit and miss, hit or miss
like there's no tomorrow, as if there's no tomorrow
when/if push comes to shove,
when/while the cat's away, the mice will play

6.1.6 *Specificity and Amplification*

There are many cases of FEIs where the variation consists broadly of some inserted or suppressed material. One version is simply a fuller version of the other, adding emphasis or precision. The extra data is often adjectival,

> cut the (umbilical) cord
> go the (full) distance
> have a (good) laugh
> in (full) bloom
> light the (blue) touch paper
> like a (hot) knife through butter
> like (greased) lightning
> put (out) to sea
> the (moral) high ground
> to (good/best) advantage

or adverbial:

> concentrate the mind (wonderfully)
> (down) on ONE's uppers
> (out) on a limb
> pass the hat (around)
> (right) on the button
> stop SOMEONE (dead) in their tracks
> turn (over) in ONE's grave

Occasionally, there is an optional prepositional phrase,

> go to hell (in a handbasket)
> twist the knife (in the wound)
> up the/shit creek (without a paddle)

catenated verb,

> a tough nut (to crack)
> give SOMEONE enough rope (to hang themselves)
> lay (to rest) the ghost of SOMEONE

expanded or augmented nominal group,

> a hair of the dog (that bit you)
> at all hours (of the day and night)
> cut the ground from under SOMEONE('s feet)
> have SOMEONE eating out of (the palm of) ONE's hand
> put flesh (and bone) on SOMETHING
> scrape (the bottom of) the barrel
> see the light (of day)

or additional catenated noun or adjective:

> a hop, skip, and jump; a hop and a skip
> all (fingers and) thumbs

signed and sealed, signed sealed and delivered
the whole (kit and) caboodle

These amplifications sometimes reflect diachronic developments.

6.1.7 *Truncation*

Amplification and truncation are two sides of the same coin, but in
the majority of cases listed below, the fuller versions are fairly
clearly attested as the original forms. Many are traditional proverbs
and sayings, downgraded from their canonical or earliest forms to
lower-level grammatical units: a compound sentence to a single
clause, or a clause to a group:

a bird in the hand (is worth two in the bush)
birds of a feather (flock together)
don't count ONE's chickens (before they're hatched)
he who pays the piper calls the tune, call the tune
let the cobbler stick to his last, stick to ONE's last
make hay (while the sun shines)
(sow the wind and) reap the whirlwind

The reduced forms can be seen in terms of ellipsis, since in many
cases an allusion to the original and fuller form remains. However,
they are institutionalized, and many can be regarded as lexical items
in their own right. *A rolling stone gathers no moss* is complicated in
that both the nominal *rolling stone* and the verb phrase *gather moss*
are institutionalized as individual items. In

a drowning man will clutch at a straw
clutch/grasp at straws

it's the (last) straw that breaks the camel's back
the last straw/final straw

the truncated forms themselves have variations. In a few cases, the
original fuller form has almost disappeared from the lexicon:

finders keepers (loser weepers)
happy the bride that the sun shines on (and blessed are the dead that the
   rain falls on)
(speech is silver but) silence is golden
butter wouldn't melt in her mouth (but cheese wouldn't choke her)

In the above cases, the reduced forms have become fossilized as the
canonical forms. Truncation can also occur on an ad hoc basis:

My mother was hysterical and my father called me a lot of unpleasant
names. I stood it for a bit and then I'm afraid I said to him that **what
was sauce for the goose** and at least I wasn't married. (OHPC:
fiction)

In one audacious move, D & B sent a questionnaire to Geoff Croughton, secretary of the Bank of England. After all, **nothing ventured** and all that. (OHPC: journalism)

6.1.8 *Reversals*

There are isolated cases of reversal within FEIs, in contrast to the normal rules concerning binomials (see Section 6.3.2):

day and night
night and day

on and off
off and on

you can't have your cake and eat it
you can't eat your cake and have it

There are no meaning distinctions here. Evidence in *CODP2* suggests that *you can't eat your cake and have it* is the earlier form, and in fact it better reflects the meaning of the proverb. Fernando and Flavell point out the illogicality of *you can't have your cake and eat it* (1981: 26): compare the more logical order of the French parallel *on ne peut pas avoir le beurre et l'argent du beurre*. And in *you can't have your cake and eat it* leads to ambiguity, since it can indicate both concomitance and sequence: if it is interpreted as sequencing, then 'having one's cake' is pointless—since it cannot be eaten. The earlier order is clearer, saying it is impossible both to eat one's cake (doing something irreversible) and then still to have it available for eating (not yet having done it). *You can't have your cake and eat it* is by far the commoner order in current British English: 10 out of the 11 tokens in OHPC are in this form, as are 135 of 138 tokens in BoE. However, Platt *et al.* (1984: 109) point out that both Nigerian and Singaporean English prefer the other, older, version.

FEIs are sometimes reversed as exploitations, with corresponding changes in meaning: see Section 6.7.

6.1.9 *Register Variation*

Variations often reflect distinctions in formality. There are several examples amongst those listed above, where variant words, more or less synonymous in general meaning, belong to different registers, for example, *beat one's breast/chest* where the first variation is more formal than the second. Section 6.7 below looks at cases where exploitations of FEIs involve the substitution of more literary or formal words.

In a few cases, one variation is an institutionalized representation of a colloquial pronunciation: the selection of the non-standard form reinforces the colloquial connotations of the FEI as a whole: these examples all involve pronouns or possessives:

knock SOMEONE dead/knock 'em dead
in your face/in yer face
on your bike/on yer bike

Take the mickey is informal in any case: *take the mick* is a further colloquialization. Note that *extract the michael*, a jocular variation incorporating more formal equivalents for *take* and *mickey*, is actually no less colloquial or informal than *take the mickey*.

6.1.10 *Variations between British and American English*

Since OHPC is a corpus of British texts, my original study looked at British English. It would be inappropriate to attempt here any rigorous analysis of lexical distinctions between British and American FEIs. However, data gathered through work towards *CCDI* can be reported briefly, and it mostly relates to idioms.

There were comparatively few cases where the verb varied:

cut a long story short (BrE), make a long story short (AmE)
flog a dead horse (BrE), beat a dead horse (AmE)
let off steam (BrE), blow off steam (AmE)
kick ONE's heels (mainly BrE), cool ONE's heels (mainly AmE)
touch wood (BrE), knock wood, knock on wood (AmE)

Far more common was variation of a noun or noun modifier. These sometimes reflected standard distinctions between British and American English:

in the driving seat (BrE), in the driver's seat (AmE)
not know ONE's arse from ONE's elbow (BrE), not know ONE's ass from ONE's elbow (AmE)
red as a beetroot (BrE), red as a beet (AmE)
throw a spanner in the works (BrE), throw a (monkey) wrench in the works (AmE)
wear the trousers (BrE), wear the pants (mainly AmE)

While *catch someone with their trousers down* is only British, *catch someone with their pants down* is found in both varieties: arguably, a British speaker's mental image might involve underwear, not outerwear. A few cases reflect other cultural distinctions:

like turkeys voting for Christmas (mainly BrE), like turkeys voting for Thanksgiving (AmE)
turn on sixpence (BrE), turn on a dime (AmE)

British *bent as a nine-bob note* and corresponding American *phoney/ queer as a three-dollar bill* reflect both cultural and lexical distinctions. In the majority of cases, the distinctions now seem idiosyncratic, although there may be historical explanations:

fall through the net (BrE), fall through the cracks (AmE)
have green fingers (BrE), have a green thumb (AmE)
if the cap fits (BrE), if the shoe fits (AmE)
keep ONE's hair on (BrE), keep ONE's shirt on (AmE)
not see the wood for the trees (BrE), not see the forest for the trees (AmE)
rub shoulders with (BrE), rub elbows with (AmE)
too big for ONE's boots (BrE), too big for ONE's britches/breeches (AmE)

British *blow one's own trumpet* corresponds to American *blow one's own horn*: the parallels appear to involve comparable musical instruments. However, *blow one's own horn* has a verb variation *toot one's own horn*, which suggests that the notional reference of *horn* is now indeterminate between a musical instrument and a car horn.

A rare case of adjective variation is British *blue-eyed boy* which corresponds to American *fair-haired boy*. There is participial variation in British *come unstuck* and the American equivalent *come unglued*.

About with spatial meaning or reference is largely a Briticism: American prefers *around*. It is therefore predictable that *(not) beat about the bush* is mainly British, *(not) beat around the bush* mainly American, although both forms are found in both varieties. Other cases of prepositional variation are more idiosyncratic:

at a pinch (BrE), in a pinch (AmE)
lead SOMEONE up the garden path (BrE), lead SOMEONE down the garden path (AmE)
on the cards (BrE), in the cards (AmE)

Finally, there are a few cases where British and American English have parallel idioms, with similar meanings, usages, and even source domains for the metaphors, but different lexis altogether:

a storm in a teacup (BrE), a tempest in a teapot (AmE)
have ONE's hand/fingers in the till (BrE), have ONE's hand in the cookie jar (AmE)
in inverted commas (BrE), quote unquote (BrE and AmE), quote end quote (AmE)

While many of these distinctions are well established, the situation in general is complex. The influence of American culture and media in Britain means that Americanisms and American variations become established in British English, or at least established in certain registers or genres of British English. For example, the mainly American *beat the bushes* 'try hard to obtain or achieve something' occurs in BofE in British journalism, admittedly with respect to American or international topics. Curiously enough, some FEIs such as *carry coals to Newcastle* and *in for a penny, in for a pound*, which intuitively feel like Briticisms, are occasionally found in American English: compare *send someone to Coventry* and *penny wise, pound foolish* which are not. And while most English FEIs exist in both varieties, they may well have different distributions, thus affecting register of use.

6.1.11 *Spelling, Homophonous, and Erroneous Variations*

Individual words in FEIs may have spelling variations, as part of the regular spelling conventions of English. This includes cases of British/American spelling variation, and in all cases it is predictable:

> a grey/gray area
> have an axe/ax to grind
> sit in judgment/judgement
> with flying colours/colors
> a nosey/nosy parker

An interesting case is that of British *sell like hot cakes*, where American English has *sell like hotcakes* (the fused spelling *hotcakes* is found increasingly in British English). However, the notional referent of the comparison in British, 'freshly baked cakes', is distinct from American, where *hotcakes* are a specific kind of pancake. There are also different stress patterns associated with *hot cakes/ hotcakes* in standard British and American usage.

Spelling variations sometimes reflect historical or etymological developments:

> rack and ruin
> wrack and ruin
>
> straight and narrow
> strait and narrow
>
> the spitting image of X
> the spit and image of X

Compare cases such as

> dull as ditchwater/dishwater
> into the wide/wild blue yonder
> plough a lonely/lone furrow

where the variant words are quasi-homophonous: similarly *be a shoo-in/shoe-in* where there is indeterminacy of form.

In fact, several FEIs have variations of spelling or form which are generally regarded as erroneous but which arise from homophony and confusion of sounds. In the following, the second form given would usually be considered deviant, although a few of these 'deviant' forms are becoming institutionalized:[2]

as opposed to
as oppose to

damp squib
damp squid

in pole position
in poll position

just deserts
just desserts

muddy the waters
muddle the waters

off ONE's own bat
off ONE's own back

strike a chord
strike a cord

to all intents and purposes
to all intensive purposes

toe the line
tow the line

whet SOMEONE's appetite
wet SOMEONE's appetite

with bated breath
with baited breath

Some of these confusions arise, perhaps, because the canonical spelling relates to a word or usage which is anomalous, and no longer found outside the FEI. For example, *toe* is not normally used as a verb, whereas the verb *tow* is well attested in collocation with words such as *rope* or indeed *line*, with literal meaning. The spelling variations in fact reflect attempts to make sense, to rationalize: they also demonstrate the dynamism of language. Note that while this kind of variation may seem marginal, any perceptions of the metaphor involved will be seriously affected.

Bolinger and Sears (1981: 249) cite *give something free reign* as an error for . . . *free rein*. This, in turn, is related to cases where FEIs

---

[2] Andrew Delahunty (personal communication) points out further examples in *have another think/thing coming* and *put a damper/dampener on something*.

are blended in error. Aitchison (1992: 250) cites *in the sleast*, and Peters (1983: 106) cites

> He was breathing down my shoulder
> I stuck my neck out on a limb
> In one ear and gone tomorrow

Tannen (1989: 41) cites

> It's no sweat off our backs
> something along those veins
> How would you like to eat humble crow?

Two further examples

> . . . were out of the door **in one clean swoop** (meeting 4 September 1996)

> It's **the thin edge of the wedge** (interviewee in a BBC news programme, 6 September 1996)

both show confusion and blends arising from near-homophony. Many more such blends get reported as 'Colemanballs':

> Aberdeen are taking this bitter pill on the chin.
> And St Helens have really got their tails between their teeth.
> I think you've hit the nose on the head.
> It's a political hot potato round their necks.
> . . . it was a can of worms in a nutshell.
> So you've finally nailed your mast to Neil Kinnock?
> (*Colemanballs* 6 (1992); *Colemanballs* 7 (1994), London: Private Eye & Corgi)

Colemanballs are discussed further in Section 10.2.1.

Finally, in a few cases, erroneous forms develop through near-homophony, and then themselves become institutionalized consciously, as jocular forms alongside the canonical originals:

> comparisons are odious
> comparisons are odorous
>
> cast aspersions
> cast nasturtiums
>
> in suspense
> in suspenders

6.1.12 *Calques and Non-Naturalized FEIs*

Although not strictly a part of the research reported here, a minor but interesting kind of variation is where FEIs from French or Latin have become assimilated into the general English lexicon, and exist alongside their translations or calques. The calques and originals typically have different frequencies or are restricted to different varieties or registers:

au contraire
on the contrary

carpe diem
seize the day

caveat emptor
(let the) buyer beware

c'est la vie
that's life

cri de cœur
a cry from the heart

en passant
in passing

fait accompli
accomplished fact

inter alia
among other things

quis custodiet ipsos custodes?
who will guard the guards?, who watches the watchdogs?

tête-à-tête
(a) head to head (face to face)

Dillard cites a further case, where *let the good times roll* and the original French *laisser les bon temps rouler* co-exist in certain Cajun contexts (1992: 133). Compare also the long-established cranberry *in lieu of* which co-exists with *in place of* and *instead of*.

6.1.13 *False Variations*

Finally, there are a few cases where, in isolation, pairs of FEIs look misleadingly as if they may be variations of one another, but in fact have different meanings:

get ONE's hands dirty (get involved)
have dirty hands (be guilty)

fill ONE's boots (get something valuable)
fill SOMEONE's boots/shoes (replace someone)

give and take (compromise)
give or take (approximately)

on the up, on the up and up (BrE, improving)
on the up and up (AmE, honest)

Ambiguity and polysemy are discussed in Sections 7.1 and 7.2. *Familiarity breeds contempt* can be compared to quasi-homophonous *familiarity breeds content* with the opposite meaning: this either represents a collision of forms or an institutionalization of a variation. Gläser (1986: 49) sees the form with *content* as a pun or ad hoc variation, but both are now commonly found.

6.2 SYSTEMATIC VARIATIONS

Simple transformations and grammatical operations were discussed in Section 5.6, as part of the routine morphological behaviour of FEIs. The following sections focus on cases where pairs or clusters of FEIs reflect deeper grammatical systems and relationships or concepts. These systematic variations, or 'systematic transformations' in Čermák's terminology (1994b: 191), display some sort of regularity. They are both syntactic and lexical. They may be predicted to occur in text, although this does not necessarily mean that they do occur.

6.2.1 *Notions of Possession*

Cowie *et al.* in the preface to the second volume of *ODCIE* (1983: pp. xxxiii–iv) draw attention to an important kind of variation in the expression of 'possession' or indication of attributes. These are variations where verbs such as *have, get, give,* and sometimes *take* or other verbs, alternate with each other:

get a raw deal
have a raw deal

get ONE's eye in
keep ONE's eye in
have ONE's eye in

give SOMEONE a good hiding
get a good hiding
receive a good hiding

have a line on SOMETHING
get a line on SOMETHING

have full play
give full play to SOMETHING
allow no play to SOMETHING (and variations)

have got cold feet
get cold feet
develop cold feet

have the measure of SOMEONE

get the measure of SOMEONE
take SOMEONE's measure (and variations)

get the cold shoulder
give SOMEONE the cold shoulder

The variations may also involve prepositional phrases headed by *with* or *without*:

have (no, an) axe to grind
with(out) an axe to grind

give SOMEONE both barrels
with both barrels

have an eye to SOMETHING
with an eye to SOMETHING

have ONE's feet on the ground
with ONE's feet on the ground

not have a stitch on
without a stitch on

not have the foggiest idea
without the foggiest idea

put ONE's feet up
with ONE's feet up

stick ONE's nose in the air
with ONE's nose in the air

6.2.2 *Causative and Resultative Structures*

In this category can be grouped cases where one variation denotes a state, process, or action, and another variation explicitly mentions the cause or result of the state, process, or action. These are causatives or ergatives: in Čermák's terminology they are 'statutory transformations' (1994*b*: 191), since they involve change from one stage or state to another. The variations typically reflect some deep transitivity patterning. In one form, the affected is mentioned as grammatical subject; in the other, the affected is mentioned as verbal or prepositional object, with the agent being mentioned as grammatical subject. The same verb may occur in both variations:

ONE's heart hardens
harden ONE's heart (towards SOMEONE)
harden SOMEONE's heart (towards SOMEONE)

steer clear of SOMETHING
steer SOMEONE clear of SOMETHING

the death knell sounds for SOMEONE/SOMETHING
sound the death knell for SOMEONE/SOMETHING

The causation is occasionally signalled explicitly by the verb *make*:

ONE's blood boils
make SOMEONE's blood boil

one's hair stands on end
make SOMEONE's hair stand on end

The transitive structures *boil someone's blood* and *stand someone's hair on end* also occur, but are much less frequent (at least in BofE) than the forms with *make*. The pair *curl someone's hair* and *make someone's hair curl* are both causatives: the variation with *make* is more emphatic. The same appears to be the case with *burn one's fingers* and *get one's fingers burned*, where the variation with *get* emphasizes result rather than process.

More commonly, the causative variation uses a different verb from the non-causative (or suppressed causative) one. The alternating verbs include *put* in its causative meaning or traditional pairings such as *raise* and *rise* or *bring* and *come*:

come to a head
bring SOMETHING to a head

get the wind up, have the wind up
put the wind up SOMEONE

go into raptures
send SOMEONE into raptures
throw SOMEONE into raptures

go through the wringer
put SOMEONE through the wringer

know the ropes
learn the ropes
show SOMEONE the ropes
teach SOMEONE the ropes

ONE's hackles rise
raise SOMEONE's hackles

the bubble bursts
prick the bubble

the wraps come off SOMETHING
take the wraps off SOMETHING

the curtain comes down on SOMETHING
bring the curtain down on SOMETHING

In a squib, Binnick (1971: 260–5) argues that while *bring* is not a true causative counterpart of *come*, since someone can come to a place without being brought there, *bring* and *come* are usually perfect counterparts in phrasal verbs: similarly with some other FEI combinations. He lists a few exceptions such as *come clean, come on strong*, and *bring something home to someone*, without counterparts. A few of his examples can be questioned: for example, *come/bring to blows* is actually restricted to the verb *come*, whereas his exception *come to pass* does in fact have a (rare) counterpart with *bring*. However, his point remains valid: that in ordinary compositional use *bring* and *come* are not necessarily a causative pairing, but in more idiomatic constructions, they typically are.

The resultative (or stative) variation is sometimes a structure with *be* as copula or auxiliary: see Pulman (1993: 256ff.) for discussion of these and their underlying roles and relationships:

> beat SOMEONE black and blue
> be black and blue
>
> have ONE's knife out (for SOMEONE)
> the knives are out (for SOMEONE)
>
> let the cat out of the bag
> the cat is out of the bag
>
> open the floodgates
> the floodgates are open
>
> set tongues wagging
> tongues are wagging
>
> take ONE's hat off to SOMEONE
> hats off to SOMEONE
>
> tie SOMEONE's hands
> have ONE's hands tied, ONE's hands are tied
>
> turn the tables
> the tables are turned
>
> wipe the slate clean
> the slate is clean (*compare* a clean slate)

Compare *see the writing on the wall/the writing is on the wall* and other active/passive structures. These variations with *be* are foregrounding result and end-state, and they can be compared to the following few cases, where the second variations may be resultatives or statives, reflecting a result/process distinction with the first variations, or else simply denote distinct activities:

> get in on the act
> be in on the act
>
> go on the warpath
> be on the warpath
>
> walk a knife edge
> be on a knife edge

6.2.3 *Aspect*

There are a number of cases where one variation is effectively a continuative, generally signalled by the verb *keep*:

cross ONE's fingers
keep ONE's fingers crossed

get a grip on SOMETHING, take a grip on something
keep a grip on SOMETHING

have ONE's ear to the ground
keep ONE's ear to the ground

have ONE's feet on the ground
keep ONE's feet on the ground
with ONE's feet on the ground

open ONE's eyes
keep ONE's eyes open

have SOMEONE on a string
keep SOMEONE on a string

have ONE's head down
keep ONE's head down

Compare the pair *hang in the air/be left hanging in the air* and also *one's heart sinks/with a sinking heart*, where the second emphasizes continuous aspect.

6.2.4 *Reciprocity*

A number of FEIs have reciprocal structures, and variations reflect the ways in which different participants are mentioned: see Table 6.3. They can be regarded as syntactic variations or transformations. An isolated case of a more lexical form of reciprocity can be seen in the cluster

show ONE's true colours, reveal ONE's true colours
see SOMEONE in SOMEONE's true colours

TABLE 6.3. *FEIs with reciprocal structures*

Singular subject	Plural subject
(X is) at loggerheads with Y	(X and Y are) at loggerheads
X changes places with Y	(X and Y) change places
(X is) in line with Y	(X and Y are) in line
X joins battle with Y	(X and Y) join battle
X meets Y's eye(s)	their eyes meet
X ties the knot with Y	(X and Y) tie the knot

where a single process is involved but the focuses differ.

Even where FEIs involve some kind of reciprocity in their semantics, transformations may not be possible, as Newmeyer points out (1972: 299f.). For example, the dual subjects in *be two peas in a pod* and *be birds of a feather* do not have single subject transformations, hence Newmeyer's hypothetical and unacceptable **Alice is a pea in a pod with (to) Sue* and **Jack is a bird of a feather with (to) Joe*.

6.2.5 *Other Case Relationships*

A very few FEIs have variations involving beneficiaries and so on, so that both ditransitive and prepositional structures are found:

drop SOMEONE a line
drop a line to SOMEONE

give SOMEONE/SOMETHING a wide berth
give a wide berth to SOMEONE/SOMETHING

lay SOMETHING waste
lay waste to SOMETHING

promise SOMEONE the earth
promise the earth to SOMEONE

Given how many FEIs contain the verb *give*, it is astonishing that so few have variations with a prepositional phrase. In most cases the 'beneficiary' or affected is mentioned immediately after the verb. In fact, some examples

give SOMEONE a run for their money
give SOMEONE a taste of their own medicine
give SOMEONE an even break
give SOMEONE an inch and they'll take a mile
give SOMEONE the runaround
give SOMEONE the third degree
give SOMEONE their head

show clearly that the prepositional structure would be unlikely for reasons of information structure. The ideational focus here is on the action or process, which is therefore in group-final position: a prepositional phrase with *to* would itself attract ideational focus by being group-final. Although the transformation is theoretically possible, it is textually unlikely: the discoursal selection of a marked and periphrastic lexical item is itself the result of an intention to focus on the action-process. Compare standard delexical uses of *give*, where the first (indirect) objects in structures such as *give someone a smile* and *give someone a shout* do not very often transform to prepositional phrases headed with *at* or even *to*.

Again, Newmeyer (1972: 300) points out that not all structures may be possible. *Give rise to, turn a deaf ear to,* and *take a shine to* do not have ditransitive transformations. He also includes here *give birth to* and *pay lip service to* in this group; in fact these expressions do occasionally have ditransitive transformations.

Variations between realizations of possessives were described in Section 5.5.3. There are also a few other cases involving permutations of some very loose notion of removal or deprivation, where the variations reflect shifts in ideational focus:

knock SOMEONE's socks off
knock the socks off SOMEONE

steal SOMEONE's thunder
steal the thunder from SOMEONE

tear a strip off SOMEONE
tear SOMEONE off a strip

6.2.6 *Delexical Structures*

Finally, here are a few cases where a verb in one variation corresponds to a cognate noun or adjective and (often) delexicalized or support verb in the other variation:

bloody SOMEONE's nose
give SOMEONE a bloody nose

circle the wagons
pull/draw the wagons in a circle

feel SOMETHING in ONE's bones
have a feeling in ONE's bones

not sleep a wink
not get a wink of sleep

pass ONE's sell-by date
be past ONE's sell-by date

rap SOMEONE on the knuckles
give SOMEONE a rap on the knuckles

ring hollow
have a hollow ring

6.3 FRAMES AND VARIATION

In this section, I want to consider cases where the variations occur within fixed frames: these will most often be noun variations. Here, clusters of FEIs share single or common structures, but the realizations of one constituent vary relatively widely, though usually still within the bounds of a single lexical set. The meanings of individual FEIs within the clusters are often identical or very similar. These kinds of FEI may be seen as realizing lexicogram-matical **frames** (compare Fillmore *et al.* (1988) and their 'formal idioms'). The crucial point is that frames are productive, and any novel realizations can be accounted for within the grammar of the frame. However, some frames appear to have constraints on the kinds of lexical realizations which are allowed, and this is discussed by Bolinger (1977: 159ff.).

Looking more closely at some frames:

down the chute
down the drain
down the pan
down the plughole
down the toilet
down the tubes/tube

in a fix
in a hole
in a mess
in a paddy
in a spot

of late
of old

on the blink
on the fritz

The expressions in each cluster are quasi-synonymous, although there may be differences in formality or distribution. The expressions are parallel in

in bloom
in blossom
in bud
in flower
in leaf

Any distinctions in meaning are entirely predictable from distinctions between the meanings of the variant nouns. This particular frame also underlies

in calf
in foal
in kitten
in lamb
in whelp

on draught
on hand
on hold
on offer
on sale
on tap
to scale
to size
to taste

The frame

in the altogether
in the buff
in the nude
in the nuddy
in the raw

reflects the fact that there are often limitations: *in the bare and *in the naked are not found, thus suggesting the controlling effect of collocational patterning and precedents. However, the motivation for *in* here is clear from its standard use in prepositional phrases denoting clothing (*dressed in green, in top hat and tails*). Compare also *in the pink* and *in the flesh*.

Another interesting frame is

on + *the* + NOUN

A number of realizations fall into sets. For example, in

on the alert
on the boil
on the bubble
on the fly
on the hoof
on the hop
on the march
on the run
on the up (BrE, improving)

the expressions represent a physical activity. Note that in

on the lam
on the loose
on the make
on the quiet, on the QT
on the rampage
on the rob
on the run (running, escaping, fleeing)
on the scrounge

the action denotes or represents an activity which is perceived by the speaker/writer as in some way contrary to societal conventions, and even in the earlier grouping there may occasionally be negative associations. However,

on the level
on the mark
on the square
on the up and up (AmE, honest)

comprise a contrasting set with entirely positive connotations.

There are a number of frame clusters based on the structure

VERB + DETERMINER + NOMINAL GROUP

where the verbs (like the prepositions in the previous groupings) are to some extent semantically depleted. Ruhl (1975, 1979) draws attention to the following, which he takes from authentic text sources:

hit the deck
hit the hay
hit the sack

hit the beach
hit the road
hit the surf

hit the newsstands

hit the bottle
hit the plum wine
hit the sauce

He argues that there are principles of metonymy and analogy governing the collocations, that *hit* is not polysemous in them, and that individual realizations should not all be regarded as individual FEIs: they are part of a broader pattern. He develops this further in a detailed examination of the verb *hit* (1989: 96ff.), where he sets out to show how *hit* is essentially monosemic, and the structure is a productive frame. Similarly, Rose (1978) draws attention to groups such as

make a fortune
make a killing
make a mint
make a pile

in exploring the semantic categories involved and the underlying constraints. An analogous group is

get the (old) heave-ho
get the (order of the) boot
get the push
get the sack
get the shove

and British dialectal *get the fire*, although I would not consider some
of this last group as FEIs since they occur fairly freely in other
structures.

Looking at more metaphorical groups, similarities may be seen in
sets such as

> spill the beans
> spill ONE's guts
> spill it

(see further discussion in Section 7.4.6) and also the group

> kick the bucket
> kick it
> kick off

Ruhl (1977: 462) discusses the consistent meaning of *kick* here:
Makkai (1977) responds to this and argues against such a reductionist approach by extending the case for similarity of meaning and
its deep conceptual nature so far that it becomes absurd and unten-
able. However, a cautious compromise position here must be right:
there is simply too much meaning in common in such clusters.

Nagy (1978) discusses 'semi-productive' groups such as *shoot the
breeze, shoot the bull*, and the continuum of semi-productivity which
he argues should be built into any model of the lexicon. Bolinger
and Sears (1981: 54) discuss less metaphorical groupings such as

> be worth while
> be worth the bother
> be worth the trouble
> be worth ONE's while

together with other less stereotyped variations. They also discuss
the set

> take fright
> take courage
> take heart

which they point out have different transformation potentials,
hence *the fright that he took* but not **the heart that he took*. This
may of course reflect the relative independence of the meaning of
the noun in these items: *fright* has its usual meaning, *heart* does not.
Nunberg *et al.* (1994: 504 ff.) list groups of families of FEIs, for
example *lose one's mind/marbles* and *clap/set/lay eyes on someone*,
arguing that their existence could be thought surprising within
the context of standard syntactic models, which assign idiosyncratic
behaviours to individual items.

Francis draws attention to a more extreme case in her discussion
of variations in BofE on the lines of *I haven't the faintest idea* (1993:

144): she observes *lack* and *display* substituting for *have*; *least, slightest, foggiest,* and *remotest* substituting for *faintest*; and *conception* and *notion* substituting for *idea* (which can also be elided in *I haven't the foggiest*). The frame can be represented as

VERB (= 'have')/*with*/*without* + (NEG) + *the* + SUPERLATIVE ADJECTIVE (+ NOUN)

but not all permutations of slot realization are possible. Complex collocational principles, as well as semantic ones, motivate such sets, and they can be compared with other cases discussed above.

All this suggests that these individual locutions can and should be integrated into a model of the general patterning of English. The frames themselves are coded or institutionalized, and there are institutionalized realizations, of which some are not compositional; these are certainly not arbitrary combinations.

6.3.1 *Similes*

Similes are essentially frames with fossilized lexis: their function is emphasis. The traditional structure is

(*as*) + ADJECTIVE + *as* + NOMINAL GROUP

and examples in OHPC include

(as) clear as crystal
dead as a doornail
as good as gold
as nice as pie
as right as rain
(as) white as a sheet

They are generally infrequent. Only one simile of the 69 recorded in the database, *as white as a sheet*, occurs in OHPC with a frequency above the significance threshold, and even this occurs only 5 times. Initial *as* is generally optional in institutionalized similes. Several have single word cognates on the model of *crystal-clear*: transforms into a structure with *than* such as *deader than a doornail* are also possible, if comparatively infrequent. See Becker (1975) for comments on and a listing of similes in English, and Mejri (1994) for a description of similes with *comme* in French, including variations.

Since similes serve to intensify adjectives, it is unsurprising that certain common adjectives, or commonly intensified adjectives, occur in frames with varying nouns:

clear as crystal
clear as day

clear as mud (ironic use)

easy as ABC
easy as pie

happy as Larry
happy as a clam
happy as a lark
happy as a pig in muck (etc.)
happy as a sandboy

plain as a pikestaff
plain as day
plain as the nose on ONE's face

quick as a flash
quick as lightning
quick as a wink

strong as a bull
strong as a horse
strong as an ox

thick as mince
thick as shit
thick as two (short) planks

thin as a lath
thin as a rail
thin as a rake
thin as a stick

white as a ghost
white as a sheet, white as snow

In the following cases, noun variations are associated with different meanings of the adjective:

clear as a bell (of sounds)
clear as crystal/day (of information)

good as gold (of behaviour)
good as new (of condition)

mad as a hatter (insane)
mad as a hornet (angry)

thick as mince/shit/two (short) planks (stupid)
thick as thieves (friendly, conspiratorial)

white as a ghost/sheet (pale, ill, frightened)
white as a sheet (pure white in colour)

Most of these are entirely transparent. A few are synchronically opaque, such as *plain as a pikestaff* and *right as rain*, and a few exploit connotations integral to the noun. A very few are oxymoronic and always ironic, such as *clear as mud*: compare *léger comme un éléphant* in French (Mejri 1994: 119). Evaluative aspects of *pure as the driven snow* are discussed in Section 9.1.3.

The other common frame associated with similes

(VERB) + *like* + NOMINAL GROUP

occurs roughly as commonly amongst database FEIs as the structure with *as*. For example:

built like a tank
get on like a house on fire
know SOMETHING like the back of ONE's hand
like getting blood out of a stone
like headless chickens, like a headless chicken
like water off a duck's back
stick out like a sore thumb
take to SOMETHING like a duck to water
work like a dog

These strings are institutionalized and have marginally higher average frequencies than realizations of the frame with *as*, but the frame is by no means so fixed or restricted.

6.3.2 *Binomial Expressions*

I want to consider one further frame: binomials, which I am using as a general term to refer to dyads or conjoined pairs, unrestricted as to wordclass, but normally occurring in fixed order as 'irreversible binomials' (Malkiel 1959; Makkai 1972). Compare the 'paired parallel phrases', mentioned by Fillmore *et al.* (1988: 507 footnote), for example *cold hands, warm hearts* and *garbage in, garbage out*. See Lambrecht (1984) for a discussion of binomials in general and German binomials in particular.

Table 6.4 shows the commonest realizations in OHPC of the pattern WORD1 and WORD2. *Of these pairings, up and down, in and*

TABLE 6.4.   *Commonest binomial structures in OHPC*

334	Trade and Industry
165	England and Wales
132	economic and monetary
112	Poland and Hungary
111	East and West
110	men and women
93	up and down
80	political and economic
75	in and out
70	black and white

out, and *black and white* are lexicalized as idiomatic units, irreversible although they also have literal meanings. These patterns show up some interesting points. Some purely compositional binomials are not irreversible but still demonstrate clear tendencies for preferred ordering: for instance, *Poland and Hungary* is five times as common as *Hungary and Poland* in OHPC (less dramatically so in BofE). It is possible to hypothesize rules or at least crude principles from these tendencies: see the discussion by Malkiel (1959). The first item is typically the one considered more positive or dominant, or logically prior; in some cases, it is the item considered 'nearer to home' or 'nearer speaker's viewpoint'. Lakoff and Johnson characterize this as the 'me-first' orientation (1980: 132f.). However, Carter and McCarthy point out that such ordering is language-specific and culture-specific (1988: 25): for example, English *come and go* contrasts with French *aller et venir*. Examples, not limited to FEIs, include:

profit and loss
home and abroad
in and out
here and there
life and death
cause and effect
men and women
women and children
British and French
French and Italian

Other pairings suggest a tendency for the shorter or monosyllabic item to precede:

law and order
bed and breakfast
time and money
fruit and vegetables
names and addresses
banks and building societies

The norm for pairs involving male/female counterparts is for the male term to precede: hence *Mr and Mrs, men and women, brothers and sisters*. There are a few exceptions such as *mother and father/ mothers and fathers*, where the female-first ordering outnumbers the male-first by around 3:1 in BofE. However, Murray Knowles points out (personal communication) that according to his corpus data, collected for a contrastive study of nineteenth- and twentieth-century children's literature, *father(s) and mother(s)* seems to have been the norm in the late nineteenth century, in contrast to *mother(s) and father(s)*in the late twentieth. This reflects a diachronic shift in the paradigm, and reinforces the fact that cultural influences underlie binomial sequencing.

This frame or structure is rule-bound, and is itself coded. Lexicalized FEIs realizing the frame usually observe the rules:

born and bred
comings and goings
cut and dried
dim and distant
drunk and disorderly
free and easy
nook and cranny
part and parcel of SOMETHING
pure and simple
tar and feather
to and fro

Rare counter-examples amongst FEIs include *black and white* (negative first), and *risk life and limb* (illogical order of the severity of the risk). *Back and forth, backwards and forwards* are indeterminate, but seem to observe the 'me-first' or 'towards speaker' orientation.

John Sinclair (personal communication) points out that many antonymic binomials, or conjoined antonyms, have a meaning along the lines of 'everything' or 'no matter what'. This can be seen in pairs, not always linked with *and*, with conjoined temporals,

from cradle to grave
beginning to end
day and night, night and day

spatials and directionals,

head to foot
left and right; left, right, and centre
search high and low
swear up and down (literally spatial)
top to toe, top to bottom
up hill and down dale

and other contrastives:

by fair means or foul
come rain or shine
flotsam and jetsam

Through thick and thin is synchronically antonymous but diachronically spatial and tautologous (*through thicket and thin wood*): it implies universality, as does the trinomial *here, there, and everywhere*.

Some conjoined antonyms imply repetition: note that the conjoined words all have dynamic meanings:

back and forth
come and go
in and out
on and off
push and pull
stop and start

Blow hot and cold implies contradiction as well as repetition; *give and take* implies reciprocity in compromise. *Dos and don'ts, ins and outs, the long and the short of it,* and *this and that* have metalinguistic reference and signal a lack of precise detail (although *ins and outs* are in fact 'details', the FEI is a substitute for detailed rehearsal of those details).

Other conjoined pairs imply strong contrast: they are set up as antonymous in the FEI context:

(be) apples and oranges
(be) chalk and cheese
(be) oil and water

Pairs linked with *or* provide more obvious contrasted alternatives:

feast or famine
fight or flight
fish or cut bait
sink or swim
trick or treat

Give or take and *hit or/and miss* both signal or denote approximation.

Linked synonyms—and cases where the same word occurs twice—are tautologous and therefore inevitably have an emphatic function or emphasis as part of their meaning: so with many linked co-hyponyms. Compare also the emphatic trinomials *every Tom, Dick, or Harry* and *lock, stock, and barrel*:

alive and kicking/well
bits and pieces
done and dusted
down and dirty
down and out
far and away
go at it hammer and tongs
high and dry
home and dry/hosed
in leaps and bounds
loud and clear
nooks and crannies

on the up and up
out and out

Belt and braces is similar, but implies superfluity. In the following set, one of the binomial elements is obsolete or old-fashioned, but a synonym or co-hyponym in diachronic terms:

at SOMEONE's beck and call
bib and tucker
bill and coo
bow and scrape
kith and kin
rack and ruin
spic(k) and span
whys and wherefores

Compare *straight and narrow* where *straight* was originally *strait* and therefore synonymous with *narrow*.

6.4 ANTONYMOUS AND PARALLEL FEIS

There are a number of individual FEI pairs or clusters where the meanings of the individual realizations are broadly antonymous: the variant words realize systematic semantic contrasts. The simplest cases involve words which are regularly opposed counterparts, for example directional antonyms such as *in/into* and *out (of)*, *off* and *on*, *up* and *down*, or reversives such as *keep* and *lose*:

from the bottom up
from the top down

get on ONE's high horse
come down off ONE's high horse

go up in the world
come down in the world

in from the cold
out in the cold

in ONE's element
out of ONE's element

keep ONE's cool
lose ONE's cool

keep track of SOMETHING
lose track of SOMETHING

lose heart
take heart

on the boil

off the boil

on SOMEONE's back
get off SOMEONE's back

swim with the tide
swim against the tide

take ONE's eye off the ball
keep ONE's eye on the ball

take up arms
lay down ONE's arms

Some pairs with *in* and *out of* were listed in Section 6.1.4.

Other pairs include contrastive or antonymous words in unaltered prepositional frames:

in private
in public

in the long run
in the short run

in the right
in the wrong

on the back burner (*compare* off the back burner)
on the front burner

on the offensive
on the defensive

to SOMEONE's credit
to SOMEONE's discredit

with a good grace
with a poor grace

There are a few cases where variant words represent a measured progression or cycle:

call it a day
call it a night

get to first base
get to second base

two strikes against SOMEONE
three strikes against SOMEONE

The last of these leads to the FEI *three strikes and you're out*, with specific meanings in baseball and (Californian) penal practice, as well as more general applications.

Motivation and rules can be discerned for these, although there seems to be a blocking rule, where the existence of an antonymous noun or adjective or other contrastive word precludes the use of a contrastive preposition: hence *in private* rather than *out of public*.

However, while phraseological frames are principled and new realizations may be hypothesized and generated, not all analogous
combinations are found. For example, Bolinger (1977: 159 ff.)
also points out that the *in/out of* contrast is not available in all cases.
Taking the case of the pairs with *lose* and *keep*, *lose one's head* and *lose
one's cool* have counterparts with *keep*. However, *lose one's marbles*
has its counterpart in *have all one's marbles*, *lose heart* in *take heart*,
and *lose face* in *save face*. *Lose one's rag* has no antonymous counterpart at all. This is in part related to questions of opacity and the
analysability of metaphors, but it is also a matter of idiomaticity.

6.5 FREE REALIZATIONS

In Sections 6.3 and 6.4, I looked at frames where there is some
vestige of lexical stability: in contrast, the clusters in this section are
more extreme. There are a very few cases where the lexis is routinely varied without any apparent limits, while the frame or syntagmatic structure and pragmatic/discoursal intention remain fixed.
Fillmore *et al.* (1988: 505 ff.) include these amongst their category
of 'formal idioms', which they define as 'syntactic patterns dedi-
cated to semantic and pragmatic purposes not knowable from their
form alone'. Their example is the frame

> *the* + COMPARATIVE + *the* + COMPARATIVE

as in *the more carefully you do your work, the easier it will get*. They
point out that formal idioms may coincide with substantive or
lexically frozen idioms such as *the bigger they come, the harder they
fall* or *the more the merrier*, as in the case of binomials.

Another such frame can be realized as

> Am I right or am I right?

Here two identical rhetorical questions are conjoined for emphasis:
the addressee's agreement is pre-empted. Similarly, a frame which
involves a rhetorical question, to which the answer is obviously yes,
may be produced in answer to a question considered unnecessary.
Some formulations are:

> Is the Pope Catholic?
> Does a bear shit in the woods?
> Do ducks swim?
> Does Dolly Parton sleep on her back?
> Does a snake do push-ups? (Fraser 1996: 176)

Sadock (1974: 138–9) describes these as pseudo-questions to be
interpreted as hints rather than affirmatives, and points out

restrictions on both use and variation. Morgan (1978: 278) adds a variation with the reverse polarity, *Do bagels wear bikinis?*, and analyses it in terms of conventionalized implicatures: 'Answer an obvious yes/no question by replying with another question whose answer is very obvious and the same as the answer you intend to convey.'

Conventionalized formulations are occasionally blended (meaninglessly if detached from their origins), as in *Is a bear Catholic?*, or exploited allusively in *the certainty of sylvan ursal defecation*. More creative formulations are rife: for example, several recent advertising campaigns make use of the frame. An advertisement for TSB was built around a rap-rhythm song which largely consisted of a series of such questions, and involved an FEI manipulation in *Are two short planks thick?*, while a cigarette advertisement included *Do giraffes have long necks?* The interest lies in the variation; the frame is consistent.

The frame

QUANTIFIER + NOMINAL GROUP + *short/shy* + *of* + NOMINAL GROUP

is used to indicate mental inadequacy or mild insanity. A conventional representation is *one card short of a full deck*, but variation is almost mandatory. The following examples are taken from various sources:[3]

a couple of blocks short of a building set
a few beers short of a six-pack
a few bricks shy of a full load
a few clowns short of a circus
a few fries short of a Happy Meal (TM)
a few marbles short of a Parthenon
a few peas short of a casserole
a few pickles short of a jar
a few planes short of an Air Force
a few sandwiches short of a picnic
a few semitones short of an octave
a few tiles short of a successful re-entry
a flying buttress short of a cathedral
a six-pack short of a case
four cents short of a nickel
nineteen cents short of a paradigm
one bit short of a byte
one board short of a porch

---

[3] At the time of writing, a monthly canonical list of these so-called 'Fulldeckisms' is published on the Internet bulletin board: rec.humor Other sites accessible via the Internet and World Wide Web are similarly collection points for such expressions.

one bun short of a dozen
one Froot Loop shy of a full bowl
one hot pepper short of an enchilada
one marble shy of a full deck
one sentence short of a paragraph
one shingle shy of a roof
one side short of a pentagon
one taco short of a combination plate
one tree short of a hammock
three fish short of a lawnmower
two coupons short of a blender
two flakes shy of a Post Toastie
two saucers short of a tea-service
two slices short of a toast rack

The creativity, humorousness, and unusualness of the realization is important, but it relies on recognition of the underlying frame and schema. There is some semblance of convention in that the first nominal group represents something without which the second, in some context at least, is incomplete or impossible (*one bun short of a dozen, one tree short of a hammock*). There are also cases of surrealism or deliberate incongruence (*three fish short of a lawnmower*) and intertextuality of realization (*one marble shy of a full deck*). Most are heavily culture-dependent, as are realizations of another frame[4]

I'm + *busier* + *than* + COMPLEX NOMINAL GROUP

The nominal group represents a person with connoted or implied problems through overactivity. Again, variation is near mandatory and intended for humour. The following selection demonstrates the preponderance of sexual and cultural references: many others include topical allusions to people in the news for sexual misdemeanours or criminal acts:

IBT (I'm busier than) a bar of soap at San Quentin
IBT a condom dispenser in Greenwich Village
IBT a dog with two dicks
IBT a five dollar hooker
IBT a flea in a dog pound
IBT a gopher on a golf course
IBT a long-tailed cat in a room full of rocking chairs
IBT a one-armed paperhanger
IBT a one-legged basketball player
IBT a prostitute in a prison
IBT a toilet in Grand Central Station
IBT a two-peckered billy goat

---

[4] These realizations are taken from a collection on the World Wide Web.

IBT a woman in the mall with her husband's credit card
IBT Captain James T. Kirk with three-breasted hookers on Risa
IBT handicapped parking at the Special Olympics

6.6 IDIOM SCHEMAS

Further along the variation continuum are FEI clusters. For example,

shake in ONE'S SHOES
quake in ONE's shoes
shake in ONE's boots
quake in ONE's boots
quiver in ONE's boots
quake in ONE's Doc Marten's

Here verbs meaning 'shake' are associated with nouns meaning 'footwear' to connote fear and apprehension. A further variation (or exploitation) occurs in

British policemen are already **quaking in their size 11s** at the thought of keeping the warring tribes apart when the European Championship comes here in 1996. (The *Guardian*, 15 May 1993)

Another case is

fan the fire of SOMETHING
fan the fires of SOMETHING
fan the flames (of SOMETHING)
add fuel to the fire
add fuel to the flame
add fuel to the flames
fuel the fire
fuel the fires
fuel the flame
fuel the flames (of SOMETHING)

Gläser (1986: 47) sees an example of *fuel the flames of* as a case of an ad hoc variation, blending *add fuel to the flames/fire* and *fan the flames*, but there is a lot of evidence for it in BofE as one amongst many variations. Arguably, the cognitive image of 'fanning' is different from 'fuelling' or 'adding fuel' and at a surface level it may imply a less direct or forceful involvement in the exacerbation of a situation. Collocationally, the variations with *flame/flames* are typically followed by a prepositional phrase with *of* and a noun which refers to a negatively evaluated situation, usually a socio-political one (*racism, bigotry, confrontation, extremism, discontent*), whereas the variations with *fire* and *fuel* have no such collocational support, though the contextual situation is similarly negatively evaluated. The main point, however, is that there is again a single, if complex, metaphor here.

Some further cases are:

hold all the aces
have all the aces
the aces are in SOMEONE's hands

pass the buck
the buck passes SOMEWHERE
the buck stops here

another nail in the coffin
a final nail in the coffin
nail down the coffin
hammer the last nail into SOMEONE's coffin (etc.)
drive the first nail into the coffin (etc.)
bolt down the coffin lid

scare the life out of SOMEONE
scare the shit out of SOMEONE
scare SOMEONE shitless
scare the pants off SOMEONE
frighten the life out of SOMEONE
be frightened out of ONE's mind
be scared out of ONE's wits

hold a pistol to SOMEONE's head
put a gun to SOMEONE's head
feel a pistol at ONE's head
with a gun to ONE's head

wash ONE's dirty linen/laundry in public (mainly British)
air ONE's dirty laundry/linen in public (mainly American)
do ONE's dirty washing in public (mainly British)
wash/air ONE's dirty linen/laundry
wash/air ONE's linen/laundry in public
launder ONE's dirty washing (mainly British)
dirty laundry/linen/washing

The last grouping contains no fixed words at all, and a further permutation occurs in the following densely metaphorical sentence:

But even the fiercest critics of the ancien regime (whose chief architects have now retired or moved on) are putting lifeboat work before **publicly laundering any dirty clothes**. (The *Guardian* (*Higher Education Supplement*), 15 October 1996)

Gross (1994: 255) discusses a further cluster *Max will beat/whale/ lick the hell/shit/living daylights/daylights/tar out of Bob*: compare the 'idiom families' listed by Nunberg *et al.* (1994: 504 ff.).

The following series of snippets from OHPC shows a gradient between the conventionalized forms *rose-coloured/rose-tinted glasses/ spectacles* and cognate lexical items:

view SOMEONE through rose-coloured lenses
look at SOMETHING through rose-coloured glasses
observe SOMETHING through rose-tinted glasses
her rose-coloured idea
a rose-tinted vision
this rosy view
[his] recollection . . . is less rosy

Barkema (1996*b*: 147) draws attention to something similar when he points out the chain

near miss
near thing
close thing
close shave
narrow shave

While the first and last items are apparently discrete items, they also represent ends of a continuum.

I am terming these kinds of FEI cluster **idiom schemas**. They have some reference in common, a metaphor in common, and cognate lexis, but without (necessarily) any very fixed structure or fixed lexis. The notion of idiom schemas can be used to explain a number of things: in particular, (extreme) variability, evaluative content, apparent compositionality, and the ease with which allusions to FEIs or exploitations are decoded. Idiom schemas represent concepts embedded in the culture and associated with particular lexicalizations. They are characterized by an underlying conceit (the relationship between tenor and vehicle) and an overlying preferred lexical realization, usually with connoted evaluation. The exact form of words may vary or be exploited, but is still tied to the underlying conceit which provides the driving or motivating force in the FEI.

It's water under the bridge is also lexicalized as *a lot of water flows under the bridge*: also *water over the dam, water under the dyke,* and *water under the mill* (see *OED*). The underlying conceit uses the metaphor of the unidirectional flowing of water with respect to a fixed point to represent the passage of time and the passing of a situation or feeling: it relates to a conceptual metaphor 'time is a moving object' (Lakoff and Johnson 1980: 42) or 'life is a journey'. The overlying realizations vary, and the same idiom schema is recognizable in

Water under the thingy. (*House of Cards.* BBC dramatization, 1990)

Soon it will be April and I am afraid I will again be very depressed and lonely at heart because that month will bring back memories of your father's illness and death as if they happened only the other day and it is eight long years that have gone by and so much has happened **under the bridge** in this period. (Vikram Seth, (1993) *A Suitable Boy*, London: Phoenix House, 42)

The development over time of this cluster and schema underscores the fact that the phenomenon of idiom schemas is part of a diachronic and dynamic process, whereby a metaphor stabilizes, destabilizes, and restabilizes.

A conventional view of metaphor may be depicted (after Searle 1979*b*: 122) as shown in Figure 6.1. In contrast, idioms and dead metaphors may be depicted as shown in Figure 6.2, with sentence meaning bypassed. However, idiom schemas may be depicted as shown in Figure 6.3, because awareness of literal meanings of the constituent lexis is maintained. In this way, metaphorical FEIs can be seen in Coulmas's words (1979*a*: 149) as 'at the same time holistic and analyzable'. Lecercle (1990: 174f.) argues for the 'bidirectionality' of metaphor, so that sentence and utterance meanings are not separated: this can be seen to happen in the

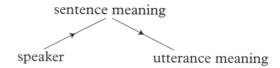

FIG. 6.1 Processing of metaphors

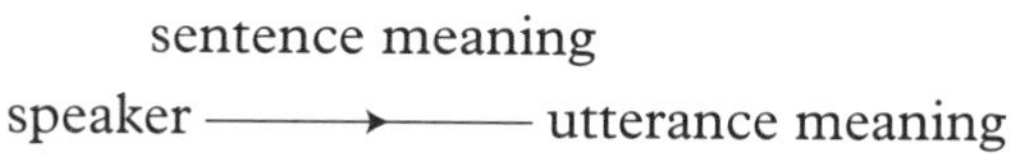

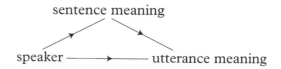

FIG. 6.2 Processing of idioms and dead metaphors

FIG. 6.3 Processing of idiom schemas

case of idiom schemas. In discussing similes and metaphors, Leech (1969: 156) talks of the open-endedness of metaphor, and its ability to allude 'to an indefinite bundle of things'. This is the case with freely formed metaphor. In contrast, the metaphors of idiom schemas are more circumscribed since by their very nature they allude to cultural stereotypes, or stereotyped situations, where evaluations, connotations, and images are givens, constrained by the contextual ideology. In fact, this can be seen in the consistent visualizations of idioms discussed by Lakoff (1987: 447ff.) and Gibbs and O'Brien (1990): see Section 2.2.1. Compare also Baranov and Dobrovol'skii (1996), who set out models and scenarios for the interpretation of idioms and the relationships between idiomatic and literal meanings. They are looking at Russian, but a similar approach could be taken with English.

It could be argued that all metaphorical FEIs and many others represent schemas: in particular, that institutionalized metaphors and proverbs are encapsulations and prepackagings of given or shared experiences: they encode ideological constructs. Compositional FEIs are simply those which have clearer schemas. In some cases, such as *bite the bullet*, the lexicalizations appear to be frozen. In other cases, lexicalizations are effectively negotiable and so variations, exploitations, truncations, and allusions are acceptable, not ill formed: they simply activate the relevant schema. Cowie (1988) discusses the processes of creativity and stability underlying lexical items of various kinds: the stability of the schemas permits creativity in their realizations. Idiom schemas can be seen as conceptualizations and semiotic hybrids. Considering this further in terms of semiotics, a metaphor such as *it's water under the bridge* is iconic in representing a physical situation and showing the resemblance between the metaphorical vehicle and tenor, whereas *water* and *bridge* are indexical, concomitants at least in the context of the schema: in cases of truncation or ellipsis one implies the other.

Idiom schemas can be tied in with frame semantics and frame theory in general: compare Brown and Yule (1983: 236ff.). For example, the schemas are not dissimilar to the sorts of frame that Minsky sets up for the interpretation of concepts, prototypes, and experiences. Minsky gives the following simplified account (1980: 1): 'Here is the essence of the frame theory: When one encounters a new situation (or makes a substantial change in one's view of a problem), one selects from memory a structure called a **frame**. This is a remembered framework to be adapted to fit reality by changing details as necessary. A **frame** is a data-structure for representing a stereotyped situation like being in a certain kind of

living room or going to a child's birthday party. Attached to each
frame are several kinds of information . . . We can think of a frame
as a network of nodes and relations . . .' Minsky then considers the
nature of the nodes or 'terminals'; the linking of frames and the
relationship this has with change of viewpoint; and the filling of
terminals with default assignments (1980: 1f.).

Such cognitive models are generated out of an artificial intelligence background rather than lexicology, but the parallels are interesting. It is possible to hypothesize that the whole corpus of
institutionalized metaphors is a series of frames. These frames
represent at one and the same time both the real-world situations
that allow the frame to be selected from memory and the metaphorical schema. Evaluations fill terminals with default values of positive or negative, or permutations such as 'positive of X, negative of
Y'. In this way, FEIs may be seen as agglomerates of cultural
information, rather than simply lexical items. A crucial point is
that the terminals, and frames, must be constructed with evaluative
content as a feature, pragmatics as well as semantics.

Fillmore has argued that frames are needed to explain understanding in addition to knowledge of the syntactic and lexical
systems (1976, 1985). In particular, he sees the frames or schemas
as involving notions such as the appropriateness of contexts, so that
speech formulae and other expressions such as *welcome aboard!*, *nice
talking to you*, and *speak of the devil* require schematic knowledge as
much as semantic knowledge: 'My point is that these expressions
too are, in a sense, indexical, in that their appearance is predictive
of a number of details of the situation of performance' (1976: 25).

Further support for idiom schemas may be found elsewhere.
Conceptual metaphors, though distinct, are related since they
draw on cultural stereotypes and are lexically realized in series of
FEIs or institutionalized metaphors: see Section 7.5. Pulman (1993)
discusses pure idioms and variations, in fact rejecting the notion of
canonical forms and also any systems or sets of syntactic and
semantic rules governing the variations: instead he postulates a
set of 'idiom rules' which govern entailment relationships. This is
entirely compatible with a notion of idiom schemas with preferred
lexical realizations. Nayak and Gibbs (1990) report research into
the role of conceptual knowledge in understanding and using
idioms, suggesting that informants are aware of their structural
and schematic properties, so that while idioms cannot be predicted,
they are perceived as motivated: moreover, neologistic blends can
be recognized. While Cacciari (1993: 36f.) points out the undesirability of relying too heavily on conceptual frameworks and so on as

a means of accounting for idiom, idiom schemas go some way towards explaining how some kinds of FEI work.

Here are some further examples. The idiom schema underlying *the knives are out* can be recognized in the following report on a World Cup qualifying round soccer match,

At last Taylor, up in the stands last night, could allow himself the broadest of grins. He had a winning team again. **The knives**, for the moment, **had been sheathed**. (The *Guardian*, 9 September 1993)

or in the punning headline to a second soccer story:

Knives ready if Souness suffers Bristol fashion. (The *Guardian*, 8 January 1994)

Another idiom schema involves the metaphor of carrots and sticks as incentives, realized in

The strategic arguments are clearly still relevant. These are uncertain times. But Cocom has devised a crude **carrot and stick** mechanism for regulating trade which has the power to make them more uncertain still. (OHPC: journalism)

Well a number of things. I've mentioned a few of them. I would have a **carrot and stick** approach. The **carrot** would be much better Park and Ride, which is what they are talking about. Now what the Labour Group are doing is super, but it doesn't go far enough. (OHPC: transcribed speech)

The career opportunity **carrot** at the end of the exacting training **stick** is, it has to be said, pretty appetising. (OHPC: journalism)

Ronald Reagan reached the limits of abuse; the macho bullying, **the stick and the carrot**. (OHPC: journalism)

No **carrot was dangled** for the SACU as a quid pro quo for any decision it may take to cancel the tour. (OHPC: journalism)

'Are you sure? It's a big **carrot he's dangling in front of** Marler's **nose**. That has unsettled Howard—all part of the well-known Buckmaster technique.' (OHPC: fiction)

More rigid are sets of synonymous variations, where the idiom schema involved is relatively clear: for example,

down the chute
down the drain
down the pan
down the plughole
down the toilet
down the tubes/tube

The idiom schema here is accompanied by a restricted lexicogrammatical frame, but further variations can be formulated and interpreted in the light of the idiom schema. Lexicographers may be forced to deal with such cases as discrete FEIs, but this is misrepresenting patterns underlying the lexicon.

Finally, here are two more examples which may indeed be simply ad hoc exploitations or represent the unfreezing of FEIs. First, *face the music*: Sue Atkins reports (personal communication) a comment on someone that 'he would not turn his back on the music'. Secondly, *dead duck*:

But Peter Bottomley, a former transport minister whose Eltham constituency takes in the wood, was more confident the Government had no plans to build the bridge. 'It is not a **live duck** this century, in my view'. (The *Guardian*, 8 July 1993)

In either case, interpretation relies on knowledge of the schemas underlying the canonical forms.

The existence of this phenomenon of variation increases the decoding and recognition problems which face non-native speakers of English—or indeed anyone unfamiliar with a particular expression. (Encoding is even more of a problem, since any parameters of the realizations of such schemas are unmapped and may be unmappable.) However, it seems that there are indeed rules or perhaps conventions: the metaphor and meaning must be maintained and the variant lexis must be recognized as belonging to a particular lexical set. Successful decoding requires recognition of the lexical pattern, the metaphoricality, and the meaning appropriate to the context.

Beyond this point, the variation phenomena simply merge into the regular metaphors and connotations of English. To give two examples, if *wrinkle one's nose* were fixed lexically, we might consider it to be some sort of FEI, meaning 'show disgust, disapproval, or displeasure': there are of course many other cases where the description of human facial expressions or body language implies emotion and attitude, and see further in Section 7.1.2. But *wrinkle one's nose* is not fixed, and other verbs are used in collocation with *nose* in this meaning:

'Surely there must have been some amount of pretence, sir,' said Burden, **wrinkling his fastidious nose**. (OHPC: fiction)

She looked down on her partly eaten meal and **her nose wrinkled** before she went on. (OHPC: fiction)

Asked what she thought of Slava Zaitsev, the man who has dressed rich

Soviet women and diplomats' wives since the Brezhnev era and the only Soviet fashion designer well known in the West, she **curled up her nose**. (OHPC: journalism)

They grin at the idea, **crinkling their noses** in mock distaste, suggesting that the monastic life holds no attraction for them. (OHPC: journalism)

The string is considered a recurrent collocation with entailed implicature, not a serious problem for interpretation. There is no real metaphor involved, just symbolism. More problematic is the case of *coat-tails*. *On someone's coat-tails* is sometimes considered an FEI. There are 5 tokens of *coat-tail(s)* in OHPC:

Dennis Hopper, who was to become an important figure in Nicholson's eventual break into major films, came in **on James Dean's coat-tails** and was devastated by Dean's death, as were Natalie Wood and their other close friend, Nick Adams. (OHPC: non-fiction)

Plenty of other good bands around the country have tried to grab **at th[e] coat-tails [of]** the Manchester scene and failed as a result. (OHPC: journalism)

By the time he was 30 politics had become his main obsession, and he was tagging **on to the coat-tails of** a local Tory MP, Alan Green, whose daughter Gilly—an extrovert with an equal hunger for politics—was to become Waddington's wife and a driving force behind his political success. (OHPC: journalism)

They have attached themselves **to the coat-tails of** that strongest of all urges in the animal kingdom, bar that to survive, the sex drive. (OHPC: non-fiction)

. . . some of it was in fact filler or **coattail** incredulity, meant simply to congratulate people for earlier funny comments and demonstrate carefree participation until a new slide came on . . . (OHPC: fiction)

Only two of these include the preposition *on*: the verbs and other prepositions collocating with *coat-tails* in all these examples suggest that the metaphor is alive: that is, it is being invoked freshly in each instance, rather than fossilized. It is a sense or use of *coat-tails*, with restricted syntax and surrounding collocational preferences, not a fixed locution or lexicalized unit. It is precisely in such cases that corpora highlight the indeterminacy of this area of lexis.

In making the case for idiom schemas, I am suggesting that what we can observe in operation is a series of semantic conceits. These have hitherto been too narrowly identified as lexical units, as opposed to semantic units, because they have a tendency to be realized in specific ways. Idiom schemas can be seen as a phenomenon of the same order as Lakoff and Johnson's conceptual metaphors. They provide a more useful and powerful notion than the traditional view of idioms as some form of peculiar morphological compound.

6.7 EXPLOITATIONS

The phenomenon of variation is institutionalized, and variations already discussed are also institutionalized, although some may be restricted to particular varieties of English or formality levels, or have very different frequencies. The other side of the coin is exploitation, the stylistic manipulation of the lexis (and semantics) of FEIs: perhaps to provide some sort of defamiliarization, and typically providing humour. In OHPC, it is most strongly associated with journalism. It is more marked and prevalent with metaphorical FEIs than any other type, since they contain the images which are most easily exploited. Exploitation of metaphorical FEIs is evidence of their compositionality: puns work by reliteralizing the FEIs, as Coulmas points out (1979a: 145). Kjellmer (1991: 123f.) further sees the ability to exploit as indicative of a user's proficiency. Gläser (1986: 47 ff.) discusses the stylistics implications.

In one kind of exploitation, one or more of the lexical items in the FEI is altered or replaced for stylistic effect, to make the FEI more appropriate in its context or simply to pun. Cases of exploitation (or adaptation) through lexical insertions are discussed in Section 6.8:

He works 18 hours a day. He rings people up at 4am his time. He **burns the candle at five ends**. He might look like this huge heavyweight boxer, but his family and friends have worried about his health for years. (OHPC: journalism)

The paper's editorial described the section as 'a nasty piece of work' which gave the police 'a considerable measure of arbitrary and unchallengeable judgement'. Using it against the hippies was like relying on '**an earthmover to crack a nut**'. (OHPC: non-fiction)

Loners are not unfortunate—they are not competing hard enough; down-and-outs are lazy and inadequate; the homeless are simply incapable of **using their own bootstraps as an elevatory mechanism**. (OHPC: journalism)

Discussing nourishment, a client complained that parsley was her 'pet noire'. Writing like that is **the real macaw**. (OHPC: journalism)

But it's odd, we had these great reviews after our Leeds show, and

I thought we totally bombed. After that one, we were ready to **throw in the moist towelette**, y'know? (OHPC: journalism)

Now, inheritance isn't a crime, and few of us (not even Mr Tony Benn) would have spat out a **silver spoon** if we had found one with our mouths at birth. (OHPC: journalism)

People are now so terrified of disqualification that they are summoning a minicab **at the drop of a Babycham**. On Friday and Saturday evenings, as a result, minicab firms offer profuse apologies but rarely a car. (OHPC: journalism)

We'll often meet around midnight, taking in a beverage or two at Highway and the Garage, and **tripping the light fantastic** (and the **fantastic lights**) at Krypton and Cosmos. (OHPC: non-fiction)

Call a spade a spade is particularly prone to substitution:

He will **call a spade a bloody shovel**. What he will do for Mrs Thatcher's view of trade unions is to reinforce all of her prejudices. As a trade union leader for the 1980s, he is a throwback to the 60s, and I will leave it to others to decide whether that means the 1960s or the 1860s. (OHPC: journalism)

The Italian press, never afraid to **call a shovel a JCB**, told Azeglio Vicini his team looked 'knackered'—a genuine translation the Brits were assured. (OHPC: journalism)

On the one hand, there are scientists who are only too willing to **call a spade a pre-spade**. (OHPC: journalism)

These are nonce-uses, features of text, although some apparent nonce-uses have themselves become institutionalized: *call a spade a shovel* is now found routinely, either with the same meaning as the canonical original, or denoting dysphemism. Compare cases where the original metaphor is reversed or inverted, again sometimes sufficiently frequently for the new form to be institutionalized:

a big fish in a little/small pond
a little/small fish in a big pond

every cloud has a silver lining
every silver lining has a cloud

poacher turned gamekeeper
gamekeeper turned poacher

rags to riches
riches to rags

a sheep in wolf's clothing
a wolf in sheep's clothing

a square peg in a round hole
a round peg in a square hole

win the battle, lose the war
lose the battle, win the war

Exploitation is sometimes so common that it forces reconsideration of the 'canonical' form of the FEI. For example, all tokens in OHPC of the proverb *beauty is in the eye of the beholder* are exploited:

Like beauty, **tawdriness is in the eye of the beholder**, and on their country's 40th birthday East Germans tend to see it through the cruelly unblinking eyes of thoroughly Westernised consumers. (OHPC: journalism)

But John Redwood, Under-Secretary for Trade and Industry, said at Question Time: '**Junkiness is in the eye of the beholder**'. (OHPC: journalism)

Its convention-dependent character means that **symbolic significance is in the eye of the beholder**. (OHPC: non-fiction)

The syntagmatic structure of the proverb remains intact, and the first example certainly refers explicitly to the original form, but the persistence of exploitation and substitution suggests that the canonical form of this FEI should be — *is in the eye of the beholder*, with an open slot in subject position to be filled by any abstract that is considered essentially subjective. In cases such as this, exploitation is a pointer to a shift in form.

A particular form of exploitation occurs in cases where lexis is replaced with more formal, literary, or euphemistic synonyms: compare the example given earlier with *using their own bootstraps as an elevatory mechanism*:

a word in ONE's ear
a word in ONE's shell-like

Bob's your uncle
Bob's your avuncular

Does a bear shit in the woods?
the certainty of sylvan ursal defecation

economical with the truth
frugal with the actualité

get ONE's finger out
extract ONE's digit

my lips are sealed
my lips are zipped

shoot the bull

shoot the BS

take the mickey
extract the michael

when the shit hits the fan
when the brown stuff hits the fan

Some of the exploitations have themselves become institutionalized.

Another form of exploitation involves the substituting items being quasi-homophonous: compare the discussion of homophonous variations in Section 6.1.11 and the exploitation with *the real macaw* above. Barkema (1996*b*: 148) discusses an exploitation of *trip the light fantastic*:

They therefore feel they are entitled to sing, throw plates and trip the light fandango during your act if they so choose (cited from *Punch*, 25 February 1992)

He points out that *fantastic* and *fandango* share morphemes, but word class has shifted. In fact, it is more complicated. It also puns on the opening line of the song *A Whiter Shade of Pale* (1967)—'We skipped the light fandango Turned cartwheels 'cross the floor'— where the original puns twice through homophony on *trip the light fandango*. The evidence in BofE is interesting: there are 41 tokens of the nominal group *light fantastic*, and 23 of these occur in headings. Of the 41, 22 collocate with *trip* as a verb and 3 with *trip* as a noun. Other collocating verbs include *rip, trick*, and *skip*, again showing pun and exploitation through rhyme or assonance. *Skip the light fantastic* is itself another allusion to the song. BofE has 3 tokens of *light fandango* of which 2 allude directly to the song, but only the third contains *skip*: all are from journalistic sources.

Finally, in another kind of exploitation, the imagery of the surface lexis of the FEI is extended in its co-text, either with individual words or with further FEIs that are thematically related. A chain of puns results, providing lexical cohesion:

The lenders would find themselves badly gored **on the horns of a property dilemma**. On the one hand they will have a large number of borrowers simply unable to pay any more, on the other, a property which is falling in value all the time. (OHPC: journalism)

Final judgement must wait until the Government has explained why the £38m payment was simultaneously **under the counter** but **above board**. (OHPC: journalism)

Lexical cohesion may, however, signal demetaphorization of the FEI:

Aston Villa are no longer **in the pink**, thankfully, their summer-pudding strip having been ditched in favour of the original claret and blue. (OHPC: journalism)

The company makes sweepers in widths of one, two and three feet, and is developing bigger versions which can be attached to fork-lift trucks for cleaning larger outdoor areas. It hopes the product—which is due to be featured in the BBC programme Tomorrow's World on Thursday—will **wipe the floor with** the more traditional brooms and industrial vacuum cleaners. (OHPC: journalism)

Compare the use of *literally* to demetaphorize: see Section 10.5. Lexical cohesion through FEIs is discussed further in Section 10.2.

Exploitations ultimately only work with full perceptions of both vehicles and tenors in the metaphors, and a vestige of lexical form. The metaphors, or idiom schemas, and frames are starting-points for the dynamic use of FEIs in interaction. Exploitations are ultimately another facet of the instability and productivity of FEIs.

6.8 INTERRUPTION AND INSERTION

The modification of FEIs by the insertion of spurious or non-canonical words is a kind of infixing. It can be regarded as exploitation, although the resulting formulations are not necessarily jocular. Interrupted FEIs can be distinguished from FEIs with open slots: in the latter case, there is a syntagmatic requirement for the insertion of an item, whereas in the former case the inserted items are governed instantially by context. Evidence in OHPC suggests that this is predominantly a phenomenon associated with metaphorical FEIs. Table 6.5 shows the proportions of FEIs recorded as interrupted, according to idiomaticity type. If secondary typological classifications are considered, the figure for metaphors rises to 68%. This can be compared to the presence of open slots in FEIs—a phenomenon particularly associated with anomalous collocations (see Table 6.6).

In discussing the insertion of adjectives in idioms, Ernst (1981) draws attention to three types. 'Domain delimiters' provide 'external modification', where the inserted adjective contextualizes the

TABLE 6.5. *Interrupted FEIs, according to idiomaticity type*

anomalous collocations	36%
formulae	12%
metaphors	52%

TABLE 6.6. *FEIs with open slots, according to idiomacity type*

anomalous collocations	56%
formulae	19%
metaphors	25%

whole FEI in much the same way that a disjunct or sentence adverbial might: his example is *Carter doesn't have a political leg to stand on*. 'Internal modification' intensifies or modifies the literal lexis, but it is entirely interpretable at the metaphorical level: for example, *we were reduced to scraping the bottom of every single barrel*. 'Conjunction modification' modifies the literal lexis and it cannot be directly interpreted at the metaphorical level, except for its pragmatic or stylistic effect: for example, . . . *that little stab of shame we feel at the end* [of Twelfth Night] *for having had such fun pulling his cross-gartered leg for so long*. Pulman (1993: 252–3) considers cases such as *I'll keep a close eye on his progress*, where *close* modifies the whole phrase, and *that turned out to be a very red herring* where *very* implies intensification of the diversion referred to. Barkema (1996*b*: 143 ff.) divides inserted items into 'additions', which are constituents of the immediate clause structure of the FEI, and 'interruptions', which are not. Nunberg *et al.* (1994: 499 ff.) relate the interruption of FEIs to their compositionality. McGlone *et al.* (1994: 184) point out that inserted items and other modifiers have to be appropriate to the meaning, that it is possible to say *he silently kicked the bucket* but not *he slowly kicked the bucket*: corpus data partially confirms this. Nicolas (1995), in a study based partly on newspaper corpus data, looks at predicate FEIs, and he observes that nearly all of the 75 items he examined were capable of interruption with an adjective or other modifer. However, there were restrictions on the kind of syntacto-semantic modification available. Most took viewpoint modifiers, but manner modifiers appeared not to be found where the nominal group in the FEI was definite and included *the*. Moreover, he found no cases where predicate FEIs took internal modifiers denoting the subject's attitude (as opposed to writer's attitude), means or instrument, or place or direction.

Corpus data shows modifiers, intensifiers, or evaluatives inserted into FEIs, collocating with either the surface lexis or the meaning: 'internal modification' and 'conjunction modification' in Ernst's terms:

England will put **the icing on the tastiest cake** in years by beating Scotland at Murrayfield on Saturday. (OHPC: journalism)

Wally, a farcically uncooperative caretaker who **puts in a regulation grumpy appearance** in each of the play's four scenes in order to enunciate his catchphrase, 'Nothing to do with me'. (OHPC: journalism)

Now this is not in order, not in a country where even the parking laws are obeyed **to the timid letter**. (OHPC: journalism)

I could **wring Camb's bloody neck**! (OHPC: fiction)

Friends rallied round yesterday as Cecil Parkinson again found himself the subject of speculation about Cabinet resignation and the Government was trying to **weather a renewed storm**. (OHPC: journalism)

The Spanish authorities were **at a total loss** as to how to handle the situation. (BofE: journalism)

And it was fairly predictable, too, that he would immediately find himself **in extremely hot water**. (BofE: journalism)

By the time we'd done a similar thing in the local church as part of the village music festival **the ice was well and truly broken**. (BofE: autobiography)

Other inserted items focus and contextualize, delimiting the relevance or truth value of an FEI. They typically collocate or accord with the context or meaning of an FEI rather than its lexis: compare Ernst's 'external modification':

At our house, as ever, we are a little late **getting our Christmas act together**. (OHPC: journalism)

Divorce **hit the financial headlines** this week. (OHPC: journalism)

The British love of comfort and chintz, Colefax & Fowler and country houses, taken together with an innate mistrust and misunderstanding of modern architecture, makes Silvestrin almost **a lone voice crying in the architectural wilderness**. (OHPC: journalism)

As the pressure grows on the US to **draw in its military horns,** so there is corresponding pressure on Japan and South Korea to take up the slack. (OHPC: journalism)

The South African can of worms was reopened yesterday when Steve Sutton, a former Wales lock, accused an unidentified Welsh Rugby Union committee member of offering him money to take part in the recent South African centenary matches. (OHPC: journalism)

The City fears that **the latest closing of government ranks** to hide divisions will prove short-lived, with potentially damaging consequences for the pound. (OHPC: journalism)

. . . an opposition stalwart who has made no secret of his distaste for a man he regards as **a Congress sheep in opposition wolf's clothes**. (OHPC: journalism)

the golden boy of British ballet . . . **born with a choreographic silver spoon in his mouth**. (OHPC: non-fiction)

The ice of mutual suspicion had been broken. (BofE: semi-scripted broadcast journalism)

Where inserted adjectives are attached to nominal groups which already contain adjectives, they are usually attached at the beginnings of the groups, hence *political hot potato*, *legal red herrings*, . . . *marital dirty linen* (all from BofE). This appears to contravene conventions for the prenominal catenation of adjectives: postdeterminer; gradable/qualitative adjectives; colour adjectives; ungradable/classifying adjectives. However, new information or contrast, as realized here in an adjective, is conventionally foregrounded by being placed first in the sequence. In this case, the canonical component adjectives represent given information, and so they adopt a classificatory adjectival position in the string, reinforcing the gestalt of the idiomatic nominal group.

In OHPC, the interruption of FEIs occurs most commonly in journalism. For example, 11 of its 19 tokens of *toe the line* occur in journalism, including all 7 of the interrupted tokens:

After a series of explosive rows with their headmaster, who felt they should **toe the education authority line**, the three lost their jobs as a result of 'redeployment'. (OHPC: journalism)

US technology is so all-pervading that firms feel they must **toe the US line**. (OHPC: journalism)

Similarly, 7 of the 29 tokens of *rock the boat* in OHPC are interrupted, and again all interrupted tokens occur in journalism:

Soviet analysts are satisfied that France and West Germany will not **rock the Eastern European boat**. (OHPC: journalism)

They know that if they **rock the political boat** they're finished; and not just in history. (OHPC: journalism)

This kind of interpolation is a stylistic device, perhaps genre-related, as well as a means of adapting the ideational content of the FEI to its context. Inserted items which signal the status of an FEI will be discussed in Section 10.5; inserted items with a grammatical function were discussed in Section 5.4.

7
Ambiguity, Polysemy, and Metaphor

This chapter considers three aspects of the semantics of FEIs: ambiguity (and homonymy), polysemy, and metaphoricality. These are surface characteristics, in contrast with non-compositionality, which is one of the key properties of FEIs: see Section 1.2.3, and, in relation to lexicalization, Section 2.3. I will not be looking at the specific meanings of FEIs, which are very much matters of the individual items. Much of the following discussion will concern metaphors, rather than FEIs in general.

7.1 AMBIGUITY AND HOMONYMY

Metaphorical FEIs have, potentially, literal counterparts, and homonymy or ambiguity is sometimes considered an essential criterion for the notional class of pure idiom (for example, Fernando and Flavell 1981: 33). FEIs without literal counterparts, such as *move heaven and earth* or *jump down someone's throat*, are therefore excluded, as they violate truth conditions. This sets up a potentially misleading division between types of metaphor, since pragmatically and discoursally *bite the bullet* and *spill the beans* have as much in common with *move heaven and earth* or *jump down someone's throat* as they do with transparent metaphors such as *stab someone in the back* or *rock the boat*, both of which also have literal equivalents.

Just as polysemous or homographic words are ambiguous when divorced from context, so are strings such as *bite the bullet* or *spill the beans*. In context, however, any ambiguity is resolved, with literal interpretations precluded. Ambiguity is therefore potential rather than actual: compare Bolinger's description of ambiguity as 'artificial and contrived' and of ambiguities as 'semantic illusions' (1976: 11). This can be seen in

They have really **bitten the bullet**, this time. It was a big step to commission the report and an even bigger one to publish it. I can't doubt their commitment . . . just hope they can achieve change. (OHPC: journalism)

This gentle nudge was never going to be enough to persuade Bobroff to **spill the beans** on his rift with the chairman of the football club, Irving Scholar, and another director, Tony Berry. (OHPC: journalism)

If no literal readings are possible for pure idioms in real contexts, then the situation does not seem very different from that of 'lesser' FEIs, which are never capable of literal interpretation. Furthermore, even though FEIs have homonymous counterparts in theory, there may be selection restrictions on subjects or realizations of other fillable slots, so rendering literal meaning impossible. Thus while the canonical form is ambiguous, the textual realization can only be metaphorical or idiomatic:

Meanwhile shareholders are in trouble. In a real crisis they may be able to do little but watch their paper wealth **go up in smoke**. (OHPC: journalism)

Hopes of a title hat-trick **hang by a thread**, but all is not quite lost. (OHPC: journalism)

The ambiguity criterion as a test for idioms cannot be valid, although it remains a feature to be further explored. It is further complicated by hyperbolic but literally plausible FEIs, such as *know something backwards* or *not lift a finger*: see Section 7.4.4 for further discussion.

Homonymy and ambiguity also depend on interpretation at the level of word or sense. *Miles from anywhere* is literally or physically impossible; however, if *anywhere* is interpreted as 'anywhere interesting or significant'—a regularly found reading—then the expression is hyperbolic but literally possible. Similarly *time flies* is impossible if *fly* is interpreted as 'move through the air on wings', but possible if it is interpreted as 'move fast': compare Weinreich (1969), who argues that idiomaticity can always be reduced to and therefore explained as polysemy. The situation becomes even more complicated where FEIs include concepts that are impossible for one group of speakers with specific world-views, but possible for a different group: for example, FEIs referring to God, heaven, or hell, or, more historically, personifications of death as in *dice with death*, *at death's door*, and *hang on like grim death*. Other FEIs that are similarly dependent on ideology include those that involve naive or superseded views of space and time such as *the sky's the limit* or *yours ever*: see Ortony (1988: 103), who discusses institutionalized metaphors involving pre-Galilean views of the universe.

Punning, of course, foregrounds and restores literal interpretation, but there is no real ambiguity of reference involved. This lexical or semantic play works equally well whether the idiom has a potential literal meaning or whether it does not:

Restaurants lose a good proportion of food through the back door and no one, so to speak, **spills the beans**. (OHPC: journalism)

The upkeep of all cars sometimes requires you to **bite the bullet** of repair bills, but with old cars, of course, that bullet can sometimes seem rather more like a howitzer shell. (OHPC: journalism)

7.1.1 *Ambiguity and Evidence*

Corpus investigations show very clearly that literal equivalents to metaphorical FEIs occur comparatively infrequently. In Section 3.2.2, I discussed how often in searching OHPC for FEI tokens, all or nearly all resulting matches for queries, even crudely specified queries, realized the target FEI type: *spill the beans* and *weather the storm* were cases in point. Such cases support the view that where metaphorical FEIs exist, their literal equivalents are avoided in free text: the idiomatic supersedes or blocks the literal. Compare Chafe's hypothesis (1968: 111) that the idiomatic meaning of a string will be commoner than its literal one: this usually proves to be true. Of course, in many cases literal uses are unlikely for real-world reasons. In literal contexts, or in corpora at any rate, people do not bite bullets, they bite food or food-like things, or their nails: they do not even spill beans very frequently, but rather coffee, beer, and other liquids. Selection restrictions merely formalize or reinforce this. The dividing-line between 'impossible' and 'possible' is valid in the abstract, but it ceases to be a meaningful distinction in practice.

A few psycholinguistic studies look specifically at ambiguity, and they tie in with general findings that idiomatic meanings are processed faster than literal ones. Van Lancker and Canter (1981) looked for phonological disambiguating clues, and they report, amongst other things, that where utterances were decontextualized, the hearer–informants inferred an idiomatic meaning regardless. (The informants made more accurate judgements when speakers deliberately set out to emphasize either a literal or an idiomatic reading.) The default reading for potentially ambiguous strings therefore appears to be idiomatic. Some other studies were interested in correlating literal meaning or likelihood of literal meaning with processing times, and so asked informants to rate FEIs according to their familiarity with the items and their assessments of the frequency of the literal and idiomatic meanings. Popiel and McRae

TABLE 7.1.   *Informant ratings for FEIs*

	Assessed frequency (literal)	Assessed frequency (idiomatic)	Assessed familiarity (literal)	Assessed familiarity (idiomatic)
beat around the bush	1.65	6.3	1.2	5.3
break the ice	4.00	5.79	3.08	4.69
kick the bucket	3.17	5.9	1.83	4.05
let the cat out of the bag	2.08	5.92	1.3	4.41
skate on thin ice	4.55	6.36	2.67	4.98
spill the beans	2.95	5.75	1.62	3.97

Source: Popiel and McRae (1988).

(1988) found that high ratings for idiomatic meanings were independent of literal meanings, and that there was greater variation with respect to intuited frequency ratings for literal meanings. Cronk *et al.* (1993) compared subjective assessments of the frequency of idiomatic uses and corresponding literal uses with an 'objective' score derived from the frequencies of the constituent words, as listed in Kučera and Francis (1967): they did not attempt to assess actual frequencies of literal or idiomatic uses of the strings in question, and it is unsurprising that they found informants' ratings to be more useful than 'objective' scores.

It is worth looking briefly at informant ratings from these last two studies for a few potentially ambiguous FEIs, chosen because their ambiguity has been discussed elsewhere in the literature. Popiel and McRae's informants rated items on a 7-point scale, where 1 is rare and 7 is very familiar, or encountered 'every day' (see Table 7.1). This suggests that informants regard idiomatic meanings as more likely, with only *break the ice* and perhaps *skate on thin ice* having plausible literal uses.

Cronk *et al.*'s informants rated items on a 5-point scale, where 5 is rare and 1 is very familiar (see Table 7.2). These are comparable findings, with literal uses consistently rated lower than idiomatic. In both studies, *let the cat out of the bag* shows the largest gap between literal and idiomatic ratings.

What does the evidence in BofE suggest? Table 7.3 gives absolute frequencies: all searches looked for very loose syntagmatic associations of constituent lexical words, with no restrictions on inflection or constituent determiners. With the exception of *break the ice* and *in hot water*, idiomatic uses are overwhelmingly more common than literal ones.

TABLE 7.2.   *Informant ratings for FEIs*

	Proportion of informants who rated literal meaning	*Familiarity with literal meaning*	*Proportion of informants who rated idiomatic meaning*	*Familiarity with idiomatic meaning*
break the ice	100%	2.8	100%	2.1
in hot water	100%	3.0	100%	2.3
kick the bucket	89.5%	3.1	85.7%	2.2
let the cat out of the bag	77.8%	3.9	100%	2.3
out on a limb	89.5%	3.8	100%	2.9
skate on thin ice	89.5%	3.2	100%	2.8
spill the beans	94.4%	3.5	100%	2.2

Source: Cronk *et al.* (1993)

Break the ice has two idiomatic meanings: 'disperse awkwardness in social interaction' (189 tokens) and, in sports contexts, 'score for the first time in a game or season' (12 tokens). *Break the ice* has a literal to idiomatic ratio of 1:3, but this reflects all BofE cases of the lemma *break* occurring within a 5-word window of *ice*, with no further syntagmatic restrictions. However, if the different structures of these matches are considered, different ratios emerge (see Table 7.4). Patterns are clear. If the string includes *the*, the ratio of literal to idiomatic is roughly 1:6. If the string is associated with an adverb particle, almost all tokens are literal (and the only idiomatic example may in fact be an ad hoc metaphor influenced by the FEI). The literal to idiomatic ratio for transitive or passive *break the ice*,

TABLE 7.3.   *BofE frequencies for literal and idiomatic meanings*

	Literal frequency	*Idiomatic frequency*
beat about/around the bush	0	109
break the ice	65	201
in hot water	181	178
kick the bucket	7	42
let the cat out of the bag	0	91
(out) on a limb	4	249
(skate) on thin ice	0	241
spill the beans	2	198

TABLE 7.4. Break the ice: *structures, meanings, and frequencies*

Structure	Literal meaning	Interaction meaning	Sports meaning
break the ice	18	152	10
break ice	6	1	1
break the ice + adverb particle	10	0	0
break ice + adverb particle	6	0	0
the ice is broken	1	31	1
the ice breaks	6	4	0
ice breaks	5	0	0
the ice breaks + adverb particle	7	1	0
ice breaks + adverb particle	6	0	0

without adverbial particle, is 1:10. Thus the absence of a determiner or the presence of a collocation with adverbial particles enhances the likelihood of a literal meaning, while transitive or passive uses are more likely to be idiomatic. The related compounds or transformations *ice-breaker* and *ice-breaking* have literal to idiomatic ratios in BofE of respectively 1:4 and 1:2 (taking *ice-breaker* 'kind of ship' as literal).

In hot water has a literal to idiomatic ratio of 1:1. However, certain collocations and structures are strongly associated with either literal or idiomatic meanings. The most important discriminator is the valency of the noun for which *in hot water* supplies a locative: when humans are in hot water, the idiomatic meaning is inferred; when inanimates or human limbs are in hot water, the literal meaning is inferred. The preceding verbs also discriminate. The idiomatic meaning is strongly associated with *be, land (someone)*, and *find oneself*, whereas the literal is associated with verbs such as *dip, dissolve, soak, wash*, and *immerse*: verbs which collocate very frequently with water in other contexts. Similarly with the dynamic transformation or variation *into hot water*: collocating verbs polarize according to meaning. The idiomatic meaning usually collocates with *get* or occasionally another verb of motion such as *run, walk*, or *stray*, whereas the literal meaning collocates with *dip, plunge*, or *put*. With respect to the discontinuous string *in—hot water*: where the slot is filled by *scalding, steaming*, and *boiling*, all realizations are literal, but where it is filled by *more, most*, and *further*, all realizations in BofE are idiomatic. (Other quantifiers such as *plenty of, a little*, and—*tablespoons of* are associated with the literal, but intensifiers such as *very* and *extremely* are mixed.) What is happening here is that collocation is reflecting the semantics of the different contexts of the literal and idiomatic meanings. The important point is that in over 300 tokens of this string, none is ambiguous at a clausal level within their co-texts.

In the case of *kick the bucket*, 3 of the 7 literal tokens are associated with the adverbial particles *over*, *along*, or *away*, and 1 has *a pile of buckets* as object, not *the bucket*. One literal token has a possessive rather than *the*, and another is passive. A further literal token occurs in the context of explaining the origin of the FEI. The only genuine, active, literal token has a cow as grammatical subject, and it occurs in conversation and provokes laughter at the implied pun. This underscores the tenacity of idiomatic meaning.

7.1.2 *The Ambiguity of Body Language FEIs*

A particular type of ambiguity is that found in body language FEIs: expressions describing a literal, physical action that connotes a reaction, emotion, social gesture, and so on. Examples include *grit one's teeth*, *hold one's breath*, *lick one's lips*, *shake hands*, and *twiddle one's thumbs*: they are different from *wrinkle one's nose* (see Section 6.6) because they are relatively fixed lexically and have institutionalized idiomatic meanings. While it is comparatively simple to separate literal from idiomatic uses of *lick one's lips*, other cases are more complex. Literal examples of *twiddle one's thumbs* may still connote idleness and boredom, and it is almost impossible to separate literal and metaphorical uses of an expression such as *take a deep breath*, where the literal action implies the metaphorical meaning 'prepare oneself for saying, doing, or hearing something'. *Put one's feet up* has both literal and metaphorical meanings. The metaphorical meaning 'relax' may involve the raising of one's feet, but does not necessarily have to. Like *in hot water*, literal and metaphorical uses are distinguished through colligation. Literal uses are associated with adjuncts of position which privilege literal interpretations. For example,

To Nell's annoyance he **put his feet up** on the dashboard and would not take them down. (OHPC: fiction)

'To tell you the truth I've retired this trip,' he says, **putting his feet up** among the radio sets. (OHPC: journalism)

Idiomatic uses are usually clause-final in OHPC, or followed by *and* or an adjunct of time or purpose:

Brew up a surprise by telling mum to **put her feet up** while you make a nice cup of tea. (OHPC: journalism)

... try one when you're **putting your feet up** after a hot Saturday morning's shopping and twenty minutes' standing on the 23. (OHPC: fiction)

After an encouraging day's work, Colin Montgomerie **put his feet up** and switched on satellite television for confirmation of his new-found status. He was disappointed. (OHPC: journalism)

Context again disambiguates. See Kövecses and Szábo (1996: 339f.) for a discussion of cultural and conceptual aspects of FEIs involving *hand* or *hands*, and see Čermák (forthcoming) for a discussion of body language FEIs in Czech, with cross-linguistic perspectives.

7.2 AMBIGUITY AND THE INTERPRETATION OF THE UNFAMILIAR

While metaphorical FEIs are hardly ever ambiguous in context, it is still true that they are potentially ambiguous in isolation, or if unfamiliar. The processing and interpretation of metaphors in general has been extensively discussed and studied, but to generalize crudely, strategies of analogy and real-world knowledge are employed, within a framework of relevance (see Grice 1975, 1989; Sperber and Wilson 1986), whereby the implicatures of the speaker/writer are decoded and the intended meaning is inferred. In the case of an unfamiliar FEI which involves an opaque metaphor, the hearer/reader may be unable to deploy either analogy or real-world knowledge. The context or co-text will typically shed light on the intended meaning, but not always. This is the problem confronting non-native speakers of a language or variety, who may also interpret FEIs in ways which native speakers do not, and see them as compositional.

To be anecdotal: I did not know the meaning of an American English FEI *on the bubble*. After I guessed at its meaning and found I was wrong, I asked a number of British speakers for their guesses. Of fifteen responses and interpretations, five thought it meant 'in an intense state of activity', that is, lexically and semantically parallel with *on the boil* or *bubbling along*. Three thought it meant 'drinking alcohol' or 'drunk': compare *on the bottle* and *bubbly* 'champagne'. Two thought it meant 'coming to a head' or 'approaching a climax': compare, perhaps, the head or froth on beer. Two others thought it meant 'borrowing money': compare, perhaps, *on the scrounge*. The remaining three responses were 'being a hanger-on on something or someone upwardly mobile' (compare *on someone's coat-tails?*);

'doing something reckless'; and 'immediately' (compare *on the spot?*). The established idiomatic meaning is actually more like *on the brink*: 'in an unstable position; in danger of bursting, collapsing, or being destroyed or defeated', which can be compared with the metaphor in *the bubble has burst*:

On the bubble where I always stay—I'm always **on the bubble**, so I'm probably one of the best scoreboard readers you'll ever meet. If I make it, it'll be by one or two shots. If I miss, it'll be by one or two shots. So I'm always right there on the edge. (BofE: unscripted broadcast journalism)

Asking people in this way about a decontextualized, unfamiliar string was entirely unfair and unscientific, but their responses suggest their use of analogizing skills and lexical knowledge, such as the frame *on the* — (see Section 6.3) and other metaphorical, extended, or non-literal meanings of *bubble* or its cognates, as much as their real-world knowledge of the physical properties of bubbles. Interestingly enough, the only example of *on the bubble* in a British source in BofE is quoting the American film-maker/actor Kevin Costner. It appears to be partially glossed in *bubbling away*, marked in scare quotes, and if so, this gloss suggests that the journalist misunderstood Costner:

Which is why Waterworld—which opens in Hollywood next Friday and which he has been feverishly trying to salvage in the cuttings and special effects rooms—could be such a potential disaster for him. Especially on the back of two rare flops, Wyatt Earp and A Perfect World. So depressed about it all is the Oscar winner that he says the idea of quitting is 'bubbling' away inside him. 'It has put it **on the bubble** quite honestly,' he says. 'If Waterworld is a success and makes tons of money it will not change how I feel—that the experience was not worth it to me ultimately,' he adds. (BofE: journalism)

This can be related to more serious discussion of the interpretation of novel or unfamiliar FEIs and proverbs. Lakoff and Turner (1989: 160ff.) see proverbs in terms of a conceptual metaphor 'generic is specific' and of the mapping of one kind of schema onto another, in particular the mapping of 'specific-level schemas onto the generic-level schemas they contain': they suggest that proverbs 'lead us to general characterizations, which nevertheless are grounded in the richness of the special case'. They regard interpretation as near-automatic, and relate it to 'The Great Chain of Being', which, crudely, is a hierarchy 'humans—animals—plants—complex objects—natural physical things': it governs the interpretation of metaphors and links innate attributes and behaviour. For example, metaphorical references to complex objects and their structural attributes correspond to 'functional behaviour'.

Honeck and Temple (1994) critique Lakoff and Turner, preferring to see interpretation in terms of problem-solving strategies. In particular, they report psycholinguistic evidence to suggest that proverb comprehension is neither quick nor automatic, and that even familiar proverbs may take longer to interpret than less metaphorical language, thus suggesting that 'proverbs are mentally effortful, and . . . they rely more on controlled than on automatic processes'.

Resnick (1982) looks at how proverbs are interpreted by children in the 8–13 age group. He takes a set of ten proverbs, all either prohibitions beginning *don't*, or following an *if —, —* pattern, and all controlled for vocabulary. Of these, only *don't count your chickens before they hatch* and *don't throw the baby out with the bathwater* occur with any frequency in corpora. The interpretation strategies which the children used seemed to involve analogy and problem-solving: Resnick points out that children seem to solve problems concretely, whereas adults seem to solve them more abstractly.

Forrester (1995) studies the comprehension of idioms by means of items of varying degrees of familiarity, together with made-up versions of idioms. These items include *fly in the ointment/smudge on the sheepskin*; *that's the way the cookie crumbles/that's the way the cheese is grated*; and *barking up the wrong tree/snarling at the wrong gamekeeper*. He observes that if the context was appropriate, the unknown or unfamiliar proverb could be interpreted idiomatically; the made-up idioms could be interpreted if they were associated with familiar idioms; and the literalness or idiomaticity of the context had no significant effect on whether or not an item could be interpreted.

What then appears to be the case is that hearers/readers apply Gricean maxims, problem-solving strategies, and analogy in constructing possible interpretations of proverbs and metaphorical FEIs. It is particularly relevant that so many FEIs fall into sets and so few are completely opaque in synchronic terms. Compare Bauer (1979), who argues that pragmatic knowledge is needed in interpreting unfamiliar noun compounds; he also points out the disambiguating role of context.

7.3 POLYSEMY

Polysemous fixed expressions are those which have two or more non-compositional meanings, in addition to any literal ones. They

TABLE 7.5.   *Polysemous FEIs, according to idiomaticity type*

	All FEIs	Polysemous FEIs
anomalous collocations	45.3%	62%
formulae	21.3%	13%
metaphors	33.4%	25%

are not much discussed in the literature, although Klappenbach (1968: 183) reports research which suggests that 8–9% of Russian FEIs are polysemous. In my own study, I treated different meanings of polysemous FEIs as separate expressions, effectively homographs. Some very common FEIs, such as *in fact*, *of course*, and *you know*, have several subtly different meanings in discourse which are mainly shown up by context. I did not describe these minutely in the database, but instead recorded only major distinctions as polysemes. For example, *you know* is treated in two entries: one for its use as a filler, and one for its use as an attention-seeking device or appeal to shared knowledge.

I found that approximately 5% of database FEIs were polysemous (compare the hypothesized 8–9% in Russian). Table 7.5 correlates polysemy with idiomaticity type, and shows that polysemy is associated more strongly with anomalous collocations than formulae or metaphors.

Correlating polysemy with grammatical types gives the results shown in Table 7.6. The proportions are markedly different, suggesting that polysemy is a feature of adjuncts rather than predicates, nominal or adjectival groups, or conventions.

TABLE 7.6.   *Polysemous FEIs, according to grammatical type*

	All FEIs	Polysemous FEIs
predicates	40%	31%
nominal groups	9%	2%
adjectival groups	2%	1%
modifiers, quantifiers	1%	1%
adjuncts, submodifiers	28%	52%
sentence adverbials	5%	5%
conventions, exclamations, and subordinate clauses	12%	5%
fillers, others	1%	3%

7.3.1 *Polysemy, Meanings, and Variations*

Most of the polysemous FEIs in the database have two meanings. The most typical cases are where one meaning is an anomalous collocation and the other a metaphor. Some examples are:

abandon ship	1. leave a ship that is sinking
	2. give up on an enterprise
out of ONE's depth	1. in water insufficiently shallow for standing
	2. in a difficult situation
tread water	1. stay upright while floating in water
	2. do nothing

Polysemous FEIs are often associated with different collocations or realizations of subject or object, and these effectively disambiguate:

X catches the sun	1. tan
PLACE catches the sun	2. be sunny, be in an open position, be exposed to sunlight
SOMETHING catches the sun	3. flash, scintillate
X clears the air	1. resolve a misunderstanding
STORM clears the air	2. make things feel fresher
BUILDING/PLACE goes up in smoke	1. catch fire, burn down
PLAN/ASPIRATION/etc. goes up in smoke	2. be destroyed
X has a go (at SOMETHING)	1. try
X has a go (at Y)	2. attack, nag
on the rocks	1. (of drinks) served with ice
	2. (of relationships, enterprises, etc.) in trouble, shaky
X puts ANIMAL out of its misery	1. kill, for humane reasons
X puts Y out of Y's misery	2. give someone the information they have been waiting for
X turns SOMETHING/Y upside down	1. change completely
X turns SOMEWHERE upside down	2. ransack, search thoroughly

Variations, parallels, or structures in OHPC are sometimes associated with just one of the meanings: compare the discussions of 'false variations' in Section 6.1.13. Apparent variations within a single FEI cluster may in fact represent different FEIs altogether:

PLANT goes/runs to seed	1. produce seeds
SOMETHING goes to seed	2. deteriorate
at liberty	1. (of people or animals) free, not confined
at liberty to VERB	2. allowed to
in/into perspective	1. realistically
in perspective	2. representationally, not out of perspective
in force	1. valid, applicable
in force, out in force	2. present in quantity (e.g., of police)
one day, some day	1. at some indefinite time in the future
one day	2. at some indefinite time in the past
X slips/gets through the net	1. evade, escape
X/SOMETHING slips/falls through the net	2. be missed or ignored

Different meanings may also operate in different clausal positions or have different clausal functions:

all in	1. (postnominal, of prices) inclusive
	2. (complement) exhausted
as usual	1. (disjunct) indicating typicality or repetition
	2. (adjunct) in the normal way
or else	1. (conjunction) prefacing contrast
	2. (convention, filler) indicating threat
without question	1. (adjunct) obediently, unquestioningly
	2. (disjunct) definitely
yours truly	1. (convention) valediction in letters
	2. (proform) reference to speaker/writer

Just under 1% of all database FEIs have 3 or more meanings: only 12 have 4 or more. Most of the more highly polysemous FEIs have slight variations in the realizations of subjects, objects, and so on, as above, although the main elements in the expression remain fixed. In context they are not ambiguous:

in play, into play	1. (of a ball) being kicked, legal to kick
into play, in play	2. happening, taking place, in existence
in play	3. while playing, during a game
on the spot	1. immediately, without delay, then and there
	2. present, actually there (man on the spot)
	3. without moving forwards (running on the spot)
	4. exactly right
on the run	1. running, escaping, fleeing
	2. in danger of defeat
	3. busy, on the hop
	4. in sequence, on the trot

The three most polysemous FEIs I found were *give way*, *in line*, and *take care*. These are complex high-frequency items. Many of their meanings are associated with distinctions in form, and so could equally well be considered different FEIs:

SOMETHING gives way to SOMETHING	1. be superseded by
SOMETHING gives way	2. collapse physically
X gives way (to Y)	3. cede, yield (in general contexts)
X gives way (to feelings)	4. lose self-control, express oneself emotionally, etc.
X gives way (to Y)	5. yield right of way, allow to pass
SOMETHING gives way to SOMETHING	6. gradually merge into and be replaced by

in line	1. in a queue
next/first/etc. in line	2. indicating order of precedence
in line for SOMETHING, in line to VERB	3. likely to have or do the thing mentioned
in line (with SOMETHING), into line	4. physically aligned
in line (with SOMETHING)	5. (of people, ideas) in accordance
in line (with SOMETHING)	6. (of amounts, directives) in keeping or proportion
in line, into line	7. (of people) behaving correctly or conventionally

X takes care of Y/SOMETHING	1. tend, care for
X takes care (to VERB, that —)	2. ensure, make certain
X takes care	3. be careful
X takes care of SOMETHING/Y	4. deal with
X/SOMETHING takes care of SOMETHING	5. destroy, expend, use
X takes care of Y	6. kill
X can take care of Xself	7. cope (in difficult situation)

SOMETHING takes care of itself	8. happen on its own, without assistance
take care (of yourself), take care now	9. valediction

7.3.2 *Polysemy and Frequency*

Different meanings of FEIs are sometimes associated with dramatic differences in frequency in OHPC. For example, the conjunction *or else* occurs in OHPC with a frequency of just over 8 per million, but as a convention and threat it occurs less than 1 per million. The conjunct *by the way* has a frequency in OHPC of 8 per million, but the homographic adjectival meaning 'irrelevant, beside the point' occurs only 3 times. In both these cases, the contrast reflects the usual distinction in frequency between grammatical and lexical items. In other cases, specialized and literal senses fail to occur, because of the topic and genre composition of the OHPC: for example, *take root*, of plants forming roots, does not occur at all, whereas a metaphorical use of *take root* 'develop, become established' occurs with a frequency of 1.6 per million. The most interesting of the disparities are indeed those where more literal meanings occur less frequently than metaphorical ones, as in

at arm's length	1. at the length of one's arms (0.6 per million)
	2. at a distance, not in close contact (1.1 per million)
hold SOMEONE to ransom	1. hold as prisoner for ransom (0)
	2. exert power over, threaten (0.5 per million)
in step, into step	1. walking together, synchronized (0.4 per million)
	2. in sympathy, taking into account (1.4 per million)
in unison	1. harmonizing (0.2 per million)
	2. together with, at the same time as (2.2 per million)

Compare the infrequency in general of literal equivalents of metaphorical FEIs.

7.3.3 *Polysemy and Ambiguity*

Very few polysemous FEIs are truly ambiguous in context. *Over someone's head* can mean 'incomprehensible' or 'without consultation, being circumvented in the hierarchy': as usual, collocation distinguishes, with the first typically following *be*, the second *go*. Only in a hypothetical and isolated example such as **it was over my head* could either meaning be possible. *It is downhill all the way* can either mean 'be very easy' (compare *be downhill*) or 'deteriorate, decline' (compare *go downhill*). Again the co-text and its evaluations indicate which meaning is intended:

Two-nil up at home against moderate opposition—**it would have been downhill all the way** for most teams. But then most teams are not lumbered with Spurs' defence. Bardsley and Francis profited from their collective inadequacy, and at 2–2 it was anybody's game. (OHPC: journalism)

Middlesbrough were without a win in seven. We expected a dour scrap, and we were not surprised. McGee settled it after only four minutes, and from then on in **it was downhill all the way**. (OHPC: journalism)

The first of these denotes ease and the second deterioration. The case of *a rolling stone gathers no moss* is sometimes cited as a rare example of an FEI with two opposed meanings or evaluative interpretations: it is discussed in Section 9.1.

7.4 METAPHORICALITY, METONYMY, AND NON-LITERAL MEANING

The following sections review the kinds of metaphors and non-literal language observed in FEIs: diachronic/synchronic considerations have to be borne in mind here. There is an extensive literature concerning the nature of metaphor. As far as FEIs are concerned, relevant discussion includes papers in the collection edited by Ortony (1979*a*; second edition 1993), such as Searle's account of metaphorical processes and institutionalized metaphors (1979*b*: 92–123), and the discussions of simile and metaphor by Ortony (1979*b*: 186–201) and Miller (1979: 202–50). From the semantics point of view, the differences between similes and metaphors are important, involving questions and degrees of truthfulness as well as perceptions of intended meaning. Lexicologically, however, similes are a fairly unimportant type of FEI. Besides, the very institutionalization of metaphorical FEIs and similes means that they are interpreted in different ways from freely formed metaphorical strings, as has been demonstrated by psycholinguistic experiments.

All metaphors, all metaphorical FEIs, are at some level untrue, flouting Grice's first maxim of Quality 'Do not say what you believe to be false' (1975: 46; 1989: 27ff.). Their rhetorical power results from the tension between their essential untruthfulness and the ways in which they could be considered to be representative of truth. Exaggeration and manipulation of reality are key features of metaphorical FEIs.

The use of *literally* to signal metaphoricality or to demetaphorize FEIs is discussed in Section 10.5.

7.4.1 *Metonymy*

Metonymy and metaphor are discrete linguistic devices, but for convenience metonymy is dealt with here and taken to include synecdoche. Of database FEIs recorded as involving metonyms, many relate to parts of the body. The particular body part represents the whole person, as well as foregrounding the physical sense or ability which constitutes the central part of the FEI's meaning. For example, in *lend an ear, ear* indicates both the person and his/ her attention; in *hard on someone's heels, heels* indicates a person and the part most (notionally) visible in running; and in *get one's head round something, head* indicates a person and his/her mind or understanding. Some further examples are:

absence makes the heart grow fonder
bums on seats
fight tooth and nail
hate SOMEONE's guts
have a nose for SOMETHING
have ONE's eye on SOMETHING
lend a hand
long in the tooth
lose ONE's nerve
not lay a finger on SOMEONE
on foot, by foot
touch a raw nerve
two heads are better than one
under the thumb of SOMEONE
a word in SOMEONE's ear

The relationship between metonymic tenor and metonymic vehicle is often governed by physiology and the real world. Sense organs denote their respective senses, and FEIs mentioning hands generally have meanings to do with holding and manipulating (see Kövecses and Szábo 1996: 339f.). In other cases, the relationship is culturally determined. By convention, *heart* indicates emotions and depth of feeling in English, and *nerve* or *nerves* audacity or bravery as well as sensitivity. This is not necessarily the case in other languages and cultures, particularly non-European ones.

Other metonymic FEIs involve objects and places that represent actions, activities, or results, or involve other part and whole relationships: they too are often culture-specific:

at the helm
at the wheel
beat swords into ploughshares
bread and circuses
daily bread
from the cradle to the grave
go under the hammer
hearth and home
on the streets
set sail
spend a penny
take the floor
take the veil
the pen is mightier than the sword
under the plough
without/not a stitch on

Finally, a very few metonymic FEIs such as *a crack shot* or *the powers that be* involve qualities or attributes that symbolize people who have those qualities and attributes.

7.4.2 *Personification*

A few FEIs involve personifications, and these are also culturally determined. The personification sometimes arises from a violation of selection restrictions. In the following list, subjects are given in cases where their animacy or inanimacy would be inappropriate in literal contexts:

dice with death
SOMETHING finds its way SOMEWHERE
SOMETHING gives birth to SOMETHING (lead to, give rise to)
SOMETHING goes begging
in the teeth of the wind
look SOMETHING in the eye
hang on like grim death
hard on the heels of SOMETHING (and variations)
laugh like a drain
like death warmed up
nature abhors a vacuum
necessity is the mother of invention

SOMETHING parts company (split, come apart)
procrastination is the thief of time
SOMETHING speaks for itself
SOMETHING speaks volumes
stare SOMEONE in the face (of obvious facts or things)
SOMETHING takes care of itself
SOMETHING tells its own tale
the eye of the storm
the pot calling the kettle black
the world and his wife
time flies
time and tide wait for no man
SOMETHING trips off the tongue

7.4.3 *Animal Metaphors*

Many FEIs contain metaphors which refer to animals, denoting and connoting supposed characteristics or qualities which are then applied to people and human situations. Interestingly, no database FEI contains *animal* or *insect*, although many contain hyponyms such as *cat*, *dog*, or *horse*: perhaps because general words such as *animal* are too neutral to engender these kinds of institutionalized metaphors, although both *animal* and *insect* are used in other contexts with metaphorical meanings. Examples of FEIs with animal metaphors include:

FEI	Connoted characteristic
as blind as a bat	weak eyesight
like a bear with a sore head	irritability
as busy as a bee, a busy bee	industry
a red rag to a bull	rage
shed crocodile tears	insincerity
dead as a dodo	obsolescence
treat SOMEONE like a dog, a dog's life	ill-treatment
eat like a horse	appetite
a leopard does not change its spots	immutability of bad qualities
as stubborn as a mule	obstinacy
eat like a pig	greediness
play possum	pretence
like sheep	slavish obedience, lack of individuality
a snake in the grass	deceitfulness, despicability

They incorporate fossilized, speciesist beliefs: they are evaluative stereotypes. Low points out that they generally refer to undesirable traits, reflecting human views of animals as lower forms of life

(1988: 133f.). Lakoff and Turner (1989: 193f.) refer to institution-alized perceptions of animals, although these are not necessarily the same as those fossilized in FEIs. In their 'Great Chain Meta-phor' (1989: 170ff.), animals form the second highest level, and are seen in terms of 'instinctual attributes and behaviour'. This can be seen in many of the FEIs just listed, where a lack of 'higher-level', or human, control and conscious restraint is implied.

7.4.4 *Hyperbole, Absurdity, and Truism*

Hyperbolic FEIs lie somewhere on a continuum between those FEIs with literal counterparts and those without. Both hyperbole and absurdity can be used as tests to separate out classes of FEIs, but a more fruitful approach is to see them simply as indicating that an FEI cannot be interpreted compositionally. FEIs that describe literally impossible processes or attributes include:

all smiles
a storm in a teacup
be neither here nor there
be nipped in the bud (of things other than plants)
breathe fire
get up SOMEONE's nose
jump down SOMEONE's throat
move heaven and earth
raise Cain
shoot the breeze
sweat blood
take ONE's life in(to) ONE's hands
the world is ONE's oyster
tie ONEself in knots
turn SOMEWHERE inside out

Fraser says that he has found no examples of 'literally uninterpre-table idioms' which undergo transformations (1970: 31), and this is not contradicted by the evidence in OHPC.

It would be perfectly reasonable to include *rain cats and dogs* in the last list. However, one (disputed) theory of the origin of the expression refers to an alleged incident when small animals were sucked up by the wind and then dropped elsewhere: similar inci-dents are reported with frogs or fish. More plausible is a second theory that the expression refers to the (former) frequent drowning of cats and dogs in flooded, inadequately drained streets during heavy rain. If either is right, the expression would then have basis in truth.[1] This typifies the problem of asserting that an FEI has no literal equivalent.

Many FEIs involve exaggerations and implausibilities, rather than actual impossibilities:

a hop, skip, and a jump (from SOMEWHERE)
a thousand and one
be coming out of ONE's ears
be paved with gold
be rolling in the aisles
be worked to death
break ONE's back to VERB
bust a gut
chilled to the marrow/bone
cold enough to freeze the balls off a brass monkey
cost an arm and a leg
eat SOMEONE out of house and home
everything but the kitchen sink
fight to the death
flog ONE's guts out (and variations)
hate SOMEONE's guts
in floods of tears
in the blink of an eye
know SOMETHING backwards
not enough room to swing a cat
not for all the tea in China
not lift a finger
one in a million
skin and bone
stink to high heaven
until the end of time
weigh a ton
would give ONE's right arm to VERB
wouldn't be seen dead VERBing
wouldn't touch SOMEONE/SOMETHING with a bargepole/ten-foot pole

These can be related to the huge number of metaphorical FEIs which describe theoretically possible actions or attributes, but which are untrue in context. *Keep something under one's hat* does not have a literal equivalent if the referent of the grammatical subject is not wearing or does not own a hat, and *catch someone red-handed* does not have a literal equivalent other than in the

---

[1] A third theory suggests that it has its origins in Norse mythology, where cats and dogs are associated with storms. A fourth theory interprets the FEI as a corruption of Greek *katadupe* 'waterfall': if correct, then the FEI would be literally uninterpretable for linguistic reasons.

context of crimes, misdemeanours, or indiscretions involving blood or red paint. A few further examples are:

a pretty (or fine) kettle of fish
be as broad as it is long
built like a tank
buzz around like a blue-arsed fly
call the shots
grasp the nettle
hold all the aces
on top of SOMEONE/SOMETHING (= very close, oppressively close, etc.)
put ONE's money where ONE's mouth is
read the riot act to SOMEONE
sweep the board
too many chiefs and not enough Indians

Truisms form another group of FEIs. They state the obvious, and achieve their rhetorical effect through litotes or understatement. These are completely truthful but they have to be interpreted in the light of what is implied in the vehicle of their metaphors. The following examples all contain negatives:

cannot hear ONESelf think
cut no ice
not a bed of roses
not be a spring chicken
not be SOMEONE's cup of tea
not hold water
not the only pebble on the beach
ONE's heart isn't in it
won't set the world on fire
be no picnic

For example, it is not possible to hear oneself think in any circumstances: the FEI's meaning arises from the fact that even if such a thing were physiologically possible, it would not be physically possible in the specific situation (itself an exaggeration). In context, other FEIs can be used in the same way:

It's . . . we're very conscious that costs that we've incurred we need to keep strapped down to a minimum, but we have to manage a forty million pound organization and you **cannot do this on the back of an envelope**. (OHPC: transcribed radio programme)

Davidson (1979: 40) points out that the negation of a metaphor is also a potential metaphor, 'the ordinary meaning in the context of use is odd enough to prompt us to disregard the question of literal truth'. Cohen (1975: 671), who Davidson follows, comments of utterances like *No man is an island* that the metaphor is essentially true, not deviant, but that the total speech act in which the sentence is embedded must be considered, since it is remarkable for the sentence to occur in that context. Fraser (1983: 34) points out that self-evident truths such as *I wasn't born yesterday* require metaphorical or pragmatic interpretations, since the alternative available reading would imply the speaker's carelessness or stupidity in making such a remark.

Similarly with other truisms such as *Business is business* and *boys will be boys*. There are only a few such which are institutionalized as FEIs, and they represent another form of absurdity. Both Lyons (1977: 417) and Davidson (1979: 40) discuss *business is business* in terms of tautology where literal truth is irrelevant: the interesting point is how the hearer/reader makes sense of the utterance. Grice (1975: 52; 1989: 33) gives tautologies as extreme examples of the flouting of the first maxim of Quantity, but nevertheless informative at the level of what is implicated. Wierzbicka (1987*a*) discusses *boys will be boys* in terms of its pragmatic function as a plea for tolerance: a more interaction-centred approach.

7.4.5 *Irony*

A very few FEIs are always used ironically. The mismatch between surface and intended meanings can be seen as a kind of metaphoricality:

a fine/pretty kettle of fish
cry all the way to the bank
big deal
God's gift to —
take the cake/biscuit
tell me about it!
need SOMETHING like a hole in the head

Irony, however, is more commonly constructed through the discoursal context. The following FEIs are often used ironically, with negative connotations or implications:

a bright spark
happ(il)y ever after
the holy of holies
ONE's heart bleeds
pearls of wisdom
ray of sunshine
whiter than white

Irony is discussed further in Section 9.1.3.

7.4.6 *Incorporated Metaphors*

Metaphoricality is widespread in the lexicon, and is one of the chief motivating forces which underlies the development of polysemy. This complicates analyses of metaphoricality in FEIs. For example, many FEIs that are classifiable as anomalous collocations contain words such as *take, give, way, in,* or *far,* where the metaphors are so deeply entrenched that they cannot be isolated from their historical and original core meanings. It can happen recursively. Expressions such as *go a long way towards (doing) something* are metaphorical, but both *go* and *way* are being used in regular metaphorical senses. *In hand* and *in one's hands* have various meanings to do with control. These meanings are also found in the more precise metaphors of *take one's life in one's hands* or *take someone/something in hand.*

This relates to the analysability of metaphorical FEIs in general. Some parts of some FEIs are more decodable than others, and so their metaphoricality is not evenly spread across the whole string. For example, *rock the boat* is a transparent metaphor, but *rock* has an analogous metaphorical meaning 'upset' institutionalized outside the FEI: compare other verbs such as *move, agitate, shake,* and *stir,* which systematically have literal meanings to do with physical movement and metaphorical meanings to do with emotional disturbance. Similarly, the metaphor of 'spilling' in *spill the beans* is simpler than that of 'beans'. That is, it is easier to draw an analogy between the action of spilling something physically and that of revealing a secret (compare *let slip* or *drop* as in *drop something into a conversation,* and *spill one's guts, spill it!*) than it is to draw one between *beans* and *secrets*: compare further discussion in Sections 2.2.1 and 6.3. Newmeyer (1972: 298–9) draws attention to this with respect to the partial compositionality of idioms: he also gives the example of *bury* as in *bury the hatchet* and *bury one's differences.* In these particular cases, *beans* and *hatchet* appear to be more heavily metaphorical than *spill* and *bury*: the idioms are asymmetrically metaphorical. This may well tie in with the fact that a number of surveys on dictionary use have suggested that users tend to look up FEIs under component nouns, as if latently aware that the nouns are the items which centrally hold the key to the metaphor. Of course, it may equally reflect users' familiarity with the common lexicographical practice of treating FEIs within the headword entry for one of their component nouns, rather than the first lexical word. See Béjoint (1981, 1994: 160ff.), Bogaards (1990, 1992), Botha (1992), and Lorentzen (1996) for further discussion.

7.5 CONCEPTUAL METAPHORS

Personification, animal metaphors, and so on are part of the cultural and ideological framework of English and its metaphorical constructs. They lead into the area of conceptual metaphors, the deep metaphors embedded in the language described by Lakoff and Johnson (1980) who showed the systematic continuum from individual meanings of single words through to sets of FEIs. One example is the metaphor cited by Lakoff and Johnson 'Life is a gambling game' (1980: 51): compare discussion of this by Dillard (1975: 61ff.). FEIs relating to card games and gambling include:

a trump card
all bets are off
come up trumps
(come) within an ace of VERBing
cover/hedge ONE's bets
do you want a bet (on it)?, don't bet on it!, I wouldn't bet on it
follow suit
have an ace up ONE's sleeve
hedge ONE's bets
hold all the aces
in the betting, out of the betting
in the running
knock spots off SOMEONE/SOMETHING
lay ONE's cards on the table
(like) a house of cards
(like) a pack of cards
lucky at cards, unlucky in love
not be playing with a full deck
on the cards
open/start a book on SOMETHING
(play ONE's cards) close to ONE's chest
play ONE's cards right
show ONE's hand
SOMETHING is a good/safe bet
the aces are in SOMEONE's hands
the cards/odds are stacked against SOMEONE
turn up trumps
what's the betting
you bet
you can bet your bottom dollar—

Lakoff (1987: 380ff.) discusses a general construct 'Anger is heat': this incorporates research carried out with Kövecses, itself reported in Kövecses (1986). Lakoff explores the ways in which various aspects of the metaphor are realized in different FEIs. For example, there are notions of heat (*hot under the collar, hot and bothered*) and of the body being a container which can explode under pressure (*make someone's blood boil, blow one's top*). This relates to another construct 'Passions are beasts inside a person', and it is realized with respect to anger in FEIs such as *get out of hand, lose one's grip,* and *breathe fire.* Lakoff explores these metaphors further to explain apparent restrictions on their semantics or contexts of use, particularly with respect to the exact degree and exact kind of anger connoted.

Kövecses and Szabó (1996) look closely at metaphors relating to fire, especially those which realize constructs such as 'anger is fire', 'love is fire', 'enthusiasm is fire', and so on. Not all their examples are FEIs, but they include:

burn the candle at both ends
catch fire, on fire
carry a torch (for SOMEONE)
fan the flames
set fire to SOMETHING
spit fire
a wet blanket

Fire in the belly and *set the world/Thames on fire* are further examples. There are other fire-based constructs they might have explored here: 'destruction is fire', 'danger is fire', or 'danger is heat', as in

crash and burn
get ONE's fingers burned
go up in smoke
a hot potato
if you can't stand the heat, get out of the kitchen
in the hot seat
like a moth to the flame
play with fire
there's no smoke without fire
too hot to handle

Many other basic conceptual metaphors can be observed in FEIs. 'Life is a vehicle' or 'situations are vehicles' can be seen in

abandon ship
a sinking ship
in the same boat
miss the boat/bus
push the boat out
rock the boat
run a tight ship

ships that pass in the night
upset the apple cart

FEIs such as *by the way* and *go round in circles* reflect 'an argument (or discourse) is a journey'. Compare the discussions by Lakoff and Johnson of other metaphors concerning journeys (1980: *passim*). A further conceptual metaphor emerging from database FEIs is 'life is a sea' or 'life is a swimming-pool' and so on. It occurs in general extended or metaphorical uses of words such as *tide*, *sink*, *drift*, and so on, in phrasal verbs such as *dive in* or *float around*, and in

a big fish in a little pond
a fish out of water
a lot of water has flowed under the bridge, it's water under the bridge
at sea (= in difficulty)
between the devil and the deep blue sea
come hell or high water
go off the deep end
go swimmingly
home and dry
in at the deep end
in deep water
keep ONE's head above water
muddy the waters
on the rocks
out of ONE's depth
pour oil on troubled waters
sink or swim
still waters run deep
swim with the tide
take the plunge
test the water, test the waters
there are other fish in the sea
tread water (= not make much progress)
uncharted waters

Clothing might be predicted to occur in FEIs that realize a construct 'clothing is concealment' or 'clothing is appearance', and certainly a few of them do:

a wolf in sheep's clothing
an iron fist in a velvet glove
draw a veil over SOMETHING
ONE's best bib and tucker
old hat
SOMETHING fits like a glove
take the veil

Interestingly, however, a number of clothing metaphors in FEIs can be characterized loosely as 'clothing is behaviour':

a feather in ONE's cap
at the drop of a hat
by the seat of ONE's pants
cap in hand
get ONE's knickers in a twist
get ONE's skates on
get too big for ONE's boots
hand in glove with SOMETHING/SOMEONE
hats off to X!, take ONE's hat off to SOMEONE/SOMETHING
have a bee in ONE's bonnet
hold on to SOMEONE's apron strings (and variations)
hot under the collar
if the cap fits, wear it
I'll eat my hat
in ONE's shoes
in plain clothes
keep SOMETHING under ONE's hat
knock SOMETHING/SOMEONE into a cocked hat
lick SOMEONE's boots
off the cuff
pull ONE's socks up
put a sock in it
put ONE's shirt on SOMETHING
scare the pants off SOMEONE
set ONE's cap at SOMETHING
shake in ONE's shoes
take the veil
take up the gauntlet
talk through ONE's hat
the boot is on the other foot
throw down the gauntlet
throw ONE's hat in the ring
trail ONE's coat

Many of these are metonyms, and indicate someone's actions, reactions, or behaviour by means of a vehicle which describes clothing or actions involving clothing.

Kövecses and Szabó (1996) argue that an awareness of under-lying metaphorical constructs is pedagogically valuable. It can help by foregrounding system and similarity, and providing a basis from which unfamiliar combinations can be understood. While they do not suggest that *all* idioms can be explicated in terms of metaphor-ical constructs, they assert that 'many, or perhaps most, idioms are products of our conceptual system and not simply a matter of language (i.e. a matter of the lexicon)'.

It is, in fact, hardly surprising that cultural constructs underlie metaphorical FEIs. After all, metaphors, especially institutionalized ones, exploit certain characteristics inherent in the vehicle and applicable to the tenor, and inevitably also exploit well-understood characteristics such as 'fire=heat' or 'fire=danger'. We make use of conventional real-world knowledge about the nature of things in order to interpret non-literal meanings. The problem is precisely as Kövecses and Szabó say (1996: 330) 'when we say that the meaning of an idiom is motivated we are not claiming that its meaning is fully predictable'. The exploration and analysis of motivations which inform metaphors and the synthesis of the motivations into systems is ultimately post hoc, providing a wise-after-the-event explanation. It has little predictive power. Even with a basic concept such as fire and related phenomena such as flames, heat, and sparks, there is a very large number of potential ideas to be exploited in FEIs and metaphors, as Kövecses and Szabó show. An unfamiliar metaphor can be interpreted by means of real-world knowledge about the source domain where this is ambiguous, but the correct metaphorical system in use can only be ascertained if or when the correct reading and hence correct target domain is known. For example, *wet blanket* can be rationalized in terms of 'fire is enthusiasm'—something that dampens enthusiasm or puts out fire—but historically and practically, it could as easily have developed a meaning 'something that prevents or stops danger, a safeguard'. Similarly, Kövecses and Szabó (1996: 344) link *have clean hands* to a structural metaphor 'ethical is clean', relating it to *he got his hands dirty*. In fact, *have dirty hands* and their later *have blood on one's hands* would be better examples: *get one's hands dirty* relates rather to their metonymy 'the hands stand for the activity', since it generally implies positively evaluated practical involvement and usually diligence, rather than unethical behaviour. Compare the discussion of ambiguity and analogy in Section 7.2.

Some recent psycholinguistics work, for example that reported in Gibbs (1992), broadly supports the validity of conceptual metaphorical constructs. However, Keysar and Bly (1995) investigated the transparency of idioms and the abilities of informants to make connections between metaphorical and literal or conceptual meanings. They chose 20 obsolete or unfamiliar idioms, which included *the goose hangs high* 'things are looking good', *to row cross-handed* 'to be self-reliant', and *to play the bird with the long neck* 'to be out looking for something or someone'. Informants were given contexts with the original, 'correct' meanings; with the opposite meanings; and with completely different meanings. Keysar and Bly suggest as a result that 'native speakers' intuitions about the transparency of idioms systematically depends on their knowledge of the stipulated meaning of the idiom. They argue that conceptual metaphors only account for a few cases and that 'intuitions [concerning transparency and conceptual metaphors] are partly a product of the links created as a result of the conventional use of the idiom'.

There are very clearly strong metaphorical systems at work—or at play—within FEIs. However, these systems need to be seen as only a partial explanation of diachronic processes. To be more than that would be to become too abstract to be meaningful. What theories of conceptual metaphors *do* offer is a very important insight into the ways in which features may be systematically transferred between source and target domains, as an explanation of motivation. They may indeed be linked into problem-solving strategies rather than providing cast-iron rules for the interpretation of the unfamiliar.

7.6 MEANINGS AND MISMATCHING

The database entries for predicate FEIs recorded the type of verbal process that they embody; for nominal groups, the type of thing that they refer to; for adjectival groups, the type of attribute; and for adjuncts, the type of circumstance. I also recorded cases where the surface lexical meaning of an FEI is different in kind from its deep idiomatic meaning: in the case of metaphorical FEIs, I routinely recorded both surface and deep meanings, even where these were not different in type. Findings are set out in the following sections.

This sort of analysis provides evidence of the kinds of metaphorical relationship embodied in FEIs, and some preliminary data with respect to the relative frequencies of the kinds of metaphorical relationship. It will be seen that there is comparative consistency in the way in which metaphors become institutionalized and fossilize into FEIs. This sheds light on the metaphorization process, suggesting that certain kinds of metaphor are more likely than others. The wholesale concrete to abstract transfer has applications when texts are considered as discourses and when their subtextual messages are analysed: compare discussions of FEIs in discourse in Chapters 9 and 10.

7.6.1 Predicate FEIs

I used Halliday's model of verbal processes (1985: 101ff.; 1994: 106ff.) as the basis for the description of predicates. It can be represented as shown in Table 7.7, using Halliday's terminology and examples, but simplifying it.

Table 7.8 shows the findings as applied to FEIs.

The verbal processes of database FEIs occur in the proportions shown in Table 7.9. This suggests that FEIs are generally descriptive and are either expressing material processes or else attributing qualities.

The most interesting cases are, of course, those where there is mismatching between the lexical meaning or process and the idiomatic meaning or process. Indeed, as Chafe (1968), Newmeyer (1974), and others have pointed out, mismatching may account for transformational deficiencies: if the deep process is intransitive, then apparently transitive verbs cannot passivize. Nunberg *et al.* (1994) develop such points further, and see transformations and structural restrictions as resulting from the kinds of metaphor embodied in idioms. Examples of mismatching in database FEIs are shown in Table 7.10. By far the commonest case is for the lexical or surface process to be an action, and the idiomatic or deep process to be something else. Mismatching occurs in approximately

TABLE 7.7. *Halliday's model of verbal processes*

material processes	event	the lion sprang
	action	the lion caught the tourist
mental processes	affection	Mary liked the gift
		the gift pleased Mary
	cognition	I know
		I believe you
		the quiet puzzles me
	perception	it hurts my ears
relational	attributive	Sarah is wise
		the fair is on a Tuesday
		Peter has a piano
	identifying	Tom is the leader
		the piano is Peter's
behavioural		Buff neither laughs nor weeps
verbal		John said I'm hungry
existential		there was a storm

Source: Halliday (1985; 1994).

TABLE 7.8. *Verbal processes and FEIs*

event	cut and run, fend for ONEself, make do
action	bring SOMEONE to justice, make money, lay SOMETHING waste
affection	feel bad, can't abide SOMETHING, hold no terrors for SOMEONE
cognition	know ONE's stuff, fail to see—, make sense
perception	see double, can't hear ONEself think
attributive	be at SOMEONE's beck and call, go hungry, hold sway
identifying	—is the operative word, the operative word is—
behavioural	pull a face, knit ONE's brow, blow (SOMEONE) a kiss
verbal	let it be known, talk shop, speak ONE's mind
existential	be the case, therein lies—

67% of predicate metaphorical FEIs. The commonest patterns of mismatch are shown in Table 7.11. The tendency is clear. Transitive material processes or concrete actions in the lexis actually denote intransitive material processes or mental or verbal processes. Both transitive and intransitive material processes in the lexis actually denote attributive (and evaluative) processes. Thus semantic metaphors are also grammatical metaphors. Compare Lakoff and Turner (1989: *passim*), who explore the conceptual metaphor 'events are actions': that is, events are described in terms of actions, or actions in the lexis/vehicle correspond to events in the denotatum/tenor.

All this is important semantically, but it is also important discoursally. There is a great difference between a text where the processes are material, contributing to a narrative and presenting clear statements about cause, circumstance, and so on, and a text where the processes are superficially material but actually grammatical metaphors for, say, mental and relational processes. Material processes are inevitably associated with fact and objective report, whereas mental and relational processes are associated more with

TABLE 7.9. *Proportions of verbal processes in FEIs*

event	23%
action	19%
affection	9%
cognition	8%
perception	2%
attributive	29%
identifying	1%
behavioural	1%
verbal	7%
existential	2%

TABLE 7.10. *Mismatching of verbal processes*

	Lexical process	Idiomatic process
be going strong	event	attributive
blow ONE's own trumpet	action	verbal
break the ice	action	verbal
fit the bill	action	attributive
follow suit	action	event
gather dust	action	attributive
go up in smoke	event	existential
hit the headlines	action	existential
jog SOMEONE's memory	action	cognition
lose ONE's heart	action	affection
make the grade	action	attributive
paint a — picture	action	verbal
put ONE's finger on SOMETHING	action	cognition
run out of steam	event	attributive
set sail	action	event
smack ONE's lips	action	affection
throw in the towel	action	event
turn SOMEONE's stomach	action	affection

evaluation and subjective comment. By disguising the second as the first, subjective opinions may appear more objective, more purely descriptive of some actual, physical situation, although in reality they communicate an interpretation and evaluation of that situation. Hence vivid FEIs such as *get hold of the wrong end of the stick, sweep something under the carpet,* and *change one's tune* use material processes as metaphors for mental processes, and *lose one's bottle, come out in the wash,* and *live from hand to mouth* use material processes as metaphors for relational ones. This may have a significant effect on a text, with a covert message quite different from

TABLE 7.11. *Commonest kinds of mismatch*

Lexical process	Idiomatic process	
action	event	13%
action	attributive	13%
event	attributive	9%
action	verbal	4%
action	affection	4%
action	cognition	3%

TABLE 7.12.   *Commonest referents of nominal FEIs*

event, situation	36%	a slip of the pen
		a shot in the arm
		a rude awakening
		funny business
		a fortune of war
person	14%	ONE's kith and kin
		a figure of fun
		the chosen few
quality	13%	airs and graces
		second nature
		turn of speed
thing	11%	hearth and home
		bits and bobs
		ONE's proudest
		possession

the surface meaning: compare the analysis of a text in these terms in Moon 1994*a* and 1994*b*: 310ff.

7.6.2 *Nominal Groups*

The commonest referents of FEIs functioning as nominal groups are shown in Table 7.12. When cases of mismatching are examined, the surface lexis typically denotes something concrete, whereas the deep meanings are more abstract. FEIs whose deep meanings denote people are usually commenting on character; such FEIs usually refer to concrete objects or animals in the surface lexis: see Table 7.13. This demonstrates the concretization of concepts and qualities typical of metaphors. Compare Lakoff and Turner (1989) and their metaphor 'states are locations', corresponding to the second grouping in Table 7.13. See Nunberg *et al.* (1994: 528ff.) for further discussion of correspondences between animate/inanimate and literal/idiomatic.

7.6.3 *Adjectival Groups*

Comparatively few database FEIs are predicative or postnominal adjectival groups. Their commonest meanings are shown in Table 7.14. The commonest cases of mismatching again involve concrete vehicles and abstract tenors: see Table 7.15.

TABLE 7.13.   *Mismatching in nominal FEIs*

Lexical meaning	Idiomatic meaning	
thing	situation, event	a Gordian Knot a can of worms a sticky wicket the tip of the iceberg cakes and ale the final curtain
place	situation, event	uncharted waters/territory pastures new hell on earth the end of the road the fast lane
thing	quality	a roving eye sticky fingers a chink in SOMEONE's armour a screw loose a short fuse
thing	person	a tough cookie a wet blanket a chip off the old block a rough diamond the salt of the earth
animal	person	a snake in the grass a lone wolf a big fish in a little pond a sitting duck the black sheep of the family

TABLE 7.14. *Commonest functions of adjectival FEIs*

describing a physical characteristic	50%	fast asleep fit and well stark naked
describing a quality	21%	free and easy holier than thou short and sweet
classifying/identifying	10%	born and bred null and void short for—
describing a situation or state	9%	flat broke over and done with ready and waiting

TABLE 7.15. *Mismatching in adjectival FEIs*

Lexical meaning	Idiomatic meaning	
physical characteristic	quality	dry as dust full of beans straight as a die wet behind the ears
physical characteristic	situation or state	all dressed up with nowhere to go cut/pared to the bone first past the post

7.6.4 *Adjuncts*

The distribution of basic adjunct types was discussed in Section 5.3.5. Mismatching is fairly mixed, but there is predictably evidence of concretization in the vehicles of the metaphors: see Table 7.16.

TABLE 7.16 *Mismatching in adverbial FEIs*

Lexical meaning	Idiomatic meaning	
place, position	circumstances, situation	at ONE's fingertips between a rock and a hard place beyond the pale in hot water in the same boat out of the woods out on a limb with ONE's back to the wall
other physical	circumstances situation	at rest in step on tap on the wane out for the count
place	manner	close to ONE's chest eyeball to eyeball on a shoestring on the side under the counter
manner	degree	in leaps and bounds by a whisker like poison with flying colours
direction	manner	from pillar to post off the top of ONE's head out of the blue straight from the shoulder
place	time	around the corner (=soon) on the horizon over ONE's dead body under the wire

8

Discoursal Functions of FEIs

The description and quantification of FEIs and their characteristics helps to define them in relation to the lexicon, but not in relation to discourse. An analysis of *the worm turns* in OHPC shows that it occurs 6 times, or once in every 3 million words, just above the significance threshold; that its clausal structure of fixed lexical subject and verb occurs in only 1% of predicate FEIs in the database; that it is metaphorical; and that while its lexical verbal process is material and denotes an event, its deep process is also relational as it implies an attribute. A look at the expression in context, however, suggests other aspects. For example, a newspaper article concerns the predilection of fashion writers and others for wearing black, but observes evidence that brighter colours may come into vogue. The last two paragraphs read:

Rifat Ozbek, whose spring collection includes some brilliantly coloured Turkish jackets believes that the tide may be turning. 'I think that black will continue, but it won't be as strong. It'll lose that fashion victim thing that it's had for the last three years. We'll be mixing it with colour and not wearing it in the black-on-black, high techy sort of way any more.'

The signs are that **the worm may indeed be on the turn**.[1] Fashion people are at last expressing boredom with their dour wardrobes and seeing something of the silly side of their obsession with black. I've even gone and bought myself a jacket in pillar box red, and after settling down from the hysteria at my own daring, I have to announce that it feels rather good. (The *Guardian*, 22 January 1987)

Compare two of the examples from OHPC:

The petit-bourgeoisie was an easy target for governments keen to raise a little more in taxes. Their common-sense ideas about life, good house-keeping and the rest were ignored by government after government, who regarded them as an over-productive milch-cow. There was a cultural bias

---

[1] This form of the FEI, *the worm (is) on the turn*, rather than *the worm is turning*, is itself a manipulation, showing cohesion with *the tide may be turning* in the previous paragraph, since *on the turn* typically collocates with *tide*, not *worm*. This further strengthens the cohesive ties in the text.

against them too: much of British theatre and cinema in the fifties and sixties was peopled by heroes and anti-heroes wrestling with the small-mindedness of the lower-middle class. It was predictable, if not predicted, that one day **the worm would turn**. Mrs Thatcher was a natural to lead the revolt of the petite-bourgeoisie. (OHPC: non-fiction)

Unlike Americans, the British never had much of a grounding in rugged individualism. They went from forelock touching feudalism to the we'll-look-after-you welfare state without a decent period of aggressive citizenship in between. **The worm has turned** and demand now swells for a separate green ministry and a food watchdog agency far from the clutches of the Ministry of Agriculture. (OHPC: journalism)

The FEI has an important evaluative component: in particular, it evaluates positively the action or behaviour of a person or group who has been negatively evaluated, typically as weak, dull, passive, or submissive (in the first example, people unimaginative enough to wear black). *The worm* relexicalizes, incorporating evaluation, the group already discussed. The predicator *turn* contrasts with the inaction or inertia previously mentioned, and refers forward to an action or situation that will be positively evaluated. The FEI functions as a discourse signal, acting as a bridge between statements of the status quo and of a new state of things, thus providing both anaphoric and cataphoric reference.

Studies of FEIs from pragmatic perspectives can of course be found. For example, those by Strässler (1982) and Lattey (1986) are rooted in the pragmatics of interaction; Sadock (1972, 1974), Morgan (1978), Gibbs (1986*b*) and others discuss idioms as speech acts and speech acts as idioms, because of their specialized language forms; Nattinger and DeCarrico (1992) discuss semi-fixed strings with respect to discoursal function; Aijmer (1996) discusses conversational routines in spoken interaction; Fraser (1996) discusses and categorizes pragmatic markers, including many examples of FEIs; and Fernando (forthcoming) will make a particular study of the discoursal properties and behaviour of idioms. But in general, studies of FEIs focus more often on their formal properties, whereas pragmatics-based lexical and collocational studies focus on the interactional properties of semi-fixed strings rather than FEIs. One of my principal aims in establishing a database was to inventorize the functions of FEIs in (corpus) text in order to explore those functions and establish correlations between function, form, and frequency. This chapter reports the findings.

8.1 A CLASSIFICATION OF TEXT FUNCTIONS

The text functions of FEIs may be classified according to the way in which they contribute to the content and structure of a text. The precise contribution is instantial and bound up with context, but it is nevertheless possible to generalize and to chart typical functions. In the model I developed for the database, I categorized FEIs according to five functions (see Table 8.1). I will discuss these functions in more detail in the following sections. Note that organizational FEIs in particular and some modalizing ones reflect the process of grammaticalization (compare Hopper and Closs Traugott 1993), whereby a string develops a specific grammatical or semi-grammatical function.

The functions of FEIs can be related to Halliday's model of the semantic components of language (for example, in Halliday 1978:

TABLE 8.1.   *Text functions of FEIs*

Category	Function	
informational	stating proposition, conveying information	rub shoulders with in the running catch sight of SOMETHING for sale
evaluative	conveying speaker's evaluation and attitude	kid's stuff a different/fine kettle of fish near the knuckle it's an ill wind (that blows nobody any good)
situational	relating to extralinguistic context, responding to situation	excuse me! long time no see knock it off! talk of the devil
modalizing	conveying truth values, advice, requests, etc.	I kid you not you know what I mean to all intents and purposes if in doubt, do nowt
organizational	organizing text, signalling discourse structure	by the way for instance talking of — be that as it may

TABLE 8.2. *Halliday's model of text components*

ideational	experiential	communication of ideas
	logical	connections between ideas
interpersonal	interactional	interrelationship between speaker and hearer
		mood
		illocution
	personal	modality
		attitude
textual	theme	thematization and thematic patterning
	information	given/new distinction
	cohesion	cohesive structure

Source: Halliday (1978); Morley (1985).

116 ff.), but they are not identical to it. Halliday's model can be represented as shown in Table 8.2, following Morley's synthesis (1985: 44–81). The model views text in terms of its semantic stratification into ideational, interpersonal, and textual or textural components: it is a model for the interpretation of ongoing dynamic discourse. Any selection has repercussions at all levels, and the levels are simultaneous. Halliday also shows how in the context of a functional grammar specific items, including multi-word items, can be linked to specific macro-functions (for example, 1985: 50; 1994: 49).

Ideational, interpersonal, and textual components operate at the highest level—at the level of discourse. In contrast, the text functions of FEIs described here are lower-level functions, reflecting the immediate effects of FEIs within their co-texts: the model developed is simply intended to provide a way of monitoring these effects. Figure 8.1 shows how FEI functions cluster with respect to the ideational and interpersonal components. The textual component, the 'enabling function', is best considered instantially in

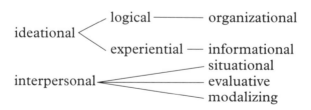

FIG. 8.1 Ideational and interpersonal, related to FEI functions

terms of the ways in which FEIs are placed topically and thematically, or contribute cohesion to their texts: see Chapter 10.

The text functions of FEIs are, of course, common to the lexicon in general, and individual words or freely formed strings may be analysed similarly as contributing information, evaluations, situational reactions, modality, or organization to their texts. FEIs are not special in this respect. Nevertheless, I want to emphasize that the roles FEIs have in real-time discourse are no less significant than their lexical, syntactic, and semantic characteristics. Neglecting or ignoring these roles may lead to discoursal ill-formedness in encoding and to misinterpretation in decoding.

8.2 DISTRIBUTION AND TEXT FUNCTIONS

Proportions of text functions in database FEIs are as shown in Table 8.3. This looks solely at primary functions. The **primary function** of an FEI is its most salient function, determined by ascertaining what kind of information is most strongly and typically conveyed by an FEI in the contexts in which it occurred in OHPC. There are many cases of multiple or secondary functions: see Section 8.8. It is important to point out in advance that if secondary functions are taken into account too, a very large number of FEIs are partly evaluative or partly modalizing, in addition to their primary function. However, in Tables 8.4–8.6, only primary functions are considered in order to simplify the discussion.

TABLE 8.3. *FEI proportions according to text function*

informational	41%
evaluative	38%
situational	5%
modalizing	10%
organizational	6%

TABLE 8.4. *FEI proportions: frequency and text function*

	<1/m	*1–10/m*	*10+/m*
all functions	72%	25%	3%
informational	29%	11%	1%
evaluative	32%	6%	<1%
situational	5%	<1%	<0.1%
modalizing	4%	4%	1%
organizational	2%	3%	1%

TABLE 8.5. *FEI proportions: text function and grammatical type*

	Inform- ational	Evalu- ative	Situa- tional	Modal- izing	Organiz- ational
predicates	21%	18%	<1%	2%	<1%
nominal groups	2%	6%	<0.1%	<1%	<1%
adjectival groups	<1%	1%	<0.1%	0.1%	<0.1%
modifiers	<1%	<1%		<0.1%	<0.1%
determiners				<0.1%	<0.1%
quantifiers	<1%	<0.1%		<1%	<0.1%
adjuncts	17%	8%	<0.1%	2%	1%
submodifiers	<0.1%	<1%	<0.1%	<1%	
disjuncts	<0.1%	<1%	<0.1%	2%	<1%
conjuncts				<1%	2%
conventions	<1%	5%	5%	1%	<1%
exclamations		<0.1%	<1%		
subordinate clauses	<0.1%	<0.1%	<0.1%	<1%	<1%
conjunctions					<1%
fillers, others	<0.1%	<0.1%	<0.1%	<1%	<1%

Text functions can be correlated with frequency bands: see Table 8.4. Proportionally more high-frequency FEIs are modalizing or organizational: this is predictable since these are the most grammatical of FEIs. The evaluative function is dramatically more common in low-frequency FEIs than middle-frequency ones. Because such expressions are infrequent, they are highly marked: this ties in with their uses as rhetorical devices for the expression of evaluations.

Correlations between syntactic type and text function are also predictable: see Table 8.5. In particular, predicate FEIs are typically informational or evaluative; nominal and adjectival groups are typically evaluative; adjuncts are typically informational; and conventions are typically evaluative or situational. The relationship between function and syntax reflects the general information structure of text, and may be set out as shown in Figure 8.2, after Halliday (1985; 1994). FEIs are realized either as whole or part rhemes (predicates in non-Hallidayan terms) or as grammatical or discoursal operators.

informational	rheme (or component of rheme)
evaluative	rheme (or component of rheme)
organizational	conjunctive adjunct
modalizing	modal adjunct

FIG. 8.2 FEI functions, related to text structure (after Halliday)

TABLE 8.6. *FEI proportions: idiomaticity type and text function*

	Anomalous collocations	Formulae	Metaphors
(all functions	45.3%	21.3%	33.4%)
informational	25%	4%	13%
evaluative	11%	9%	18%
situational	1%	4%	<1%
modalizing	5%	3%	1%
organizational	3%	2%	<1%

Finally, a correlation of text functions with idiomaticity type shows metaphors and formulae to be typically evaluative, and anomalous collocations to be most typically informational: see Table 8.6.

8.3 INFORMATIONAL FEIS

Informational FEIs are vehicles for conveying new information and contribute to a discourse propositionally. Some examples are:

behind bars
by default
clear ONE's throat
down tools
face to face
fast asleep
for sale
in flower
in the red
ONE's kith and kin
on sale
set foot SOMEWHERE
step by step
ONE's waking hours
wide awake
wear and tear

The information conveyed may be of various kinds. It may describe a process, state, or quality, in which case the FEI typically takes the form of a predicate, adjectival group, or postnominal qualifier:

It was a great thrill to **catch sight of** my team-mates as I got near to the pavilion. If you're going to bat for any reason, it's for the respect of your team-mates. (OHPC: journalism)

Industrial production came to a standstill as factory workers **downed tools** and went off across the Wall. (OHPC: journalism)

General Wojciech Jaruzelski may be back **in the running** for the post of Polish president. (OHPC: journalism)

The gallery holds about 500 works, and there are 1,000 **in reserve**. (OHPC: journalism)

The information may be circumstantial in nature, and describe time, place, manner, or circumstances and so on. Such FEIs typically take the form of adjuncts:

Then, at about 6.50pm, the gunmen opened fire **at close range** from behind some foliage. (OHPC: journalism)

The state of London's traffic—moving, if at all, as though axle-deep in a vast lake of porridge—has provoked one firm of couriers to turn back to making deliveries **on foot**. (OHPC: journalism)

On Saturdays, they dress up and go into town for a night out **on the razzle**. (OHPC: journalism)

Other types of information conveyed include the simple naming of entities, quantification, and description:

Upholstered furniture came under fire, with quality problems in a third of all purchases within five years. Early signs of **wear and tear** caused most difficulties. (OHPC: journalism)

Rising at 5.30 in the morning, her **waking hours** are devoted to her horses. (OHPC: journalism)

Sergeant Roy Eglinton and WPC Sharon Giles were trying to arrest a man on suspicion of being **drunk and disorderly**. (OHPC: journalism)

It has already been seen that informational FEIs are the commonest type of FEI in the database (41%), and that 70% of informational FEIs are in the lowest frequency bands, with 27% in the middle ones—a distributional spread almost identical to that observed across FEIs in the database in general. Conveying information is a very basic language function, and informational FEIs are the most basic of all. However, correlating discourse function with idiomaticity type shows that a comparatively high proportion of informational FEIs were classified as anomalous collocations—just under 60%, compared with just over 45% in the database as a whole—whereas comparatively few of them were formulae—just under 10%, compared with 21%. The proportion of metaphorical informational FEIs is 31%, which is fairly close to the 33% of database metaphors. Speculating why they should be distributed like this sheds light on the behaviour of FEIs in text. The conveying of information is a creative, text-forming process, and is less likely to be marked and stereotyped. Anomalous collocations are classifiable as FEIs largely on the grounds that they are lexicogrammatically non-compositional: they are often unmarked and uninteresting 'ways of saying things', adding little to the text stylistically. Formulae, on the other hand, are by definition stereotypes. They repeat familiar ideas, clichés, or thoughts, and even where they are used to convey new information, as in the case of some similes, they do so by appealing to cultural norms. Marked repetition in general is associated with corroboration, emphasis, and appeals to norms or shared views, rather than information-giving.

8.4 EVALUATIVE FEIS

Evaluative FEIs communicate the evaluations of the speaker/writer, rather than simply furthering the narrative, and examples include:

a tall order
come unstuck
do the trick
down to earth
drag ONE's feet, drag ONE's heels
get off to a flying start
have/with SOMETHING to show for —
in the doldrums
make the grade
over the top
second to none
strike a balance
the icing on the cake
to good effect
SOMEONE's trump card
work wonders

Many evaluative FEIs constitute the rhemes of clauses, appearing in the forms of predicates or after copulas:

After 12 years in power, the Tories had **run out of steam**. (OHPC: journalism)

I think this government is really trying to wash its hands of the national museums and galleries. The only exception is this Imperial War Museum, which **speaks for itself**. (OHPC: journalism)

His serve was never quite **up to scratch** and his timing on the ball lacked conviction. (OHPC: journalism)

We believe these improvements will ensure that The Independent remains **second to none** in the breadth and depth of its coverage. (OHPC: journalism)

Others appear as nominal groups, or in prenominal position:

His seat in the Lords is, for him, only **the icing on the cake**. (OHPC: journalism)

But The Company of Heaven plc—launched at Aldeburgh and in the USA last year, and now introduced to London at the start of the Spital-fields Festival—is a bit of **a lame duck** in the concert hall. (OHPC: journalism)

To have the affairs of a club of such majesty as Manchester United conducted in a **hole and corner** manner has sickened more than many of their vast, worldwide following. (OHPC: journalism)

Only a few FEIs that operate as adjuncts are evaluative:

His fondness for the lyrically enigmatic and illogical, however, can lead him **up a few gum-trees** here and there. (OHPC: journalism)

Our company was expanding into overseas markets **in leaps and bounds**. (OHPC: journalism)

In contrast, evaluations are conveyed by a relatively large number of FEIs functioning as whole clauses, conventions, or prefacing clauses:

Thus it is advisable that the period of bridging finance is minimized if the mortgagee is not to suffer disproportionate expense in servicing this short-term loan. Yet **there is a silver lining to this particular cloud**. If a bridging mortgage is being used for the purpose of purchasing the mort-gagee's sole or main residence, at the discretion of the Inland Revenue, it too may qualify for mortgage interest relief and this can be claimed retrospectively. (OHPC: non-fiction)

A Foreign Ministry statement said: '**It is high time** for the civilised world to act in unity and see to it that Saddam Hussein will not be able to pursue his irresponsible designs.' (OHPC: journalism)

Even where proverbs are downgraded to predicates, they typically retain evaluative content:

The internal row is essentially between the leaders and the ranks. Mr Lech Walesa and his coterie of aides show every sign of seeking **to have their cake and eat it**. Just prior to Wednesday's vote, the leadership was treading a fine line, pledging support for the President, while avoiding being seen to vote for him. (OHPC: journalism)

There is only one glimmer of hope, although pessimists say it could be **clutching at straws**. (OHPC: journalism)

Evaluative FEIs are often metaphorical. Whereas 33% of database FEIs in general were classified as metaphors, 47% of evaluative FEIs are metaphors. Moreover, 24% of evaluative FEIs were classified as formulae, but a number of these are similes or proverbs with metaphorical content. The picture is more marked if dual classifications and subclassifications are considered, since 89% of all database FEIs with any metaphorical or simile content have some evaluative function. This suggests that the use of institutionalized metaphors is stylistic, bound up with evaluation, and centred on the interaction: see further discussion of evaluation and FEIs in Chapter 9.

8.5 SITUATIONAL FEIS

Situational FEIs are typically found in spoken discourse as they are responses to or occasioned by the extralinguistic context: they may also be illocutionary speech acts. They are therefore constrained by real-world sociocultural factors. They generally appear syntactically as conventions, clauses, and exclamations. Examples include:

excuse me
go for it
good luck
good morning
I beg your pardon
it's a small world
no problem
put a sock in it
see you
up yours
walls have ears
well done

They may be grouped according to function, and the following is intended simply to show the range. For example, greetings and valedictions:

Hello, **good afternoon** I'm just ringing in response to the previous caller you had on actually. (OHPC: transcribed radio programme)

'**So long**, René, take care of her,' Craig called as they pushed him out through the waves and the tiny outboard motor carried him on. (OHPC: fiction)

In view of the recent arson attacks, both at the Upper School and the playgroup, I wonder if some of today's pupils would feel like repeating this act of charity? **Yours sincerely** [etc.] (OHPC: letter in journalism)

and apologies, congratulations, commiserations, thanks, acknowledgements, and so on:

Excuse me, Colonel, I meant no offence. (OHPC: fiction)

'I'm sorry'. 'Oh **never mind**. Shit, hell.' (OHPC: fiction)

'Well, I'm really grateful to you, **thank you very much** for giving me your time,' he told her with his most plausible smile. (OHPC: fiction)

There are also palliatives and other miscellaneous ritual utterances, such as *touch wood*, *bless you* (as a response to someone's sneezing), and toasts:

'**Least said, soonest mended**,' Aunt Rose said, gazing meaningfully at the nursemaid. 'There's **no harm done** and they didn't get far. No need to make too much of it now.' (OHPC: fiction)

These are mostly conventionalized utterances, routines, and gambits. They are typically formulaic, compositional strings of words with pragmatic functions: see Aijmer (1996) for discussion of, in particular, rituals of thanking and apologizing. Of those situational FEIs classified as anomalous collocations, some are grammatically ill formed, such as *good morning*, *so long*, and *thank you*, and others simply defective collocations—diachronically, they are elided or reduced relics of grammatical and formulaic utterances. Only rarely are situational FEIs metaphorical, and these include a few cases such as *walls have ears* and *talk of the devil* which are used to comment on the situation itself.

8.6 MODALIZING FEIS

Modalizing FEIs are hyperpropositional: they indicate modality. This is typically epistemic or deontic in nature, although some FEIs may be regarded as conative or volitive.[2] Examples include:

as we know it
at all
at any price
believe you me
full well
I mean

---

[2] The following makes use of a very simple model of modality: cf. the much more delicate terminology and categories used by Palmer (1986).

if need be
in effect
in principle
in the short run
more or less
no doubt
on no account
or so
to all intents and purposes
up to a point

The majority of FEIs that function as disjuncts are modalizing:

You couldn't **by any stretch of the imagination** call Arthur Miller's *After The Fall* a comedy. (OHPC: journalism)

I mean Leonardo, **without question** one of the most outstanding geniuses the world has ever known . . . (OHPC: interview in journalism)

These rules are **by and large** irrelevant in dealing with the terminally ill patient who is, **in a sense**, in a special class. Such a patient is, **by definition**, going to die sooner rather than later. (OHPC: non-fiction)

Modalizing FEIs also occur as adjuncts, postnominal groups, and submodifiers:

The result is equivalent to abandoning consequentialism **in all but name**. (OHPC: non-fiction)

Mr Hart said it was 'perverse **in the extreme**' to demand a regular review of any new head's performance but not to make any extra performance incentive payments. (OHPC: journalism)

This time our backs are **well and truly** against the wall. Last week the press had us as favourites, now we are underdogs. (OHPC: journalism)

In addition, some predicate FEIs, adjectival groups, and complete clauses are modalizing:

Like influenza and sexual desire, the alternative press **comes and goes** in cycles. (OHPC: journalism)

How much time he'll spend at the English bar is **open to question**. (OHPC: journalism)

This was to have been a carve-up reflective of Ferrasse's absolute power. But suddenly **all bets are off**. (OHPC: journalism)

Sir Geoffrey Howe, as tight-lipped as you can get without surgical assistance, muttered: '**No comment**. I have made my support clear on earlier occasions.' (OHPC: journalism)

Over half of modalizing FEIs were classified as anomalous collocations, and around a third are formulaic. They are therefore relatively unmarked in text in comparison with the few modalizing FEIs that are metaphorical, for example *on the cards*, *by a long chalk*, and *by the skin of one's teeth*. Since the modality conveyed by FEIs in their discourses is important, the following looks more closely at its different kinds.

8.6.1 *Epistemic Modalizers*

Two-thirds of the FEIs that I classified as modalizing are primarily epistemic. They can loosely be described as representing the speaker/writer's commitment to the truth value of the discourse. There are many shadings within this group, and I will only describe major types.

A few epistemic FEIs are existential, and vehicles for a proposition that states the way things are. Examples include *be the case*, *under way*, *bear witness to something*, and *the state of play*:

This in fact seems to be very much the situation which anthropologists have found in pre-capitalist systems, and this **was the case** with the Malagasy people I studied. (OHPC: non-fiction)

In 1986 the scheme was well **under way**, affecting in Northern Ireland alone round 218 miles of watercourse, which was stripped of vegetation over many reaches. (OHPC: non-fiction)

Many epistemic modalizers are used to indicate likelihood and probability (*(as) like as not*, *on the cards*, *a foregone conclusion*) or improbability (*in a month of Sundays*):

Grandini isn't alone in designing the car, though. There is a Bertone version **on the cards** and it's believed both Pininfarina and ItalDesign have also put forward proposals. (OHPC: journalism)

The final victory of May 1945 came only just in time. It was **touch-and-go**, not **a foregone conclusion**. (OHPC: non-fiction)

Related to these are expressions such as *to come*, *on the verge of —*, and *on the horizon* which indicate futurity in different ways:

Sometimes they would take journalists to the front line; sometimes they would risk their lives to help reporters. Or they would rob them or threaten to execute them. One day, in years **to come**, they would kidnap them, too. (OHPC: non-fiction)

. . . Korda was having problems raising cash to fund production, and his British Lion company was **on the verge of** bankruptcy. (OHPC: non-fiction)

Another area where trouble could be **on the horizon** is religion. (OHPC: journalism)

Frequentative FEIs generally express epistemic modality, for example *from time to time, in — cases, as usual,* and *once in a blue moon*: these overlap with the previous subgroupings:

In many cases, Hume says, actions are virtuous because of the motives which produce them. (OHPC: non-fiction)
From time to time the authorities got wind of these breaches of regulations and punished clubs. (OHPC: non-fiction)

Many modalizing FEIs add emphasis. Some add it to the propositions conveyed in their co-texts, for example *at any price, come rain or shine, by far, far and away,* and *like nobody's business*:

I would not have his job **at any price**. (OHPC: journalism)
Prost drove **by far and away** his best race of the season. (OHPC: journalism)

Others add emphasis by indicating certainty or drawing attention to the veracity of the utterance, for example *mark my words, I kid you not, it stands to reason, there's no mistaking,* and *no doubt*:

It stands to reason, therefore, that outlay on buildings and equipment should be kept to the minimum required for the efficient production of healthy crops and livestock. (OHPC: non-fiction)
No firm decision is expected until after another forum in January. But **there can be no mistaking** the determination of the EC's DGXV, responsible for financial institutions and company law. (OHPC: journalism)
Mark my words, at this very moment, someone is trying to cash in on this supermarket trolley fetish with some useless bit of equipment or other. (OHPC: journalism)
The favourite means of breaking the ice are a 14lb weight, a pick-axe or an anchor, but the latest method is a chainsaw. **I kid you not**. The start of a canal competition on really freezing winter days sounds like a giant swarm of killer bees on the loose. (OHPC: journalism)

Related to these are expressions with which speakers/writers engage more directly in the interaction by negotiating meaning and truth values. For example, *in a (very) real sense/in any real sense, I take it, you're joking,* and pre-emptive *needless to say*:

But until that happened, he was debtor of the company only and no asset of his was, **in any real sense**, available for the payment of the firm's creditors. (OHPC: journalism)

Needless to say, mismanagement on an international scale has been the legacy of our generation in Europe. (OHPC: non-fiction)

Other modalizing FEIs negate, deny, or cast doubt, for example *in no sense, not always, no way*, and *be open to debate*:

We are **in no sense** promoting or supporting the introduction of the legislation. (OHPC: journalism)

Whether this indicates that men are more adept at driving, or simply more confident about the test, is **open to debate**. (OHPC: journalism)

Some FEIs indicate ignorance, disclaim knowledge, or defer judgement: for example *no comment, not that I know, that's news to me*, and *time will tell*:

British Waterways fisheries officer John Ellis said: 'The pollution **is news to me**. I shall have to investigate the matter with the NRA.' (OHPC: journalism)

What the repercussions will be in South Africa—where the ageing president, Danie Craven, has threatened to support rebel tours—**only time will tell**. (OHPC: journalism)

A few modalizing FEIs indicate corrections and modifications, for example *I tell a lie*, and some uses of the polysemous FEIs *at least, in fact*, and *I mean*. *Jump to conclusions* typically indicates correction and criticism of someone other than the speaker/writer. See Kay (1992) for an extended discussion of *at least*, and Aijmer (1996: 223 f.) for discussion of *in (actual) fact*:

. . . we're really beginning to understand now that what people are doing when they program indeed, **I mean as it were** the ace programmers, are expressing their intention for whatever's to be done in the task the computer's to perform clearly. (OHPC: transcribed radio discussion)

It's likely that you have been misled in some way or another and **are jumping to conclusions**, so don't worry too much. (OHPC: journalism)

While many modalizing FEIs emphasize, many others mitigate or downtone by indicating vagueness and retreating from definite assertion, for example, *in part, sort of, in a way*, and *more or less*: 'surface markers of detachment' (Stubbs 1996: 208):

Bewator employs just 45 people but it is on the success of small, growing companies of this type that Sweden's industrial future success will **in part** depend. (OHPC: journalism)

Yet that **in a way** is what you would expect. Unemployment is inevitably a lagging indicator and despite the continued fall you can just see signs of a slight deceleration. (OHPC: journalism)

Life has returned to normal, **more or less**. (OHPC: journalism)

Some FEIs indicate the range of reference by emphasizing inclusiveness: *all told, warts and all,* and *across the board*. FEIs such as *and all that jazz* and *and so on* indicate inclusiveness or category membership through vagueness (see Channell 1994: 119ff. for a discussion of this). Other FEIs indicate degree, such as *well and truly* and the frames *to a — degree* and *to a — extent*:

We have been accused of dragging our feet, but to have adopted the review committee's proposals **warts and all**, without further consultation, would have been precipitate—even foolhardy. (OHPC: journalism)

That applies **across the board**: self-confessed fundamentalists are as rare as Druids. (OHPC: journalism)

One of the most reliable chores of journalism comes around with jingle bells **and all that jazz**, the idea of a backwards glance at this sporting life no longer thought to be threadbare but conveniently original and therefore the source of considerable enthusiasm. (OHPC: journalism)

The council was supposed to provide a coordinated direction of the war, and so, **to some extent**, it did. (OHPC: non-fiction)

Some FEIs signal generalizations or approximations, restatements, and summaries, for example *on the whole, as a (general) rule,* and *in effect*:

Warnie's career there had **on the whole** been happy and successful. (OHPC: non-fiction)

As a general rule, where extradition proceedings are before a magistrate, the entire case, including all the evidence which the parties wish to adduce, should be presented to the magistrate before either side applies for a prerogative remedy. (OHPC: journalism)

For many years it might have seemed as if doctor really did know best. But Mrs Thatcher, **in effect**, rendered the BMA impotent by excluding it from the NHS review consultation process . . . (OHPC: journalism)

Finally, some modalizing FEIs provide frames with which the truth value of the associated proposition can be focused or delimited, according to the topic or aspect denoted by the inserted word, for example, *in — terms/in terms of —* and *on the — front*. These can be compared to the topicalizing insertions described in Section 6.8:

She can negotiate and play around with her own budget—currently about 20 million, small **in TV terms** but an increase. (OHPC: journalism)

In terms of sheer physical size, the volcanoes are the most impressive feature of Mars. (OHPC: non-fiction)

It is a strange choice for a dollar-wise nation, given the 1990 botch-up **on the lire front**. (OHPC: journalism)

8.6.2 *Deontic Modalizers*

While modalizing FEIs are very often epistemic, a substantial number are deontic. They express such things as advice, advisability, directions, and warnings. Proverbs in particular express advice, and examples include *prevention is better than cure* and *better safe than sorry*. Other expressions that convey advisability and necessity include *if needs be*, *if I were you*, *may as well*, *be a good bet*, and *would do well to —*:

Prevention is better than cure. A better quality of life comes from better health. (OHPC: official leaflet)

Last year there were six weeks of industrial action, and **if needs be**, are you prepared to do the same again? (OHPC: transcribed radio programme)

FEIs that convey warnings, reprimands, and other kinds of exhortation include *had better watch —*, *at one's peril*, and *have no business —*, *get your finger out* and *shut your face*:

You'd better watch it, young lady, Pat was skinny at your age and now look at her! (OHPC: non-fiction)

The prudent pilot, for example, allows plugs to soldier on unchecked **at his or her peril**. (OHPC: journalism)

The US **has no business** interfering in Panama. (OHPC: journalism)

Excellent, so **keep your mouth shut** or I'll have you shot and remember—failure is a sign of weakness. (OHPC: fiction)

8.6.3 *Other Kinds of Modalizer*

A small number of modalizing FEIs are conative and indicate ability and potential. These include *have a crack at*, *at pains to —*, and *do one's level best to —*:

For having found fame in rock music and the cinema he has been given the chance **to have a crack at** Romeo. (OHPC: journalism)

Mrs Thatcher was **at pains to** emphasise the Government's commitment to the National Health Service. (OHPC: journalism)

A few further modalizing FEIs are volitive, indicating intention and preference; a few others are optatives or expressions of hope. They include *would rather, if only, be bent on, wouldn't mind, have it in mind to* —, and *keep one's fingers crossed*:

Given the choice, I **would rather** be a paramedic than anything else, but not under these conditions. (OHPC: journalism)

I half **had it in mind** to invite you to come and work for me here in Vienna. (OHPC: fiction)

In more than 3,000 hours of flying, this was my Worst Day so far. Why 'so far'? Well, I **keep my fingers crossed** and plan to do my best to make sure that I'll be prang-free for the rest of my flying career. (OHPC: journalism)

8.7 ORGANIZATIONAL FEIS

Like modalizing FEIs, **organizational** FEIs are hyperpropositional. They organize texts by signalling logical connections between propositions, deixis, prefaces, summaries, and opinions, and so on. Some examples are:

all in all
as yet
be that as it may
by the same token
by the way
for example
in consequence (of —)
in question
in the circumstances, under the circumstances
in the event
let alone
only part of the story, not the whole story
on the one hand, on the other (hand)
talking of —

The commonest syntactic type is the conjunct:

On the other hand, Moscow was one of the world's largest holders of gold bullion. (OHPC: journalism)

For example, diseases such as diabetes, rheumatism, and arthritis all have links with diet. (OHPC: non-fiction)

Other organizational FEIs are adjuncts, or multi-word prepositional heads of adjuncts:

. . . we would consider how best we might contribute to the arms control process **in the light of** the changed circumstances. (OHPC: journalism)

When a person purports to act **on behalf of** another, but without his authority, the latter may subsequently ratify the act of the former . . . (OHPC: non-fiction)

There are also a few conjunctions:

British disarmament, or rather reduction of armaments, was not initiated as an example to others. **Still less,** when originally planned, was it carried beyond the margin of safety. (OHPC: journalism)

Companies making specialized or high-technology products are under particularly strong pressure to export **in order to** reach a sufficiently large market. (OHPC: journalism)

Some FEIs functioning as prenominal groups or proforms are organizational because they are deictic:

A choice of viewing on **any given** day offered a perspective on her own feelings . . . (OHPC: fiction)

As with modalizing FEIs, organizational FEIs are typically anomalous collocations or formulaic. Only a few can be classified as metaphorical: exceptions include *in a nutshell, in the face of something,* and *the other side of the coin.* Again, this is significant with respect to the markedness or saliency of such items in text.

The following considers the principal kinds of organization which FEIs establish; Chapter 10 considers organization by focusing on texts.

8.7.1 *FEIs that Organize Propositional Content*

Many organizational FEIs control the continuity of text content: in this respect they are like informational FEIs. Some indicate logical connections and relations, for example by conveying purposes, reasons, causes, circumstances, and results, and examples include *thanks to —, in the light of —, on the grounds that —, in the event, in spite of, in case —,* and *with a view to*:

Queen's Park Rangers beat Coventry one nil, **thanks to** a Les Ferdinand goal. (OHPC: journalism)

In spite of the sharp recession induced by US economic sanctions, General Noriega has played a skilful game of counter-propaganda. (OHPC: journalism)

To take her to dinner **with a view to** persuading her to go back to Dorset with him? (OHPC: fiction)

FEIs that indicate time or place organize by locating texts temporally and spatially. For example, *in the meantime, to date, from that time onwards*, the classical narrative opening *once upon a time* which also organizes as a preface, and *in (some)one's neck of the woods*:

He had no answer, but **in the meantime** the manager appeared and asked me to come into the office. (OHPC: non-fiction)

Once upon a time there was a man who thought he could be a dragon-master. (OHPC: fiction)

Other deictic FEIs organize by distinguishing, disambiguating, or otherwise identifying: *(the) one and only*, *one another*, and *the —s of this world*:

I headed for the white gleam of a village in the distance and was grateful to find that the **one and only** store sold iced drinks. The storekeeper asked if I was German. (OHPC: non-fiction)

It is not, however, easy to contemplate putting whole federations out of action. That is a bullet on which **the Arthur Golds of this world** have steadfastly failed to bite. (OHPC: journalism)

Some FEIs express connections and similarities, such as *in the same way*, *by analogy*, and *in comparison with —*. Others indicate relevance and pertinence, for example *in relation to —*, *with respect to —*, and *to do with*:

Snappy, short news sequences certainly helped promote some of the big names but this was on a small scale **in comparison** with the United States where a few outstanding sportsmen became Hollywood stars. (OHPC: non-fiction)

It is all **to do with** the horrendously complicated system of green currencies used to calculate the tax on UK farm exports and the subsidy on imports, known as monetary compensatory amounts. (OHPC: journalism)

A few indicate exceptions, for example *not counting*, *save for*, and *leaving to/on one side* and variations. These overlap with epistemic modalizers which delimit the range of reference (see Section 8.6.1):

We went to the pictures no more than once or twice a week, **not counting** Saturday mornings; though if it was good we sometimes stayed round to see it again. (OHPC: fiction)

Leaving the technology issue to one side, there is also scant evidence in the local population of commercial attitude at the level required. (OHPC: journalism)

Finally, some organizational FEIs function as concessives, for example *after all*, *even if*, *at any rate*:

Retraining, they say, is the key to the future: **after all**, 75 per cent of the work force of the year 2000 is already at work now. (OHPC: journalism)

We had also one advanced (for those days, **at any rate**) feminist, Mrs Lucas. (OHPC: non-fiction)

8.7.2 *FEIs that Organize the Discourse*

Other organizational FEIs organize texts at a metadiscoursal level. One such group comprises boundary markers, and it includes such expressions as *by the way, that's all, talking of —, that's that, so much for —,* and *now for —/now for something completely different.* These are comparable with the gambits discussed by Keller (1979), and with the formulae marking the beginnings and ends of macro speech acts, for example ones used to establish or conclude a conversation, to which Van Dijk draws attention (1977: 238 ff.):

While the majority of guests are British, there are Belgians and Dutch whom you will enjoy getting to know over lunch or dinner. **Talking of food**, calorie counting is to be recommended, otherwise I'm afraid the waistline will suffer a little. (OHPC: non-fiction)

By the way I shall send another paper to Perris at the end of the week. (OHPC: non-fiction)

And now for something completely different: cheap and cheerful claret. (OHPC: journalism)

Some organizational FEIs indicate sequencing of different kinds in their texts, for example *to begin with, in the first/second place, in passing, as follows.* The pair *on the one hand* and *on the other (hand)* both sequence and signal a contrast:

To begin with, however, let us note that the definition allows for two distinct types of incommensurability. (OHPC: non-fiction)

In passing, one might notice that Yeats had very few Europeans among his acquaintances . . . (OHPC: non-fiction)

. . . to strike a balance between the need for worker autonomy within the enterprise **on the one hand**, and the need for economic co-ordination at higher economic levels **on the other** . . . (OHPC: non-fiction)

Many organizational FEIs function as prefaces or signals of additional information, clarification, suggestions, and so on. These include *in addition, what's more, for example, to boot, a case in point, in other words, far be it from me to —,* and *I tell you what* (compare modalizing FEIs):

Strangely unfunny and in bad taste **to boot**. (OHPC: journalism)

. . . the European Community is giving Poland a $1bn stabilisation fund to help it 'manage' the value of the zloty in the early months of economic reform. **In other words**, Poland will have funds to intervene to support its currency. (OHPC: journalism)

I think, Bill, really you . . . **far be it from me to** try and teach you your job, but you ought to have perhaps gone back a little bit and wondered why we were all in this position . . . (OHPC: transcribed radio discussion)

A number of organizational FEIs focus or foreground the ensuing information or point, for example *not least, above all, let alone, not to mention,* and *more to the point*:

It was a reminder that Christmas is, **above all**, a time for tradition. (OHPC: journalism)

None of these issues rates a mention, **let alone** a conclusion. (OHPC: journalism)

What must she think of us? **More to the point** is what we thought of her. (OHPC: journalism)

Some organizational FEIs signal counter-arguments, contrasts, denials, and rebuttals: for example, *on the other hand, on the contrary, at the same time, all very well, beg to differ, as against,* and *then/ there again. In retrospect* and *with hindsight* signal opinions or observations that contrast with previous perceptions:

In our interpretation, a gradual faunal change is not justified. **On the contrary**, the evidence appears to underscore a catastrophic scenario. (OHPC: fiction)

'And the site on the airfield is well, well away from the village and none of you will actually see it.' '**I beg to differ**. I mean my house is actually right next to it and also the people that live at Shilton Edge Farm and you can see it from the airfield or the Kencot Road . . . ' (OHPC: transcribed radio discussion)

With hindsight, it is becoming clear that his complaints last month were backed by clever logic. (OHPC: journalism)

Some FEIs signal summaries and conclusions, for example *at the end of the day, in short, to cut a long story short, in a nutshell,* and *in a word. The rest is history* functions as a summary and boundary marker by appealing to shared knowledge of consequences or events:

At the end of the day, the decision to foster isn't one which can be taken lightly. (OHPC: journalism)

That, **in a nutshell**, is it: a strategy pitched somewhere between 'conservativism' and the radicals who want every regulation thrown out of the window tomorrow. (OHPC: journalism)

At the 1981 Salzburg Easter Festival, the Herbert von Karajan Foundation in Salzburg teamed up with Sony, Philips, and the Polygram group to announce the imminent launch of the compact disc. **The rest is history**. (OHPC: non-fiction)

Some FEIs signal quotation: *in X's words* and *as X puts it*. Others indicate attribution of sources and opinions. *As far as X is concerned* and *in the eyes of X* can refer either to the speaker/writer or to someone else, whereas *if you ask me* and *I am bound to say* can only refer to the speaker/writer. A few distance by attributing a remark to the community in general: *as they say* and *as rumour has it*. Such attribution and distancing can also be regarded in terms of modality:

As the writer Anthony Burgess puts it, while many British playgoers thought *Waiting for Godot* absurd, the French considered it an outstanding contribution to the Theatre of the Absurd. (OHPC: journalism)

As far as Henry was concerned they could fill the whole thing in with concrete. (OHPC: fiction)

I'm bound to say that when considering some examples of modern architecture I enthusiastically join those who say, 'God bless the Prince of Wales'. (OHPC: journalism)

In Warsaw, **rumour has it** the lower floors of the Communist Party Central Committee's infamous concrete headquarters will be rented out to a Western bank. (OHPC: journalism)

If you follow my meaning, *if you catch my drift*, and variations have functions in maintaining or checking on comprehension, as well as signalling the need for inference or consideration of subtext:

It was a lot of sort of hippies pulling together to pull something off— hardly your Daily Mirror love nest, **if you get my drift**. (OHPC: attributed speech in non-fiction)

Finally, a number of FEIs have functions in plane-changing (Sinclair 1983): that is, they comment on the selection of lexis itself. Examples include *to put it mildly*, *in — parlance*, *for the sake of argument/discussion/—*, *if you'll pardon the expression*, and *for want of a better word*. See Section 10.5 for discussion of the signalling of FEIs:

Morale, **to put it mildly**, is not running high. (OHPC: journalism)

In structural engineer's parlance, crack widths of less than 1mm (1/16in) are termed very slight and those less than 5mm (3/16in) are termed 'slight'. (OHPC: journalism)

It will be assumed **for the sake of argument** that this patient had not indicated or is unable to indicate a desire that treatment on the ventilator be terminated. (OHPC: non-fiction)

. . . research and design in the direction of (**for want of a better word**) socialized architecture. (OHPC: non-fiction)

8.8 MULTIPLE FUNCTIONING

Nearly 47% of FEIs in the database are classified as having two or more text functions: that is, they contribute to their texts in two or more ways. Note that I was recording functions for types rather than individual tokens, and so some of the apparent ambiguity or duality of function might be resolved on a case-by-case basis. As in the case of idiomaticity types, multiple classification may be seen as a measure of the effectiveness of the classification model. It has clearly proved impossible to assign one, and only one, function to each FEI; on the other hand, it might have been surprising if this had been possible. FEIs, as with other kinds of grammatical and linguistic categories, operate on different levels at the same time.

Table 8.7 shows the distribution of unique and multiple assignments according to text function. Bracketed percentages represent cases where FEIs have unique assignments. It can be seen that informational FEIs frequently also have evaluative content. Examples of such FEIs include *steer clear (of someone/something), come under fire,* and *in jeopardy.* These expressions further the narrative, conveying new information, but some evaluation is intrinsic to their meanings. For example, the person or thing avoided in *steer clear (of someone/something)* is negatively evaluated, and so are the situations of 'coming under fire' or being 'in jeopardy':

Hongkong Bank **steered clear of** the mania to lend to third-world countries that peaked in the early 1980s. (OHPC: journalism)

Charlton immediately **came under fire**, his decision to withdraw Brady from the fray seen to be cavalier and grossly insensitive. (OHPC: journalism)

TABLE 8.7 *FEIs with unique and multiple functions*

Primary function	Secondary function				
	Inform- ational	Evalu- ative	Situa- tional	Modal- izing	Organiz- ational
informational	(18%)	11%	<1%	8%	3%
evaluative	5%	(22%)	<1%	10%	1%
situational	<1%	1%	(3%)	1%	<1%
modalizing	1%	1%	<1%	(6%)	1%
organizational	<1%	<1%	0	2%	(3%)

Many informational and evaluative FEIs have modalizing secondary functions, typically epistemic. For example, *on stream, take*
place, and *come to light* further the narrative and make statements
about the way things are or seem. Similarly, *the tip of the iceberg* and
go/run deep evaluate and modalize by suggesting the extent of the
phenomenon:

The fully fledged system of departmental reports will come **on stream** in
1991. (OHPC: journalism)

But had the market boom continued a few more weeks, the whole thing
might never have **come to light**. (OHPC: journalism)

The usually veiled criticism contained in the report material, and the open
comment coming to light in denunciations and court prosecutions, have
necessarily to be regarded as **the tip of the iceberg**. (OHPC: non-fiction)

As with the overlap between disjuncts and conjuncts (see Section
5.3.6), it is not always possible to separate modalizing and organizational functions. Both occur in expressions such as *to say the least,*
at present, in the end, in general, in any case, and *at least*, which
function as signals of modifications, opinions, generalizations, or
summaries and also comments on the extent of the truth value of
the associated text:

There is a hill in St Albans, I think it's called St Peter's Church hill, and it is
very, very severe **to say the least**. (OHPC: transcribed radio journalism)

This could be an accident, or possibly a subtle directorial ploy on the part
of the French director Robert Enrico, in charge of the other half of the
film. **In any case**, the effect is the same. (OHPC: journalism)

Finally, a few informational and evaluative FEIs also have some
organizational function. For example, *the pros and cons* gives information and also signals contrasted aspects of the matter under
discussion. Similarly, *last but not least* evaluates and signals the
end of a sequence, and *the conventional wisdom* both evaluates and
signals an appeal to shared beliefs:

To see why, start with a look at **the pros and cons** of Mr Codd's creation.
His relational model is a theory of what data is and how it can be retrieved.
[etc.] (OHPC: journalism)

They did, however, tend to draw upon academic illusionism, early
modernism, or **last but not least**, on mass-media imagery. (OHPC:
non-fiction)

It was **conventional wisdom** in the 1960s that a trade gap could be closed,
without sacrificing growth, by a lower pound. (OHPC: journalism)

8.9 CROSS-FUNCTIONING

Individual FEIs may be predicted to perform their canonical primary or secondary functions in most of the contexts in which they are used—conveying information or evaluations, emphasizing, stating logical relationships, and so on. In contrast, cross-functioning operates instantly and relates to the behaviour of individual FEIs in individual contexts. **Cross-functioning** is the phenomenon whereby a speaker/writer uses FEIs in functions other than their canonical ones, thereby foregrounding or thematizing the selection. A typical case is that of informational or evaluative FEIs used as signalling devices: a text organizer or speech gambit. For example, a newspaper column begins:

I must **nail my colours to the mast**. I'm a very keen advocate of all sorts of sport for all sorts of people at all ages, but intensive sport or intensive training for sport could surprisingly, [*sic*] have side-effects. (*Daily News* (Birmingham), 4 June 1987: 10)

Nail one's colours to the mast is used here to preface and to emphasize frankness, not simply to convey information: it is followed by the report of what is being transmitted frankly and clearly. This example may be compared functionally, though not lexically, to a more conventional, unmarked opening of another newspaper article: 'Let me straightaway declare an interest' (The *Guardian*, 26 February 1988), prefacing the interest declared.

The examples of *the worm turns* at the beginning of this chapter may be seen as cases of cross-functioning. In the following example, an FEI is used—and exploited—in the opening sentence of an article when the writer underlines his frankness and signals the statement of his particular ideas or beliefs:

To the question, what are universities for? I would shake **the bees from my bonnet** and answer from under it that they exist in order to advance knowledge and understanding of three great provinces of thought and learning: the human world (including the past and present states of civilization), the natural world, and the technologies, which enable us to put our science at the disposal of our civilization. (Philip Brockbank, *University of Birmingham Bulletin*, 16 November 1987)

Similarly, *the tip of the iceberg* is canonically evaluative and modalizing, but in the following example it functions as a preface, signalling an expansion:

Brian Raymond, a solicitor who defended Clive Ponting and has figured in several major murder trials, believes these cases are **the tip of the**

iceberg in police manipulation of the Press. 'A journalist's ear is bent, through unattributable briefings, with very much the police view of the case. Unless the defence is aware, the way the trial is reported can be very heavily influenced.' (OHPC: journalism)

Such uses can also be observed in spoken interaction. In the course of a discussion on political scandals, a TV presenter prompted with

Are there any **skeletons left in the cupboard** to come out? Has **the last cat in the bag been let out?** (*Central Weekend,* 7 January 1994)

In a BBC television interview during the 1987 general election campaign, David Dimbleby made three consecutive attempts to interrupt the politician he was interviewing and to grab the turn. He used FEIs in order to do so (in addition to evaluating the interviewee's remarks): 'You're just beating around the bush', 'You want the best of both worlds', and 'You're trying to have it both ways'. A friend of mine used a truncated proverb as preface and attitude marker to communicate news concerning someone who had been threatening his family: 'It never rains. Andrew's been released [from police custody] and he's decided to plead not guilty.' As a proposition decoded either literally or metaphorically, *it never rains* is meaningless. To make sense, it must be interpreted in the light of the full proverb and the supposed universal truth, evaluation of things, and deontic content that the full proverb expresses. In the same way, FEIs, especially proverbs and sayings, can be used as closing turns in exchanges, providing summaries and evaluations. Similar points have been made by Schegloff and Sacks (1973: 306–7) and Stubbs (1983: 24), who lists 'cliché-cum-proverbs' such as *'still, that's life'*, *'well, that's the way it goes'*, and *'but something may turn up—you never know'*.

These are examples of the cross-functioning of informational and evaluative FEIs. The cross-functioning of other kinds of FEIs is rarer, but occurs. A sports report in The *Daily Mirror* of 3 February 1987 about the sacking of a footballer is accompanied by a photograph and the caption *On yer bike!* (this is later repeated in the opening paragraph as a quotation). Another sports report about the British Grand Prix in The *Daily News* (Birmingham) of 8 July 1988, is headlined *Now you see them* . . . . The expressions *on your bike* and *now you see them, now you don't* are both normally situational FEIs, contextually determined by extralinguistic factors, yet here they function as information-giving summaries. Such cases can be compared to the use of spoken discourse markers in written text. These are described by McCarthy (1993) with respect to fanzine data, in particular the marker *well*, but also *now, mind you, still, after all, I mean,* and *okay,* and McCarthy draws attention to the ways in which the writers are reproducing conversational styles in written media.

Cross-functioning adds an extra layer of function: primary function is not lost sight of, but rather the interplay between primary function and cross-function underlines the textual significance of FEIs. The instance of *it never rains* cited above is not simply a preface but establishes the tenor of the succeeding information by means of the denotational and connotational value of the FEI, suggesting a coincidence of several bad things. Such uses of FEIs as prefaces, summaries, and signals in general may be regarded as cohesive devices, and this will be explored in more detail in Chapter 10.

9
Evaluation and Interactional Perspectives

This chapter looks at FEIs in relation to interaction and the inter-personal component of discourse (Halliday 1978: 128 ff.; Halliday and Hasan 1989: 20 and *passim*; Morley 1985: 44–81). The selection and use of FEIs is not simply a matter of the lexical realization of meaning, but part of the ongoing dynamic interaction between speaker/writer and hearer/reader within the discoursal context. Moreover, many FEIs may be seen as culture-bound stereotypes, indexing (in Hallidayan terms) language through experience.

9.1 EVALUATION AND ATTITUDE

FEIs are used to convey a speaker/writer's attitude towards the condition, situation, or thing that he or she is describing: they therefore represent his/her intrusion into the situation. This may be expressed directly by stating a judgement, as is the case with primarily evaluative FEIs, or indirectly through the evaluative or axiological components of other kinds of FEI. Attitude may also be expressed as modality, through modalizing FEIs, and through FEIs functioning as exclamations.

Krzeszowski (1990) argues that all linguistic items can be assessed on an axiological scale and that axiology is a crucial factor in establishing the coherence of a discourse, with the good–bad dimension at least as important as the true–false dimension is at the sentence or utterance level. Krzeszowski also points out that meta-phorical concepts are more likely to be axiologically loaded than non-metaphorical ones. The evaluative component of FEIs, parti-cularly metaphors, helps to explain why FEIs are selected in the first place.

In theory, evaluation in FEIs as with other lexical items is of two kinds. It may be centred on the speaker/writer, and thus project his/her personal interpretation of something as good or bad. Alternatively, it may be centred on the culture at large, and thus project general norms of good and bad. The difference can be seen by considering *drag one's feet*, as in

Other reports have suggested that some arms factories are deliberately obstructing the process of conversion from military to consumer production. It also appears that the army is **dragging its feet** in teaching officers about the new defensive military doctrine formulated by the Kremlin. (OHPC: journalism)

The FEI denotes inaction and encodes the speaker/writer's interpretation of inaction and its consequences as bad. This contrasts with *go bust*:

His bank, Lincoln Savings and Loan, **went bust** recently along with hundreds of other American savings banks that made bad loans, mostly in real estate. (OHPC: journalism)

where the FEI refers to a situation that is evaluated more generally as bad. The distinction may be seen as one between evaluative referends and evaluative referents. FEIs falling into the first category tend to be pure evaluatives, whereas FEIs falling into the second category tend to be informationals with secondary evaluative functions. In both cases the speaker/writer is persuading the hearer/reader to share his/her orientation towards the situation or to acknowledge the conventionalized cultural interpretation of the situation.

In practice, the distinction becomes blurred, and it is not always possible to identify the exact nature and locus of the evaluation. Compare Telija's discussion of the distinction with respect to lexicography (1992), in which she points out that these two kinds of evaluation, respectively 'emotional' and 'rational', are frequently confused: this may be because they are often impossible to separate. Even when referring to cultural norms, evaluatives have emotional content, and even when expressing personal opinions, evaluatives appeal to shared norms. For example, in the following

How many environmentalists, as they drive back up the motorway, having admired the birdlife of the Levels through a brand-new pair of binoculars, pause to consider that they are really **having their cake and eating it too**, as they enjoy a top-quality environment which may be preserved only because the quality of the lives of its inhabitants holds out little promise of advancement. (OHPC: non-fiction)

the use of a form of the proverb *You can't have your cake and eat it* encodes both the writer's opinion of the hypocrisy of the environmentalists and a reference to shared values or norms—that it is wrong or foolish to expect to have two mutually incompatible things at the same time.

The category of evaluative FEIs is, of course, especially associated with the transmission of attitude. Positive evaluation is implied in

I thought the way we were taking corners was getting stale, so we had decided to vary them from near to far post. It **did the trick**, as they looked dangerous. Paul Kee did well making some great saves to keep us in the game. (OHPC: journalism)

The drawings of the Royal Institute of British Architects form one of the less well-known collections in London. Architectural historians have already raided it **to good effect**, notably Mark Girouard for his book on the sixteenth-century architect Robert Smythson and Jill Lever, the curator of the collection, for the book she wrote with Margaret Richardson, The Art of the Architect. (OHPC: journalism)

while negative evaluation is implied in

Stores remained **in the doldrums**, with the latest retail sales figures confirming the difficulties of the high street. (OHPC: journalism)

In a new analysis, the influential magazine, Power in Europe, estimates that the bill cannot be less than £15bn and could be a lot higher. If this turns out to be the case it **makes a mockery of** the £2.5bn provision the Government is making to indemnify the privatised industry against 'unforeseen' decommissioning costs. (OHPC: journalism)

In each pair, the first example is oriented towards the evaluated real-world situation and the second towards the writer's own evaluation, although again the overlap is apparent.

The evaluative components of FEIs may be complex, but they are vital to semantic and discoursal well-formedness. Mel'čuk (1995: 178) points out that *make a mountain out of a molehill* means 'grossly exaggerate a minor problem' (or difficulty), and it cannot be extended to, say, 'grossly exaggerate someone's merits or successes'. To develop his point: the FEI itself implies a negative evaluation of the action of exaggeration, but the thing exaggerated must be something that is evaluated as bad or onerous, and not something innately good.

My database recorded cases where FEIs normally transmit either positive or negative evaluations, including cases where the evaluation relates to only one part of the expression: for example, the person, thing, or situation mentioned as the verbal object. About a third of all database FEIs are canonically either positive or negative in orientation. Table 9.1 correlates these FEIs with idiomaticity type. Evaluative orientations are more strongly associated with metaphors than other kinds of FEI.

It emerges that negative assignments are roughly twice as common as positive ones. The same kind of distribution was also observed in the compilation of *CCDI*, which systematically recorded negative and positive evaluations. It is possible that negative evaluations are simply more salient, and so negative orientations are more likely to be noticed: the proportions reflect human error or bias. However, it is equally possible that negatively evaluating FEIs are indeed commoner than positively evaluating ones or neutral ones. If this is the case, it may be because FEIs are periphrastic and used as politeness devices or euphemisms: see further below. Note that there appear to be some distinctions here between British and American English: some FEIs which evaluate negatively in British English are neutral or even positive in American. For example, evidence in BofE suggests that in British English *labour of love* often has negative connotations, mildly denigrating the activity in question: *labor of love* in American is more usually neutral or positive.

There are a few problematic cases where the FEI can be either approbatory or deprecatory, although the selection of the FEI entails in context a particular selection of orientation. For example, *wash one's hands of something/someone* denotes giving up, dissociating, or desisting. Such an action may be perceived as good or bad, the subject of the verb as right or wrong, and the object of the preposition as bad and wrong or good and unfairly treated, according to the sympathies of the speaker/writer. In the following,

Why does Mr Rifkind stand for it? He could, if he wished, **wash his hands of** the whole operation and go off to make his fortune at the bar. As it is, he may find himself impeded at every stage from carrying out the policies which his heart and his shining intelligence must tell him are needed. (OHPC: journalism)

TABLE 9.1. *FEIs: orientation and idiomaticity type*

	Anomalous collocations	Formulae	Metaphors
(total in database	45.3%	21.3%	33.4%
positive	14%	5%	15%
negative	22%	8%	36%

Angry claims that South Oxfordshire District Council **is washing its hands of** Littlemore over work needed at Peers sports centre have been made. The district council says it will not start the £30,000 upgrading work unless Oxford City agrees to take over the work and the loan charges when Littlemore becomes part of the city. Littlemore member of South Oxfordshire District Council, Mrs Bessie Ledger said she was very angry—and so are people in the community. She told the full council meeting 'We are still in south Oxfordshire. Littlemore people have paid you their poll taxes. You should not **wash your hands of** Littlemore just because it will be part of the city next year.' (OHPC: journalism)

the first implies a positive evaluation of the action and actor/agent and the second a negative one. The exact orientation has to emerge through other factors in the co-text and, perhaps, through the metaphor itself.

Metaphors frequently hold the keys to the orientation of the expression, as in the case of negatively evaluated *drag one's feet/ heels* or *spill the beans*, where real-world knowledge about the metaphorical image and its connotations colours and clarifies evaluation, thus reinforcing claims about the partial composition-ality of such FEIs. However, this is sometimes complicated. The orientation of *wash one's hands of someone/something* is determined idiolectally as well as instantially. If interpreted in the light of its Biblical origins—Pilate's refusal to accept further responsibility for Jesus, accompanied by his symbolic washing of his hands (*Matt.* 27: 24; Flavell and Flavell 1993*a*: 55)—the action denoted is more likely to be evaluated as bad. If interpreted synchronically, then the notional and general action of washing hands is more likely to be evaluated positively, and the action denoted in the FEI as good. Similarly, the precise evaluation implied in *break the mould* depends on whether interpretation of the metaphor focuses on the previous situation which can never be recreated or regained and never surpassed (according to *OED*, the original interpretation); or on a new situation where there are open-ended possibilities because an obsolete or restrictive state of affairs has been ended (a later interpretation). That is, does the speaker/writer selecting *break the mould* imply the negative aspects of loss and destruction or the positive ones of potential, radical change, and opportunity? Both idiolect and diachrony need to be taken into account in discussing evaluation.

Another complex case is the proverb *a rolling stone gathers no moss*, discussed by Milner (1969: 380); Meier (1975: 237); Lakoff (1987: 451); Obelkevich (1987: 48); Flavell and Flavell (1993*b*: 224f.). This proverb has two opposed meanings and evaluations. One meaning, perhaps the commoner meaning, can be glossed crudely as 'people who move around a lot will never acquire wealth, position, stability, and so on': it evaluates rolling stones and mobility negatively (moss = asset and sign of stability = good). The other meaning can be glossed as 'people who move around a lot will never grow stale and dull': it evaluates rolling stones and mobility positively (moss = encumbrance and sign of sluggishness = bad). The different meanings may be associated with dialect: Obelkevich observes the positive evaluation in Scotland, the negative in England, although Lakoff observes both meanings in American English. The FEI *gather moss*, apparently a truncated form of the proverb, connotes stasis or sluggishness, normally therefore evaluating moss as bad and mobility as good. The name of the rock group *The Rolling Stones* presumably evaluates rolling stones and hence mobility as good, regardless of whether the name is a deliberate subversion of one meaning of the proverb it alludes to, or else a straightforward reflection of the other. The intricacy of the evaluative content is shown further in the song *Like a Rolling Stone*, where the narrator evaluates negatively the addressee's dysfunctional situation by catenating its different aspects such as isolation, dispossession, and degradation:

> Princess on the steeple and all the pretty people
> They're drinkin', thinkin' that they got it made
> Exchanging all kinds of precious gifts and things
> But you'd better lift your diamond ring, you'd better pawn it babe
> You used to be so amused
> At Napoleon in rags and the language that he used
> Go to him now, he calls you, you can't refuse
> When you got nothing, you got nothing to lose
> You're invisible now, you got no secrets to conceal
>
> How does it feel
> How does it feel
> To be on your own
> With no direction home
> Like a complete unknown
> Like a rolling stone?
>
> (B. Dylan, *Highway 61 Revisited* (1965))

We infer a negative evaluation for *like a rolling stone*: an illocutionary purpose of the song is, arguably, to disabuse the addressee and get her to acknowledge reality; yet one implication in the song is that the addressee regards her situation and its freedom, symbolized as the rolling stone, as desirable.

9.1.1 *Evaluation and Modality*

Modal choices—and in the context of the present study, modalizing FEIs—are interpersonal choices in terms of Halliday's model of meaning (1978: 128 ff.). When epistemic, they realize the speaker/writer's attitude and commitment with respect to the discourse. They concern meaning, and are involved with the negotiation and communication of such things as probability (including certainty and possibility) and mitigation of the message. As such, their close relationship with direct evaluatives may be seen: compare Stubbs (1986; 1996: 196 ff.), who discusses the interaction between modality, evaluation, commitment, and so on. Deontic modalizers realize the speaker/writer's attempt to direct and control: the deontic cannot be separated from evaluation, which may involve strategies of suasion.

The range of modal meanings that FEIs convey was discussed in Section 8.6, together with their syntactic forms. This section simply considers two examples in detail in order to show how epistemic modalizers relate to their interactions and express evaluation, opinion, and attitude. Both examples are taken from the transcript in OHPC of a single broadcast of a Radio Oxford discussion programme and phone-in: *A* is the interviewee, *B* the interviewer.

The first example shows how FEIs fit into patterns of mitigation and argument:

A: I think the process that I've just explained would allow that anyway, because what I would do, if I just go back over it again, supposing **for argument's sake** by the end of February we've agreed which one we think it's going to be, we then . . . I then go to the home. My staff meet every resident. We write to all their relatives, as in early March.

B: But basically you're telling them that it's almost **an accomplished fact** and [um] they probably don't have too much **room for manoeuvre**.

A: **To a certain extent** that's true. Absolutely. The Council has decided to close an elderly person's home. From that moment in time they will have the opportunity to express their views to Councillors, to myself, to my staff. We will, when we go to committee in April, say all this. We'll report all this to the Council. You're dead right, closing down a service of this kind is controversial and very difficult and has to be handled very sensitively.

B: Well, sensitively is one way of putting it. I think [um] effectively and with a powerful hand is another way of doing it.

A begins by attempting to present a scenario in neutral and non-sensational terms: *for argument's sake* establishes the hypothetical nature of his scenario. *B* re-interprets it (*basically*) using two anomalous collocations, as a case of lack of choice: his is a more definite view, though none the less modalized and mitigated by *almost* and *probably*. *A* is forced to agree (*that's true, absolutely*, and *you're dead right*), but he prefaces his agreement with *to a certain extent*, showing hesitation or reluctance, and downtoning his agreement with *B*'s interpretation. The final sentence of his turn also attempts to mitigate the situation described. *B* changes plane (Sinclair 1983) by commenting on *A*'s lexis and relexicalizing it to be more definite and more negatively evaluative (in this context), in keeping with his discoursal role as antagonist.

The interview continues with a discussion of a Day Centre for the mentally handicapped that was threatened with closure but reprieved:

B: Yes. Now why did it get a reprieve? Because the name was put in the Press early, before any irrevocable decisions had been made, and people there at that centre **got their act together**. They did an excellent job of lobbying. I was quite impressed by what they did. I'm sure a lot of Councillors were gob-smacked, and what happened is that Councillors were caught **on the hop**. They had to make policy **on the hoof** and they reprieved that place. And I think that's a wonderful example of people actually having power over the decisions.

A: **I mean** if I could make a general point. Firstly, I was . . . I too was, if I can use the expression, gob-smacked at the strength of feeling that was expressed at the Social Services Committee and subsequently at the Policy Services Committee as well. Social Services . . . the world of Social Services don't have as strong a lobby as the Education lobby, or the Environment lobby, nationally or traditionally, and **in a way** I think the awfulness of the situation got people to the point of saying **enough's enough**, and that was to me very healthy, absolutely healthy. That's the power of living in a democracy.

B: Yes, to you it was healthy. Yesterday I had three Councillors here in the studio. We were talking about budget decisions and after the microphones closed at the end of the programme they commented about that home in Blenheim Road in Kidlington, and to them it wasn't healthy. They didn't like that one bit.

B establishes forcefully his positive evaluation of grass-roots action in his first turn. Positively evaluating lexis includes the FEIs *get one's act together* and *on the hoof*, as well as the single-word items *excellent*, *impressed*, *wonderful*, and so on: *caught on the hop* parallels *on the hoof* but contrasts by implying a negative evaluation of the previous inertia of the councillors. *B*'s evaluation, through politeness, enforces the agreement of *A*, who as Director of Social Services must professionally support closures and cuts while mitigating their severity. The delicacy of his position is reflected in his use of hesitation markers and mitigators: *I mean*, *in a way*, and *I think*, as well as his echoing and tentative acceptance of *B*'s *gob-smacked*. He employs a deontic proverb *enough's enough* to summarize public reactions; by reporting it he distances himself from it, but he then evaluates positively (*very healthy, absolutely healthy*) the reaction and attitude. *B* once again attacks *A*'s lexis in order to contradict *A*'s evaluation of the situation.

The uses of FEIs here cannot be separated from other modal devices and strategies, but clearly have roles in developing the argument. *A* is the weaker participant here, forced into a defensive position. This is shown in his use of modalizers and his desperate attempts to construct a positive evaluation for a situation that is widely evaluated negatively. In contrast, the FEIs used by *B* are informational and evaluative, and reflect his control of the discourse and attitude (compare further examples in the next section). In other texts, FEIs are used in different ways to express modality and attitude—in particular, by distancing—and this will be seen later.

9.1.2 *Negotiation of Evaluation*

Chapter 10 will discuss how FEIs are used in relexicalizations or restatements to convey evaluations, as in

I said before I went that they **were putting the cart before the horse**. **You know**, they were doing the applications before the research. (conversation, 29 March 1988)

where *put the cart before the horse* is expanded and restated (after a signalling FEI) in order to make its relevance more apparent. More particularly, relexicalizations sometimes use FEIs as loci for the negotiation of evaluations and interpretations. The following example is taken from another transcript of a Radio Oxford discussion programme: again, *A* is the interviewee, *B* the interviewer:

A: We work with people who have fallen through the existing nets of provision [um] generally because their problems are so multiple that no particular one agency can deal with them. For example, somebody might [um] be homeless, but no hostel in town will take them on because perhaps they have a mental illness or a drug problem, or perhaps they are in trouble with the courts [um] we can return to that hostel with the person saying 'Don't worry about these other problems, just fill in the bits you can, the accommodation, and we'll sort out the other bits.' Meanwhile, we'll be trotting them along to probation or a solicitor or whatever and getting that side of things dealt with, etc. etc., so we try to stitch together some sorts of packages for people who otherwise fall through.

B: So you're **scraping the bottom of the barrel**?

A: [laugh] That's a . . . in some ways a very unkind way of putting it, but yes.

Here, *(scraping) the bottom of the barrel* classifies and evaluates *A*'s clientele and her work, described in the previous turn. This evaluation prompts a plane-changing response, but it is accepted. *B* promotes and clarifies the topic of the homeless by deliberately selecting a dysphemistic FEI and hence schema: not necessarily through lack of sympathy for the referents but as a strategy to control the discourse and stimulate the discussion. The same provocativeness can be seen in another extract from the broadcast cited in Section 9.1.1:

A: [omitted text] It'll involve us developing visiting schemes, under eight services, helping families in different ways, improving services for disabled children, developing family centres, and a new specific— this'll . . . might amuse you this—a new specific responsibility for us to inspect and register the care practices of private schools in the County, and Oxfordshire has got the biggest number of those in the whole country. We have to register them. [um] I don't know if you remember the Esther Rantzen programme, I think three months ago, where they uncovered all sorts of misdeeds at a school in . . . I think it was Cuckham Grange [*sic*: probably an error for 'Crookham Court'] or somewhere in Berkshire. Well this is very much responsibilities placed on us to ensure that the care practices in residential schools, boarding schools, are **up to scratch**. So we've got a whole heap, as it were . . .

B: **Can of worms**

A: Well **a can of worms**, or a heap of possibilities, whichever way that you want to put it, but the Children Act [*sic*] in total . . . we are going to spend something like another four hundred thousand in nineteen ninety one, in the new financial year, which is good news.

B: But, forgive me, that just seems like it's **a drop in the bucket**.

A: Well it's **a drop in the bucket** in one sense, but it's on top of what we're already doing with our Children's Services, which are very good quality services now in the County. And it's a step. The following year that doubles up, and so on and so on. [etc.]

A is characterizing the duties laid on Social Services with the lexicalization *a whole heap (of . . .*), but *B* pre-empts this with a reformulation, *can of worms*, which he offers as a correction. It evaluates negatively, apparently referring to hypothesized further 'misdeeds' to be uncovered, rather than simply synonymous with *a whole heap*. *A* repeats this formulation, then repeats his original one; while he seems to accept both formulations, his reversion to his original topic and the positive evaluation underlying *heap of possibilities* shows his rejection of the negative *can of worms* and any more specific topic. He evaluates a budget allocation positively, as *good news*. *B* intervenes and uses *a drop in the bucket* as coreferential with *four hundred thousand*, thus changing the evaluation to negative. *A*'s response is again to pre-empt or avoid overt dispute. He repeats the negative evaluation as if accepting it, and then, as before, he uses it to preface his continuation of his account of the situation in altogether more positive terms. The inherent evaluations of individual items are not negotiated here, but the evaluations themselves are negotiated by the selection of different FEIs.

This can be compared to the discussion by Drew and Holt (1995) of idioms and other FEIs used to signal topic transition in conversation. They report and analyse cases where multiple FEIs are produced, associating them with disagreements between speakers: 'It appears that one or both speakers employ idiomatic formulations of their position in an attempt to close the matter by getting the other participant to agree with that position.' In an earlier paper (1988), they also observe idioms occurring at points in an interaction where a complainant is attempting to get a sympathetic response from an uncommitted addressee: see Section 10.4 for discussion. Their data provides further evidence of the negotiation of evaluation through FEIs, with inherent evaluations unquestioned.

9.1.3 *Subversion of Evaluation*

The canonical evaluative orientation of FEIs cannot always be taken for granted, and corpus evidence shows that in context evaluations are sometimes modified in the co-text or framing narrative, perhaps through the addition of a negative or modal. In particular, FEIs denoting actions or situations that are conventionally and culturally marked as good or bad may be used in contexts where their polarity is reversed and the evaluation renegotiated instantially. In

And then Robson's assistant, Don Howe, chose to **rock the boat**. He did the game a service. (OHPC: journalism)

the normally negatively evaluated consequences of 'rocking the boat' are seen as good. Another example is

David Edgar identifies two rather different responses to the realisation that Thatcherism was not just a temporary aberration. 'One was that what art should be doing was to re-assert the old certainties and express and underline old truths and continue to act, if you like to caricature it, as the dance band on the Titanic, playing as the ship went down.

'Or some writers felt they had earned the right in the Seventies, and now had the duty, to participate in the reassessment of the Left, if necessary by **washing dirty linen in public**. Most writers have done a bit of both. I was more inclined to the latter than the former.' (OHPC: journalism)

Washing dirty linen in public expands *the reassessment of the Left*, and forms part of the exposition of the second of *two rather different responses*: it is therefore in an antithetical relationship with the first response, the re-assertion of *the old certainties*, which is particularized in a non-institutionalized metaphor *continue to act . . . as the dance band on the Titanic, playing as the ship went down*. *Washing dirty linen in public* has an evaluative component. The full proverb with its prohibition or warning (*Don't wash . . ., One doesn't wash . . .*) leads naturally to its being negative; in this context, however, it is positive. It is instantially interpreted with respect to the concepts *right* and *duty*; it contrasts with the negative evaluation implied in the first 'response' and lexically realized in *old* and the dance-band metaphor; and since the speaker associates himself with the activity, it naturally projects the speaker's positive evaluation of his own achievements.

A similar process can be seen in the following example, from a short article on Tony Hoare, Professor of Computing at Oxford University, and the only European on a list of 'hi-tech geniuses' published by *The Wall Street Journal*:

Now 59, he does not mind being thought of as existing in **an ivory tower**. 'Some have to be **ivory tower** thinkers and others have to **get their hands dirty** on the product line.'

He does worry, though, that the Government is putting too much emphasis on research linked to industry, as opposed to academic research. 'Applied research provides for the future, but without pure research, we won't know what that future is going to be,' he said. 'The understanding the pure brings makes applied research easier. Otherwise, at best, we're doing cooking.' (The *Independent on Sunday*, 30 May 1993)

It too involves a contrastive relationship, this time with both parts expressed by FEIs. *Ivory tower* and *get one's hands dirty* are not syntactically parallel, but they are semantically antonymous, reflecting the later contrast between *academic research* and *research linked to industry*, or between *pure* (*research*) and *applied research*. *Ivory tower* and *get one's hands dirty* both evaluate, in addition to introducing new information. The typically negative evaluation of *ivory tower* is here subverted, and the typically positive evaluation of *get one's hands dirty* is downplayed.

A further case shows how, although proverbs conventionally operate as speech acts, promoting the inherited wisdom of the culture, the wisdom may not be accepted:

The name of the game is 'demerging', in which the predator gambles that the sum of the parts of a company is greater than the whole. BAT has spent the past two decades using the cash generated by its 'core' business, tobacco, to diversify into other activities like financial services, paper, and retailing. Tobacco was carrying health warnings in the West and it seemed prudent not to **put all your corporate eggs into one basket**. But they don't teach that at Harvard Business School any more. The buzz philosophy now is get back to your core business. (OHPC: journalism)

Evaluation can be subverted through irony: note that Leech sees irony pragmatically in terms of an Irony Principle, as a politeness device (see Section 9.2): 'The I[rony] P[rinciple] is a "second-order principle" which enables a speaker to be impolite while seeming to be polite; it does so by superficially breaking the C[ooperative] P[rinciple], but ultimately upholding it' (1983: 142). The simile *pure as driven snow* theoretically evaluates positively, but it typically occurs in BofE in broad negative or ironic contexts, where someone is being evaluated negatively and criticized for their behaviour:

Judge a man on the merits of his judicial knowledge and his opinion as a jurist. We all have skeletons in our closets. Look at some of the men sitting on that committee. None of them are **pure as driven snow**. (BofE: transcribed unscripted radio journalism)

It doesn't look like nonsense to me! Obviously you see yourself as the virtuous bishop, **pure as driven snow**, and Stephen as the hard-drinking, shady dean who's a terrible cross for you to bear, but let me ask you this: has it ever occurred to you that you might have got everything wrong? (BofE: fiction)

A more subtle way in which evaluations can be subverted is by disturbance of the prevalent or typical semantic prosody of the item (Louw 1993, after Sinclair). For example, in *fan the flames (of something)* and variations, 'something' is normally realized by a word denoting a negatively evaluated situation or feeling, usually a socio-political one (*racism, bigotry, confrontation, extremism, discontent*) (see Section 6.6). The following is an isolated example in BofE where 'something' is realized by *optimism*, which is conventionally evaluated as desirable and positive:

President Clinton **fanned the flames of optimism** in Northern Ireland yesterday with a simple but emphatic message to the men of violence: 'You are the past, your day is over.'

In fact, the unusualness of the collocating evaluation sets up an expectation of irony, either in the writer or in the situation described, and this is borne out in the next few paragraphs:

On a day of set-piece political theatre, the US president—the first to set foot in Northern Ireland—was able to spring a few surprises, going walk-about and shopping on the Shankill near the scene of an IRA atrocity which claimed 10 lives, and the Falls Road, where he shook hands publicly for the first time with the Sinn Fein president Gerry Adams.

The 'accidental' encounter outside a cake shop fooled nobody but spoke volumes about the sensitivities which still surround contacts with Sinn Fein. John Major is yet to follow the president's lead and shake hands.

It was the briefest of encounters. Afterwards Mr Adams said he had told the president: 'Cead mile failte (one thousand welcomes). Welcome to West Belfast.' Mr Clinton replied: 'Nice to see you. I look forward to seeing you this evening.'

He was referring to a reception at Queen's University, where care was taken to ensure that political enemies such as Mr Adams and the Democratic Unionist leader Ian Paisley all met Mr Clinton without meeting one another. (BofE: The *Guardian*, 1 December 1995)

9.1.4 *Ideology and Shared Evaluations*

Metaphors and proverbs, informational and evaluative FEIs, appeal to shared knowledge and to shared values, and they encode the speaker/writer's relationship with the ideological context of the discourse. (This can be compared to the use of modalizing FEIs, which adjust the speaker/writer's relationship with the discourse by increasing or decreasing degrees of certainty and so on.) FEIs represent institutionalized sociocultural values. By selecting an FEI, a speaker/writer is invoking an ideology, locating a concept within it, and appealing to it as authority. This is less prominent in cases where FEIs are simply descriptive, than in cases where they express evaluations of situations or behaviour, or are directive in intent.

Obelkevich discusses how proverbs represent authority (1987: 44): 'What defines the proverb, though, is not its internal layout but its external function, and that, ordinarily, is moral and didactic:

people use proverbs to tell others what to do in a given situation or what attitude to take towards it. Proverbs, then, are 'strategies for situations'; but they are strategies with authority, formulating some part of a society's common sense, its values and ways of doing things . . . That air of authority is heightened by another feature, their impersonality.' While he specifically excludes proverbial phrases and idioms from consideration, regarding them as expressive rather than directive, much the same can be said of other FEIs. Proverbs more obviously appear to cite authority (and are therefore distanced), but other FEIs may effectively do so too.

Evaluative FEIs and proverbs clearly show appeals to authority and the contextual ideology, and this can be seen in the following example:

Livewire is not primarily about awards, but aims to encourage young people to think about self-employment and to provide assistance in the form of individual advisers. The awards, at both local and national level, provide a focus but remain **the icing on the cake**. (OHPC: journalism)

The evaluative and metaphorical FEI *the icing on the cake* could be glossed as 'peripheral but pleasant; something extra but not essential': less emotive forms of words. It alludes to a cultural schema where the stereotype involves an equation with an ancillary, sugary, decorative coating to a food that is itself peripheral rather than staple: it does not even have the same connotations that jam on bread might have. Part of the shared schema is that icing is even nicer than cake, and this is accepted, not challenged, even though in the real world many people dislike the sickly sweetness of icing. Such real-world ambivalence is irrelevant to the metaphorical schema, and corpus evidence for the FEI suggests that the inherent evaluations of *icing* and *cake* in the metaphor pass unquestioned, although other issues may be raised.

In another example,

The picture I have in mind is that of **live and let live**. People's lives are their own affairs. They may be moral or immoral, admirable or demeaning, and so on, but even when immoral they are none of the state's business, none of anyone's business except those whose lives they are. All that politics is concerned with is providing people with the means to pursue their own lives, i.e., with helping them satisfy their wants and realize their goals. The state should therefore act on welfarist grounds alone and shun all ideal-regarding principles. (OHPC: non-fiction)

live and let live is only weakly metaphorical, but like many other proverbs it represents something such as a course of action that is accepted as wise or advisable by the culture (albeit only in certain situations). The proverb here provides a recommendation as a preface that is then relexicalized in more specific terms (and the schema is later explored critically, if not challenged), but the prevailing orthodoxy is already set out and taken for granted.

Proverbs and metaphors can be related both to Barthesian mythologies, and to the linguistic encoding of power relations that Fairclough discusses (1989: 33): 'Ideological power, the power to project one's practices as universal and 'common sense', is a significant complement to economic and political power, and of particular significance here because it is exercised in discourse.' Appeals and challenges to FEIs therefore become appeals and challenges to the culture and its ideology, channelled through the FEIs. They can be seen as respectively maintaining the status quo or attempting to subvert it. The norm is the former, and their discoursal uses depend on it.

Appeals to shared values and knowledge that are inherent in FEIs can be compared to appeals to other authorities. In other realizations, such appeals may take the form of precise citations and hence modal distancing through reporting; of impersonal and passive structures such as *it is apparent* or *may be compared*; or simple appeals to non-specific *they*. The effect of invoking the schema involved in, say, *live and let live* is much the same.

The notion of idiom schemas (see Section 6.6) can be broadened to take into account other types of FEI and other features. In this way, instead of simply consisting of metaphorical conceits with implied connotations, tied to preferred lexicalizations, the schemas encompass canonical evaluations as institutionalized in the culture: compare Carter's discussion of the connotations and ideology of *life in the fast lane* (1993: 140). I am arguing here that FEIs such as metaphors, proverbs, and many other formulae or collocations operate as discourse devices by appealing to socioculturally conditioned schemas. This then gives access to predetermined evaluation defaults which inform the discoursal position. Such schemas are rhetorically powerful, coercing agreement and pre-empting disagreement.

Many of the most powerful schemas involve metaphors of various kinds, and any discussion of metaphor should be related to the extensive research that has been carried out on metaphor and discourse: in particular, on the way in which argument may depend crucially upon constructs that are metaphorical in nature and origins. Metaphor is then seen as a key phenomenon through which the ideology of a discourse is mediated: see Kress (1989); Martin

(1989: 26). Much of this work concerns fundamental lexical and grammatical metaphors that are more or less subliminal: compare the conceptual metaphors of Lakoff and Johnson (1980), discussed in Section 7.5, and grammatical metaphor or mismatching discussed in Section 7.6. Metaphor is ubiquitous, not peripheral. Metaphorical FEIs and proverbs represent cultural schemas, with entailed evaluations, and they are marked selections within the paradigm available at a given point in text. It is, in fact, possible to see the sociocultural system of FEI schemas in their ideological constructs as a cryptotype in Whorfian terms, to the extent that the metaphors and evaluations are subliminal, covert, and accepted: notwithstanding the fact that canonical evaluations are sometimes subverted instantially.

9.2 POLITENESS

Many uses of FEIs in text can be related to the pragmatics of politeness. This applies to both written texts and spoken interaction, although the relationships between the discourse participants are qualitatively different. I want first to consider issues of face and person, and how FEIs are used to maintain or threaten face, particularly in spoken interaction. I then want to consider issues of politeness and the ways in which FEIs are used to create solidarity between discourse participants, in particular by being periphrastic.

9.2.1 *Face, Person, and FEIs*

The use of linguistic rituals to preserve or threaten face have been well documented (Brown and Levinson 1987; Leech 1983). It is clear that many FEIs are simply realizations of these rituals, for example situational FEIs. Emphasizing and downtoning modalizers make contributions by enabling the speaker to negotiate the truth value of his/her utterance. So much is reasonably straightforward. More complex is the way in which other kinds of FEI relate to politeness strategies, and in this the correlation between person and use of FEIs needs to be explored.

Strässler sees idioms (in his terms) as speech acts that establish social relationships (1982: 126 ff.): he restricts his study to spoken interaction. He argues that idioms may only be used in certain social situations, and that their use reflects the power relationships of the discourse participants. This is shown grammatically by the co-selection of idioms and person. He finds few examples of idioms used in the first person (which would imply self-abasement and hence loss of face), and in the second person, they are only used of someone considered less powerful and therefore open to loss of face. Low (1988: 139) points out that some metaphors/FEIs are more likely to be used in third-person structures or reports, because they might appear rude in other kinds of structure: to use his examples, *he really gets on my nerves at times* . . . is less impolite than *you really get on my nerves*, and *I shall now hit the roof* is unlikely if not impossible.

McCarthy and Carter (1994: 110ff.), supporting Strässler's findings, further relate person and idiom selection to conventions of narrative. They comment: 'To say to someone "I'm sorry if I've put your nose out of joint" expresses a dominance and confidence on the part of the speaker and a potential abasement of the listener which an alternative non-idiomatic rendition (e.g. "I'm sorry if I've caused you difficulties/upset you in some way") seems to neutralize.' There is another reason for the discoursal ill-formedness of hypothetical 'I'm sorry if I've put your nose out of joint'. The expression *put someone's nose out of joint* carries strong implications that the person who has been offended is overreacting, and therefore to use the FEI as an apology would negate or undermine the apology and so breach interactional etiquette.

Looking purely at unscripted conversational data in BofE for *put someone's nose out of joint* (2 tokens) and 3 loosely synonymous FEIs *rub someone up the wrong way* (3 tokens), *step/tread on someone's toes* (19 tokens), and *put someone's back up* (9 tokens), there does indeed seem to be a strong correlation between person and pragmatic use. Many occur with negatives and modal structures (conatives, volitives, deontics) and with generic pronoun references:

A: She would never do it in front of anybody.
B: Mm.
A: She didn't want to **put anybody's . . . nose out of joint**.

I feel that you got . . . to be careful you don't **tread on their toes**.

A: It isn't really good . . . good politics is it for anybody to
B: Mm
A: go against the wishes of the local . . . If . . . if . . . you're **putting the local community's backs up** . . . you . . . you're going to have antigo antagonism.

The first and third examples are associated with relexicalizations which reinforce the message.

Only 5 of the 33 tokens for these expressions occur in the first person, and in 4 cases, the semantic co-text implies not wanting to do this or regretting having done it, and with reference to third parties not present in the interaction—not the addressee. There is only one case in an apology, and it is cross-functioning as a pre-emptive preface, mitigating a comment which might be interpreted as aggressive, and clearly showing self-abasement so as not to threaten addressee's face:

A: Yeah. When you say you've tried everything . . .
B: Well I feel like I have I probably haven't . . .
A: No well you see . . . I . . . **I'm sorry** I don't know a way to be . . . tactful about this so if I . . .
B: Yeah . . .
A: **tread on your toes I'm really sorry** . . .
B: No . . .

However, all these FEIs—*step/tread on someone's toes* to a lesser extent than the others—carry implications that the affected person in the FEI is overreacting. Compare an expression such as *put one's foot in it*, where the FEI refers to tactless behaviour without specific reference to any other (syntactic) participant. Of 12 tokens in BofE, 3 are first person, although all these refer contextually to an action which has affected a third party. It seems to me that an apology such as 'I'm sorry if I've put my foot in it' could only be discoursally ill formed in terms of inappropriate formality level, not in terms of face-threatening. However, I have found very few cases in BofE conversational data where an apology is formulated with *sorry* and an FEI. The following both have metalinguistic reference, and do not refer to previous actions which have caused offence:

Because one was did feel th Oh . . . I'm . . . **I'm sorry I'm putting words into your mouth**. Did you feel sort of privileged at th actually living there and er having all this?

A: We've still got this enormous problem . . . you're not you know . . . you're . . . you're unable we're . . . unable to find half the money that we need this year. We're not . . . going to be able to cut it by half unless we totally change what . . . we're doing which no-one was asking to do . . . So . . . so . . . so the budget . . . that . . . that we **I'm sorry I've . . . slightly lost my track** . . .
B: We were talking about the . . .
A: The cost . . .
B: The cost. Comparing the costs . . .
A: Yes. Oh that was the One of the arguments I was able to . . . use knowing that we were cheaper is to say [etc.]

In the first, one speaker with clear and deliberate self-abasement uses it to acknowledge his appropriation of the other speaker's turn, and then proceeds to hand back the turn. The second also shows self-abasement in appealing for a prompt.

There are of course many cases in corpus data where FEIs are used in first and second person. FEIs in the first person are generally used as mitigators, appealing for sympathy, so real loss of face is not at issue:

We've got demand for Home Care **coming out of our ears**. (OHPC: transcribed radio discussion)

And we have done something about it, **grasped the nettle**, and I believe that in a short while we're going to solve this problem, and it won't be thanks to you and the Conservative Party. (OHPC: transcribed radio discussion)

Compare the use of a first person FEI cited by Brown and Levinson (1987: 82 ff.): 'It's no skin off my teeth, but I think you might want to take a look at what your son is up to in the gooseberry patch.' Brown and Levinson observe that the FEI denies risk to the speaker's face, but will be perceived as threatening the addressee's face. Note that the FEI is associated with the hedging formula *I think* and distancing *might*, which may mitigate.

FEIs in the second person in OHPC often occur in expressions of solidarity and sympathy, and therefore show politeness:

But what happens if a site gets known as a place where the troublemakers are likely to aim for? Then you've got **a real hot spot on your hands**, don't [*sic*] you? (OHPC: transcribed radio discussion)

However, they also sometimes occur in personal attacks, where face is under threat:

I've been on this Gipsy Working Party since you lost control of this Council for the last five years and you've **fought tooth and nail all the way down the line** to resist every gipsy site that came in . . . you've used every manoeuvre that you could possibly do to resist it. (OHPC: transcribed radio discussion)

These uses of FEIs can be compared to the examples given in Section 9.1.2 where evaluations are negotiated through FEIs. The last two examples given show the speaker in control, either prompting and furthering the discussion or attacking. Compare also FEIs which almost always occur in face-threatening acts, expressing speaker's impatience with addressee, and so on: for example, exclamations such as *don't give me that, what are you playing at?*, and *get stuffed!*, and the FEIs cited by Fraser (1996: 185f.) as 'displeasure markers' such as *for the love of God/Mike* and *in God's/heaven's name*.

The relationship between person and the selection of FEIs is delicate and cannot be separated from other interactional patterns and processes. Strässler, and McCarthy and Carter are right: there does seem to be some kind of idiom-avoidance in certain kinds of interaction. But inevitably, certain kinds or formality levels of language are avoided in accordance with the precise power relationship between the participants in the interaction. In framing apologies, it is impolite and inappropriate to use face-threatening language: similarly, with other discourse situations such as advising or sympathizing. This is not necessarily a problem of idiom use but rather of lexical choice in general. Idioms and other FEIs have connotative or evaluative semantic content, as has been seen, and this could be directly face-threatening. If they are avoided where there is obvious inequality between speaker and hearer, with speaker of lower status, it may be because of the semantics and connotations of the individual items and because of the relative informality of idioms in general, or because idioms are evaluative, and forceful evaluation in such circumstances is perceived as inappropriate or impolite. It remains to be seen if idiom-avoidance in such interactions applies to all FEIs equally, or if it is mainly associated with ones which evaluate negatively.

9.2.2 *Periphrasis*

FEIs, especially idioms, are inherently periphrastic, and express politeness through their very indirectness. They may also express politeness through euphemism: compare Fernando's observation (1978: 325) of euphemism in idioms as a reason for their selection. Brown and Levinson (1987: 216) find euphemism to be 'a universal feature of language usage', and Leech (1983: 147f.) sees it as evidencing the 'Pollyanna Principle', which prefers pleasant topics, views, and formulations to unpleasant ones. *Powder one's nose, have one's fingers in the till* (etc.), *at rest* (= dead), *on the game*, and *not be all there* are examples of euphemistic FEIs. Warren (1992) establishes a taxonomy of euphemisms, of which the commonest types by far are particularizations and metaphors, accounting for nearly three-quarters of her data. *Powder one's nose* and *have one's fingers in the till* are particularizations, since, like metonyms, they denote actions associated with the idiomatic meaning; *at rest* and *on the game* are metaphors. *Not be all there* is a case of understatement—one of Warren's minor types—although it also has some metaphorical content. All this may appear to conflict with the fact that negatively evaluating FEIs outnumber positives; in fact, it really shows that negative FEIs are simply periphrastic devices to convey negative evaluations more politely and less overtly or face-threateningly than simplex items.

More widely, FEIs, especially metaphors and proverbs, convey opinions and evaluations indirectly and periphrastically while appealing to cultural norms: they are polite by being vague. (See Channell (1994) for a detailed discussion of vague language and its pragmatic functions.) In many discourse situations, they avoid loss of face both on the part of the speaker/writer (by pre-empting disagreement) and of the hearer/reader (by presenting a schema with which he/she is culturally bound to agree), at the same time, avoiding overt commitment by the speaker/writer to the evaluation. Norrick discusses the use of proverbs as a strategy whereby personal commitment and refutation are both avoided (1985: 27ff.), and this can be seen in

As a reward for quality work and exceptional non-absenteeism, two of the workers had been given tickets for a play currently showing at the Maly Theatre. The women would have much preferred tickets for the circus, but of course **one couldn't look a gift-horse in the mouth**. (OHPC: fiction)

It is clear, too, that he believes government should commit extra resources to universities. But he is not a one-eyed government critic. 'I'm old-fashioned, I believe in the independence of universities. But one has to be realistic about this. The taxpayer provides a lot of the money necessary to keep higher education in business. **The Government pays the piper. To some extent the Government must have a say in the selection of tunes the piper plays**.' (OHPC: journalism)

The proverbs in these examples are associated with other strategies of detachment such as impersonal *one* and *of course*, which here signal generalization and 'consensual truth' (Schiffrin 1987: 275ff.).

Low discusses metaphor (1988) and its 'two central but opposing roles' of on the one hand clarifying and explicating, and on the other hand creating 'a shielded form of discourse' (Lerman's terms, cited by Low). By selecting an FEI, the speaker/writer retreats and shelters behind shared values, thus coercing agreement and pre-empting disagreement. The selection is semantic, but it also reflects interpersonal aspects of the interaction. In referring to someone *jumping the gun* or *spilling the beans*, speakers/writers are appealing to schemas which represent shared experience and sociocultural values, and which hold understandings of the typical consequences of hasty action or of indiscretion. Because the implicit evaluation is indirect, it is therefore more polite: compare the discussion by Brown and Levinson of conventionalized indirectness (1987: 70f.). The speaker/writer avoids saying anything specific which may be perceived as overly judgemental or just wrong. Negative evaluation can also be expressed indirectly through irony as a politeness device: see Section 9.1.3.

Although FEIs avoid face-threatening acts, thus manifesting politeness and solidarity, their indirectness can sometimes be seen as a face-threatening act: compare Bertuccelli Papi's discussion (1996) of insinuation in mainly literary texts, and compare the use of irony. Moreover, the very indirectness and lack of specificity of FEIs can be seen as obfuscation and covertness, since periphrasis can lead to concealment and suppression of information. Kress and Hodge (1979: *passim*) describe ways in which certain syntactic transformations such as passivization, detransitization, and nominalization may be used to do precisely this, particularly in withholding information about causality and agency. Something comparable seems to happen with FEIs. It can be seen by examining the mismatching between surface lexis and deep semantics in their metaphors: see Section 7.6. For example, with regard to predicate FEIs and the verbal processes they embody, transitive material processes in the surface lexis tend to be associated with intransitive material processes or mental or verbal processes in the idiomatic meaning; surface material processes are also associated with deep attributive processes. Similarly, other metaphorical FEIs tend to have concrete vehicles associated with abstract tenors.

Mismatches of this kind in verbal processes may appear to be precisely the opposite of the detransitization transformation described by Kress and Hodge in that they concretize and perhaps transitize something that notionally affects only one participant. In fact, they represent a kind of double-bluff. They make something seem more definite by depicting specific concrete situations and relating them to the specific situation mentioned in the text, yet they do so superficially and in order to achieve indirectness. The schemas are more concrete and at the same time more general and more abstract: they are analogies not equations. This can be seen in

Then only last week, the Director of Public Prosecutions for Northern Ireland and Sir Patrick Mayhew, the Attorney General (both, incidentally, with spotless criminal records) agreed that no one should be prosecuted for attempting to pervert the course of justice—not because these things hadn't happened, but because putting them in the spotlight of British Justice would 'not be in the public interest'. That is to say: it might open up **a can of worms**. (The *Guardian*, 3 February 1988)

where *can of worms* is explicitly signalled (*'that is to say'*) as a relexicalization and explication but actually refers indirectly and imprecisely to an awkward state of affairs. Thus although appearing to clarify, FEIs may in fact be doing the opposite.

9.2.3 *Solidarity*

The selection of FEIs, particularly metaphors and proverbs, can be seen as part of a discourse of familiarity, enforcing an acknowledgement of common ground between the discourse participants by appealing to shared sociocultural schemas and evaluations. FEIs allow evaluations to be expressed politely, but also increase solidarity between the speaker/writer and hearer/reader: they can be the 'parallel' pragmatic markers, indicating solidarity, which Fraser (1996: 185f.) discusses. This is particularly evident in certain genres and subgenres. For example, the dialogues in television soap operas or demotic police dramas are often constructed with heavy densities of FEIs, which demonstrate the solidarity and camaraderie between the participants and lack of a necessity to avoid face-threatening acts (or, in some situations, to encode risks to face). Puns and exploitations of FEIs further solidarity: Brown and Levinson (1987: *passim*) talk about jokes and other forms of linguistic humour in terms of positive politeness, although Zajdman (1995) points out that humour itself can be face-threatening. FEIs are used to increase solidarity in journalism, and this can be seen in the following, the opening of a newspaper article about the designer Philippe Starck:

What really **gets up the noses of** the more easily irritated members of the design profession about Philippe Starck is that it is impossible to write him off as all mouth and no talent. Yes of course his cheeky-chappie 'I can design a chair in 15 minutes' rent-a-quote style is infuriating.

It is unsubtle, even naive. What is more it runs quite counter to all the received wisdom about what grown-up design should be. He is not in the least interested in all that politically correct stuff about teamwork, ergonomics, or in fact making responsible noises about anything. Most of all he is not convinced by the idea that there needs to be more to design than makings things look, and feel, good. (The *Guardian*, 15 June 1993)

Gets up the noses of is thematized in a cleft structure, thus drawing attention to the alleged annoyingness of Philippe Starck (lexically reinforced in the cohesive *irritated* and *infuriating*). The evaluation expressed in the FEI is presented as that of other people, not the writer/journalist, and the second part of the cleft structure sets up the expectation that the evaluation will eventually be reversed. The FEI is therefore used to establish as one of the themes of the piece the dichotomy between the 'annoyingness' of Philippe Starck and his achievements, realized respectively as *mouth* and *talent*. (The secondary headline text is also instrumental in setting up expectations and eventual evaluations: 'He is a stylist of genius, a Le Corbusier meets Flash Gordon, cool enough to impress the architects and seductive enough to touch a popular chord. But is Philippe Starck a designer?') The interpersonal content of the FEI is evident and creates a camaraderie, 'the illusion of oral mode' (Fowler 1991: 63) which is reinforced by the pre-emptive *yes of course* . . .   In this way the writer binds the reader in a closer relationship. What could or should be a piece of analytical exposition becomes hortatory (see Martin (1989: 16 ff. and *passim*) for an account of this): an examination of the thesis in the headline text 'But is Philippe Starck a designer' and of the meaning and function of design in general.

Get up someone's nose is dysphemistic. Dysphemism is a strategy for increasing solidarity through frankness, reversing norms of politeness, although it is none the less indirect. Dysphemistic FEIs include *kick the bucket, up the duff,* and *be banging away like a shithouse door*. The use of dysphemisms and other depreciatives is culturally and interpersonally bound: Wierzbicka (1992: 373 ff.), for example, relates such uses in Australian culture to the Australian ethos, particularly in terms of 'mateship', openness, and disrespect for authority. In

I don't necessarily now demand to speak to him which I used to I've now got used to his assistants and I know that I can say things to them in the same way and it'll get to him. But I always now prefix my conversations with It's that **thorn in your side** again because I don't know you know years and years ago if you had a problem you might have said I think I'll write to the chief executive and you wrote. Well I don't do that any more. (BofE: unscripted conversation)

the speaker reports deliberately using a negatively evaluating, self-referential, and therefore self-abasing FEI *thorn in someone's side* as a politeness strategy. In journalism, FEIs sometimes reflect lack of deference and respect, but they also establish intimacy and conversational tone as well as appealing to shared values and culture: as

Cohen, points out, the use of metaphor creates an intimacy between 'maker' and receiver (1979: 6).

Valerie Grundy (conference discussion: Lyon, 1989) commented that the use of FEIs is an example of insiderism—including the hearer/reader, excluding others, we against they. This is true of allusive language in general, and it can be seen in a couple of examples taken from a posthumously published article by Oscar Moore, a personal account of his experience of Aids, where FEIs are exploited and manipulated in cohesive chains of imagery:

The media viewed the emerging crisis through the stained-glass window of its neo-Victorian Thatcherite pieties, while we, furious at its warped perspective, stared at ourselves from behind rose-tinted mirror shades.

We had gone from the envied social butterflies of an international fashion, music, nightclub trail to the moths singed in our own candle as we burnt it at every end. The rudest shock was to discover that for all our well-placed 'sisters', we had no political clout, no voice in the corridors of power. (The *Guardian*, 21 September 1996)

These examples demonstrate how insiderism is promoted through rhetoric and humour, metaphor and wordplay, closing the gap between writer and reader. Extreme solidarity and insiderism may then be compared to antilanguages: 'typically used for contest and display, with consequent foregrounding of interpersonal elements of all kinds' (Halliday 1978: 180). While antilanguages are inherently unstable and motivated by challenges to the status quo and norms, their purpose is to demonstrate and maintain solidarity within a group. FEIs peculiar to certain registers or dialects, and ephemeral catchphrases in particular, are instances of lexical differentiation that represent the distinction between 'we' and 'they'.

More generally, the use of indirectly evaluative FEIs can be seen as solidarity. Evaluations are polite, indirect, and distanced by being encoded in terms of shared assumptions and values, but confirm the common ground. In this way, discoursal space and mutual attitude are negotiated. FEIs may therefore be markers in a discourse of solidarity, perhaps overlying a discourse of authority, as described by Lee (1992: 144ff.). They are characterized by being lexical givens, so that their familiarity encourages intimacy and solidarity, thus helping, in Kress's terms (1989: 12), the speaker/writer to bridge or eliminate the differences created in the text.

9.2.4 *Maxims of Idiom Use*

Searle posits a neo-Gricean maxim (1979*a*: 50): 'Speak idiomatically unless there is some special reason not to.' This can be related to FEIs since they are bound up with conventions and norms of interaction. In particular, the conventionalized implicatures that they embody may be exploited in the polite communication of evaluation. The 'special reason' not to speak idiomatically and therefore to avoid idiom use may be as Strässler argues (1982: 119) when he expounds Grice's maxims of conversation and relates them to idiom use:

When applied to idioms, the two requirements of the maxim of quality read as follows:

1. Do not use an idiom if you believe you are in a social situation which does not allow such usage.

2. Do not use idioms if you are not sure about the present social situation.

Since the maxim of quality relates to truth values, I suggest a third requirement:

Do not use an idiom if its conventional evaluations and connotations are untrue or inappropriate.

In this way, the demands for politeness in face-to-face conversation and indeed in written contexts can be met.

9.3 FEIS AND SPEECH ACTS

I now want to look briefly here at FEIs as speech acts. I will not be relating FEIs methodically to the kinds of speech act models described by Searle (1969, 1975), Sadock (1974), and Levinson (1983), but a few points should be made. The simplest cases of FEIs as speech acts occur with situational FEIs: see Section 8.5. They are direct performatives, with associated illocutionary and perlocutionary force, and they include directives, commissives, and expressives: warnings, requests, and promises, as well as greetings, valedictions, apologies, thanks, and other socioculturally determined routines. They are clearly communicatively important.

Wierzbicka's approach to the analysis of FEIs lends itself to analysis in terms of speech acts. She discusses the illocutionary forces of FEIs, in particular greetings and valedictions, and directives, deconstructing *how dare you!* and *go (and) jump in the lake* in terms of semantic formulae (1986: 102f.). Similarly, in the course of her discussion of Australian English, she draws attention to the FEIs *no worries* and *good on you*, analysing them from pragmatic and cultural perspectives (1992: 388–91), concluding: 'Generally speaking, I would suggest that the set of commonly used interjections and illocutionary fixed expressions of a given language reflects in an illuminating and remarkably reliable way the "national character" and the prevailing ethos of the users of this language. Rigorous semantic analysis of such expressions may therefore enable us to find some hard evidence to support purely impressionistic observations about such matters, often dismissed as vague and subjective.' Her concern is with situational and non-metaphorical FEIs, rather than curiosities such as *not know whether one is Arthur or Martha*, *flash as a rat with a gold tooth*, and *so bare you could flog a flea across on it*. However, her approach, with its focus on interpersonal and cultural considerations, can be extended to other kinds of FEI.

In a number of books dealing with aspects of syntax and semantics, Wierzbicka has developed a way of representing the meanings of words and the concepts underlying them (1985, 1986, 1987*b*, 1988, 1992). These are extended, discursive explications that use a severely restricted defining vocabulary, comparable to a set of lexico-semantic primitives or universals to express meanings as combinations of irreducible elements and concepts. In this way, near-synonyms and co-hyponyms can be properly distinguished without cultural prejudice, and illocutionary force can be properly represented. In particular, she sets out to do this extensively for speech act verbs in English (1987*b*). Her explication of *beg* runs (1987*b*: 52 f.):

I want something (X) to happen that will be good for me
I know I can't cause it to happen
I feel something because of that
I know that you can cause it to happen
I assume that you don't want to do it
I say: I want you to do it
I know that you don't have to do what I say I want you to do
I don't want to stop saying that I want this to happen
I say this, in this way, because I want to cause you to do it
I think of you as someone who can cause me to feel something more
than good or something more than bad

Such explications are accompanied by examples from written texts and by a more conventional discussion of meaning components. These definitions are inappropriate for ordinary dictionaries, but they enable meaning to be methodically deconstructed by unpacking the bundles of assertions, beliefs, assumptions, implications, and relationships that make up speech act verbs.

This methodology can be applied to the analysis of FEIs: for example, *you can't have your cake and eat it* which in its canonical form is deontic and a speech act. The following keeps within Wierzbicka's defining vocabulary:

I know X is good and Y is good
If you do X, you cannot do Y
If you do Y, you cannot do X
You want to do both X and Y, but it is not possible
It is wrong to try to do both X and Y
Some people say it is bad to try to do both X and Y
I say you can do X or you can do Y, but you cannot do both
I say you have to say to yourself which one you want to do
I say: you can't have your cake and eat it

Beg the question itself functions like a speech act verb. Its meaning is complex: the evidence in OHPC suggests two meaning areas that are distinct at their extremes but shade into one another. To regard the expression as polysemous would be to imply ambiguity in the examples. This is not the case: rather, the meanings represent different applications of a common semantic core (in synchronic terms). The first meaning area can be paraphrased as 'assume in one's argument or assertion something that cannot be assumed or that has not been proved': it is modalizing:

Since marriage has an 'essentially heterosexual character', the criteria used to assess 'womanhood' must, Ormrod J. asserts, be biological. For, he reasons, only a biological female 'is naturally capable of perform- ing the essential role of a woman in marriage'. Besides **begging the whole question** by using the word 'heterosexual', the tautology of this explanation is striking. (OHPC: non-fiction)

The other meaning area can be paraphrased as 'raise or invite a question about something': it is organizational. This is always asso- ciated with a question in the co-text, often unanswered, and can be related to the use of *beg* in strings such as *beg comparisons*:

Although Sotheby's will not comment on the Dorrance guarantee, the sale **begs the question** of whether auction houses should act as bankers as well as agents for clients. (OHPC: journalism)

The meanings expressed in these examples are distinct. However, meanings in some other cases are indeterminate, both involving the notion of the defectiveness of a proposition or argument and signalling a question that encodes the missing point. The following occurs in a discussion of science fiction films:

Why the decline? Tudor's suggestion is that it is due to a shift in public attitudes, from regarding science as a mysterious and imponderable threat to seeing it as a banal fact of life (a progress mirrored, one might say, in public reactions to the Apollo space programme: initial fascination giving way to a sense of the routine).

There is clearly much to be said for this view, though it **begs certain questions**—why, for example, should 1932 have been the genre's most fruitful year? (OHPC: journalism)

The situation is further complicated by another use where *beg the question* has the meaning 'evade the question, wriggle out of answering': this meaning is sometimes regarded as solecistic. There is no clear evidence of it as an isolated meaning in OHPC, although many tokens of *beg the question* imply negative evaluation and some degree of deliberate avoidance of an issue.

The various meaning areas can be integrated and represented by means of a Wierzbicka-style analysis. The common core of *beg the question* might be represented as

I think that there is something wrong with what you are saying
I say: you beg the question, or what you are saying begs the question

The logical use might continue

You speak about X, and speak as if X is true
I think that X may not be true
I think that what you say may not be true
I think that this is bad
I say you do not know that X is true
I say this because I want to cause people to think that the way you speak about X is wrong

but an alternative use in conjunction with a question might continue

I think that you have not said something that is important
I do not say that this is bad
I assume that people want to know more
I say you have not spoken about X
I expect that you will now say more about X

or, where avoidance of an issue is implied,

I think that you have not said the thing that you should have said
I think that you have not said the thing that you were asked
I think that you have not said everything that you know
I assume that you can say more
I say it is bad and wrong that you do not say more

It can now be seen that individual tokens with indeterminate meanings may be represented in similar formats as permutations of such statements.

Many other uses of FEIs can be seen as speech acts, either direct or indirect. Since proverbs in the abstract have deontic functions, they can be categorized as directives. In real text, however, they occur comparatively rarely as direct performatives, except sometimes in journalistic headlines and headings, as for advice columns, or horoscopes: see the examples of horoscopes given in Section 4.9 which use proverbs and other FEIs to give warnings and advice, both as direct and indirect performatives. The following example is a directive at second hand:

The warning to the Health Secretary is clear. For once, **look before you leap**. Make sure back-up services are in place. Cut beds only because it will benefit patients, not because it will save money. (BofE: journalism)

Elsewhere, FEIs featuring in directives are most likely to be indirect performatives, expressed by means of appeals to shared values, and sometimes signalled explicitly as deferring to (cultural) authority:

Within the Rolling Stone thing, I mean, part of it has you as the chief designer and you have to accept the notion that **two heads are better than one** . . . (OHPC: transcribed discussion)

In considering idioms as speech acts, Strässler sets up felicity conditions for their use in spoken interaction and lists types of infelicity (1982: 126ff.). He sees the locutionary act as the production of the idiom, the illocutionary the assessment of the social situation, and the perlocutionary the invoking of the social hierarchy and the consequences of this. This, however, seems to be only part of the picture. The crucial evaluative components in idioms and proverbs mean that they realize another kind of social control. The illocutionary act may then be seen as deference to authority and negotiation of opinion and evaluation, and the perlocutionary act the maintenance of consensus. Thus the ideological content of idioms in particular and FEIs in general may be integrated with speech act theory, underlining their importance in discourse.

9.4 STYLISTICS AND INTERACTION: INTEREST AND BANALITY

The stylistics of FEI use is an area in its own right (see Gläser 1986). I will look at it only briefly here: full stylistics treatment needs detailed exploration of texts in relation to genre and intertextuality, and in relation to other choices of lexis. Meier (1975: 231) rightly emphasizes the importance of rhetorical or stylistic aspects of FEIs, and these may be seen in terms of their interactional effects on reader/hearer.

Leech considers hyperbole as part of an Interest Principle (1983: 146–7). In this: 'conversation which is interesting, in the sense of having unpredictability or news value, is preferred to conversation which is boring and predictable.' While the 'fixedness' of FEIs may appear to imply predictability, their selection is unpredictable and therefore 'interesting'. Amongst other things, the use of FEIs may have entertainment value and provide humour (see Section 10.2.3), promoting solidarity and grabbing attention. For example, Roger McGough's poems often include puns or exploitations of FEIs, as in

> Then the vandals moved in
> deflowered the verges
> **put the carp before the horse**
> and worse

('Vandal', *after the merrymaking* (1971), London: Jonathan Cape, 42)

Similarly, Flann O'Brien's fictions of conversations between Keats and Chapman, shaggy dog stories, end with puns that frequently involve FEIs:

Keats was once presented with an Irish terrier, which he humorously named Byrne. One day the beast strayed from the house and failed to return at night. Everybody was distressed, save Keats himself. He reached reflectively for his violin, a fairly passable timber of the Stradivarius feciture, and was soon at work with chin and jaw.

Chapman, looking in for an after-supper pipe, was astonished at the poet's composure, and did not hesitate to say so. Keats smiled (in a way that was rather lovely).

'And why should I not **fiddle**,' he asked, '**while Byrne roams**?' (*The Best of Myles* (1968), London: Grafton, 194–5)

Such marked uses of FEIs can be seen as anarchic uses of language, like antilanguages, or what Lecercle describes as 'lalangue' (1990: 37–40 and *passim*): metaphors, puns, and other 'remaindered' aspects of language, where the instability of language is most evident.

While the use of periphrastic FEIs can be seen as evidencing an enriched range of pragmatic devices, it is also sometimes seen as cliché, evidencing an impoverished vocabulary. Clichés are often associated with FEIs and other stereotyped phrases and collocations,

with many idioms labelled 'cliché' in dictionaries and other reference books. Clichés are condemned as empty rhetoric, without real
meaning, communicating subliminally or interpersonally without
proper ideational content: at times, there is a political subtext, and
this is discussed by Orwell in his essay *Politics and the English language* (1946/1962), and by Zijderveld, who examines clichés in various semiotic forms (1979). (These discussions can be related to
discussions of metaphor and ideology by Kress and Hodge (1979),
Kress (1989), and Martin (1989).) Yet cliché is not a formal category
of lexical item but rather a reflection of an individual's stylistic
judgement, nor is it a static category but one that changes over
time. See Howarth (1996: 12 ff.) for a critical discussion of the term.

   In certain kinds of text, FEIs and other lexis deemed informal are
written in scare quotes to distance the writer from his/her lexical
choice:

If you are interested, do come along to one of our regular Wednesday
evening 'get togethers' at the Keys Club, Cornwall Street, and give us the
'once over'. The evenings start at 9.00 pm and all prospective new members will be met on the door and 'looked after' on their first evening by our
host or hostess of the week who will tell them all about the club.
   Do come along. Its [*sic*] great fun once you have **'broken the ice'** and
you are more than welcome.
   Looking forward to seeing you. (BofE: ephemera)

In fact there is a strange dissonance here between the welcome in
the message, realized in a generally informal mode of addressing,
and the apparent need to distance lexis. Similarly, *proverbial* is used
to signal FEIs and the relevant schema, distancing and pre-empting
possible criticism of lexical choice as cliché (see further in Section
10.5):

According to this theory, the abnormal protein acts as **the proverbial
bad apple**, corrupting its neighbours one by one: the protein does not
synthesise new copies of itself as it would if it were replicating in a
conventional sense. (BofE: journalism)

The Senate read **the proverbial writing on the wall** and told the President there was too little support. (BofE: non-fiction)

At the end of the day has been condemned as cliché and ridiculed
for vacuity. It is comparatively common in OHPC, with a frequency
of around 6 per million words. Functionally, it is organizational and
signals a conclusion, summary, or opinion; it also modalizes by
referring to future time (or to a later point in time). This example
from written text is relatively unexceptionable:

Vermuyden had faced remarkable difficulties, not least the age-old problem of clients who want the profit **at the end of the day**, but who are not prepared to lay out sufficient capital to achieve it. (OHPC: non-fiction)

An example from spoken interaction has a different effect:

At the end of the day though, the championship I think, tells you who is the best team of any one year and [um] that's the professional's choice I think, if you said at the start of the year which trophy we'd like to win, we would have said the championship, [um] we were top I think after two games and we fell away a bit since but [um] the time to be tops after twenty two, so lets hope we can get up there. (OHPC: transcribed radio programme)

Here *at the end of the day* is part of a series of fillers and other markers of hesitation or distance which indicate the speaker's production difficulties. It is this kind of use which is responsible for dislike of the expression. Although its interpersonal function is not meaningless, heavy densities of similar fillers in a text may indeed obscure the message, but perhaps through communicative incompetence rather than, necessarily, anything more sinister.

This suggests another way of looking at clichés, as production devices. Cowie (1992: 9ff.) sees the incidence of FEIs and semi-fixed expressions in newspaper reports or editorials as partly driven by time constraints as well as by stylistics. Uses of 'clichéd' FEIs can therefore be seen as interpersonal strategies which enable the communication of the message, and as discoursally and pragmatically of importance.

Cohesion and FEIs

Cohesion makes texts into text. It is the enabling system of ties or links within a text that makes it possible to interpret its elements as meaningful and relevant; it is both meaning-oriented and text-oriented. In *Cohesion in English*, Halliday and Hasan (1976) describe how first the grammatical system and then the lexical system provide the cohesive ties which enable text. Hasan presents reorganized models of cohesion in Hasan (1984) and in Halliday and Hasan (1989: 70–96). These later models blur the 1976 distinction between grammatical and lexical cohesion, and redefine the notion of lexical cohesion in terms of 'general' and 'instantial', and of 'identity chains' and 'similarity chains' (1984: 201 ff. and 1989: 84 ff.). The notion of collocation as a cohesive force is weakened, and the concept of lexical cohesiveness is made more robust by analysis in terms of specific relations such as synonymy and hyponymy, rather than general relatedness of topic as evidenced in the vocabulary. Other discussions and models of cohesion include those of Hoey (1991), de Beaugrande and Dressler (1981), and Sinclair (1993): these allow effective explorations of texts as dynamic processes and of textual organization, and variously show up weaknesses in Halliday and Hasan's original model.

In spite of the admitted weaknesses in Halliday and Hasan's original model, it is the one which lends itself most to a focus on different kinds of lexical item and it is the most convenient model to apply in an exploration of the ways in which FEIs provide cohesion in their texts. In this chapter, the cohesive effects of FEIs are grouped into the grammatical (in terms of Halliday and Hasan's 1976 model); the lexical (principally repetition and consistency of lexical sets); and the semantic (substitution and other endophoric identity). These groupings are intended primarily as headings for the discussion of different kinds of cohesive phenomena. However, it should be noted that the cohesiveness of FEIs is always partly lexical, since they are a lexically determined subset of the lexicon. Moreover, their cohesiveness is often complicated since metaphors may be tied through their surface lexis or deep meanings, or both.

10.1 GRAMMATICAL COHESION

Grammatical cohesion is provided in text through such processes as reference, substitution, and ellipsis; also conjunction, although Halliday and Hasan see this as both grammatical and lexical (1976: 6 and 226ff.), and Hasan separates it out altogether in her revised models (1984: 185; Halliday and Hasan 1989: 82). Amongst database FEIs, organizational ones (see Section 8.7) provide grammatical cohesion, either referentially by tying texts to contexts in time and space, or conjunctively by showing the logical connections between propositions or signalling kinds of information, and so on. The following subsections examine more closely how FEIs provide cohesion through reference and conjunction, and as the latter is the larger phenomenon, it will be dealt with first. FEIs also provide cohesion through substitution: this is discussed in Section 10.3 as part of the general semantic cohesiveness of FEIs.

10.1.1 *Cohesion through Conjunction*

The conjunctive roles and functions of FEIs can be seen in the following examples, taken from Halliday and Hasan's *Cohesion in English* itself:

The linguistic patterns, which embody, and **at the same time** also impose structure on, our experience of the environment, **by the same token** also make it possible to identify what features of the environment are relevant to linguistic behaviour and so form part of the context of situation. (1976: 21)

Texture is a matter of degree. It is almost impossible to construct a verbal sequence which has no texture at all—but this, **in turn**, is largely because we insist on interpreting any passage as text if there is the remotest possibility of doing so. We assume, **in other words**, that this is what language is for; whatever its specific function may be in the particular instance, it can serve this function only under the guise of text. (1976: 23)

This affects our notion of a text. Up to now we have been discussing this on the assumption of an all-or-nothing view of texture: either a passage forms text, or it does not . . . But **in fact** there are degrees of texture, and if we are examining language from this point of view, especially spoken language, we shall **at times** be uncertain as to whether a particular point marks a continuation of the same text or the beginning of a new one. (1976: 24–5)

But in the analysis of texts, relations within the sentence are fairly adequately expressed already in structural terms, **so that** there is no need to involve the additional notion of cohesion to account for how the parts of a sentence hang together. (1976: 146)

The highlighted FEIs represent all four of the categories of conjunction that Halliday and Hasan set out (1976: 238 ff.). The first category is additive: conjoining new or additional information. *By the same token* is both additive and internal: that is, the relationship is within the communication process rather than within the content of the text. It indicates comparison and similarity. The cohesive tie is provided through the establishment of parallels and interinvolvement between the fact that 'linguistic patterns' encode 'our experience of the environment' and the fact that they enable the identification of salient and relevant factors in the environment. *In other words* is also additive and internal, and it is an example of expository apposition. It provides a cohesive tie between 'we insist on interpreting any passage as text [etc.]' and its relexicalization or reformulation expressed as 'We assume . . . that this is what language is for'.

In fact exemplifies the second of Halliday and Hasan's types of conjunction: adversative, indicating 'contrariness to expectations'. In their terms, it is internal, and a contrastive avowal. It ties the 'all-or-nothing view of texture' with 'there are degrees of texture', promoting the second proposition as contrastive and a corrective to the first.

The third kind of conjunction is causal, indicating reasons, results, and purposes. The conjunction *so that* is a general causal conjunction, in this case linking condition and corollary as steps in an argument, and tying the assertion about relations within the sentence being 'well expressed in structural terms' with the conclusion that it is accordingly unnecessary to invoke additionally the notion of cohesion.

At the same time, in turn, and *at times* can be regarded as temporal, the fourth of Halliday and Hasan's categories of conjunction, in that they indicate time reference or sequence, and provide cohesive ties through this. However, both expressions are complex. *In turn* is also deictic, or has a function in clarifying reference. *At the same time* is partly additive, and ties 'impose structure on' to 'embody', indicating that they occur together. In other contexts, *at the same time* can be adversative:

The Lytton commission laboriously toured the Far East. At the end of 1932 it reported. It found that many of the grievances were justified. **At the same time** it condemned the Japanese method of redressing these grievances. (OHPC: non-fiction)

This occurrence of *at the same time* ties in an adversative relationship the quasi-incompatibles, the acceptance of the grievances and the condemnation of action taken over them.

A clearer case of temporal conjunction is presented by, say, *at last*:

These attacks went virtually unreported in the Western media and have been conveniently ignored by those who have since sought to justify the US/China game of condemning Vietnam for an invasion that was, in fact, an act of self-defence. The truth of this episode is **at last** dawning in America, as a speech by the Democratic Majority leader, Senator George Mitchell, recently made clear. (OHPC: journalism)

At last ties the earlier state of affairs—lack of reporting—with a changed situation, and it is partly adversative too in this context: this is reinforced by adversative *in fact* in the previous sentence.

Halliday and Hasan also describe a small heterogeneous group of what they term 'continuatives' (1976: 267 ff.). Their examples include the FEIs *of course* and *after all*, which provide cohesion within a text, and do not always link with the external topic. They may be grouped with the boundary markers and other FEIs described in Section 8.7. While such items are complex and strongly interpersonal, their conjunctive functions in most cases can be related to those described above.

10.1.2 *Cohesion through Reference*

Cohesion through reference is largely provided by means of the grammatical system. Halliday and Hasan categorize it (1976: 37 ff.) into personal (*I, he, her, its,* etc.); demonstrative (*this, the, here, then,* etc.); and comparative (*same, equal, other, such, likewise,* etc.). Many of these items are located within the nominal group, but this is an infrequent position for FEIs and relatively few FEIs can be related to these functions.

Personal reference is provided by a few periphrastic FEIs, for example *what's his/her name, yours truly, our friend,* and *the powers that be*. They do not always provide endophoric cohesion; however, cohesive functions can be seen in:

So as you will see this leaves a hole as big as a goat's backside in the programme, and Dulcie wrote to Jas and I that unless one of us would write another ballet, and a longish one at that, the University Ballet wouldn't be able to go to JHB!!! Jas can't, so of course **yours truly** will have to do it . . . (OHPC: letter in non-fiction)

'Don't blame you for getting out,' said Rush. 'You probably didn't like listening to **our friend** from overseas.' (OHPC: fiction)

In the first example, *yours truly* is coreferential with the writer and with *I* in the previous sentence. In the second example, *our friend* . . . is coreferential with someone present in the preceding narrative situation.

FEIs with demonstrative reference fall into two groups. First, deictics with endophoric discoursal reference, such as *in question*, *in hand* (as in 'the job in hand'), and *at issue*:

To prolong the life of a seal, the Spanish will mount an operation which could cost several tens of thousands of pounds, and involve the deployment of a crack army unit and the latest military technology. The animal **in question** is a rare Monk Seal which lives off the Chafarinas, a group of islands belonging to Spain near the North African coast. (OHPC: journalism)

Mr Hans-Dietrich Genscher, Foreign Minister and leading Free Democrat, said he was appalled at the discussion 'as if the subject **at issue** were the stock market quotation of a major company instead of the future of 17m people'. (OHPC: journalism)

In question ties 'the animal' to the seal previously mentioned, and *at issue* locates 'the subject' as well as indicating that it is disputed.

Other FEIs locate in time and space, and are therefore deictic. These include *in — years'/months'/etc. time*, *the — of the moment*, and *— neck of the woods*:

The real boost for cellular radio will come **in two to three year's time** with the introduction of the Europe-wide service. (OHPC: journalism)

B: Yes, this, this is your, **your neck of the woods** [*A*—], what's, what's happening?
A: Right, well I work in quite a number of Community Centres across the City, and Northway Community Centre which has a bar with quite a large turnover . . . (OHPC: transcribed radio programme)

In two to three year's time ties the proposition temporally to the extralinguistic or discoursal situation. *Your neck of the woods* ties with preceding and following mentions of Northway Community Centre.

FEIs do not really provide cohesion through comparative reference. Comparative and contrastive FEIs such as *as against —*, *in comparison*, *as opposed to —* and *in contrast* are structurally conjunctive, and their cohesion lies in the conjunction of the associated propositions rather than in the strings themselves. FEIs such as *(as different as) chalk and cheese* and *like two peas in a pod* indicate similarity and dissimilarity, but as general qualities, not for deixis.

10.2 LEXICAL COHESION

Halliday and Hasan explain lexical cohesion as 'the cohesive effect achieved by the selection of vocabulary' (1976: 274). They consider it in terms of two principal groupings: reiteration (repetition, synonymy, and hyponymy) and collocation. Their notion of collocation has been shown to be weak and insufficiently rigorous for formal analysis of the lexical organization of texts (Carter 1987: 73f.; Hoey 1991: 6ff.). However, one of the most interesting aspects of the lexical cohesiveness of FEIs is the way in which their lexis and meanings interact with their co-texts, and this is most easily considered in terms of collocation. The notion of collocational cohesiveness is therefore retained in the following discussion.

10.2.1 *Lack of Cohesiveness and Incongruity*

Where (broadly) metaphorical FEIs are concerned, it is their very lack of cohesion which signals their metaphoricality and anomalousness. The lexico-semantic content of the text sets up contextual constraints whereby any literal value for the metaphor is excluded. For example, in

They build on the introduction of general management into the NHS five years ago, which has seen all managers from region down to hospital move on to rolling contracts and performance-related pay. That has undoubtedly improved the management of the service. But it has also reduced the managers' willingness to **rock the boat** in public—over resources, for example—however hard they may argue in private. (OHPC: journalism)

Yesterday's return was seen by the company as a sign of a widespread back-to-work movement which could spread to thousands of workers at the three sites today. But Roger Lyons, assistant general secretary of the union MSF, said yesterday: 'British Aerospace **are clutching at straws** in advance of an important meeting tomorrow which will mobilise support for the strikers . . . ' (OHPC: journalism)

references to boats and straws are incongruent, and there is no lexical cohesiveness between the FEIs and their co-texts. Compare the discussion of ambiguity in Section 7.1.

Many metaphorical FEIs incorporate nominal groups with *the*, for example *bite the bullet, carry the can, jump the gun, spill the beans,* and *take the bull by the horns*. Although these FEIs violate truth conditions, if interpreted literally, and have no lexical cohesion with their contexts, *the* signals shared or given information, which must be retrieved indirectly from the context via the meaning of the FEI, rather than directly as in ordinary discourse. Gumpel comments (1974: 34): 'the *definitive* sense characterizing an idiom is made explicit through the *definite* form of the article.' In this way incongruent items are made cohesive. Fellbaum (1993) discusses determiners in idioms at length, pointing out that demonstratives may be substituted for *the* in quasi-compositional FEIs where the reference of the nominal group has already been established.

While metaphorical FEIs are typically lexically incongruent, they may be topicalized or made more coherent or cohesive through, for example, the insertion of adjectives, possessives, demonstratives, and the like: see Section 6.8. For example, in

Under **the sweep of William Glock's new broom** at the BBC, groups such as the Vesuvius and Melos ensembles had been catching up on modern developments throughout the decade; the London Symphony Orchestra was at its all-time peak and the metropolis seemed full of players who actually wanted to do new music. (OHPC: journalism)

Thus it is advisable that the period of bridging finance is minimised if the mortgagee is not to suffer disproportionate expense in servicing this short-term loan. Yet **there is a silver lining to this particular cloud**. If a bridging mortgage is being used for the purpose of purchasing the mortgagee's sole or main residence, at the discretion of the Inland Revenue, it too may qualify for mortgage interest relief and this can be claimed retrospectively. (OHPC: non-fiction)

the insertion of respectively a possessive or demonstrative contextualizes the deixis of the *new broom* and *cloud*.

Incongruence of FEIs in their co-texts sometimes leads to unwitting juxtaposition with other metaphors and locutions, creating humour. This is pointed out by Chiaro (1992: 20f.), who sees it as accentuating cohesion, albeit unintentionally. She cites an example given by Scherzer:

In his search for economic and military aid, Anwar Sadat has not exactly been greeted by [*sic*] **open arms**. (CBS News report, 10 June 1975)

Such accidental cohesion is particularly associated with spoken discourse and the generation of humour. In conversation, it may lead to a stretch of wordplay and punning, and at the very least, the foregrounding of the lexical selection in the interaction. In broadcasting, there is no opportunity to repair the selection, even where inadvertent or inappropriate, as when the anchorperson in the BBC television news coverage of the Townsend Thoresen ferry disaster in 1987 asked the reporter at the scene 'Could the captain have done anything? Or was he just in the same boat as everyone else?'

Humour can arise through unplanned lexical cohesion, or through the mixing of lexically incongruent metaphors, and the Colemanballs column in *Private Eye* is populated with examples. Simpson analyses them as communicative errors (1992: 286) and in terms of breaches of Gricean maxims. He draws particular attention to metaphorical blends and mixed metaphors which flout the Maxim of Quality (1992: 296 ff.). Some examples of Colemanballs were quoted in Section 6.1.11, and two further examples are:

Do you think we **are out of the wood** yet, or are there more hiccups to come? (*Colemanballs* 4 (1988), London: Private Eye & Andre Deutsch)

The proof of the pudding is in the eating and Villa aren't pulling up any trees. (*Colemanballs* 5 (1990), London: Private Eye & Corgi)

Such incongruence may be distinguished from incoherence or false cohesion that arises pathologically. For example, Rochester and Martin cite the following (1979: 94 f.) in their discussion of cohesion in the speech of schizophrenics and thought-disordered speakers:

Interviewer: **A stitch in time saves nine**. What does that mean?

Patient: Oh! that's because all women have a little bit of magic to them / I found that out / and it's called, it's sort of good magic / and nine is sort of a magic number / like I've got nine colors here you will notice / I've got yellow, green, blue, gray, orange, blue, and navy / and I've got black / and I've got a sort of clear white / the nine colors to me they are the whole universe / and they symbolize every man, woman, and child in the world.

There is superficial lexical cohesion here, but no semantic coherence.

More normally, the lexical incongruence of FEIs is accompanied by semantic congruence, and this leads to a crucial point. Cohesiveness of text is desirable, particularly in polemical or discursive non-literary writing, where clarity is important and conjunction bound up with control of the developing argument. But metaphors, proverbs, and so on interrupt and complicate the cohesive flow, even where topicalized through inserted items. The same can be said of ad hoc metaphors, although in this case the analogies that they realize extend their texts ideationally as well as enriching them rhetorically. Through the operation of Gricean maxims, such interruption or complication is interpreted as coherent and cohesive rather than disruptive: see Sperber and Wilson (1986: 238f.), who discuss how a proverb is made relevant through implicature, since if a request to hurry up is met with the response *more haste less speed*, the response will be interpreted as a traditional piece of wisdom, 'attributable . . . to people in general', and 'wise in the circumstances'. FEIs are also cohesive interpersonally—that is, with the dynamic interaction—by maintaining interest, establishing focus, and appealing to shared knowledge and values.

10.2.2 *Extended Metaphors*

Although it is typical for metaphorical FEIs to be lexically incongruent, there are cases where the lexis of FEIs is deliberately developed and made cohesive with the lexis of their co-texts, as in

The lenders would find themselves badly gored **on the horns of a property dilemma**. On the one hand they will have a large number of borrowers simply unable to pay any more, on the other, a property which is falling in value all the time. (OHPC: journalism)

Final judgement must wait until the Government has explained why the £38m payment was simultaneously **under the counter** but **above board**. (OHPC: journalism)

Gored is cohesive collocationally with the literal meaning of *horns* in *on the horns of a dilemma*: *dilemma* is cohesive as a signal of and preface to the two alternatives. *Counter* and *board* in *under the counter* and *above board* are co-hyponyms in the same lexical set, and *under* and *above* are antonyms. Such cases of congruence may be motivated rhetorically, sometimes for entertainment value, sometimes not. The following examples are not purely humorous:

It is time, perhaps only a week ahead of the mid-term reshuffle, to have a look at the centrepiece of the Government's economic policy, its Medium Term Re-election Strategy (MTRS). There are two important questions. The first is whether it can navigate the undoubtedly choppy waters and **deliver the goods**. The second question is who is the best person to have as Chancellor for the **home stretch**. (OHPC: journalism)

The impression created by Topol is that anything is fair game, in or out of government, Civic Forum or not. It is better, he believes, to **rock the boat** than keep it **on an even keel**. (OHPC: journalism)

In each case, the FEIs are lexically cohesive. The first example extends the image of the journey as a metaphor for successful handling of situations and their outcomes: *deliver the goods* collocates with *navigate*, *choppy waters*, and *the home stretch* within a general metaphorical schema. The second example exploits a nautical image in contrasting *rock the boat* and *on an even keel*.

In a more complex case, an FEI is made the locus or vehicle for a metaphor that crucially underpins the argument of the text, an article (by Will Hutton) on economics in The *Guardian* of July 1990, part of OHPC. The thesis addressed by the writer is stated in the opening paragraph:

There is a new economic alibi at large. The British do not save enough. There has been some sort of change in our economic performance, we are all asked to recognise, but the difficulty is that we are just not thrifty enough to capitalise on it.

The premise that the British people's failure to save is responsible for Britain's economic problems is explored further by the writer. He then rejects it, citing Keynes in support of the rejection:

The Keynesian point was simple. Saving cannot itself be a dynamic element in the economy because it is an abstention of activity; it only ceases to be an abstention of activity if it is translated through the financial system into spending.

And, as the plans of those who abstain from activity are governed by a wholly different set of expectations from those who spend; and as the rate of interest, which might be expected to broker between their parallel but different sets of demands, is governed by yet another set of expectations, the economy should be thought of as permanently in search of a point of balance which it can never find.

He continues with the proverb *Don't put the cart before the horse*, developing it through both the visual or surface image and its conventionalized illocutionary function as an admonition concerning sequencing, logic, causes and effects, and so on. (After this, the article continues the refutation in a more straightforward way.)

To regard savings as the animating force in this scheme of things is to **put the cart before the horse**. The **horse** is the growth of national income, propelled by the level of spending; the **harness** linking **horse** and **cart** the financial system, and bringing up the rear is the **cart** of saving. The **horse** is larger the greater the level of investment; and the larger the **horse** the larger the **cart** of savings it can support. But there is no god-given identity between the two, the linkages being wholly determined by the nature of the **harness** the financial system.

It is a rough and ready analogy, of which doubtless Keynes and Keynesians might disapprove, but it serves an important illustrative purpose. For when the lack of savings is bemoaned, what is actually complained of is the excess of spending. And what lies behind the excess of spending is not a collapse in the character of the British, but a transformation in the structure of the financial system, the **harness** linking **horse** and **cart**.

horse	=	growth of national income
(force propelling horse	=	level of spending)
harness	=	financial system
cart	=	savings

FIG. 10.1 *Put the cart before the horse:* metaphor and analogues

For the financial system in the Keynesian scheme of things is not just a neutral inanimate object; it is an **engine** in its own right, whose capacities and decisions—to continue the analogy—actually propel the **horse**. If the **cart** of savings has become smaller, then it is because it has been induced by the **harness** of the financial system. We save less because we can borrow more; and what we borrow we spend.

The antithesis to the contention concerning 'British lack of thriftiness' is represented in 'Saving cannot itself be a dynamic element in the economy': grounds for the antithesis are given through the analogy realized by the proverb. *Don't put the cart before the horse* notionally represents the writer's opinion, and this is tied into the semantic and discoursal context through explicit statements of the analogy: see Figure 10.1. In fact, the argument turns critically on *harness*: the financial system itself, essentially the subject-matter of the column. It changes the image of the harness into that of an engine: crucially, something that is dynamic—not passive and constraining—and has potential, although harnesses and engines in the real world are quite different kinds of entity, and horses and engines would be more natural parallels. The original image itself becomes distorted in the argument, although it still serves to make a point about flawed logic and sequencing, by saying that neither horse nor cart, national income nor savings, are independent of or separable from the harness–engine and system in general. Thus the basic proverb and its extensions provide cohesive ties that hold together the developing argument.

10.2.3 *Humour and Puns*

Some of the texts cited above are reasonably serious in intent; in contrast, other kinds of text deliberately use FEIs as the loci for humour, as Gläser (1986: 48f.) points out. The humour arises through cohesion or false cohesion from puns based on the lexis or phonology of the FEI in question. For example, jokes, riddles, and so on may be built around an idiom:

The days of graffiti **are numbered—the writing is on the wall**. (Nash 1985: 41)

'Someone's bound to **smell a rat**,' as the diner said when he found a mouse in his stew. (Nash 1985: 53)

Abstinence is **the thin end of the** pledge. (Nash 1985: 38)

How do you start a teddy-bear race? **Ready, teddy, go**! (children's joke)

In the first of these, humour arises from the juxtaposition of two crudely synonymous FEIs: *someone's days are numbered* and *the writing is on the wall*. These are further tied by the inserted *graffiti* in the first which is lexically and semantically cohesive with the literal denotation of the second: the second functions as an explanation of the first. The second example relies on cohesion between the literal meaning of *smell a rat* and the situation described: *rat* is co-hyponymic with *mouse*, and *smell* is appropriate collocationally in contexts relating to food and eating. The third example is compositionally meaningless, but *pledge* ties with *abstinence* collocationally, and *the thin end of the wedge* phonologically. The fourth example also relies on phonology: the alteration of the formula *ready, steady, go!* and repetition of *teddy-bear* and *teddy*. Puns are discussed in detail by Nash (1985) and Chiaro (1992): the above examples merely indicate the role of cohesion in constructing humour.

These are jokes framed or formulated according to the subgenre of jokes, but there are other kinds of pun involving FEIs, which similarly function interpersonally. Some examples are given in Section 6.7 in the course of discussing exploitations of the lexis of FEIs. They rely on a process of demetaphorization for their effect, as well as lexical cohesion through collocation and co-hyponymy. In

Steve Bell, the Wolves and England striker, is not one to '**blow his own trumpet**' but he did recently have a go with a saxaphone [*sic*]. (OHPC: journalism)

literal meaning is foregrounded while other rhetorical characteristics of FEIs are retained. Similarly,

After nearly 20 years in university teaching, I have finally realised why universities are known as **ivory towers**. It must be because we are hanging on **by the skin of our teeth**. (letter in The *Guardian*, 24 February 1987)

[sc. on the third Annual Heritage Open Day in Britain] Many contemporary architects are bravely inviting verbal **stone throwers** into their **glass houses**, opening their homes or offices. In Hammersmith, west London, Richard Rogers is opening his famous office. (The *Guardian*, 14 September 1996)

The first of these shows cohesive ties through collocation and iteration. *Universities* is tied synonymically to *ivory towers* (which also evaluates), and *ivory* is tied through co-hyponymy with *teeth*. The whole text evaluates the sociopolitical situation in question by means of the pun. The second example exploits the proverb *people in glass houses shouldn't throw stones*, and equates *glass houses* with *homes or offices*, alluding to the contemporary, sometimes criticized, architectural use of glass as a building material.

Although puns are usually meaningful to some extent at both literal and metaphorical levels, in the following case the idiomatic meaning is lost:

Few pursuits are quite as esoteric as catching numbers **in their prime**. Mathematicians have been searching relentlessly for ever bigger prime numbers (those like 2, 3 and 5 that can only be divided evenly by themselves and by 1) for thousands of years as if they were looking for the Holy Grail. (The *Guardian*, 6 September 1996)

Punning on FEIs may take other semiotic forms and involve visual imagery. Advertisements provide examples, both in magazines and on television, and one example will suffice. A TV advertisement shows a stereotypical scene from a Western: two gunfighters walking towards each other along a street. One prepares to fire but finds the other has drawn an icecream rather than a gun and has started to eat it. The voice-over comments *'Another one bites the Feast'*, exploiting *bite the dust*, itself of Western origin, through the pararhyme of *Feast* (the name of the icecream) and *dust*. This can be compared to a frequent technique in television journalism, where a reporter uses an idiom or other metaphor, juxtaposed with film showing visually whatever is mentioned in the lexis of that idiom or metaphor.

10.2.4 *Headings and Headlines*

Headings and headlines are an important source of puns involving FEIs, although in some cases cohesiveness is superficial and purely lexical. For example, newspaper headlines and headings use idioms, formulae, and sayings, as well as citations and catchphrases. A cursory glance at The *Guardian* of 8 June 1993 provided the following, among many others:

Partners **held over a barrel** (a story about two pub lessees and the quadrupling of their rent)

Why Labour should be wary of brothers **under the skin** (comment on relationship between the Labour Party and the unions)

Paying the piper, calling the tune (leader, comment on union vote against proposal for election reform by John Smith/Labour Party)

The ties vary in kind and depth. The headline in the first of these examples is both lexically cohesive with and semantically appropriate to its story; so too with the second. In the third, the ties are semantic and not lexical at all. All the stories are, to different degrees, about serious issues, situations, or events, and of the headlines, the second and third are not intended as humorous at all.

The selection and use of stylistically marked FEIs as headlines, slogans, and other attention-seeking devices cannot be separated from other lexical choices that are made. Words are often alliterative and, especially in headlines, monosyllabic; syntax may be aberrant, with articles and auxiliaries elided, or nouns catenated in modifier sequences. There is a particular tension between story headlines and stories in newspapers: headlines can be seen as an integral part of the journalistic story frame, attracting attention and arousing interest in readers. See Brown and Yule (1983: 139f.), Crystal and Davy (1969: 177ff.), and Fowler (1991: 156ff.) for further discussion of titles and headlines. They are important: the lexical choices involved are significant, establishing expectations cataphorically and initiating readers into the following texts with which they are cohesive. While newspaper headlines and headings are not necessarily selected by the writer responsible for the associated story, the two elements must be considered together, as single subdiscourses, from the reader's point of view. Newspaper headlines typically have roles in establishing the interpersonal relationship between newspaper and its readership, the 'mode of address' (Hartley 1982: 88ff.), and they promote 'the illusion of oral mode' (Fowler 1991: 63).

Three principal ways in which FEIs in headlines are made formally cohesive with their stories are through lexis, topic, and phonology. In extreme cases there is virtually no semantic cohesion with the topic. Headlines seem to be simply punctuation or signals: they are initiating turns that operate interpersonally, not ideationally. For example,

First past the Post

Sir—Referring to M.E. Matthews' letter and Friday collected post, I can confirm that this is quite a regular occurrence with my post from King's Lynn, Norfolk.

With an 18p [sc. first-class] stamp, Friday postmarked letters are always delivered Monday, and Saturday mail is delivered Tuesday.

However, all is not gloom as a letter I received from Kings Lynn postmarked January 17 arrived on the 20th with an 18p stamp. It was delivered with one from Mablethorpe, Lincs postmarked Doncaster, January 17 with a 13p stamp.

Who is kidding who about first class postage? (letter, *Daily News* (Birmingham), 3 February 1987)

The meaning of the headline FEI has little to do with the contents of the letter. However, *first* is tied cohesively with *first class* and, by synonymy in this context, with *18p stamp*. *Post* in the headline is tied cohesively through homonymy with the set of words *post, stamp, mail, postmarked, delivered, letter, postage*, and so on.

In other cases, the cohesive ties are mainly topical. A report on the English football team and its manager in The *Guardian* of 15 June 1993 is headed *England comes in from the cold but Taylor still draws heat*. The antithesis and the situations described by *in from the cold* and *draw (the) heat* are lexically cohesive through antonymy of *heat* and *cold*, and they summarize the two main topics of the story, but there are no further lexically cohesive ties.

In the next example, the headline is tied through both topic and lexis to the story. An editorial in The *San Francisco Chronicle* of 26 February 1993 which discusses the presence of US troops in Somalia has the headline *Somalia's rocks and hard places*: this is cohesive with the topic and the editorial's rehearsal of the problems faced in Somalia. These problems are evaluated and lexically signalled by *rocks* and *hard places*. The deictic *Somalia's* is tied lexically through repetition in the text with references to *Somalia*. The rest of the headline is tied lexically with the full form of the FEI at the end of the closing paragraph:

For the moment, the best we can hope for is that diplomatic efforts succeed in restoring order while U.S. forces are still present. But the longer the United States remains in Somalia, the more it will look like a colonial occupation force, no matter what its intentions. More and more, Somalia is looking like the proverbial space **between a rock and a hard place**.

Between a rock and a hard place thus functions as both an opening and a closing gambit, as well as a cohesive device and a means of evaluation.

There may be constraints on the use of FEIs, puns, and so on in headlines to certain kinds of story. For example, the following seems to break some convention:

Knives out at funeral

Mourners at the funeral of an armed robber killed by police marksmen set about reporters and photographers with knives, boots, and fists yesterday, leaving five of them in need of hospital treatment by the time police arrived. (The *Guardian*, 7 August 1987)

Finally, there are other kinds of heading that involve FEIs: in particular, the titles of books, films, and so on. There are innumerable examples, and among many, mention may be made of David Lodge's trilogy *Changing Places*, *Small World*, and *Nice Work*, all formulae or anomalous collocations; the films *To Catch a Thief*, *Life is a Bed of Roses*, and *Nine Lives are not Enough*, all forms of proverbs; and the British TV situation comedies *On the Up*, *One Foot in the Grave*, and *Birds of a Feather*, all metaphors or part proverbs. The cohesive ties are complicated, since much longer texts, some non-verbal in part, are involved, but they are none the less there.

10.3 SEMANTIC COHESION

While all cohesive ties are semantic, since they make texts meaningful, some endophorically cohesive uses of FEIs fall together and are more conveniently considered under a separate heading. In these cases, FEIs (typically informational or evaluative FEIs) are used as relexicalizations, opening or closing gambits, and so on. They provide cohesion through substitution or conjunction. In terms of Halliday and Hasan's 1976 model, they are both grammatically and lexically cohesive: compare the blurring of the categorization of cohesive ties as grammatical or lexical in Hasan's revised models of cohesion. In the previous section I concentrated on lexical ties, but I introduced the loose concept of 'topical' cohesion particularly with respect to the relationship between headlines and their associated stories. It is this kind of tie which characterizes the sorts of cohesion I shall discuss in the following sections.

Because FEIs are to some extent non-specific items, they can therefore be used in a variety of contexts. FEIs, especially metaphors, avoid precision by appealing to given schemas with shared evaluations, and thus meanings can be transacted or negotiated interactionally. FEIs are used existentially as synonymous (or antonymous) with each other or with other stretches of text, even though there are theoretically distinctions in meaning. This can be related to the concepts of actual (instantial) and virtual (canonical) synonymy discussed by de Beaugrande and Dressler (1981: 58) and to the description by McCarthy (1988) of how synonymous and antonymous relations are set up in context.

10.3.1 *Relexicalization and Substitution*

FEIs are used in relexicalizations—or reformulations—of situations or states that are encoded in the co-text. An example of this was given above, where *put the cart before the horse* was used as the locus for an extended metaphor. They are essentially condensed paraphrases of the advice or proposition contained elsewhere in the texts. These textual uses of FEIs involve lexical substitution, and the re-interpretation and encoding of a wider, looser stretch of language in the FEI. Halliday and Hasan write (1976: 89): 'Substitution . . . is a relation within the text. A substitute is a sort of counter which is used in place of the repetition of a particular item.' Although they are talking here of proforms such as *one* and *do*, and of coreferentiality and avoidance of repetition, the point may be extended to lexical substitution: FEIs are very much counters set down in text, albeit marked. In this respect, FEIs can be related to the kinds of discourse-organizing noun, such as *cause, claim, idea, reason, suggestion,* which function anaphorically and metadiscoursally: crucially, some hold evaluations. See, for example, Winter (1977; 1994) and Francis (1986; 1994) for further discussion. McCarthy considers uses of idioms and other expressions as organizational and signalling devices (1991: 83): he observes that they are used in informal discourses for functions performed by more formal vocabulary in written argumentation.

The following example comes from an article on expert systems development and its relationship with traditional software development. It is the first of two parallel labelled subsections in which negative and positive viewpoints are set out and contrasted:

The Negative

The negative argument usually runs as follows.

Expert systems development costs are high, development times are long, and the resulting systems consume large amounts of computing resources. This tends to lead one to think that knowledge engineering methodologies are effective only for small and relatively simple applications. For applications of any real complexity, expert systems software is generally hard to understand, debug and maintain.

In more general terms, knowledge engineering has been described as a scientific **cul-de-sac** which diverts attention from the more important and deeper questions of AI. **In short**, expert systems are **at best** either **a re-invention of the wheel** obscured by a new and fashionable jargon, or **at worst a dead end** which is diverting scarce resources from more important issues. (*Computer Bulletin*, December 1987: 11)

The FEIs here facilitate the message. The structure of the argument is controlled: a preface, followed by a paragraph outlining the arguments, followed by the 'more general' paragraph which contains two summaries or interpretations, each introduced by a hyperpropositional FEI. (The following subsection, outlining the positive argument, follows much the same pattern.) The first summary contains a metaphor centred on *cul-de-sac*, with the inserted prenominal focuser scientific. The second summary expands this slightly as two groups, prefaced by the parallel and contrastive FEIs *at best* and *at worst*. One group contains a nominalization of the expression *reinvent the wheel*, which evaluates negatively, and the other a further negatively evaluating FEI (*be*) *a dead end*, which is tied through synonymy with *cul-de-sac*. *Dead end* is accordingly a restatement of a clarification of a summary of an argument.

In the next example, an FEI is used to evaluate a situation, and then relexicalized to explain the situation further. *You know*, a conventionalized appeal to shared knowledge (compare Schiffrin 1987: 267ff.), signals the tie and equation:

I said before I went that they **were putting the cart before the horse**. **You know**, they were doing the applications before the research. (conversation, 29 March 1988)

These last two examples demonstrate general–particular patterns in text: compare Hoey (1983: 134ff.). The FEIs encode a generalizable situation, one familiar to the hearer, which is then relexicalized more precisely. The example from *Computer Bulletin* is a particular segment of a larger-scale pattern, but it also contains its own general–particular pattern.

Relexicalization is often less heavily signalled, and the tie simply indicated through proximity. In the next example, the FEI precedes the stretch with which it is tied:

Academic freedom stands little chance against this onslaught. **The final twist of the knife**, the removal of tenure, will make it almost impossible to protect traditional freedoms. (*AUT Bulletin*, January 1988)

The nominalization of *to twist the knife* is used to evaluate the more specific event *the removal of tenure*. The apparent pleonasm and tautology of these groups foregrounds the evaluation inherent in *the final twist of the knife.* In fact, although the FEI could be omitted, *the removal of tenure* could not: there is no other reference in the text which explains what is encoded as *twist of the knife.*

In the following example, three proverbs form the structure of the argument in the opening of the following editorial concerning the political situation, censorship and repression, in South Africa: the first proverb is also exploited in the heading:

Out of sight, but much in mind

Two years ago the problems of South Africa were problems for all the world: because the world could see them daily, in their mounting violence, on television screens. Then came the State of Emergency. The pictures vanished. News copy was censored. Newspapers in South Africa were muffled, or banned. And some 30,000 blacks were locked away. Problems over? In one way, for a time, it almost seemed so. **Out of sight was out of mind**. Pressure for sanctions abated. Mrs Thatcher was seen to smile triumphally.

Appearances, however, **were always deceptive**. Behind the pall of censorship the townships were still simmering in revolt. And yesterday, for any doubters, **actions** again **spoke louder than words**. Mr P. W. Botha renewed his State of Emergency just two days after the end of a strike by black trades unions which had brought much of the country to a halt. The problem of South Africa hasn't gone away, and two years of television remission have done nothing to ease or address it. [continued] (The *Guardian*, 11 June 1988)

The exploited proverb of the headline establishes an abstract of the editorial—that something is not forgotten in spite of not being visible—with adversative *but* signalling the exploitation and linking the contrasting pairs *out of/in* and *sight/mind*. It ties lexically with the non-exploited occurrence in the first paragraph *out of sight was out of mind* by means of both repetition and antonymy. *Out of sight* in both instances is iterated through collocation or substitution in the contrasting original situation (. . . *were problems for all the world: because the world could see them daily . . . on television screens*) and in the later 'synonymous' situation (*pictures vanished* and *blacks were locked away*, and even *News copy was censored . . . Newspapers were . . . banned*). *Out of sight* then becomes equated with *Problems over* and the proverb's continuation *out of mind*. It is set up rhetorically as a false equation, through the series of modalizers *in one way, for a time, it almost seemed so*; through the headline's *but much in mind*; and even, given the newspaper's political sympathies, the reference to Mrs Thatcher smiling.

The second paragraph opens with the second of the proverbs, here inflected: *Appearances were always deceptive.* This signals in lexicalized form the falseness of the equation. *Appearances* ties cohesively into the chain centred on *out of sight*. The whole proverb is relexicalized in the specific event encoded in the next sentence: *behind the pall of censorship the townships were still simmering in revolt*. *Appearances* is tied to *the pall . . .* , and *deceptive* is by implication tied to *behind, censorship, still*, and so on. The third proverb *actions speak louder than words* is a distant semantic relative of the second: the *actions/words* dichotomy is presented as another encoding of the *appearances/reality* dichotomy. The renewal of the State of Emergency—the specific realization of *actions*—is then taken as indicative of the 'problem' not having gone away, and so it is tied cohesively with the 'problem' set out in the first paragraph, with *simmering in revolt*, and with *a strike . . .* The second part of the third proverb, *spoke louder than words* is tied lexically with the co-textual references to the media and censorship. It is slightly unsatisfactory from an ideational point of view, since one of the points made is that censorship has enforced no words at all: moreover, there has been no reference to speech-making. In this can be seen justification for one of the criticisms levelled at the use of idioms, proverbs, and other formulae or 'clichés' in text: that the rhetorical effect is prioritized over meaningfulness.

10.3.2 *Prefaces*

Many FEIs are marked lexical choices, and it is therefore not surprising that they are used at rhetorically significant points in text—in effect, as boundary markers. This section considers their uses when text-initial or paragraph-initial, prefacing the following text. Occurrences in headlines may also be seen as prefaces, although in this case there is (theoretically) cohesion with the whole of the following text, not just part of it.

In Section 8.9, I gave examples of FEIs functioning as prefaces to illustrate the cross-functioning of FEIs. In a further example, a proverb occurs as an opening gambit in an editorial concerning dental health in Britain, and the first paragraph is

If **it is an ill wind which blows nobody any good**, it is also a wind of exceptional benevolence which does not blow someone, somewhere, a bit of harm. The livelihood of people who make false teeth, it was reported yesterday, is a threatened by a glorious upsurge in dental health. It is expected that the rate of total tooth loss will drop . . . to 6 per cent by 2028 . . . According to Professor Martin Downer of the Institute of Dental Survey, the market for replacement dentures may be finished by 2041. (The *Guardian*, 30 May 1991)

There is lexical cohesion in the first sentence, where *wind* and *blow* in the proverb are repeated in the main clause, *nobody* is replaced by *someone*, and *ill* and *any good* are tied to the antonymous strings *of exceptional benevolence* and *a bit of harm*. The exploited relexicalization of the proverb contained in the main clause of the first sentence then forms the springboard for the following text. The result of the 'wind' is equated with the general situation; the implication that it is not *a wind of exceptional benevolence* sets up the expectation that the situation is not perfect. By the time the reader meets *a glorious upsurge in dental health*—the situation equated with the wind's consequences—*a bit of harm* has already been interpreted as the threat to the livelihood of false teeth makers. Such prefatory uses of FEIs signal content and also the writer's attitude.

Another case of cross-functioning occurs in the following opening of a newspaper column:

Do not, as they say, **hold your breath**, but the much-maligned American legal system might just have located the Achilles heel of this country's insane gun laws. (The *Guardian*, 8 November 1993)

Don't hold your breath is typically used as a modalizer to express doubt and evaluate negatively someone else's opinion or wish. Here, it is organizational too and is altogether more positive: 'it might happen' without the conventionalized implication 'but it's unlikely'. The signalling of the FEI with *as they say* underlines the conventional status of the string and reinforces its rhetorical effect, while distancing.

10.3.3 *Summaries and Evaluations*

Text-final or paragraph-final position is also significant for FEIs, but in this case they are likely to be used with anaphoric reference, as summaries and overt evaluations. The newspaper column starting with *I must nail my colours to the mast*, cited in Section 8.9, ends with this paragraph:

Odd isn't it that the over-zealous pursuit of health and physical prowess, like anything, is not good for us. Another lesson that **moderation in all things** is a good rule to follow. (*Daily News* (Birmingham), 4 June 1987: 10)

There is cohesion in the antonymous tie between *moderation* and *over-zealous*, as well as other references in the preceding text to excessiveness of exercise. The first sentence in the final paragraph is cohesive with one in the first, *intensive sport or intensive training for sport could surprisingly have side-effects*: the second sentence is cohesive with both by means of a cause–consequence or problem–solution relation. The proverb is deontic, offering advice. It is also evaluative, and offers both advice and evaluation as a conclusion and as a summary of the argument of the whole column.

The following is a simple case of a proverb used to summarize and evaluate:

Never again
Journalists at TV-am have voted overwhelmingly against backing the sacked technicians.
So what will their union, the NUJ, do?
Damn all!
When journalists at Wapping voted against a strike in support of the printers NUJ vengeance knew no bounds.
They sent pickets down to harass working journalists, threatened them with expulsion and fined them huge sums.
Yet they achieved precisely nothing.
It's a case of once bitten twice shy. (The *Sun*, 20 February 1988: typographical variation not reproduced)

Once bitten twice shy relexicalizes and is tied with the headline *never again*. Its preface, the formula *It's a case of . . .* , ties the evaluating proverb with the situation just described. *Once bitten* is tied by substitution and metaphor with the action taken by the NUJ over Wapping and the outcome. *Twice shy* is tied similarly with the apparently parallel situation at TV-am and the NUJ's hypothesized or actual lack of action. The parallels are further underlined by the proverb's internal parallelism and contrast, and it functions as a coda: see Section 10.4.

Finally, another editorial uses a proverb to summarize and evaluate, this time in paragraph-final position. The editorial concerns US protests at alleged subsidizing of the European Airbus by the relevant governments, on the grounds that this is unfair competition. The stance of the editorial is already established in the heading: *Airbus must be backed*. The first of two paragraphs ends:

There is nothing in the GATT rules governing international trade which forbid [sic] Government support as long as signatories seek to remove adverse effects on trade. Well, **it takes two to tango**. (The *Guardian*, 4 February 1987)

The proverb as summary is signalled by the prefatory and concessive use of *well*. The proposition contained in the previous sentence also functions as a conclusion, in presenting a judgement on the rights and wrongs of the case: this is reinforced by the proverb. The reciprocity of the proverbial proposition refers back not only to the two sides involved in the dispute, but also to the parallelism between the Airbus situation and a comparable situation, already mentioned, in the US, where there is heavy funding by the US of the aviation industry (apropos of defence). A second strand in the editorial is the motivation underlying US protests, set out in the opening sentences of the editorial, and formulated with metaphors:

The Reagan administration can be excused an occasional show of mercantile machismo. It has a trade deficit of £112 billion hanging round its neck and a strongly protectionist Congress biting at its heels.

The situation, described through personification or metonymy, is returned to in the opening of the second paragraph:

The interesting point is why the Americans should be **making such a song and dance** now.

This follows immediately after *it takes two to tango*, with which it is lexically cohesive. *Making such a song and dance* is tied by substitution with other references to the US protests: anaphorically to *aggressive tactics* and *claims* in the first paragraph, cataphorically to *fuss* towards the end of the second. The FEI also conveys attitude and implies a lack of real justification or cause: in this respect it is cohesive evaluatively with a later lexical selection *fuss* as well as with the general argument of the editorial.

10.4 SPOKEN INTERACTION

It can be predicted that there will be differences in the uses of FEIs in written and spoken language, just as there are sharp distinctions in the lexis and grammatical structures of written and spoken language (see, for example, Biber 1988). This indeed appears to be the case, and the distinctions may be shown by considering just one of the spoken texts in OHPC—a set of transcripts of several broadcasts of a Radio Oxford discussion programme and phone-in. FEIs are here used less often in a highly mannered way for rhetorical and stylistic effect; they are used more often as devices to maintain, promote, or repair the discourse. Situational FEIs are still rare, but modalizing and organizational FEIs abound as downtoners, hedges, and emphasizers, and boundary markers and connectives. Informational and evaluative FEIs are used as interactional devices in conveying new information or evaluations and negotiating meanings, by appealing to shared knowledge and values.

This can be seen in the following, the opening address by the Director of Social Services of Oxfordshire County Council on the day after the Council's announcement of budgets cuts:

Well **I think**, [*B*—], if I was to try and sum it up I'd say that the Social Services settlement was **the best of a bad job**. [um] once the government announced their capping limits later on . . . late last year, the County Council knew it was **in trouble** and back in December the Social Services Committee faced cuts of **something like** three and a half million. Well, on Tuesday of this week [um] the settlement [um] gave us what is **in effect** [um] a balanced budget—a lot of money in, a lot of money out. **In other words**, we've been funding from within our own budget new developments that'll come **on stream** next year and it's a very complicated budget and it contains some quite [um] controversial [um], which **no doubt** we'll go through **in a minute**, but overall [um], given the total financial situation, I'm a relieved man today.

The FEIs can be grouped according to their text functions: see Table 10.1. *I think* is also organizational here, functioning as a preface. The commonest use is that of modalizers: three of the four mitigate or downtone, retreating from certainty. In terms of cohesion, *I think*, *in other words*, and *in a minute* have conjunctive functions, signalling cataphorically the succeeding discoursal events. *In other words* typically signals a reformulation, but here it signals something that may rather be considered new information. *The best of a bad job* sets up expectations both of a comparatively satisfactory outcome and a negatively evaluated situation. *Best* ties with positively evaluated *balanced* (*budget*), *relieved*, and perhaps *new*

TABLE 10.1. *FEIs realizing text functions*

informational	on stream
evaluative	the best of a bad job
	in trouble
modalizing	I think
	something like
	in effect
	no doubt
organizational	in other words
	in a minute

(*developments*); *bad job* ties with *in trouble, cuts,* and *total financial situation. On stream* forms part of a chain that includes *new, 'll come,* and *next year.*

In spoken interaction, lexical cohesion through extended metaphors is normally deliberate, marked, and foregrounded, but the following case from the transcripts seems comparatively unforced:

A: The majority of people who come in are angry because they can't get anywhere. It doesn't matter how hard they try, the system **knocks them down**. You know, they might just **get up a little way** and then some bureaucracy **knocks them down again** and they're back where they started.

B: Without betraying any secrets, or identifying any particular people, can you give us general cases that would illustrate this? I mean what happens with some of those people when they try to get **on their feet**? They are **knocked down** again?

On one's feet follows on naturally from the metaphor used by the previous speaker. *B* also sets up expectations for the following speaker: that is, an account of further difficulties encountered, and a movement from general to detail or example. The threefold repetition of *knock . . . down* reinforces cohesion. Sinclair regards this kind of repetition as verbal echo, often indicating co-operation and convergence on the part of the speakers (1993: 15f.): compare also Tannen (1989: 36ff. and *passim*), who sees repetition as evidence of patterning and structure in conversation.

In the following example, the discussion concerns John Major's failure to appoint women to his first cabinet:

B: Are you prepared to accuse him of insincerity?

A: I'm, no, I'm prepared to **give him the benefit of the doubt** for the moment. I think we'll wait and see.

B: What's **the doubt**? What's **the doubt that you're giving him the benefit of**?

A: **The doubt** is that he perhaps didn't take into consideration of the women who are available. I mean people like Linda Chalker and [um] so on [um] that's **the doubt** and **that doubt** is going to be either borne out or shown to be wrong by the rest of John Major's incumbents, so at the moment I'll certainly **give him the benefit of the doubt**.

B: All right. [continued]

Give someone the benefit of the doubt—in particular, *doubt*—provides a motif or framework for this part of the discussion. *B* exploits it to stimulate the discussion: *What's the doubt that you're giving him the benefit of* seems an anomalous transformation. It may be compared to the manipulation of *put the cart before the horse* in Section 10.2.2, where *put the cart before the horse* is manipulated. That example is more marked because it involves a metaphor where both image and meaning are exploited. Both examples are, however, utilitarian in being strategies for developing the discoursal argument.

FEIs are frequently used in relexicalizations, as in

> You know, it's all very well to put the blame on everybody else, but you try and try and try. You **bend over backwards**. The vicar's tried I don't know how many times to talk to him, offer him this and that, but he won't have it.

where the hyperbole of *bend over backwards* iterates and reinforces repeated *try*. Another example shows cohesion through iteration across turns and an interruption:

B: Oh, that was confidential. Oh yes, I wouldn't tell anybody.
A: Of course not!
B: It's **between you and me**.
A: [laugh] These things are very difficult, very sensitive. I can't say any more than that.

Between you and me is tied to *confidential* and *wouldn't tell anybody*, and again the iteration has a reinforcing function.

It has already been seen that FEIs are used as summaries and evaluatives. McCarthy (1992: 59ff.) and McCarthy and Carter (1994: 111) draw attention to this in relation to the structure of oral narrative, as set out by Labov (1972). They observe idioms used at points where the teller is evaluating, and in codas where the narrative worlds and real worlds are linked or where a story or narrative subsection is signalled as ending. Similarly, Drew and Holt (1995) explore 300 idioms and other FEIs in a corpus of telephone conversations, and find strong evidence of idioms being used to signal topic transition, summarizing or assessing a segment of the conversation: 'the production of an idiom is mutually oriented to or by participants as bring one topic to a close and providing an opportunity for introducing a next topic' (1995: 124). This can be seen in:

A: And it's just like dead easy going. And yet everybody else is really . . . complic This had been some unbelievable complications externally. Like me and . . . Barry haven't got a problem with it . . .
B: Mm . . .
A: we just see each other when we see each other. But everybody else . . . [laughs] is freaking out. And it's like I said to Harry and what have you you . . . know Barry and I are old enough to look after ourselves so sort

of No. That's . . . it. So I've **put Harry's back up** . . . [laughs] I've fallen out with Larry. I've fell out with my mum. [laughs] When I do it I do it **big time**. Really I do. So that only leaves Lily really . . . [laughs]

B: She's all right. [laughs]

A: I've only got one friend left. Bless her. Yeah. Lily and Milly. Milly isn't too . . . good at the moment . . . She er . . . she's got something wrong with the . . . discs in her back. A couple of them have slipped and like the stuff like the . . . jelly stuff if you like in between them that's all rotting. (BofE, unscripted conversation, names changed)

Drew and Holt's data and other corpus examples suggest strongly to me that it is the *evaluation* function which is the key here. The FEIs are being slotted into a natural point at which a section of the conversational narrative is wound up, through evaluation, preparatory to moving onto a new topic or to ending the conversation altogether: compare some of the examples from written text set out above. Idioms are selected precisely because they are evaluative, and they are cross-functioning as boundary markers.

In an earlier paper (1988), Drew and Holt look at idioms with respect to the formulation of complaints, observing that idioms occur in segments where summaries or assessments are being made by the speaker/complainant, perhaps after listing the grounds of the complaint. Crucially, Drew and Holt say that idioms occur at points where the sympathies or affiliation of the addressee have not yet been displayed. They suggest that the metaphorical character of idioms is important here: ' . . . idiomatic expressions remove the complaint from its supporting circumstantial details. This may give such expressions a special robustness: since they are not to be taken literally, they may have a certain resistance to being tested or challenged on the empirical facts of the matter' (1988: 406). Again, their data here strongly supports other, broader, observations in other kinds of discourse. Idioms are used as evaluatives, to establish shared views and pre-empt disagreement. In Drew and Holt's data, idioms are a means by which the speaker/complainant moves towards the alignment of the hearer and a common interpretation or evaluation of the situation, by enforcing the shared view inherent in the idioms.

In all this, it appears that many uses of FEIs in spoken interaction may well be qualitatively different from those in written text. Cohesiveness is less prominent, and in particular, conjunctive cohesion less clearly marked as a separate phenomenon; yet at the same time there is clear evidence of cohesive patterns. Modality is expressed more often though fillers than through primary clause elements, and informational and evaluative FEIs are used as production strategies. This is another area in which further genre-based studies of FEIs are needed.

10.5 SIGNALLING OF FEIS

Finally, I want to consider briefly how FEIs as linguistic items are made cohesive through structures where the speaker/writer comments metalinguistically on his/her choice of lexis. A word such as *phrase*, *catchphrase*, or *expression* may be used in the immediate co-text: these words tend to co-occur in OHPC with citations, colloquialisms, or clichés, rather than institutionalized FEIs. The following example uses *bromide*:

And since this was obviously the case, it might be profitable for the scum to pursue a little knowledge, for as the **bromide** declared, **a little knowledge is a dangerous thing**. (OHPC: fiction)

To coin a phrase co-occurs with clichés, and *if you'll pardon the expression* with strings considered indelicate, although neither occurs specifically with FEIs.

FEIs themselves may be used to signal other FEIs. Schiffrin discusses the use of *y'know* to acknowledge consensual truths (1987: 267ff.), and cites

Y'know they say **an apple a day keeps the doctor away.**

Similarly, the formula *as they say*:

Well, **as they say, the rest is history**, or quite a bit of it. (OHPC: journalism)

Truth, as they say, is stranger than fiction. (OHPC: fiction)

The mind boggles, as they say. (OHPC: fiction)

The FEI tag *if you like* occurs largely in conversation and oral narrative. It is used widely in contexts where meaning is being negotiated, for example in relexicalizations or in vague formulations, but in the following examples it is used to comment on the FEI just selected, distancing the speaker from his/her selection:

Because at the end of the day the most logical structure is the clinical directorate structure because that firmly puts the clinician in the er **in the driving seat if you like**. (BofE: unscripted conversation)

A: It's not a problem at the present time erm and therefore it's not being addressed.

B: Mm.

A: I think it's sort of it's **on the back burner if you like**. (BofE: unscripted conversation)

Another such FEI tag is *so to speak*. In BofE it is used mainly in spoken interaction and journalism, again after an FEI, to acknowledge that an item might be thought too trite or poorly selected, to acknowledge a pun, or to signal the appropriateness of a literal reading of an idiom:

Impotence and infertility are travelling **hand in hand (so to speak)**. (BofE: journalism)

Queensland promises to be the scene of much investment activity, with large-scale mining and gas infrastructure projects **in the pipeline, so to speak**. (BofE: journalism)

Now Martin being the youngest and I mean the . . . youngest 'cos . . . he was . . . he . . . he's twelve years younger than my . . . sister . . . which meant . . . he was a babe . . . he . . . he as I say he was . . . the ba And of course my mum and dad split up and then my . . . sister . . . about six months . . . Yeah. He was about six months. My mum and dad split up . . . and then my sister left home which . . . sort of **left me holding the baby so to speak**. (BofE: unscripted conversation)

Again, these items are being used as distancing devices, downtoning colloquialisms that are thought too marked or potentially inappropriate for their discourses, or seeking to attribute to other sources a form of wording or its ideational or ideological content.

Inserting *proverbial* signals the idiomatic status of the accompanying string. The adjective *proverbial* occurs 21 times in OHPC, never with the meaning 'of or relating to proverbs', and never signalling proverbs. Instead, it modifies nominal groups in idioms, or simply metaphorical or connotative uses of nouns:

I'm so dead tired these days I **sleep like the proverbial log**. (OHPC: fiction)

. . . getting more broke and, generally speaking, **going even further down the proverbial toilet**. (OHPC: journalism)

The cat is **snug as the proverbial bug in a rug**, on top of the nice warm boiler. (OHPC: journalism)

The much more extensive evidence in BofE supports this, and further suggests that, in addition to signalling FEIs which might be considered clichés, it often signals exploitations: in this way it is used to create even further distance between speaker/writer and their choice of lexis, at the same time as it draws attention to it. BofE data also suggests that *proverbial* is far commoner in journalism than conversation (unlike the euphemism *proverbials*). The much rarer item *proverbially* has a similar signalling function:

[in Puerto Rico] Half a mile down a road bordered by illegal and hallu-cinogenic compana flowers, we found an hospitable one-roomed shack and took to its domino table and local rum supply **like proverbial ducks to agua**. (BofE: journalism)

Why aren't all schools run in this fashion? Apparently the parents never **smell the proverbial rodent**, even when the children iron their own socks. (BofE: journalism)

Most would-be actors do part-time menial work, such as waiting in restaurants, selling in shops or even loo-cleaning, to pay the rent while their real career is still **proverbially waiting in the wings**. (BofE: journalism)

Nicolas (1995: 243) observes that in his data, *proverbial* always follows *the* or another definite deictic, even if this results in a non-standard form of the FEI so interrupted: he is only looking at predicate FEIs. BofE largely supports Nicolas's claim: the cano-nical forms of three of the above examples have *a* and not *the* (in a fourth, an indefinite plural alternates with canonical *a*).

Literally is also used as a signal, but in this case it is inserted or appended in order to demetaphorize or intensify: it is discussed in detail by Powell (1992). In OHPC, *literally* is used to indicate that a metaphorical FEI should be interpreted as having its ordinary compositional meaning (compare *so to speak*) or to emphasize vera-city by suggesting that the accompanying image is not hyperbolic. Both functions can be seen in the following examples, and some signal puns as well:

And last autumn the world began to change **literally hour by hour**. (OHPC: journalism)

It's nice to say this year it's come back home to Shrewsbury—**literally a stone's throw down** the road. (OHPC: transcribed radio journalism)

Will secretaries, with powerful information technology **literally at their fingertips**, take over some of the tasks now done by managers or other office-based professional staff; or will managers, once they have a key-board, have less need for secretarial staff? (OHPC: non-fiction)

. . . that in its confidence of beauty and arrogance **literally took my breath away**. (OHPC: fiction)

It's easy to recall the horrendous noise as we traversed the ground and the earth clods, probably sent up by the propeller blades, crashing against the fuselage as we **literally ground to a halt**. (OHPC: journalism)

In being used to signal the lexical, stylistic, or semantic nature of the associated text, *literally, proverbial,* and other expressions are providing cohesive ties between FEIs and their co-texts. While they foreground the incongruence of the lexis, they are, ironically, at the same time minimizing the lack of cohesion by drawing attention to it. They are therefore far from insignificant as cohesive devices.

11
Afterword

Three main conclusions can be drawn from this account of English FEIs. First, further corpus-based studies are needed in order to make the picture of FEIs more accurate and complete. Second, existing models and descriptions need to be revised in the light of emerging corpus evidence, in particular with respect to form and variation. Third, the significance of the roles of FEIs in discourse should not be underestimated.

Clearly, future research will need to use much larger corpora than OHPC. This has, however, provided a starting-point, so that tendencies can be observed, hypotheses set out, and further evidence or corroboration sought. Cross-corpus comparisons will reveal the extent to which the tendencies and distributions observed in OHPC are borne out more widely. In particular, studies with larger corpora are needed to explore the question of FEIs and genre. My data suggested some general points: for example, the density of metaphors and proverbs seems to be greater in journalism than other text types, and pure idioms seem to be less common in spoken interaction than is often thought. My data also suggested that some individual items have individual genre preferences: this needs to be looked at in more detail.

Further corpus studies, using larger corpora, are needed to explore the formal characteristics of FEIs: their patterning, transformational defectiveness, inflectability, person (and gender), clause position or clause type, and so on. While OHPC suggested much, many FEIs occurred too infrequently to be adequately described. At the same time, OHPC provided massive evidence of the instability of the forms of FEIs. More studies of lexical and syntactic variation are needed, to ascertain which FEIs repeatedly show up in real text as frozen and which as fluid; and to classify and correlate the different kinds of variation. It may then be possible to separate out formal classes, to determine robustly which FEIs could indeed be logged as 'big words', uninflectable, unvariable, and uninterruptable, and at the same time to develop 'rules' governing other more flexible kinds of item.

This leads into the principal theoretical area for further research: the area of typology and categorization. The FEI typology I developed was a means to an end, intended simply to provide a framework for my research. Typology is inherently abstract, and FEIs represent real chunks of language which do not conform neatly to abstract categories. I do not believe that it will be possible to identify the set of FEIs in English as a discrete grouping of vocabulary items—assuming such a thing is desirable in the first place—nor to categorize them definitively until the English lexicon has been mapped out, including the collocational, colligational, and transformational or inflectional patterns associated with individual meanings of individual words. Such a mapping in itself would lead to a better understanding of lexicalization and of the systematic nature of lexicogrammatical frames. FEIs may well prove eventually to be the exceptions in the lexicon, the residue, but many alleged or potential FEIs are in reality single-word items with severe co-textual or contextual restrictions; others are institutionalized metaphorical conceits.

As far as semantics is concerned, my data suggests that very few metaphorical FEIs are ambiguous between literal and idiomatic meanings. Either there is no or almost no evidence for literal equivalents, or there are strongly divergent collocational or colligational patterns associated with either literal or idiomatic uses: this applies too to the different meanings of polysemous FEIs. Virtually no tokens are ambiguous at the level of clause and sentence, and this has implications for psycholinguistic research into the processing of FEIs, which too often seems to have proceeded from an assumption that items are ambiguous; in reality they are not.

As far as pragmatics is concerned, my data suggests the importance of FEIs in relation to discourse and text: in particular, in terms of cohesion, evaluation, and politeness. It is significant that FEIs provide cohesive ties within texts, and that metaphorical FEIs function as indices of intertextuality. It is significant that many FEIs have strong evaluative content; there are interesting implications if there really do prove to be more negatively evaluating FEIs than positive ones. An examination of politeness, face, and FEIs must involve correlations with grammatical person, and here again corpora larger than OHPC are needed to chart restrictions and patterns of use. Finally, it is appropriate to re-emphasize here that FEIs have roles as enabling devices in discourse: they are not redundant, nor necessarily casual or meaningless lexical choices.

I have deliberately focused on FEIs synchronically, but diachronic aspects still need to be explored. How far are current syntactic,

lexical, or semantic anomalies the product of historical development? To what extent do FEIs freeze and unfreeze over time? The
development of historical corpora of English will provide evidence
of earlier processes, while the development of series of very large and
readily accessible text corpora of current English will provide oppor-
tunities to observe FEI behaviour and changes over comparatively
short periods such as five years and less. The evidence so far is that
changes are rapid.

I set out to demonstrate what could be learned from a corpus
about FEIs, and to demonstrate that FEIs are a phenomenon of
discourse as well as the lexicon. I found that existing descriptions
of FEIs do not account adequately for their characteristics as
observed in corpora and in text. There are implications for such
fields as artificial intelligence, semantics, text linguistics, and
cross-linguistic and cross-cultural studies, and there are practical
applications in lexicography, pedagogy, and translation. There is
much more which could be added here; but that might only open
cans of worms, and, as they say, enough is enough.

References

Aarts, J. (1991), 'Intuition-based and observation-based grammars', in K. Aijmer and B. Altenberg (eds.), *English Corpus Linguistics*, London: Longman, 44–62.

Abeillé, A. (1995), 'The flexibility of French idioms: a representation with lexicalized tree adjoining grammar', in M. Everaert, E.-J. van der Linden, A. Schenk, and R. Schreuder (eds.), *Idioms: Structural and Psychological Perspectives*, Hillsdale, NJ: Lawrence Erlbaum Associates, 15–42.

Aijmer, K. (1996), *Conversational Routines in English: Convention and Creativity*, London: Longman.

Aisenstadt, E. (1979), 'Collocability restrictions in dictionaries', in R. R. K. Hartmann (ed.), *Dictionaries and their Users* (Exeter Linguistic Studies 4), Exeter: University of Exeter, 71–4.

—— (1981), 'Restricted collocations in English lexicology and lexicography', *ITL Review of Applied Linguistics*, 53, 53–61.

Aitchison, J. (1987a), 'Reproductive furniture and extinguished professors', in R. Steele and T. Threadgold (eds.), *Language Topics: Essays in Honour of Michael Halliday*, II, Amsterdam: John Benjamins, 3–14.

—— (1987b), *Words in the Mind*, Oxford: Basil Blackwell.

—— (1992), *The Articulate Mammal* (3rd edition), London and New York: Routledge (reprint of 1989 edition published by Unwin Hyman).

Akimoto, M. (1983), *Idiomaticity*, Tokyo: The Shinozaki Shorin Press.

Alexander, R. J. (1978), 'Fixed expressions in English: a linguistic, psycholinguistic, sociolinguistic and didactic study' (part 1), *Anglistik und Englischunterricht*, 6, 171–88.

—— (1979), 'Fixed expressions in English: a linguistic, psycholinguistic, sociolinguistic and didactic study' (part 2), *Anglistik und Englischunterricht*, 7, 181–202.

Alford, D. (1971), 'Kicking the habit', *Linguistic Inquiry*, 2/4, 573.

Allerton, D. (1984), 'Three (or four) levels of word cooccurrence restriction', *Lingua*, 63, 17–40.

Alt, N. V. (1991), 'Non-finite clauses in English verb complementation', Unpublished Ph.D. thesis: University of Birmingham.

Altenberg, B. (1991), 'The London–Lund Corpus: research and applications', *Using Corpora* (Proceedings of the Seventh Annual Conference of the University of Waterloo Centre for the New OED and Text Research), 71–83.

—— and Eeg-Olofsson, M. (1990), 'Phraseology in spoken English: presentation of a project', in J. Aarts and W. Meijs (eds.), *Theory and Practice in Corpus Linguistics*, Amsterdam: Rodopi, 1–26.

Amosova, N. N. (1963), *Osnovy Angliiskoi Frazeologii*, Leningrad: University Press.

Arnaud, P., and Moon, R. E. (1993), 'Fréquence et emploi des proverbes anglais et français', in C. Plantin (ed.), *Lieux Communs: Topoï, Stéréotypes, Clichés*, Paris: Kimé, 323–41.

Atkins, B. T. S. (1992), 'Tools for computer-aided lexicography: the Hector Project', in F. Kiefer, G. Kiss, and J. Pajzs (eds.), *Papers in Computational Lexicography: Complex '92*, Budapest: Research Institute for Linguistics, Hungarian Academy of Sciences, 1–59.

Bahns, J., Burmeister, H., and Vogel, T. (1986), 'The pragmatics of formulas in L2 learner speech: use and development', *Journal of Pragmatics*, 10/6, 693–723.

Baranov, A. N., and Dobrovol'skii, D. O. (1996), 'Cognitive modeling of actual meaning in the field of phraseology', *Journal of Pragmatics*, 25/3, 409–29.

Bar-Hillel, Y. (1955), 'Idioms', in W. N. Locke and A. D. Booth (eds.), *Machine Translation of Language*, New York and London: Technology Press of MIT, John Wiley and Sons, and Chapman and Hall, 183–93.

Barkema, H. (1996*a*), 'The effect of inherent and contextual factors on the grammatical flexibility of idioms', *Synchronic Corpus Linguistics* (Papers from the Sixteenth International Conference on English Language Research on Computerized Corpora, Toronto 1995), Amsterdam: Rodopi, 69–83.

—— (1996*b*), 'Idiomaticity and terminology: a multi-dimensional descriptive model', *Studia Linguistica*, 50/2, 125–60.

Bauer, L. (1979), 'On the need for pragmatics in the study of nominal compounding', *Journal of Pragmatics*, 3/1, 45–50.

—— (1983), *English Word-formation*, Cambridge: Cambridge University Press.

Becker, J. D. (1975), *The Phrasal Lexicon* (Artificial Intelligence Report No. 28: Report No. 3081), Cambridge, Mass.: Bolt, Beranek, and Newman.

Béjoint, H. (1981), 'The foreign student's use of monolingual English dictionaries: a study of language needs and reference skills', *Applied Linguistics*, 2/3, 207–22.

—— (1989), ' "Codedness" and lexicography', in G. James (ed.), *Lexicographers and their works* (Exeter Linguistic Studies 14), Exeter: University of Exeter, 1–4.

—— (1994), *Tradition and Innovation in Modern English Dictionaries*, Oxford: Oxford University Press.

Benson, M., Benson, E., and Ilson, R. (1986), *The BBI Combinatory Dictionary of English*, Amsterdam and Philadelphia: John Benjamins.

Bertuccelli Papi, M. (1996), 'Insinuating: the seduction of unsaying', *Pragmatics*, 6/2, 191–204.

Biber, D. (1988), *Variation across Speech and Writing*, Cambridge: Cambridge University Press.

—— and Finegan, E. (1991), 'On the exploitation of computerized corpora in variation studies', in K. Aijmer and B. Altenberg (eds.), *English Corpus Linguistics*, London: Longman, 204–20.

Binnick, R. I. (1971), 'Bring and come', *Linguistic Inquiry*, 2/2, 260–5.

Blackwell, S. (1987), 'Syntax versus orthography: problems in the automatic parsing of idioms', in R. Garside, G. Leech, and G. Sampson (eds.), *The Computational Analysis of English*, London: Longman, 110–9.

Bloomfield, L. (1935), *Language*, London: Allen and Unwin (first published 1933, New York: Holt).

Bobrow, S. A., and Bell, S. M. (1973), 'On catching on to idiomatic expressions', *Memory and Cognition*, 1, 343–6.

Bogaards, P. (1990), 'Où cherche-t-on dans le dictionnaire?', *International Journal of Lexicography*, 3, 79–102.

—— (1992), 'French dictionary users and word frequency', in H. Tommola, K. Varantola, T. Salmi-Tolonen, and J. Schopp (eds.), *Euralex '92* Proceedings, I (studia translatologica ser. A, 2), Tampere: University of Tampere, 51–61.

Bolander, M. (1989), 'Prefabs, patterns, and rules in interaction? Formulaic speech in adult learners' L2 Swedish', in K. Hyltenstam and L. Obler (eds.), *Bilingualism across the Life-Span*, Cambridge: Cambridge University Press, 73–86.

Bolinger, D. (1976), 'Meaning and memory', *Forum Linguisticum*, 1/1, 1–14.

—— (1977), 'Idioms have relations', *Forum Linguisticum*, 2/2, 157–69.

—— and Sears, D. A. (1981), *Aspects of Language* (3rd edition), New York: Harcourt Brace Jovanovich.

Botelho da Silva, T., and Cutler, A. (1993), 'Ill-formedness and transformability in Portuguese idioms', in C. Cacciari and P. Tabossi (eds.), *Idioms: Processing, Structure, and Interpretation*, Hillsdale, NJ: Lawrence Erlbaum Associates, 129–43.

Botha, W. (1992), 'The lemmatization of expressions in descriptive dictionaries', in H. Tommola, K. Varantola, T. Salmi-Tolonen, and J. Schopp (eds.), *Euralex '92* Proceedings, II (studia translatologica ser. A, 2), Tampere: University of Tampere, 465–72.

Breidt E., Segond, F., and Valetto, G. (1996), 'Local grammars for the description of multi-word lexemes and their automatic recognition in texts', in F. Kiefer, G. Kiss, and J. Pajzs (eds.), *Papers in Computational Lexicography: Complex '96*, Budapest: Research Institute for Linguistics, Hungarian Academy of Sciences, 19–28.

Briscoe, E. J. (1990), 'English noun phrases are regular: a reply to Professor Sampson', in J. Aarts and W. Meijs (eds.), *Theory and Practice in Corpus Linguistics*, Amsterdam: Rodopi, 45–60.

Brown, G., and Yule, G. (1983), *Discourse Analysis*, Cambridge: Cambridge University Press.

Brown, P., and Levinson, S. C. (1987), *Politeness: Some Universals in Language Usage* (2nd edition), Cambridge: Cambridge University Press.

Burgess, C., and Chiarello, C. (1996), 'Neurocognitive mechanisms underlying metaphor comprehension and other figurative language', *Metaphor and Symbolic Activity*, 11/1, 67–84.

Cacciari, C. (1993), 'The place of idioms in a literal and metaphorical world', in C. Cacciari and P. Tabossi (eds.), *Idioms: Processing, Structure, and Interpretation*, Hillsdale, NJ: Lawrence Erlbaum Associates, 27–55.

—— and Levorato, M. C. (1989), 'How children understand idioms in discourse', *Journal of Child Language*, 16, 387–405.

—— and Tabossi, P. (1988), 'The comprehension of idioms', *Journal of Memory and Language*, 27, 668–83.

—— —— (eds.) (1993), *Idioms: Processing, Structure, and Interpretation*, Hillsdale, NJ: Lawrence Erlbaum Associates.

Carter, R. (1987), *Vocabulary*, London: Allen and Unwin.

—— (1993), 'Language awareness and language learning', in M. P. Hoey (ed.), *Data, Description, Discourse: Papers on the English Language in Honour of John McH. Sinclair*, London: HarperCollins, 139–50.

—— and McCarthy, M. J. (1988), *Vocabulary and Language Teaching*, London: Longman.

Čermák, F. (1988), 'On the substance of idioms', *Folia Linguistica*, 22/3–4, 413–38.

—— (1994a), 'Czech Idiom Dictionary', in W. Martin, W. Meijs, M. Moerland, E. ten Pas, P. van Sterkenburg, and P. Vossen (eds.), *Euralex '94* Proceedings, 426–31.

—— (1994b), 'Idiomatics', in P. A. Luelsdorff (ed.), *Prague School of Structural and Functional Linguistics*, Amsterdam and Philadelphia: John Benjamins, 185–95.

—— (1994c), 'On the nature of universality in phraseology and idiomatics', *Z problemów frazeologii polskiej i słowiańskiej*, VI Warsaw: PAN Slawistyczny Ośrodek Wydawniczy, 15–20.

—— (forthcoming), 'Somatic idioms revisited', *Europhras 95*.

Chafe, W. (1968), 'Idiomaticity as an anomaly in the Chomskyan paradigm', *Foundations of Language*, 4, 109–27.

Channell, J. (1994), *Vague Language*, Oxford: Oxford University Press.

Chiaro, D. (1992), *The Language of Jokes*, London and New York: Routledge.

Chin, D. (1992), 'Pau: parsing and understanding with uniform syntactic, semantic and idiomatic representations', *Computational Intelligence*, 8, 456–76.

Chomsky, N. (1965), *Aspects of the Theory of Syntax*, Cambridge, Mass.: MIT Press.

Choueka, Y., Klein, S. T., and Neuwitz, E. (1983), 'Automatic retrieval of frequent idiomatic and collocational expressions in a large corpus', *ALLC Journal*, 4/1 (Association for Literary and Linguistic Computing), 34–8.

Church, K. W. (1988), 'A stochastic parts program and noun phrase parser for unrestricted text', *Proceedings of the Second Conference on Applied Natural Language Processing*, Austin, Tex., 136–43.

—— and Hanks, P. W. (1990), 'Word association norms, mutual information, and lexicography', *Computational Linguistics*, 16/1, 22–9.

—— Gale, W., Hanks, P. W., and Hindle, D. (1991), 'Using statistics in lexical analysis', in U. Zernik (ed.), *Lexical Acquisition: Using On-line Resources to Build a Lexicon*, Englewood Cliffs NJ: Lawrence Erlbaum Associates, 115–65.

—— —— —— —— and Moon, R. E. (1994), 'Lexical substitutability', in B. T. S. Atkins and A. Zampolli (eds.), *Computational Approaches to the Lexicon*, Oxford: Oxford University Press, 153–77.

Cignoni, L., and Coffey, S. (1995), 'Looking for preselected multiword units in an untagged corpus of written Italian: maximizing the potential of the search program DBT' (Report No. ILC-IRC-1995-1), Pisa: Istituto di Linguistica Computazionale, CNR.

Clausén, U. (1996), 'Idiom i bruk', *Språket Lever: Festskrift till Margareta Westman*, Stockholm: Svenska Språknämnden, 36–42.

Cohen, T. (1975), 'Figurative speech and figurative acts', *Journal of Philosophy*, 72, 669–84.

—— (1979), 'Metaphor and the cultivation of intimacy', in S. Sacks (ed.), *On Metaphor*, Chicago and London: University of Chicago Press, 1–10.

Colombo, L. (1993), 'The comprehension of ambiguous idioms in context', in C. Cacciari and P. Tabossi (eds.), *Idioms: Processing, Structure, and Interpretation*, Hillsdale, NJ: Lawrence Erlbaum Associates, 163–200.

Coulmas, F. (1979a), 'Idiomaticity as a problem of pragmatics', in H. Parret, M. Sbísa, and J. Verschueren (eds.), *Possibilities and Limitations of Pragmatics* (Proceedings of the Conference on Pragmatics, Urbino 1979), Amsterdam: John Benjamins, 139–51.

—— (1979b), 'On the sociolinguistic relevance of routine formulae', *Journal of Pragmatics*, 3, 239–66.

—— (ed.) (1981), *Conversational Routine*, The Hague: Mouton.

Coulthard, R. M. (1985), *An Introduction to Discourse Analysis*, (2nd edition), London: Longman.

Cowie, A. P. (1988), 'Stable and creative aspects of vocabulary use', in R. Carter and M. J. McCarthy, *Vocabulary and Language Teaching*, London: Longman, 126–37.

—— (1992), 'Multiword lexical units and communicative language teaching', in P. Arnaud and H. Béjoint (eds.), *Vocabulary and Applied Linguistics*, London: Macmillan, 1–12.

—— (ed.) (forthcoming), *Phraseology: Theory, Analysis, and Applications*, Oxford: Oxford University Press.

—— and Howarth, P. (1996), 'Phraseology—a select bibliography', *International Journal of Lexicography*, 9/1, 38–51.

Cronk, B. C., Lima, S. D., and Schweigert, W. A. (1993), 'Idioms in sentences: effects of frequency, literalness, and familiarity', *Journal of Psycholinguistic Research*, 22/1, 59–82.

—— and Schweigert, W. A. (1992), 'The comprehension of idioms: the effects of familiarity, literalness, and usage', *Applied Psycholinguistics*, 13, 131–46.

Cruse, D. A. (1986), *Lexical Semantics*, Cambridge: Cambridge University Press.

Crystal, D. (1988), *The English Language*, London: Penguin.

—— (1991), 'Stylistic profiling', in K. Aijmer and B. Altenberg (eds.), *English Corpus Linguistics*, London: Longman, 221–38.

—— and Davy, D. (1969), *Investigating English Style*, London: Longman.

Cutler, A. (1982), 'Idioms: the colder the older', *Linguistic Inquiry*, 13, 317–20.

Danchev, A. (1993), 'A note on phrasemic calquing', in P. Zlateva (ed. and trans.), *Translation as Social Action: Russian and Bulgarian Perspectives*, London and New York: Routledge, 58–62.

Dasgupta, P. (1993), 'Idiomaticity and Esperanto texts: an empirical study', *Linguistics*, 31/2, 367–86.

Davidson, D. (1979), 'What metaphors mean', in S. Sacks (ed.), *On Metaphor*, Chicago and London: University of Chicago Press, 29–45.

de Beaugrande, R., and Dressler, W. (1981), *Introduction to Text Linguistics*, London: Longman.

Dillard, J. L. (1975), *American Talk*, New York: Random House.

—— (1992), *A History of American English*, London: Longman.

Drazdauskiene, M.-L. (1981), 'On stereotypes in conversation, their meaning and significance', in F. Coulmas (ed.), *Conversational Routine*, The Hague: Mouton, 55–68.

Drew, P., and Holt, E. (1988), 'Complainable matters: the use of idiomatic expressions in making complaints', *Social Problems*, 35, 398–417.

—— —— (1995), 'Idiomatic expressions and their role in the organization of topic transition in conversation', in M. Everaert, E.-J. van der Linden, A. Schenk, and R. Schreuder (eds.), *Idioms: Structural and Psychological Perspectives*, Hillsdale, NJ: Lawrence Erlbaum Associates, 117–32.

Dunning, T. (1992), 'Accurate methods for the statistics of surprise and coincidence', Report No. MCCS-91-223, Las Cruces, N. Mex.: Computing Research Laboratory, New Mexico State University.

Ernst, T. (1981), 'Grist for the linguistic mill: idioms and "extra" adjectives', *Journal of Linguistic Research*, 1/3, 51–68.

Estill, R. B., and Kemper, S. (1982), 'Interpreting idioms', *Journal of Psycholinguistic Research*, 11/6, 559–68.

Everaert, M., and Kuiper, K. (1996), 'Theory and data in idiom research', (abstract for the Thirty-Second Meeting of the Chicago Linguistic Society), http://humanities.uchicago.edu/humanities/cls/conf

Fairclough, N. (1989), *Language and Power*, London: Longman.

Fass, D. (1991), 'met*: a method for discriminating metonymy and metaphor by computer', *Computational Linguistics*, 17/1, 50–90.

Fellbaum, C. (1993), 'The determiner in English idioms', in C. Cacciari and P. Tabossi (eds.), *Idioms: Processing, Structure, and Interpretation*, Hillsdale, NJ: Lawrence Erlbaum Associates, 271–95.

Fernando, C. (1978), 'Towards a definition of idiom: its nature and function', *Studies in Language*, 2/3, 313–43.

—— (forthcoming), *Idioms and Idiomaticity*, Oxford: Oxford University Press.

—— and Flavell, R. (1981), *On Idiom: Critical Views and Perspectives* (Exeter Linguistic Studies 5), Exeter: University of Exeter.

Fillmore, C. J. (1976), 'The need for a frame semantics within linguistics', *Statistical Methods in Linguistics*, Stockholm: Skriptor, 5–29.

—— (1985), 'Frames and the semantics of understanding', *Quaderni di Semantica*, 12, 222–54.

—— Kay, P., and O'Connor, M. C. (1988), 'Regularity and idiomaticity in grammatical constructions: the case of *let alone*', *Language*, 64/3, 501–38.

Flavell, L., and Flavell, R. (1993*a*), *Dictionary of Idioms and their Origins*, London: Kyle Cathie.

—— —— (1993*b*), *Dictionary of Proverbs and their Origins*, London: Kyle Cathie.

Flores d'Arcais, G. B. (1993), 'The comprehension and semantic interpretation of idioms', in C. Cacciari and P. Tabossi (eds.), *Idioms: Processing, Structure, and Interpretation*, Hillsdale, NJ: Lawrence Erlbaum Associates, 79–99.

Forrester, M. A. (1995), 'Tropic implicature and context in the comprehension of idiomatic phrases', *Journal of Psycholinguistic Research*, 24/1, 1–22.

Fowler, R. (1991), *Language in the News*, London and New York: Routledge.

Francis, G. (1986), *Anaphoric Nouns* (Discourse Analysis Monographs 11), Birmingham: English Language Research, University of Birmingham.

—— (1993), 'A corpus-driven approach to grammar', in M. Baker, G. Francis, and E. Tognini-Bonelli (eds.), *Text and Technology: in Honour of John Sinclair*, Philadelphia and Amsterdam: John Benjamins, 137–56.

—— (1994), 'Labelling discourse: an aspect of nominal-group lexical cohesion', in R. M. Coulthard (ed.), *Advances in Written Discourse Analysis*, London: Routledge, 83–101.

Fraser, B. (1970), 'Idioms within a transformational grammar', *Foundations of Language*, 6/1, 22–42.

—— (1983), 'The domain of pragmatics', in J. C. Richards and R. W.

Schmidt (eds.), *Language and Communication*, London: Longman, 29–58.

—— (1996), 'Pragmatic markers', *Pragmatics*, 6/2, 167–90.

—— and Ross, J. R. (1970), 'Idioms and unspecified NP deletion', *Linguistic Inquiry*, 1, 264–5.

Garside, R. (1987), 'The CLAWS word-tagging system', in R. Garside, G. Leech, and G. Sampson (eds.), *The Computational Analysis of English*, London: Longman, 30–41.

—— Leech, G., and Sampson, G. (eds.) (1987), *The Computational Analysis of English*, London: Longman.

Gibbs, R. W. (1980), 'Spilling the beans on understanding and memory for idioms in conversation', *Memory and Cognition*, 8/2, 149–56.

—— (1985), 'On the process of understanding idioms', *Journal of Psycholinguistic Research*, 14/5, 465–72.

—— (1986a), 'Skating on thin ice: literal meaning and understanding idioms in conversation', *Discourse Processes*, 9, 17–30.

—— (1986b), 'What makes some indirect speech acts conventional?', *Journal of Memory and Language*, 25, 181–96.

—— (1992), 'What do idioms really mean?', *Journal of Memory and Language*, 31, 485–506.

—— and Gonzales, G. P. (1985), 'Syntactic frozenness in processing and remembering idioms', *Cognition*, 20, 243–59.

—— Nayak, N., Bolton, J. L., and Keppel, M. E. (1989a), 'Speakers' assumptions about the lexical flexibility of idioms', *Memory and Cognition*, 17/1, 58–68.

—— —— and Cutting, C. (1989b), 'How to kick the bucket and not decompose: analyzability and idiom processing', *Journal of Memory and Language*, 28, 576–93.

—— and O'Brien, J. (1990), 'Idioms and mental imagery: the metaphorical motivation for idiomatic meaning', *Cognition*, 36, 35–68.

Gläser, R. (1984), 'Terminological problems in linguistics, with special reference to neologisms', in R. R. K. Hartmann (ed.), *LEXeter '83 Proceedings* (Lexicographica Series Maior 1), Tübingen: Max Niemeyer, 345–51.

—— (1986), 'A plea for phraseo-stylistics', in D. Kastovsky and A. Szwedek (eds.), *Linguistics across Historical and Geographical Boundaries 1: Linguistic Theory and Historical Linguistics*, Berlin, New York, and Amsterdam: Mouton, 41–52.

—— (1988), 'The grading of idiomaticity as a presupposition for a taxonomy of idioms', in W. Hüllen and R. Schulze (eds.), *Understanding the Lexicon*, Tübingen: Max Niemeyer, 264–79.

Glass, A. L. (1983), 'The comprehension of idioms', *Journal of Psycholinguistic Research*, 12/4, 429–42.

Glassman, L., Grinberg, D., Hibbard, C., Meehan, J., Reid, L. G., and van Leunen, M.-C. (1992), *Hector: Connecting Words with Definitions*

(SRC Research Report 92a), Palo Alto, Calif.: Digital Equipment Corporation Systems Research Center.

Glucksberg, S. (1993), 'Idiom meanings and allusional content', in C. Cacciari and P. Tabossi (eds.), *Idioms: Processing, Structure, and Interpretation*, Hillsdale, NJ: Lawrence Erlbaum Associates, 3–26.

Greene, B. B., and Rubin, G. M. (1971), *Automatic Grammatical Tagging of English*, Providence, RI: Brown University Department of Linguistics.

Grice, H. P. (1975), 'Logic and conversation', in P. Cole and J. Morgan (eds.), *Syntax and Semantics 3: Speech Acts*, New York: Academic Press, 41–58.

—— (1989), *Studies in the Way of Words*, Cambridge, Mass. and London: Harvard University Press.

Gross, M. (1993), 'Local grammars and their representation by finite automata', in M. P. Hoey (ed.), *Data, Description, Discourse: Papers on the English Language in Honour of John McH. Sinclair*, London: Harper-Collins, 26–38.

—— (1994), 'Constructing lexicon-grammars', in B. T. S. Atkins and A. Zampolli (eds.), *Computational Approaches to the Lexicon*, Oxford: Oxford University Press, 213–63.

Guarino Reid, L., and Meehan, J. R. (1994), *Inside Hector: The Systems View* (SRC Research Report 123), Palo Alto, Calif.: Digital Equipment Corporation Systems Research Center.

Gumpel, L. (1974), 'The structure of idioms: a phenomenological approach', *Semiotica*, 12/1, 1–40.

Halliday, M. A. K. (1966), 'Lexis as a linguistic level', in C. E. Bazell, J. C. Catford, M. A. K. Halliday, and R. H. Robins (eds.), *In Memory of J. R. Firth*, London: Longman, 148–62.

—— (1978), *Language as Social Semiotic*, London: Edward Arnold.

—— (1985), *An Introduction to Functional Grammar*, London: Edward Arnold.

—— (1993), 'Quantitative studies and probabilities in grammar', in M. P. Hoey (ed.), *Data, Description, Discourse: Papers on the English Language in Honour of John McH. Sinclair*, London: HarperCollins, 1–25.

—— (1994), *An Introduction to Functional Grammar* (2nd edition), London: Edward Arnold.

—— and Hasan, R. (1976), *Cohesion in English*, London: Longman.

—— —— *Language, Context, and Text: Aspects of Language in a Social–Semiotic Perspective*, Oxford: Oxford University Press (originally published 1985, Deakin University, Victoria).

—— and James, Z. L. (1993), 'A quantitative study of polarity and primary tense in the English clause', in J. M. Sinclair, M. P. Hoey, and G. Fox (eds.), *Techniques of Description: Spoken and Written Discourse. A Festschrift for Malcolm Coulthard*, London and New York: Routledge, 32–66.

—— McIntosh, A., and Strevens, P. (1964), *The Linguistic Sciences and Language Teaching*, London: Longman.

Harris, Z. (1991), *A Theory of Language and Information*, Oxford: Oxford University Press.

Hartley, J. (1982), *Understanding News*, London and New York: Routledge.

Hasan, R. (1984), 'Coherence and cohesive harmony', in J. Flood (ed.), *Understanding Reading Comprehension*, Newark, Del.: International Reading Association, 181–219.

Hatim, B., and Mason, I. (1990), *Discourse and the Translator*, London: Longman.

Hausmann, F. (1985), 'Kollokationen im deutschen Wörterbuch. Ein Beitrag zur Theorie des lexicographischen Beispiels', in H. Bergenholtz and J. Mugdan (eds.), *Lexikographie und Grammatik*, Tübingen: Max Niemeyer, 118–29.

Healey, A. (1968), 'English Idioms', *KIVUNG* (Journal of the Linguistic Society of the University of Papua New Guinea), 1/2, 71–108.

Hockett, C. F. (1958), *A Course in Modern Linguistics*, New York: Macmillan.

Hoey, M. P. (1983), *On the Surface of Discourse*, London: George Allen and Unwin.

—— (1991), *Patterns of Lexis in Text*, Oxford: Oxford University Press.

—— (1993), 'The case for the exchange complex', in M. P. Hoey (ed.), *Data, Description, Discourse: Papers on the English Language in Honour of John McH. Sinclair*, London: HarperCollins, 115–38.

Honeck, R. P., and Temple, J. G. (1994), 'Proverbs: the Extended Conceptual Base and Great Chain Metaphor Theories', *Metaphor and Symbolic Activity*, 9/2, 85–112.

Hopper, P. J., and Closs Traugott, E. (1993), *Grammaticalization*, Cambridge: Cambridge University Press.

Howarth, P. A. (1996), *Phraseology in English Academic Writing*, (Lexicographica Series Maior 75), Tübingen: Max Niemeyer.

Hudson, R. (1980), *Sociolinguistics*, Cambridge: Cambridge University Press.

Jackendoff, R. (1988), *Semantics and Cognition*, Cambridge, Mass. and London: MIT Press.

—— (1991), *Semantic Structures*, Cambridge, Mass. and London: MIT Press.

—— (1995), 'The boundaries of the lexicon', in M. Everaert, E.-J. van der Linden, A. Schenk, and R. Schreuder (eds.), *Idioms: Structural and Psychological Perspectives*, Hillsdale, NJ: Lawrence Erlbaum Associates, 133–65.

Johansson, S., and Hofland, K. (1989), *Frequency Analysis of English Vocabulary and Grammar*, Oxford: Oxford University Press.

Jones, S., and Sinclair, J. M. (1974), 'English lexical collocations', *Cahiers de Lexicologie*, 24, 15–61.

Katz, J. J. (1973), 'Compositionality, idiomaticity, and lexical substitution', in S. Anderson and P. Kiparsky (eds.), *A Festschrift for Morris Halle*, New York: Holt, Rinehart, and Winston, 357–76.

—— and Postal, P. M. (1963), 'Semantic interpretation of idioms and sentences containing them', *M.I.T. Research Laboratory of Electronics Quarterly Progress Report*, 70, 275–82.

Kay, P. (1992), 'At least', in A. Lehrer and E. F. Kittay (eds.), *Frames, Fields, and Contrasts: New Essays in Semantic and Lexical Organization*, Hillsdale, NJ: Lawrence Erlbaum Associates, 309–31.

Keller, E. (1979), 'Gambits: conversational strategy signals', *Journal of Pragmatics*, 3, 219–38.

Keysar, B., and Bly, B. (1995), 'Intuitions of the transparency of idioms: can one keep a secret by spilling the beans?', *Journal of Memory and Language*, 34, 89–109.

Kiparsky, P. (1976), 'Oral poetry: some linguistic and typological considerations', in B. A. Stolz and R. S. Shannon (eds.), *Oral Literature and the Formula*, Ann Arbor: University of Michigan, 73–106.

Kjellmer, G. (1987), 'Aspects of English collocations', in W. Meijs (ed.), *Corpus Linguistics and Beyond* (Proceedings of the Seventh International Conference on English Language Research on Computerized Corpora), Amsterdam: Rodopi, 133–40.

—— (1991), 'A mint of phrases', in K. Aijmer and B. Altenberg (eds.), *English Corpus Linguistics*, London: Longman, 111–27.

Klappenbach, R. (1968), 'Probleme der Phraseologie', *Wissenschaftliche Zeitschrift der Karl-Marx Universität, Leipzig*, 17, 172–87.

Kövecses, Z. (1986), *Metaphors of Anger, Pride, and Love*, Amsterdam and Philadelphia: John Benjamins.

—— and Szabó, P. (1996), 'Idioms: a view from cognitive semantics', *Applied Linguistics*, 17/3, 326–55.

Krashen, S., and Scarcella, R. (1978), 'On routines and patterns in language acquisition and performance', *Language*, 28/2, 283–300.

Kress, G. (1989), *Linguistic Processes in Sociocultural Practice*, Oxford: Oxford University Press (originally published 1985, Deakin University, Victoria).

—— and Hodge, R. (1979), *Language as Ideology*, London: Routledge and Kegan Paul.

Kronasser, H. (1952), *Handbuch der Semasiologie*, Heidelberg: Carl Winter Universitätsverlag.

Krzeszowski, T. P. (1990), 'The axiological aspect of idealized cognitive models', in J. Tomaszczyk and B. Lewandowska-Tomaszczyk (eds.), *Meaning and Lexicography*, Amsterdam and Philadelphia: John Benjamins, 135–65.

Kučera, H., and Francis, W. N. (1967), *A Computational Analysis of Present-Day American English*, Providence, RI: Brown University Press.

Kuiper, K. (1996), *Smooth Talkers: the Linguistic Performance of Auctioneers and Sportscasters*, Hillsdale, NJ: Lawrence Erlbaum Associates.

—— and Haggo, D. (1984), 'Livestock auctions, oral poetry and ordinary language', *Language in Society*, 13, 205–34.

—— and Tillis, F. (1985), 'The chant of the tobacco auctioneer', *American Speech*, 60/2, 141–9.

Kunst, A. E., and Blank, G. D. (1982), 'Processing morphology: words and clichés', in R. W. Bailey (ed.), *Computing in the Humanities*, Amsterdam, New York, and Oxford: North-Holland Publishing Company, 123–31.

Labov, G. (1972), *Language in the Inner City*, Oxford: Basil Blackwell.

Lakoff, G. (1987), *Women, Fire, and Dangerous Things*, Chicago and London: University of Chicago Press.

—— and Johnson, M. (1980), *Metaphors We Live By*, Chicago and London: University of Chicago Press.

—— and Turner, M. (1989), *More than Cool Reason: A Field Guide to Poetic Metaphor*, Chicago: University of Chicago Press.

Lamb, S. M. (1962), *Outline of Stratificational Grammar*, Berkeley: ASUC.

Lambrecht, K. (1984), 'Formulaicity, frame semantics, and pragmatics in German binomial expressions', *Language*, 60, 753–96.

Lattey, E. (1986), 'Pragmatic classification of idioms as an aid for the language learner', *IRAL*, 24/3, 217–33.

—— and Heike, A. E. (1990), *Using Idioms in Situational Contexts: A Workbook*, Tübingen: Francke.

Laver, J. (1970), 'The production of speech', in J. Lyons (ed.), *New Horizons in Linguistics*, Harmondsworth: Penguin, 53–75.

Lecercle, J.-J. (1990), *The Violence of Language*, London and New York: Routledge.

Lee, D. (1992), *Competing Discourses: Perspective and Ideology in Language*, London: Longman.

Leech, G. N. (1969), *A Linguistic Guide to English Poetry*, London: Longman.

—— (1983), *Principles of Pragmatics*, London: Longman.

—— (1991), 'The state of the art in corpus linguistics', in K. Aijmer and B. Altenberg (eds.), *English Corpus Linguistics*, London: Longman, 8–29.

Lefevere, A. (1993), in P. Zlateva (ed., and trans.), *Translation as Social Action: Russian and Bulgarian Perspectives*, London and New York: Routledge, 58–62.

Lesk, M. (1986), 'Automatic sense disambiguation using machine-readable dictionaries: how to tell a pine cone from an ice cream cone', *Proceedings of SIGDOCI*, 24–6.

Levinson, S. C. (1983), *Pragmatics*, Cambridge: Cambridge University Press.

Levorato, M. C. (1993), 'The acquisition of idioms and the development of figurative competence', in C. Cacciari and P. Tabossi (eds.), *Idioms: Processing, Structure, and Interpretation*, Hillsdale, NJ: Lawrence Erlbaum Associates, 101–28.

Lorentzen, H. (1996), 'Lemmatization of multi-word lexical units: which entry?', in M. Gellerstam, J. Järborg, S.-G. Malmgren, K. Norén, L. Rogström, and C. R. Papmehl (eds.), *Euralex '96* Proceedings, Göteborg University, 415–21.

Louw, B. (1993), 'Irony in the text or insincerity in the writer?—the diagnostic potential of semantic prosodies', in M. Baker, G. Francis, and E. Tognini-Bonelli (eds.), *Text and Technology: in Honour of John Sinclair*, Philadelphia and Amsterdam: John Benjamins, 157–76.

Low, G. D. (1988), 'On teaching metaphor', *Applied Linguistics*, 9/2, 125–47.

Lyons, J. (1977), *Semantics*, Cambridge: Cambridge University Press.

McCarthy, M. J. (1988), 'Some vocabulary patterns in conversation', in R. Carter and M. J. McCarthy, *Vocabulary and Language Teaching*, London: Longman, 181–99.

—— (1991), *Discourse Analysis for Language Teachers*, Cambridge: Cambridge University Press.

—— (1992), 'English idioms in use', *Revista Canaria de Estudios Inglese*, 25 (Universidad de la Laguna), 55–65.

—— (1993), 'Spoken discourse markers in written text', in J. M. Sinclair, M. P. Hoey, and G. Fox (eds.), *Techniques of Description: Spoken and Written Discourse. A Festschrift for Malcolm Coulthard*, London and New York: Routledge, 170–82.

—— and Carter, R. (1994), *Language as Discourse: Perspectives for Language Teaching*, London: Longman.

McCawley, J. (1971) (writing as Quang Phuc Dong), 'The applicability of transformations to idioms', *Papers from the Seventh Regional Meeting of the Chicago Linguistic Society*, 200-205.

McEnery, T. (1992), *Computational Linguistics: A Handbook & Toolbox for Natural Language Processing*, Wilmslow: Sigma.

McGlone, M. S., Glucksberg, S., and Cacciari, C. (1994), 'Semantic productivity and idiom comprehension', *Discourse Processes*, 17/2, 167–90.

Makkai, A. (1972), *Idiom Structure in English*, The Hague: Mouton.

—— (1977), 'Idioms, psychology, and the lexemic principle', in R. J. Di Pietro and E. L. Blansitt, Jr. (eds.), *The Third LACUS Forum*, Columbia, SC: Hornbeam Press, 467–78.

—— (1993), 'Idiomaticity as a reaction to *l'Arbitraire du Signe* in the universal process of semeio-genesis', in C. Cacciari and P. Tabossi (eds.), *Idioms: Processing, Structure, and Interpretation*, Hillsdale, NJ: Lawrence Erlbaum Associates, 297–324.

Malkiel, Y. (1959), 'Studies in irreversible binomials', *Lingua*, 8, 113–60.

Martin, J. H. (1990), *A Computational Model of Metaphor Interpretation*, Boston, Mass.: Academic Press.

—— (1996), 'Computational approaches to figurative language', *Metaphor and Symbolic Activity*, 11/1, 85–100.

Martin, J. R. (1989), *Factual Writing*, Oxford: Oxford University Press (originally published 1985, Deakin University, Victoria).

Matthews, P. H. (1974), *Morphology*, Cambridge: Cambridge University Press.

Meehan, J. R., Moon, R. E., and Reid, L. G. (1993), 'Multi-word units and corpus lexicography', Manuscript, Palo Alto, Calif.: Digital Equipment Corporation Systems Research Center.

Meier, H. H. (1975), 'On placing English idioms in lexis and grammar', *English Studies*, 231–44.

Mejri, S. (1994), 'Séquences figées et expression de l'intensité: essai de description sémantique', *Cahiers de Lexicologie*, 65, 111–22.

Mel'čuk, I. A. (1988), 'Semantic description of lexical units in an explanatory combinatorial dictionary: basic principles and heuristic criteria', *International Journal of Lexicography*, 1/3, 165–88.

—— (1995), 'Phrasemes in language and phraseology in linguistics', in M. Everaert, E.-J. van der Linden, A. Schenk, and R. Schreuder (eds.), *Idioms: Structural and Psychological Perspectives*, Hillsdale, NJ: Lawrence Erlbaum Associates, 167–232.

—— with Arbatchewsky-Jumarie, N., Elnitsky, L., Iordanskaja, L., and Lessard, A. (1984), *Dictionnaire explicatif et combinatoire du français contemporain: Recherches lexico-sémantiques*, I, Montréal: Les Presses de l'Université de Montréal.

—— and Žolkovskii, A. K. (1984), *Tolkovo-kombinatornyj slovar' sovremennogo russkogo jazyka: Opyt semantiko-sintaksičeskogo opisanija russkoi leksiki*, Vienna: Wiener Slawistischer Almanach.

Miller, G. A. (1979), 'Images and models, similes and metaphors', in Ortony, A. (ed.), *Metaphor and Thought*, Cambridge: Cambridge University Press, 202–50.

Milner, G. M. (1969), 'Quadripartite structures', *Proverbium*, 14.

Minsky, M. (1980), 'A framework for representing knowledge', in D. Metzing (ed.), *Frame Conceptions and Text Understanding*, Berlin and New York: Walter de Gruyter, 1–25.

Mitchell, T. F. (1971), 'Linguistic "goings on": collocations and other lexical matters arising on the syntagmatic record', *Archivum Linguisticum*, II (ns), 35–69.

Moberg, L. (1996), 'Om engelskans stundom välgörande inflytande på svenskan', *Språket Lever: Festskrift till Margareta Westman*, Stockholm: Svenska Språknämnden, 216–21.

Moon, R. E. (1988), 'Time and idioms', in M. Snell-Hornby (ed.), *Zürilex '86 Proceedings*, Tübingen: A. Francke, 107–15.

—— (1992a), 'Textual aspects of fixed expressions in learners' dictionaries', in P. Arnaud and H. Béjoint (eds.), *Vocabulary and Applied Linguistics*, London: Macmillan, 13–27.

—— (1992b), '*There is reason in the roasting of eggs*: a consideration of fixed expressions in native-speaker dictionaries', in H. Tommola, K. Varantola, T. Salmi-Tolonen, and J. Schopp (eds.), *Euralex '92 Proceedings*, II

(Studia Translatologica ser. A, 2), Tampere: University of Tampere, 493–502.

—— (1994*a*), 'The analysis of fixed expressions in text', in R. M. Coulthard (ed.), *Advances in Written Discourse Analysis*, London: Routledge, 117–35.

—— (1994*b*), 'Fixed expressions and text: a study of the distribution and textual behaviour of fixed expressions in English', Unpublished Ph.D. thesis: University of Birmingham.

—— (1996), 'Data, description, and idioms in corpus lexicography', in M. Gellerstam, J. Järborg, S.-G. Malmgren, K. Norén, L. Rogström, and C. R. Papmehl (eds.), *Euralex '96 Proceedings*, Göteborg University, 245–56.

Morgan, J. L. (1978), 'Two types of convention in indirect speech acts', in P. Cole (ed.), *Syntax and Semantics*, 9, New York: Academic Press, 261–80.

Morley, G. D. (1985), *An Introduction to Systemic Grammar*, London: Macmillan.

Nagy, W. (1978), 'Some non-idiom larger-than-word units in the lexicon', in D. Farkas, W. M. Jacobsen, and K. W. Todrys (eds.), *Papers from the Parasession on the Lexicon, Fourteenth Regional Meeting of the Chicago Linguistic Society*, 289–300.

Nash, W. (1985), *The Language of Humour*, London: Longman.

Nattinger, J. R., and DeCarrico, J. S. (1992), *Lexical Phrases and Language Teaching*, Oxford: Oxford University Press.

Nayak, N. P., and Gibbs, R. W. (1990), 'Conceptual knowledge in the interpretation of idioms', *Journal of Experimental Psychology: General*, 119, 315–30.

Needham, W. P. (1992), 'Limits on literal processing during idiom interpretation', *Journal of Psycholinguistic Research*, 21/1, 1–16.

Negreneau, A. (1975), 'Idiomaties françaises, idiomaties roumanies', *Cahiers de Lexicologie*, 27/2, 117–28.

Newmark, P. (1991), *About Translation*, Clevedon, Philadelphia, and Adelaide: Multilingual Matters.

Newmeyer, F. J. (1972), 'The insertion of idioms', in P. M. Peranteau, J. N. Levi, and G. C. Phares (eds.), *Papers from the Eighth Regional Meeting of the Chicago Linguistic Society*, 294–302.

—— (1974), 'The regularity of idiom behavior', *Lingua*, 34, 327–42.

Nicolas, T. (1995), 'Semantics of idiom modification', in M. Everaert, E.-J. van der Linden, A. Schenk, and R. Schreuder (eds.), *Idioms: Structural and Psychological Perspectives*, Hillsdale, NJ: Lawrence Erlbaum Associates, 233–52.

Norrick, N. R. (1985), *How Proverbs Mean: Semantic Studies in English Proverbs*, Berlin, New York, and Amsterdam: Mouton.

Nunberg, G., Sag, I. A., and Wasow, T. (1994), 'Idioms', *Language*, 70/3, 491–538.

Obelkevich, J. (1987), 'Proverbs in social history', in P. Burke and

R. Porter (eds.), *The Social History of Language*, Cambridge: Cambridge University Press.

Odlin, T. (1991), 'Irish English idioms and language transfer', *English World-Wide*, 12/2, 175–93.

Ortony, A. (ed.) (1979*a*), *Metaphor and Thought*, (2nd edition, 1993), Cambridge: Cambridge University Press.

—— (1979*b*), 'The role of similarity in similes and metaphors', in A. Ortony (ed.), *Metaphor and Thought*, Cambridge: Cambridge University Press., 186–201.

—— (1988), 'Are emotion metaphors conceptual or lexical?', *Cognition and Emotion*, 2, 95–103.

—— Schallert, D., Reynolds, R. E., and Antos, S. J. (1978), 'Interpreting metaphors and idioms: some effects of context on comprehension', *Journal of Verbal Learning and Verbal Behavior*, 17, 465–77.

Orwell, G. (1946), 'Politics and the English language', reprinted (1962), in *Inside the Whale and Other Essays*, Harmondsworth: Penguin.

Palmer, F. R. (1986), *Mood and Modality*, Cambridge: Cambridge University Press.

—— (1990), *Modality and the English Modals* (2nd edition), London: Longman.

Pawley, A. (1986), 'Lexicalization', in D. Tannen and J. E. Alatis (eds.), *Languages and Linguistics: The Interdependence of Theory, Data, and Application* (Georgetown University Round Table on Languages and Linguistics 1985), Washington, DC: Georgetown University Press, 98–120.

—— and Syder, F. H. (1983), 'Two puzzles for linguistic theory; nativelike selection and nativelike fluency', in J. C. Richards and R. W. Schmidt (eds.), *Language and Communication*, London: Longman, 191–225.

Pedersen, V. H. (1986), 'The translation of collocations and idioms', in L. Wollin and H. Lindquist (eds.), *Translation Studies in Scandinavia* (Proceedings from the Scandinavian Symposium on Translation Theory (SSOTT), II, 1985), Malmö: CWK Gleerup, 126–32.

—— (1992), 'English influence on modern Danish vocabulary and its implications for Danish/English lexicography', in J. E. Nielsen (ed.), *Words that Teem with Meaning: Copenhagen Views on Lexicography* (Copenhagen Studies in Translation 2), Copenhagen: Museum Tusculanum Press, University of Copenhagen, 93–114.

Peters, A. M. (1983), *The Units of Language Acquisition*, Cambridge: Cambridge University Press.

Platt, J., Weber, H., and Ho, M. L. (1984), *The New Englishes*, London: Routledge and Kegan Paul.

Popiel, S. J., and McRae, K. (1988), 'The figurative and literal senses of idioms, or all idioms are not used equally', *Journal of Psycholinguistic Research*, 17/6, 475–87.

Powell, M. J. (1992), 'Folk theories of meaning and principles of conventionality: encoding literal attitude via stance adverbs', in A. Lehrer and E. F. Kittay (eds.), *Frames, Fields, and Contrasts: New Essays in Semantic and Lexical Organization*, Hillsdale, NJ: Lawrence Erlbaum Associates, 333–53.

Pulman, S. (1993), 'The recognition and interpretation of idioms', in C. Cacciari and P. Tabossi (eds.), *Idioms: Processing, Structure, and Interpretation*, Hillsdale, NJ: Lawrence Erlbaum Associates, 249–70.

Radford, A. (1988), *Transformational Grammar*, Cambridge: Cambridge University Press.

Reagan, R. T. (1987), 'The syntax of English idioms: can the dog be put on?', *Journal of Psycholinguistic Research*, 16/5, 417–41.

Renouf, A. (1987), 'Lexical resolution', in W. Meijs (ed.), *Corpus Linguistics and Beyond* (Proceedings of the Seventh International Conference on English Language Research on Computerized Corpora), Amsterdam: Rodopi, 121–32.

—— and Sinclair, J. M. (1991), 'Collocational frameworks in English', in K. Aijmer and B. Altenberg (eds.), *English Corpus Linguistics*, London: Longman, 128–43.

Resnick, D. A. (1982), 'A developmental study of proverb comprehension', *Journal of Psycholinguistic Research*, 11/5, 521–38.

Rochester, S., and Martin, J. R. (1979), *Crazy Talk: A Study of the Discourse of Schizophrenic Speakers*, New York: Plenum Press.

Romaine, S. (1988), *Pidgin and Creole Languages*, London: Longman.

Rosch, E. (1975), 'Cognitive representations of semantic categories', *Journal of Experimental Psychology: General*, 104, 192–233.

Rose, J. H. (1978), 'Types of idioms', *Linguistics*, 203, 55–62.

Ross, J. R. (1970), 'Two types of idioms', *Linguistic Inquiry*, 1/1, 144.

Ruhl, C. E. (1975), 'Primary verbs', in A. Makkai and V. B. Makkai (eds.), *The First LACUS Forum*, Columbia, SC: Hornbeam Press, 436–45.

—— (1977), 'Idioms and data', in R. J. Di Pietro and E. L. Blansitt, Jr. (eds.), *The Third LACUS Forum*, Columbia, SC: Hornbeam Press, 456–66.

—— (1979), 'Alleged idioms with *hit*', in W. Wölck and P. L. Garvin (eds.), *The Fifth LACUS Forum*, Columbia, SC: Hornbeam Press, 93–107.

—— (1989), *On Monosemy*, New York: State University of New York.

Sadock, J. M. (1972), 'Speech act idioms', in P. M. Peranteau, J. N. Levi, and G. C. Phares (eds.), *Papers from the Eighth Regional Meeting of the Chicago Linguistic Society*, 329–39.

—— (1974), *Towards a Linguistic Theory of Speech Acts*, New York: Academic Press.

Sampson, G. (1987), 'Evidence against the "Grammatical/Ungrammatical" distinction', in W. Meijs (ed.), *Corpus Linguistics and Beyond* (Proceedings of the Seventh International Conference on English Language Research on Computerized Corpora), Amsterdam: Rodopi, 219–26.

Schegloff, E. A., and Sacks, H. (1973), 'Opening up closings', *Semiotica*, 8/4, 289–327.

Schenk, A. (1995), 'The syntactic behaviour of idioms', in M. Everaert, E.-J. van der Linden, A. Schenk, and R. Schreuder (eds.), *Idioms: Structural and Psychological Perspectives*, Hillsdale, NJ: Lawrence Erlbaum Associates, 253–71.

Schiffrin, D. (1987), *Discourse Markers*, Cambridge: Cambridge University Press.

Schweigert, W. A. (1986), 'The comprehension of familiar and less familiar idioms', *Journal of Psycholinguistic Research*, 15/1, 33–45.

—— (1991), 'The muddy waters of idiom comprehension', *Journal of Psycholinguistic Research*, 20/4, 305–14.

—— and Moates, D. R. (1988), 'Familiar idiom comprehension', *Journal of Psycholinguistic Research*, 17/4, 281–96.

Searle, J. R. (1969), *Speech Acts*, Cambridge: Cambridge University Press.

—— (1975), 'Linguistics and the philosophy of language', in R. Bartsch and T. Vennemann (eds.), *Linguistics and Neighboring Disciplines*, Amsterdam and Oxford: North-Holland Publishing Company, 89–100.

—— (1979*a*), *Expression and Meaning: Studies in the Theory of Speech Acts*, Cambridge: Cambridge University Press.

—— (1979*b*), 'Metaphor', in A. Ortony (ed.), *Metaphor and Thought*, Cambridge: Cambridge University Press, 92–123.

Simpson, P. (1992), 'The pragmatics of nonsense: towards a stylistics of *Private Eye's* Colemanballs', in M. Toolan (ed.), *Language, Text and Context*, London and New York: Routledge, 279–305.

Sinclair, J. M. (1983), 'Planes of discourse', in S. N. A. Rizvil (ed.), *The Two–Fold Voice: Essays in Honour of Ramesh Mohan*, Salzburg Studies in English Literature, Salzburg: Universität Salzburg.

—— (1984), 'Naturalness in language', in J. Aarts and W. Meijs (eds.), *Corpus Linguistics: Recent Developments in the Use of Computer Corpora in English Language Research*, Amsterdam: Rodopi, 203–210.

—— (1986), 'First throw away your evidence', in G. Leitner (ed.), *The English Reference Grammar*, Tübingen: Max Niemeyer (reprinted in Sinclair 1991).

—— (1987), 'Collocation: a progress report', in R. Steele and T. Threadgold (eds.), *Language Topics: Essays in Honour of Michael Halliday*, II, Amsterdam: John Benjamins, 319–31.

—— (1991), *Corpus, Concordance, Collocation*, Oxford: Oxford University Press.

—— (1993), 'Written text structure', in J. M. Sinclair, M. P. Hoey, and G. Fox (eds.), *Techniques of Description: Spoken and Written Discourse. A Festschrift for Malcolm Coulthard*, London and New York: Routledge, 6–31.

—— Jones, S., and Daley, R. (1970), *English Lexical Studies*, University of Birmingham, for Office for Scientific and Technical Information.

Smith, G. W. (1991), *Computers and Human Language*, New York and Oxford: Oxford University Press.

Sorhus, H. B. (1977), 'To hear ourselves—implications for teaching

English as a second language', *English Language Teaching Journal*, 31/3, 211–21.

Sperber, D., and Wilson, D. (1986), *Relevance*, Oxford: Basil Blackwell.

Stock, O., Slack, J., and Ortony, A. (1993), 'Building castles in the air. Some computational and theoretical issues in idiom comprehension', in C. Cacciari and P. Tabossi (eds.), *Idioms: Processing, Structure, and Interpretation*, Hillsdale, NJ: Lawrence Erlbaum Associates, 229–47.

Strässler, J. (1982), *Idioms in English: a Pragmatic Analysis*, Tübingen: Gunter Narr.

Stubbs, M. (1983), *Discourse Analysis*, Oxford: Basil Blackwell.

—— (1986), ' "A matter of prolonged field work': notes towards a modal grammar of English', *Applied Linguistics*, 7/1, 1–25.

—— (1996), *Text and Corpus Analysis*, Oxford: Basil Blackwell.

—— and Gerbig, A. (1993), 'Human and inhuman geography: on the computer-assisted analysis of long texts', in M. P. Hoey (ed.), *Data, Description, Discourse: Papers on the English Language in Honour of John McH. Sinclair*, London: HarperCollins, 64–85.

Svartvik, J., and Quirk, R. (1980), *A Corpus of English Conversation* (Lund Studies in English), Lund: CWK Gleerup.

Svensén, B. (1993), *Practical Lexicography*, Oxford: Oxford University Press (trans. J. B. Sykes and K. Schofield: originally published in Swedish in 1987).

Swinney, D. A., and Cutler, A. (1979), 'The access and processing of idiomatic expressions', *Journal of Verbal Learning and Verbal Behavior*, 18, 523–34.

Tannen, D. (1989), *Talking Voices: Repetition, Dialogue and Imagery in Conversational Discourse*, Cambridge: Cambridge University Press.

Telija, V. N. (1992), 'Lexicographic description of words and collocations: feature–functional model', in M. Alvar Ezquerra (ed.), *Euralex '90 Proceedings*, Bibliograf: Barcelona, 315–20.

—— and Doroshenko, A. V. (1992), 'The motivational basis in the semantics of idioms and ways of its presentation in the computer data base', in H. Tommola, K. Varantola, T. Salmi-Tolonen, and J. Schopp (eds.), *Euralex '92* Proceedings, II (studia translatologica ser. A, 2), Tampere: University of Tampere, 433–9.

Thun, H. (1975), 'Quelques relations systématiques entre groupements de mots figés', *Cahiers de Lexicologie*, 27/2, 52–71.

Titone, D. A., and Connine, C. M. (1994), 'Descriptive norms for 171 idiomatic expressions: familiarity, compositionality, predictability, and literality', *Metaphor and Symbolic Activity*, 9/4, 247–70.

Toury, G. (1986), 'Monitoring discourse transfer', in J. House and S. Blum-Kulka (eds.), *Interlingual and Intercultural Communication: Discourse and Cognition in Translation and Second Language Acquisition Studies*, Tübingen: Gunter Narr, 79–94.

Van Dijk, T. A. (1977), *Text and Context: Explorations in the Semantics and Pragmatics of Discourse*, London: Longman.

Van Lancker, D., and Canter, G. J. (1981), 'Idiomatic versus literal interpretations of ditropically ambiguous sentences', *Journal of Speech and Hearing Research*, 24/1, 64–9.

———— and Terbeek, D. (1981), 'Disambiguation of ditropic sentences: acoustic and phonetic clues', *Journal of Speech and Hearing Research*, 24/3, 330–5.

Verschueren, J. (1987), *Pragmatics as a Theory of Linguistic Adaptation* (International Pragmatics Association Working Document 1), University of Antwerp.

Voutilainen, A., Heikkilä, J., and Anttila, A. (1992), *Constraint Grammar of English: A Performance-Oriented Introduction*, University of Helsinki, Department of General Linguistics.

Wardhaugh, R. (1986), *An Introduction to Sociolinguistics*, Oxford: Basil Blackwell.

Warren, B. (1992), 'What euphemisms tell us about the interpretation of words', *Studia Linguistica*, 46/2, 128–72.

Wasow, T., Sag, I., and Nunberg, G. (1983), 'Idioms: an interim report', in S. Hattori and K. Inoue (eds.), *Proceedings of the XIIIth International Congress of Linguistics*, Tokyo: Comité International Permanent des Linguistes, 102–15.

Weinreich, U. (1963), 'Lexicology', in T. Sebeok (ed.), *Current Trends in Linguistics*, I, The Hague: Mouton, 60–93.

—— (1969), 'Problems in the analysis of idioms', in J. Puhvel (ed.), *Substance and Structure of Language*, Berkeley, Calif.: University of California Press, 23–81.

Wierzbicka, A. (1985), *Lexicography and Conceptual Analysis*, Ann Arbor, Mich.: Karoma.

—— (1986), 'Metalanguage for illocutionary meanings', *Journal of Pragmatics*, 10/1, 67–108.

—— (1987a), 'Boys will be boys: "radical semantics" vs. "radical pragmatics"', *Language*, 63, 95–114.

—— (1987b), *English Speech Act Verbs*, Sydney: Academic Press.

—— (1988), *The Semantics of Grammar*, Amsterdam and Philadelphia: John Benjamins.

—— (1992), *Semantics, Culture, and Cognition*, Oxford: Oxford University Press.

Wilensky, R., and Arens, Y. (1980), *PHRAN—a Knowledge-based Natural Language Understander* (ERL Memorandum No. UCB/ERL M80/34), Berkeley, Calif.: University of California, Electronics Research Laboratory.

Willis, D. (1993), 'Grammar and lexis: some pedagogical implications', in J. M. Sinclair, M. P. Hoey, and G. Fox (eds.), *Techniques of Description: Spoken and Written Discourse. A Festschrift for Malcolm Coulthard*, London and New York: Routledge, 83–93.

Winter, E. O. (1977), 'A clause relational approach to English texts', *Instructional Science*, 6/1, 1–92.

Winter, E. O. (1994), 'Clause relations as information structure: two basic text structures in English', in R. M. Coulthard (ed.), *Advances in Written Discourse Analysis*, London: Routledge, 46–68.

Wood, M. M. (1981), *A Definition of Idiom*, MA thesis: University of Birmingham (published 1986, Indiana University Linguistics Club).

Yorio, C. (1989), 'Idiomaticity as an indicator of second language proficiency', in K. Hyltenstam and L. Obler (eds.), *Bilingualism across the Life-Span*, Cambridge: Cambridge University Press, 55–72.

Zajdman, A. (1995), 'Humorous face-threatening acts: humor as strategy', *Journal of Pragmatics*, 23, 325–39.

Zgusta, L. (1967), 'Multiword lexical units', *Word*, 23, 578–87.

—— (1971), *Manual of Lexicography*, The Hague: Mouton.

Zijderveld, A. C. (1979), *On Clichés: The Supersedure of Meaning by Function in Modernity*, London: Routledge and Kegan Paul.

DICTIONARIES

CCDI: Moon, R. E. (ed.) (1995), *Collins Cobuild Dictionary of Idioms*, London and Glasgow: HarperCollins.

CCDPV: Sinclair, J. M., and Moon, R. E. (eds.) (1989), *Collins Cobuild Dictionary of Phrasal Verbs*, London and Glasgow: HarperCollins.

CCELD: Sinclair, J. M., Hanks, P. W., Fox, G., Moon, R. E., and Stock, P. F. (eds.) (1987), *Collins Cobuild English Language Dictionary* (1st edition), London and Glasgow: HarperCollins.

CODP2: Simpson, J. A. (1992), *The Concise Oxford Dictionary of Proverbs* (2nd edition), Oxford: Oxford University Press.

ODCIE: Cowie, A. P., and Mackin, R. (1975), *Oxford Dictionary of Current Idiomatic English*, 1; Cowie, A. P., Mackin, R., and McCaig, I. R. (1983), *Oxford Dictionary of Current Idiomatic English*, 2 (new editions 1993), Oxford: Oxford University Press.

ODEP: (1970), *The Oxford Dictionary of English Proverbs*, Oxford: Oxford University Press.

OED: Simpson, J. A., and Weiner, E. S. C. (eds.) (1989), *Oxford English Dictionary* (2nd edition), Oxford: Oxford University Press.

Index